The Science of
Stress Management

The Science of Stress Management

A Guide to Best Practices for Better Well-Being

AMITAVA DASGUPTA

ROWMAN & LITTLEFIELD
Lanham • Boulder • New York • London

Published by Rowman & Littlefield
A wholly owned subsidiary of The Rowman & Littlefield Publishing Group, Inc.
4501 Forbes Boulevard, Suite 200, Lanham, Maryland 20706
www.rowman.com

Unit A, Whitacre Mews, 26-34 Stannary Street, London SE11 4AB

British Library Cataloguing in Publication Information Available

Library of Congress Cataloging-in-Publication Data

Names: Dasgupta, Amitava, 1958– author.
Title: The science of stress management : a guide to best practices for
   better well-being / Amitava Dasgupta.
Description: Lanham, MD : Rowman & Littlefield, [2017] | Includes index.
Identifiers: LCCN 2017038463 (print) | LCCN 2017048222 (ebook) | ISBN
   9781538101216 (electronic) | ISBN 9781538101209 (cloth : alk. paper)
Subjects: LCSH: Stress (Psychology) | Stress management. | Well-being.
Classification: LCC BF575.S75 (ebook) | LCC BF575.S75 D267 2017 (print) | DDC
   155.9/042—dc23
LC record available at https://lccn.loc.gov/2017038463

♾™ The paper used in this publication meets the minimum requirements of
American National Standard for Information Sciences—Permanence of Paper
for Printed Library Materials, ANSI/NISO Z39.48-1992.

Printed in the United States of America

For Thor

Contents

Preface

There is no way to avoid stress in life. Thus the goal is to manage stress effectively and avoid many stress-related physical and mental illnesses. Stress activates the sympathetic nervous system, causing the release of epinephrine and norepinephrine from the adrenal glands. These hormones are collectively called catecholamines, and they prepare the body within seconds for "fight or flight" response. However, the hypothalamic-pituitary-adrenal axis is also activated in response to stress, which eventually results in the secretion of cortisol and other stress hormones, also from the adrenal glands. Cortisol provides long-term response to stress but also increases oxidative stress.

Chronic stress increases the risk of major depression, anxiety, and other mental disorders, including age-related dementia, Alzheimer's disease, and Parkinson's disease. Women are more susceptible to stress-related depression than men. Moreover, chronic stress increases the risk of cardiovascular diseases, including myocardial infarction (heart attack), which is the number-one killer in the United States and other developed countries. In addition, chronic stress increases the risk of stroke, cancer, type 2 diabetes, and many other chronic illnesses. However, proper stress management protects us from these stress-related illnesses. Studies have shown that stress management can reduce cortisol response during stress by improving coping skills, thus improving quality of life. Chronic stress can reduce brain volume, but effective stress management through exercise, yoga, and meditation can reverse such stress-induced brain damage by increasing gray matter volume in regions of the brain that are affected by chronic stress.

There are many excellent books on the market that give practical tips on effective stress management strategies. However, this book is different because all effective approaches of stress management discussed in this book are backed by solid science, as evidenced by published papers in prestigious peer-reviewed medical journals. This book is written for a general audience, with all medical jargon explained in simple terms so that readers do not need to have a scientific background to enjoy reading it. However, for readers with advanced science and medical backgrounds, I provide an extensive list of scientific papers at the end of the book in the notes section. The purpose of this decision is to convince every reader that all important statements made throughout the book are based on extensive research. Moreover, advanced readers (graduate students doing research in psychology, biology, or medicine, medical students, nurses, physicians, health-care professionals, social workers, or anyone with an advanced science background) can read original scientific papers for in-depth information on any topic if desired.

The book has ten chapters. In the first chapter I explain how stress kills silently and why stress management is essential for a healthy body and mind. Although women experience more stress than men, women's approach to stress management (tend and befriend) is superior to men's response (fight or flight). Human studies indicate that the hormone oxytocin, which is secreted from the brain, in conjunction with female reproductive hormones may be related to a different pattern of response by women to stress because oxytocin can counteract the negative effects of the stress hormone cortisol. These aspects of the stress response are discussed in chapter 2.

In chapter 3, I explain why pets are excellent stress busters. Pets offer unconditional love, and petting a cat or dog lowers blood pressure as well as cortisol levels in the blood. Walking a dog is also a great form of exercise. However, social networking, laughter, volunteering, and taking vacations can effectively reduce stress as well. These stress management modalities are discussed in chapter 4. Exercise is essential for good health, but exercise also reduces stress. Moreover, meditation and yoga are very effective in stress management. Exercise, yoga, and meditation can also increase the volume of gray matter in areas of the brain that are damaged by stress. See chapter 5 for details.

Aromatherapy and massage are very effective at reducing stress, as reflected by lower blood pressure and lower cortisol levels. Music therapy is likewise effective for reducing stress. These stress management approaches are discussed in chapter 6. Making love to your spouse or significant other is an excellent stress buster—see chapter 7 for details. Because stress increases oxidative stress and lowers the antioxidant defense of the body, eating fruits and vegetables is essential for restoring antioxidant levels in the body. In chapter 8, foods rich in antioxidants are discussed, along with antioxidants present in tea and coffee. An apple a day indeed keeps the doctor away. Drinking in moderation not only reduces stress but also reduces the risk of cardiovascular disease, stroke, type 2 diabetes, age-related dementia, and possibly Alzheimer's disease. However, heavy drinking is a health hazard. These topics are discussed in chapter 9. In chapter 10, I discuss how eating chocolate in moderation can reduce stress.

I would like to thank my wife, Alice, for putting up with me for the last twelve months as I devoted long hours in the evenings and on weekends to writing this book. If readers enjoy the book, my hard work will be duly rewarded.

Amitava Dasgupta
Houston, Texas

1

Adverse Effects of Stress on Mind and Body

The word "stress" comes originally from physics, where it is defined as a pressure or tension applied to a material object. In engineering, stress is a component of Hooke's law, where it is defined as a measure of internal forces acting within an elastic system. In economics, stress describes physical and mental symptoms arising from indebtedness. However, in biology, there is no universally accepted definition of stress, though Hans Selye's definition of stress as "the nonspecific response of the body to any demand for change" is widely accepted. In psychology, stress is defined as a dynamic process that occurs when an individual appraises situational demands that exceed available resources. In a work situation, stress may be due to excessive job demands, tight deadlines, or working for a supervisor with a difficult personality. Law enforcement professionals are highly stressed due to exposure to work-related dangers, such as fighting crime and scrutiny by the media. Professionals working with information technology define their stress as "technostress," which is a negative impact on workers due to high demand and the security-related issues associated with it. Nurses and physicians are also subjected to significant work-related stress.[1]

AMERICANS ARE STRESSED OUT

It is common knowledge that Americans are stressed out, but levels of stress have been on the rise over the last twenty-six years. In one study based on surveying 3,387 Americans eighteen years old and older in 1983 and surveying

1

2,000 adults in both 2006 and 2009, the authors observed that scores on the Perceived Stress Scale (PSS) increased by up to 30 percent between 1983 and 2009 in different demographic categories. Overall, PSS scores increased by 29 percent in men and 18 percent in women from 1983 to 2009. Interestingly, stress levels in people sixty-five years old and older did not change significantly in the past twenty-six years. Major findings of this study include the following:

- In general, women reported higher stress levels than men.
- Psychological stress levels increased in a graded fashion with decreasing education and incomes in all three surveys, but stress scores were higher in 2006 and further increased in 2009 compared to 1983, indicating overall increased stress at all education levels in the past twenty-six years.
- In the 2009 survey, people with advanced degrees reported approximately 30 percent lower stress levels, people with bachelor's degrees 25 percent lower stress levels, and finally people with a high school diploma 15 percent lower stress levels, compared to people with no high school diploma.
- Increased socioeconomic status is associated with lower overall stress levels. For example, in the 2006 survey, the average stress score was 25 percent lower for people earning more than $75,000 and 15 percent lower for people with earnings in the $50,000–$75,000 range, compared to people earning less than $25,000.
- In the 1983 and 2006 surveys, employed people reported less stress than unemployed people.
- In all three surveys, retired people reported less stress than employed people. Interestingly, psychological stress decreased in a graded fashion with increasing age. This may be due to maturity because as we grow older, we interpret events as less stressful and have better coping skills. The youngest people (below twenty-five years) reported the highest stress levels in all three surveys.
- Minorities may experience more stress than Caucasians, but the difference did not achieve statistical significance.

However, the authors cautioned that these results should be interpreted carefully because of methodological differences (the 1983 survey was conducted by phone, while the 2006 and 2009 surveys were conducted online).[2]

The American Psychological Association started a national survey in 2007 (conducted by the Harris Poll) to estimate stress levels among Americans. Although overall stress levels decreased from 2007 (average score 6.2 on a scale of 1–10, where 1 represents no stress and 10 represents extreme stress; a score of 3.9 or below is desirable) to 2012 (average score 4.8), the stress scores for Americans increased again in 2015 (average score 5.1). Moreover, a significant percentage of people reported experiencing ex-

> Overall stress levels in America increased by up to 30 percent in the past twenty-six years for various demographics.

treme stress (24 percent of people surveyed in 2015 and 20 percent of people surveyed in 2016). People with annual earnings of $50,000 experienced more stress than people with higher incomes. Women on average reported higher stress levels than men. Minorities also reported experiencing more stress. Money was the number-one cause of stress reported by people in all surveys. In addition, women were more likely than men to report money (64 percent of women vs. 57 percent of men) and family responsibilities (56 percent of women vs. 42 percent of men) as major sources of stress in their lives.[3]

Consistent with this report, various other surveys conducted by the American Psychological Association also indicate that stress levels in America are increasing because 44 percent of respondents reported that their stress had increased over the past five years. Significant sources of stress include money (75 percent), work (70 percent), the economy (67 percent), relationships (58 percent), family responsibilities (57 percent), family health issues (53 percent), personal health concerns (53 percent), job stability (49 percent), housing costs (49 percent), and personal safety (32 percent). In addition, many Americans are experiencing the emotional and physical toll of stress, as 42

> According to surveys conducted by the Harris Poll on behalf of the American Psychological Association, money, work, and the economy are major causes of stress in Americans.

percent reported irritability or anger; 37 percent fatigue; 35 percent lack of interest, motivation, or energy; 32 percent stress headache; 24 percent stomach upset; and 17 percent change of appetite due to stress.[4]

Although women on average experience more stress than men, women are capable of coping with stress better than men. While men prefer a classical "fight or flight" approach in response to stress, women use a different approach known as "tend and befriend." This gender difference in stress management skills is discussed in detail in chapter 2.

NPR (National Public Radio), the Robert Wood Johnson Foundation, and the Harvard School of Public Health in 2014 also conducted a national poll to assess the burden of stress in America. About half of the respondents (49 percent) reported having a stressful event in the past year. When asked about stress the previous month, 26 percent people reported a great deal of stress, 37 percent some stress, 23 percent not much stress, and only 14 percent no stress, indicating that a majority of Americans are stressed out. People in poor health (60 percent) reported a great deal of stress. Single parents (35 percent) and parents with a teen (34 percent) were also highly stressed. In addition, highly stressed people reported that stress affected their family life (75 percent), health (74 percent), and social life (68 percent). The impact of stress on health included poor emotional well-being, difficulty sleeping, and difficulty in concentrating and decision making. People with chronic illnesses also reported worsening of symptoms as a result of a great deal of stress. The most common stress management approaches included spending time with family or friends (71 percent), prayer or meditation (57 percent), spending time outdoors (57 percent), and healthy eating (55 percent). However, more than half of respondents reported no initiative toward stress management. Only 35 percent of respondents reported seeking professional help for stress management.[5]

STRESS-RELATED VISITS TO PRIMARY CARE PHYSICIANS

Approximately 60–80 percent of visits to primary care doctors in the United States have been estimated to be stress related. Unfortunately, stress management counseling by U.S. primary care physicians was the least common type of counseling (3 percent), compared to counseling about nutrition (16.8 percent), physical activity (12.3 percent), weight reduction (6.3 percent), and tobacco cessation (3.7 percent). The low rate of counseling on stress management is a potentially missed opportunity, suggesting that physician counseling about stress has not been incorporated into primary care despite the fact that a high prevalence of depression among patients going to their primary care physicians has led to primary care being described as the "hidden mental health system." It has been

> An estimated 60–80 percent of visits to primary care physicians are stress related.

well documented in the medical literature that stress is linked to both initial diagnosis and the clinical course of depression.[6]

POSITIVE STRESS (EUSTRESS) VS. DISTRESS

Although the word "stress" is usually interpreted negatively, some stress may have positive effects. Eustress is associated with a transient increase in cortisol levels, the main stress hormone, and is beneficial to health. Therefore, eustress is a positive psychological response to a stressor. However, when stress is associated with adverse life events such as the death of a spouse, getting a divorce, or being fired from a job, such high stress levels usually exceed the coping skills of a person. Such stress is defined as distress because such stress is associated with prolonged high cortisol levels, which are harmful to both body and mind.

> Dr. Dhabhar commented that "a hassle a day may keep the doctor away."[7]

Some commonly encountered eustresses include the following:

- High school graduation and making the decision to attend a college or university
- First experience of leaving home to attend a college or starting a new job
- Choosing a major in college
- The decision to get higher education or professional education (medical school/law school/business school), etc.
- Job interview
- First day in a new job
- First date or blind date
- Marriage
- Pregnancy and childbirth
- Waiting for a promotion
- Outstanding achievement
- For parents, a child starting school or leaving home for college

Eustress may improve health directly through hormonal and biochemical changes.[8] Moreover, two different persons may interpret the same stressor differently.[9] For example, difficult math problems on a take-home final exam may cause eustress for a student very good at mathematics but distress for another student not so good at mathematics. Stress may also affect males and females differently. Medical students are constantly exposed to stress, but in one study based on 114 medical students, the authors observed high attendance and better day-to-day performance in female medical students when exposed to more stress in comparison to male students. The authors concluded that stress has more beneficial effects in females compared to males.[10]

In general, an inverted-U model is applied to describe the relationship between job stress and performance. Almost no stress in a job may cause boredom. As the pressure increases, a person

> Stress may motivate women to perform better than men in medical school.

enters the area of best performance known as the "optimum stress level," but with more pressure, performance may deteriorate, and finally, with excessive pressure, a person may experience burnout. High stress also leads to anxiety and unhappiness. Three major approaches can be taken to deal with stress:[11]

- Action oriented: where we deal with stress by changing the work environment or situation, such as looking for a different job or the same job in a better work environment.
- Emotion oriented: where we do not have power to change the situation but we can manage stress by interpreting the situation in a more emotionally positive way (personality plays an important role in emotion-oriented stress management, as some people may feel burnout in a job situation whereas others may cope by using positive emotion).
- Acceptance oriented: when we have no control of the stressful situation and have no power to avoid it, the goal is to survive.

Work stress and its associated problems cost organizations in the United States an estimated $200 billion or more each year in things such as decreased productivity, absenteeism, turnover, worker conflict, health-care costs, and worker compensation claims. Most people complain about work and report work-related stress as a major source of stress in their lives. The nursing profession is a very demanding job. However, whether a nurse may feel eustress or distress is dependent on personality traits. In one study involving 158 nurses, including intensive care unit nurses who worked more than forty hours a week, the authors observed that despite the demands of their work situation, these nurses reported a high degree of a positive psychological state of hope. The authors concluded that the capability of focusing on the essential tasks of their jobs facilitated active and pleasurable engagement (eustress) in these nurses. The authors further commented that when people believe that their action will lead to positive results, they may be more willing to accept job-related stress and report pleasurable engagement with their assignments.[12]

Personality may determine whether a person is going to burn out when exposed to work-related stress. In one study based on forty health-care professionals involved in psychiatry and elderly care (nurses, nursing aides, work leaders, and social workers/therapists), the authors observed that twenty professionals experienced burnout, while another twenty professions did not experience any burnout. The authors observed that health-care professionals who did not report any burnout had excellent emotional stability and tended to be trustful, unsuspecting, forgiving, accepting, easygoing, and drawn to lively social situations, and they expected fair treatment and good intentions from others. They also managed life events and emotions in a realistic, adaptive manner and could tolerate frustration. They were generally satisfied with their lives. However, burned out health-care professionals had low emotional stability and sometimes unrealistic expectations when dealing with others. These professionals also showed higher levels of anxiety than non-burnout professionals. People with high anxiety and neuroticism may perceive their work environment as more threatening and may react in a very emotional way during a stressful work situation.[13]

> Personality traits may determine whether a person experiences burnout when facing the same job-related stress. People who are anxious and high in neuroticism (feelings of anxiety, anger, envy, guilt, and depressed mood) are more susceptible to burnout due to work-related stress.

In another study, the authors investigated the role of personality traits in job burnout using 296 nurses. The authors observed that personality differences explained why some nurses were burned out but others were not when facing similar job-related stress. Nurses higher in extraversion perceived more personal accomplishments and enjoyed their jobs, while nurses higher in neuroticism were more likely to experience burnout. Extraversion includes such traits as talkativeness, social poise, assertiveness, and venturesomeness. Individuals high in extraversion are cheerful and energetic because they engage in activities to overcome stressful situations.

> People high in extraversion are cheerful and energetic, which may protect them from job-related stress because they also have positive emotion, social support, and optimism to deal with stressful situations.

People low in extraversion are usually quiet and reserved, and individuals higher in neuroticism have more negative views of themselves and others and may feel distressed and nervous. In this study, the authors also observed that nurses higher on extraversion had a positive mood, which protected them from job-related stress, while nurses higher on neuroticism experienced negative mood, which may contribute to their bleak outlook for the future, lower social support from others, and lack of ability to cope with job-related stress, which may eventually cause burnout.[14]

POSITIVE EMOTIONS IMPROVE HEALTH AND RESILIENCE

Positive emotion can be defined as feelings that reflect a state of pleasurable engagement with life, such as joy (happiness), contentment (tranquility, serenity), interest, gratitude, and love. Although positive emotions may appear more transitory in life than negative emotions such as sadness, anger, doubt, fear, anxiety, and others, research has shown that the overall emotional baseline of most people is slightly positive. In one study based on thirty dual-earning couples with school-age children, the authors observed that mild positive emotion was generally characteristic of both mother and father from the time they left for work to the time they went to bed on weekdays. Interestingly, mothers were more emotionally expressive than fathers, but mothers' positive emotions dropped during the evening period (5–8 p.m.), when the most salient feature of dinner was children's vocal expression of distaste for the food.[15]

People who experience warmer, more upbeat emotions live longer and healthier lives. Studies have shown that individuals who experience positive emotions more frequently have fewer colds, reduced inflammation, and lower risk of cardiovascular diseases. Moreover, positive emotion increases overall feelings of well-being and lowers physiological responses to stress as reflected by lower cortisol output and reduced cardiovascular response (such as lower blood pressure). Positive emotions may also reduce the risk of stroke. Sleep problems are associated with impaired cognitive functions, chronic illnesses, mental health problems, and premature mortality. In a study based on 736 men and women (aged fifty-eight to seventy-two years), the authors observed that positive emotions such as feelings of happiness and

> People who experience positive emotions more frequently are happier, healthier, and live longer. Moreover, these people can cope with stressful situations better and enjoy a good night's sleep.

enjoyment, as well as eudaemonic well-being (purposeful engagement with life), were directly associated with a good night's sleep in these subjects. In contrast, negative psychological factors, including financial strain, social isolation, low emotional support, negative social interactions, and psychological distress, caused poor sleep quality. Disturbed sleep patterns were also associated with reduced psychological well-being.[16]

Dr. Barbara L. Fredrickson proposed the "broaden and build" theory of positive emotion. According to this theory, positive emotions are evolved adaptations that function to build long-lasting physical and intellectual resources for people. Positive emotions can also counteract negative emotions. In general, positive emotions arise in response to diffuse opportunities rather than threats, and such emotions broaden people's attention and thinking in a positive manner. Therefore, the personal resources accrued sometimes unintentionally through the frequent experience of positive emotions increase little by little with time, which has overall positive effects on our physical and emotional well-being.[17]

Although positive emotions are often viewed as subtle and fleeting experiences, positive emotions do not need to be intense or prolonged to produce beneficial effects. Prospective correlation studies have shown that people who, for whatever reason, experience positive emotions more than others show increases over time in optimism, tranquility, friendship development, and marital satisfaction. Positive emotions also make people happy, and studies have shown that people who are happier also achieve better life outcomes, including financial success, supportive relationships, mental health, and physical health, as well as better coping skills during stressful life events. Positive emotions also increase life satisfaction by building resilience. In one study based on eighty-six students

> Positive emotions help people build resilience, which protects them against depressive symptoms and also improves overall satisfaction with life.

where the authors measured emotions daily for one month, positive emotions predicted increases in both resilience (ability to bounce back from negative experiences by flexible adaptation to the ever-changing demands of life) and life satisfaction. Interestingly, negative emotions had weak effects and did not interfere with positive emotions. The authors concluded that happy people become more satisfied with life not simply because they feel better but because they develop resources for living well.[18]

Positive emotions significantly improve coping skills during stressful life situations. Positive emotions unlock human cognition and encourage people to think more freely, thoughtfully, and creatively and at the same time enable a wider range of coping skills to deal with stress. In one study based on U.S. college students (eighteen men and twenty-eight women) before and after the September 11, 2001, terrorist attack in New York, the authors observed that, amid the emotional turmoil generated by the terrorist attack, subtle positive emotions such as gratitude, interest, love, and others appeared to protect some students against depression by improving their coping skills during the crisis.[19]

Studies have shown that people who experience more frequent positive emotions than others have better coping skills during stress, even when working in highly stressful professions such as public school teachers, physicians, and military spouses. Postdoctoral fellows also experience high stress levels. In one study based on two hundred postdoctoral research fellows, the authors observed that fellows who experienced positive emotions more frequently than others had higher resilience, which protected them from depressive symptoms even during highly stressful situations. The authors commented that positive emotions may enhance resilience directly as well as indirectly through the mediating role of coping strategies, especially through adaptive coping. Although stress is unavoidable, implementing programs that increase positive emotions among postdoctoral fellows may improve their coping skills in response to significant stress.[20]

Positive emotions can be induced, for example, by loving-kindness meditation. In one study based on 139 working adults, where half of the participants practiced loving-kindness meditation (68 subjects) and others (71 subjects) were placed in a waiting list control group, the authors observed that meditation produced positive emotions daily in the subjects, and the magnitude of the positive emotions increased over time. Moreover, meditation increased the personal resources of these subjects (increased mindfulness, purpose in life, and social support and decreased illness symptoms). These increments in personal life resources were also associated with increased life satisfaction and reduced depressive symptoms in the subjects.[21] Positive emotions can also be fostered through showing kindness to other people, appreciating simple beauties in life such as a beautiful sunset and nature, volunteering, having a new hobby, accepting one's limitations, and setting achievable goals in life.

CAN MONEY BUY HAPPINESS?

Happiness or subjective well-being is a positive emotional state of mind that increases life satisfaction. A happy person experiences positive emotions frequently and negative emotions infrequently. Personality factors such as extraversion, positive self-esteem, optimism, the ability to bond with others, and internal locus of control all contribute to happiness. Although GDP (gross domestic product) is widely held to be correlated with citizens' welfare, it is not correlated with happiness. According to the World Happiness Report, Canada ranked fifth (Switzerland ranked first) and Mexico ranked fourteenth, ahead of the United States, which was in fifteenth place. Moreover, in the last fifty years, the happiness of Americans did not change, but in European countries the level of happiness increased with increasing economic growth.

Work is necessary to pay bills, and good earnings contribute to a person's self-esteem, but the number of hours an average American works per week exceeds the average number of hours a European works per week. Because Americans spend more time at work, it reduces time available to connect with friends, family, and romantic partners. Research has indicated that people are most happy during socialization as well as during an intimate relation with a romantic partner, and people are least happy while commuting to work and during working hours. Therefore, working long hours to make more money does not translate into more happiness, but spending time with loved ones or spending time making social connections is strongly associated with greater happiness.[22]

Income appears to have a surprisingly modest impact on an individual's happiness. According to the experience-stretching hypothesis, the mundane joys of life such as sunny days, cold beer, and chocolate bars may have a greater impact on happiness than dining in a very expensive restaurant. In one study, the authors reported that money impairs people's ability to savor positive emotions and the experiences of daily life. The authors observed that wealthier individuals reported lower savoring ability.[23] Interestingly, people who spend money on others are happier than people who spend money on themselves.[24]

Although money does not buy happiness, poverty is not desirable because it may negatively impact life. Based on a survey of more than 450,000 people, the authors in one study observed that although emotional well-being increases with income, beyond an annual income of $75,000, there is no significant change in emotional well-being with increasing income. The authors commented that although low income exacerbates emotional pain, increases in income above the $75,000 threshold no longer improve overall emotional well-being. Higher income may increase life satisfaction but not happiness.[25] In another study based on a survey of 104 physician executives, only 3 percent of respondents stated that bonuses could be used to improve satisfaction, while the majority of respondents opined that personal growth, effective communication, personal communications, and work-life balance were key factors in improving job satisfaction and happiness.[26]

> People who spend money on others are happier than people who spend money only on themselves. A 2010 report indicates that beyond an annual income of $75,000, there is no significant change in emotional well-being with higher income.

THE OVERALL BURDEN OF STRESS

Stress is a major public health issue not only in the United States but also worldwide. The global burden of stress-related mental illness is expected to rise in the coming decade. The World Health Organization (WHO) Global Burden of Disease survey estimates that by the year 2020, depression and anxiety disorders, including stress-related mental health conditions, will be second to heart diseases in regard to disabilities among people. The disability caused by stress is just as great as disabilities caused by workplace accidents and other common medical conditions such as diabetes, hypertension, and arthritis. A survey in the United States found that 17.3 percent of the general population had experienced an episode of major depression and 24.5 percent of people suffered from anxiety disorders at some time in their lives. Depressed people also show higher mortality due to heart attack compared to nondepressed individuals. Work-related stress and home-related stress are two major sources of stress in the general population. Moreover, home-related stress may impact job performance. More than nineteen million Americans are inflicted with stress-related disorders each year, which costs the United States more than $42 billion every year for additional health care. People suffering from stress-related illnesses are three to six times more likely to visit a doctor and six times more likely to be hospitalized compared to nonsufferers.

It has been estimated in the Property and Casualty Insurance Edition of *Best's Review* that $150 billion of revenue is lost to stress annually due to lower productivity, absenteeism, poor decision making, and stress-related illnesses. The Washington Business Group on Health has found that 46 percent of all employees are severely stressed and 33 percent of Americans are suffering from insomnia.

> More than nineteen million Americans are inflicted with stress-related disorders each year, which costs the U.S. economy more than $42 billion every year in extra health-care costs.

In the United Kingdom, the Mental Health Foundation reported that stress costs British industries three billion British pounds per year.[27]

Although it is reasonable to feel stressed once a week or a few times per month, experiencing work- and/or home-related stress on a regular basis (chronic stress) is associated with both physical and mental illness. Although optimistic people may have better coping skills for stress, it is important for everyone to effectively manage stress on a regular basis to avoid stress-related illnesses. The goal of this book is to empower readers with scientifically proven, effective approaches that can be easily adopted in their lives. Personal preference should dictate which stress management approach is most suitable for each person.

STRESSORS OTHER THAN PSYCHOLOGICAL STRESS
Although stress usually means "psychological stress," there are other sources of stress, such as the following:

- Chronic illness
- Exposure to excessive noise, sunlight, extreme heat or cold, or air pollution
- Exposure to some household chemicals, poison, or certain medications such as anticancer drugs

Noise can be a significant source of stress. Studies have indicated that workers who are exposed to air traffic noise are more prone to develop hypertension. Another study demonstrated that children who live in a noisy "airport community" tend to have higher blood pressure than children who do not live in a noisy community.[28]

Exposure to sunlight during the summer months can add additional stress to the skin. The ultraviolet radiation of sunlight is composed of ultraviolet A (UVA: wavelengths of 320–400 nm), ultraviolet B (UVB: 280–320 nm), and ultraviolet C (UVC: 100–280 nm). Only UVA and UVB reach the surface of the earth because the atmosphere absorbs the most harmful UVC, which has the shortest wavelength. UVA is responsible for tanning while UVB is more damaging, causing cataracts and skin cancer, including melanoma. Actinic keratoses, also known as solar keratoses, which appear as rough scaly patches with discoloration of the skin (pink or flesh colored to dark brown) when exposed to the sun, occur more commonly in fair-skinned people. If a skin rash or skin problem due to sunburn does not respond to home therapy and persists over a week, or if a rash is painful, you should consult your doctor immediately. Ceratin medication can also cause photosensitivity, and certain diseases such as porphyria can make the skin very sensitive to sunlight.

> Caucasians are at an increased risk of experiencing sunburn (including skin cancer), especially individuals with lighter hair color (blond or redhead) and freckles. More than 90 percent of cases of melanoma are diagnosed in Caucasians.

The ultraviolet index (UV index) is an international standard to measure the strength of the ultraviolet radiation of the sun at a particular place or on a particular day. The higher the index, the greater the danger (six or higher indicates a high UV index, and eleven or greater represents an extreme case). Usually the UV index is higher in countries located at the equator and decreases with increasing latitude. Therefore, the number of days in a year with a high or extremely high UV index in Boston is significantly lower than in Houston. Skin must be protected when the UV index is high in your city by wearing clothes with a light color (or white) and covering most parts of your body.

> UV radiation of the sun is highest between 10 a.m. and 4 p.m. Watch your local weather or read your local newspaper for the daily UV index, and avoid direct exposure to the sun during times when the UV index is high (six or higher). If the UV index is extremely high (eleven or greater), try to stay indoors between 10 a.m. and 4 p.m.

Sunscreen must be used during a trip to the beach or while sunbathing. Despite public education, only about three out of ten adults in the United States routinely practice sun protection behavior, although women and elderly persons are more likely to use such protection. Sunburn is still an epidemic in the United States, with 34.4 percent of U.S. adults experiencing sunburn annually.[29]

Air pollution, especially in big cities, can cause additional stress. Smog, which is a combination of fog and smoke, may also cause significant air pollution, especially during winter months in big cities. The air quality of any U.S. city on a particular day is usually published in the local newspaper and is also available from the local weather station. When air quality is poor, it is better to avoid outside air as much as possible by staying indoors. In addition, a face mask can be helpful in significantly reducing the harmful effects of breathing polluted air. Trees can significantly reduce air pollution. Therefore, even if you live in an urban area, if your neighborhood has many tall trees, your air quality may be better than downtown. In general, rural areas of the United States have better air quality than urban areas. Reducing exposure to polluted air is advisable because chronic exposure to polluted air increases the risk of respiratory diseases (e.g., asthma, chronic obstructive pulmonary disease, lung cancer) and cardiovascular diseases (e.g., heart attack, heart failure). Moreover, elderly people, pregnant women, infants, and people with chronic diseases are more susceptible to the deleterious effects of ambient air pollution.[30]

Household chemicals should be properly stored in a childproof way because accidental poisoning of children due to access to household chemicals may cause life-threatening situations. In the United States, unintentional poisoning in children due to ingestion of household chemicals is common, with the most commonly reported exposures involving cosmetic personal care products (perfume, cologne, and aftershave) and household cleaning substances (bleach and alkaline corrosives).[31] A case of near fatality in a child who ingested nail polish remover has also been reported.[32] Many household cleaning products and laundry detergents are toxic and may cause stress to the human body if exposed directly. Therefore, protective masks and gloves should be used during house cleaning and while doing the laundry. Solvent abuse and glue sniffing is becoming a popular practice among some adolescents. Similar to drug or alcohol abuse, glue sniffing and solvent abuse may cause serious harm to the body. Adolescents should thus be counseled properly regarding the dangers of such abuse.

A NEWER STRESSOR: INTERNET ADDICTION

The Internet has positively changed the world by providing information at our fingertips, online businesses such as buying airline tickets and booking hotels, entertainment, and social networking with people worldwide. While healthy Internet use is defined as using the Internet for a specific time with no cognitive or behavioral difficulty, problematic Internet use—also referred to as Internet addiction, Internet dependency, or pathological Internet use—is defined as excessive use of the Internet without any purpose. The common features of problematic Internet use include spending excessive time on the Internet (more than five hours per day or thirty hours per week for nonessential Internet use), the desire to spend more time on the Internet, staying online much longer than intended, and often ignoring sleep or hunger to stay online. Moreover, losing track of time while on the Internet, irritability when not using the Internet, overjustification of or concealing Internet use, withdrawal from social life and physical activity, and failed attempts to cut time on the Internet are all indicative of Internet addiction. Although time spent on the Internet for non-work-related matters can be used to evaluate whether a person is addicted to the Internet, other approaches such as various questionnaire-based psychological scales used for assessing addiction or questionnaires specifically designed for diagnosis of Internet addiction can also be used by mental health professionals to diagnose Internet addiction.

Like any addiction, Internet addiction increases people's stress levels. Studies have shown that parental stress level has some correlation with adolescent Internet addiction. In one study, the authors observed that young males with an Internet gaming addiction reported greater stress in everyday life as well as chronic stress for a longer period of time compared to nonaddicts. Moreover, subjects addicted to the Internet showed attenuated cortisol response, higher heart rate, and greater negative effects in response to stress compared to normal subjects.[33]

In a study conducted by Dr. David Greenfield based on eighteen thousand individuals who logged on to the ABC News website, the author concluded that 5.7 percent of individuals met the criteria for Internet addiction. In other smaller studies, the prevalence of Internet addiction varied from 6 to 14 percent. Study participants were mostly addicted to chat rooms, pornography, online shopping, and e-mail. Approximately one-third said they used the Internet as a form of escape or to improve their mood on a regular basis. In addition, people addicted to the Internet admitted to feelings of losing control of their time spent on the Internet. Moreover, 75 percent of people addicted to the Internet admitted to feelings of intimacy for someone they met online, compared to 38 percent of nonaddicts who reported similar feelings, indicating that people addicted to the Internet may prefer to live in a virtual reality.

In general, males are more prone to Internet addiction than females. In one study based on 9,265 respondents, the authors reported that more men than women accessed pornography at least once (20 percent of men versus 12 percent of women).[34] In another study based on 713 adults, the authors reported that perceived addiction to Internet pornography, but not pornography use itself, was uniquely related to the experience of psychological distress.[35]

Most U.S. businesses provide Internet access to their employees, and almost all companies (82.6 percent) have Internet access policies in place outlining appropriate and inappropriate use of the Internet in the workplace. Despite such policies, employees abuse their Internet access; as a result, more than 60 percent of companies out of 224 companies surveyed disciplined their employees for inappropriate use of the Internet, while more than 30 percent of companies had terminated employees for inappropriate use. Accessing pornography, online chatting, gaming, investing, or shopping at work were leading causes of disciplinary action or termination.[36] In another study based on telephone interviews of 2,513 adults (mean age 48.5 years), the authors observed that 5.9 percent of respondents felt that their relationship suffered due to spending excessive time on the Internet, 8.7 percent attempted to conceal nonessential Internet use, 3.7 percent felt preoccupied by the Internet when offline, 13.7 percent found it difficult to stay away from the Internet for several days at a time, 8.2 percent used the Internet to relieve bad moods or to escape problems, 12.3 percent attempted to cut time on the Internet, and 12.4 percent stayed online longer than intended often or very often. Overall, approximately one out of eight people (12.5 percent) met at least one criterion for problematic Internet use. Individuals with problematic Internet use are highly likely to suffer from mood and anxiety disorders.[37]

> Spending more than five hours per day or more than thirty hours per week on the Internet for nonessential tasks is usually considered problematic use of the Internet.

Current U.S. data indicate that 93 percent of adolescents and young adults (aged twelve to twenty-nine years) use the Internet regularly. As a result, Internet addiction is more problematic for adolescents and young adults compared to older adults. Among adolescents and young adults, the prevalence of Internet addiction can be as high as 26.3 percent. Internet addictions in adolescents and young adults may have negative health consequences, including excessive daytime sleepiness due to poor sleep quality at night, depression, attention deficit hyperactivity disorder, problematic alcohol use, or injury. In addition, Internet addiction has been associated with negative academic consequences such as missed classes, lower grades, and even academic dismissal.[38] Moreover, Internet addiction is associated with decreased family communication, loneliness, shyness, and increased stress. Internet use is highest among young adults (aged sixteen to twenty-four years), and being of this age group may be considered a risk factor for Internet addiction. Interestingly, adolescent girls use the Internet to meet new people, to join various groups, and for personal networking, while adolescent boys use the Internet for surfing or to play violent games. Female students also spend more time on the Internet for academic study than male students. Problematic Internet use is likewise associated with loneliness and dating anxiety among young adults.[39]

> Internet addiction is associated with poor grades and academic difficulties in students. Moreover, these young adults may not socialize with friends and, as a result, may experience loneliness, emotional problems, and increased stress.

Internet Addiction Alters the Brain's Chemistry

Internet addiction, like any other addiction, may also alter brain chemistry. In one study based on seventeen adolescent subjects suffering from Internet addiction and sixteen normal subjects with no such addiction (control), the authors observed abnormal white matter in brain scans (whole-brain voxel-wise analysis of fractional anisotropy) of individuals addicted to the Internet, but no such abnormality was observed in controls. The areas of the brain where white matter abnormality was observed are responsible for emotion, self-control, and decision making. Moreover, such abnormality may be linked to behavioral impairment. Other studies have shown decreased gray matter density in various parts of the brain of subjects with Internet addiction. Students addicted to the

> Internet addiction in adolescents may cause abnormal changes in the brain, leading to emotional instability, poor attention span, and impaired self-control.

Internet showed less efficiency in information processing and lower impulse control than normal subjects. A positron emission tomography (PET) study of the brain also revealed that people who were addicted to Internet games had neurological abnormalities that had some similarities with people addicted to drugs. Therefore, all these findings indicate that Internet addiction may cause structural and functional changes in the brain regions responsible for emotional processing, attention span, decision making, and cognitive control.[40]

Cell Phone Addiction and Stress

Addiction to cell phones (e.g., smart phones) is similar to addiction to the Internet. The current fascination with cell phones, for better or worse, appears to be encouraging people to spend relatively more time with cell phones and less time with fellow human beings. Such fascination is more intense among young adults, especially among college students, compared to older adults because 67 percent of young adults (aged eighteen to twenty-four years) own cell phones compared to 53 percent of all adults. Research suggests that college students consider cell phones a significant part of their lives. Based on a large-scale survey of 2,500 U.S. college students, the authors observed that 60 percent of students admitted that they may be addicted to cell phones. Moreover, many young adults aged eighteen to twenty-nine (77 percent according to one survey) prefer to use cell phones for Internet access, thus replacing laptop or desktop computers for such access. Studies have shown that college students spent an average of 420 minutes (seven hours) on their cell phone daily. However, in a more recent study based on 164 college students, the authors observed that females spent an average of 600 minutes (10 hours) on their cell phone every day compared to 459 minutes (7.7 hours) per day spent by males. Time spent texting was the most common activity, but females spent more time texting than males (105 minutes for females compared to 84 minutes for males). After texting, sending e-mails and being on social media were the most common activities on cell phones. Most likely, the addictive part of cell phone use is related to time spent on various social networking sites such as Facebook, Instagram, and Pinterest. However, activities such as talking, sending e-mails, and texting may not be addictive.[41]

Various psychological questionnaires such as the Applied Mobile Phone Use Habit Survey or the Adapted Cell Phone Addiction Test can be used to evaluate whether a person is addicted to cell phones. In one study based on

301 college students and 362 non-college students, the authors observed that 10–20 percent of subjects exhibited problematic cell phone use, and their behavior satisfied a number of criteria for addiction. In addition, more than 40 percent of respondents in the study used their cell phones to help them feel relaxed, to improve mood, and to escape problems. The authors concluded that, like Internet addiction, cell phone addiction is a behavioral addiction that should be taken seriously by the psychological community.[42] Cell phone addiction is also associated with anxiety, stress, sleep disturbances, and (to a lesser extent) depression.[43]

Cell phone addiction is more common in young adults. Cell phone addiction increases psychological stress and anxiety and causes sleep disturbances. Cell phone addiction may also, to a lesser extent, increase the risk of depression.

FREQUENT CONSUMPTION OF ENERGY DRINKS MAY INCREASE STRESS

Energy drinks are frequently marketed targeting young adults with declarations of increasing mental and physical energy levels as well as providing a short-term boost to mood and performance. However, some energy drinks contain almost three times the caffeine of an average carbonated soda. Although the acute mood effects associated with consuming energy drinks is often positive, regular consumption of energy drinks is associated with undesirable mental health effects such as anxiety, depression, and possibly mood disorders. In one study based on 136 undergraduate students, the authors observed that male students in general consumed more energy drinks than female students. Moreover, students consumed energy drinks when they felt stressed out. However, consuming energy drinks on a regular basis was associated with lower academic performance.[44] In another study based on 502 young males and 567 young females, the authors observed that energy drink consumption (100 mL/day) was significantly associated with anxiety (though not depression) in males but not in females.[45]

Regular consumption of energy drinks may increase anxiety and stress levels and negatively impact academic performance in young adults.

In one review article, the authors included twenty studies investigating the effects of energy drinks on mental health and commented that although some studies reported no association, the majority of studies observed negative mental health consequences of consuming energy drinks on a regular basis. One study reported higher stress levels in regular energy drink consumers (i.e., those who consumed more than one energy drink per week) compared to nonregular users (i.e., those who consumed one or fewer energy drinks per week). Drinking three or more energy drinks per day was associated with sleep disturbances. Studies have also reported higher anxiety levels in regular energy drink consumers compared to nonconsumers, as well as a positive association between regular energy drink consumption and depression, self-harming, and even suicidal thoughts in tenth-grade students from Turkey.[46]

MEASURING PSYCHOLOGICAL STRESS

Although feeling stressed out may be subjective, researchers must have quantitative methodologies to evaluate the magnitude of psychological stress in different situations. Biological variables such as cortisol, norepinephrine, and epinephrine measured in biological fluids (serum urine, saliva), as well as blood pressure, heart rate, and respiratory rate, are valid quantitative approaches to measuring stress levels. Moreover, various questionnaires have been developed to assess an individual's stress level. These questionnaires are designed based on various factors such as daily hassles, happiness ratings, an individual's perception of the present and the future (optimism or pessimism), personality traits, depressive life events, and so on. Although these questionnaires can assess stress using certain scoring methods, such an approach has limitations, such as the subjective bias of an individual toward assessment of her or his true psychological state. Moreover, a person may not disclose his or her addiction to alcohol or drugs even when secrecy of response is assured. People may also avoid disclosing personal matters such as stress with a relationship. As a result, newer biomarkers of stress have been developed to assess the stress level of a person objectively.[47]

The Trier Social Stress Test (TSST) is a laboratory-based standardized test that is widely used to induce psychological stress in human subjects during stress-related studies. The protocol for the TSST was originally developed by Kirschbaum and colleagues at the University of Trier. In general, several hormones, including adrenocorticotropin (ACTH), cortisol, vasopressin, beta-endorphin, epinephrine, and growth hormone, are increased in response to psychological stress, but levels of luteinizing hormone and testosterone are decreased. However,

> The Trier Social Stress Test (TSST) is a laboratory-based standardized method that is widely used in stress research. Cortisol, a stress hormone, is the main biomarker of stress. However, salivary alpha-amylase is also a useful marker of stress response.

there are large interindividual variations. In the TSST, the hypothalamic-pituitary-adrenal axis (HPA axis) is activated in test subjects by inducing psychological stress. In general, there is an anticipatory period (ten minutes) and then a test period of ten minutes where subjects have to deliver an impromptu speech for a job interview and perform mental arithmetic (serial subtraction) in front of an audience of supposed experts. Participants are also informed that they will be videotaped and later evaluated by professionals. The response to such psychological stress in test subjects is measured by determining serum levels of ACTH, growth hormone, prolactin, and total cortisol (before and after psychological stress). Alternatively, salivary cortisol is also measured. In addition, heart rate response may be monitored. In general, concentrations of ACTH, growth hormone, prolactin, and cortisol are significantly increased in response to psychological stress in test subjects compared to baseline values (pretest values). Salivary cortisol may increase two- to fourfold from the baseline value.[48] However, there are modified versions of the TSST where only some of the parameters described in the original TSST are measured. Several investigators have used the TSST where only salivary cortisol (noninvasive because no blood is drawn) was measured.

Although cortisol response is a widely accepted measure for the TSST, salivary alpha-amylase is also a useful marker of stress response because it is a noninvasive surrogate marker of sympathetic nervous system activity. Moreover, it has been suggested that salivary alpha-amylase may serve as an index of dysregulation of the autonomic nervous system in patients with mental disorders.

Laboratory stressors such as the TSST induce reliable psychological stress responses, which are mainly assessed using biological parameters such as cortisol. In one study, the authors investigated whether emotional stress response correlates with the physiological parameters measured. The authors initially reviewed data from 358 studies and further evaluated data from 49 studies and found significant correlations between cortisol response and emotional stress response in approximately 25 percent of the studies. The authors concluded that stress reactivity is a complex phenomenon involving several response systems—namely, cognitive, emotional, psychological, and behavioral responses—which may explain significant differences between studies. The authors suggested that future studies should also include personality traits that may significantly influence stress response.[49]

PHYSIOLOGICAL RESPONSE TO STRESS

Homeostasis is the tendency of an organism to maintain physiological equilibrium in the body so that blood pressure, heart rate, oxygen content of the blood, and blood pH, as well as concentrations of electrolytes, sugar, hormones, and many other biochemical parameters, are maintained within normal physiological ranges. Stress disrupts this physiological equilibrium through activation of a specific part of the nervous system, which then through chemical messengers activates adrenal glands to secret various stress hormones, including cortisol.

In general, the nervous system can be broadly divided into the central nervous system (the nervous system that consists of the brain, including optic nerves, and the spinal cord) and the peripheral nervous system (nerves and ganglia outside of the brain and spinal cord, but these nerves do go to and from the central nervous system). The peripheral nervous system can be subdivided into the voluntary nervous system (somatic nervous system) and the involuntary nervous system (autonomic nervous system). The autonomic nervous system is vital to maintaining homeostasis because this nervous system controls vital functions of the body, including heart rate, blood pressure, breathing, maintaining water and electrolyte balance, production of body fluids (saliva, sweat, and tears), secretion of stomach acid and food processing, and urination. The autonomic nervous system has two divisions, the sympathetic nervous system and the parasympathetic nervous system. Stress activates the sympathetic nervous system and prepares the body for a stress response, while the parasympathetic nervous system calms the body and attempts to restore homeostasis during stress relief.

The midlevel part of the brain, known as the limbic system (consisting of the thalamus, hypothalamus, amygdala, and pituitary gland), plays a vital role in stress response. Walter Cannon, an American physiologist, first described the "fight or flight" phenomenon in humans and animals as a survival mechanism in response to external threat. In response to perceived threat, sensory nerves (present in the eyes, ears, and other sensory organs) send the information to the amygdala (fear is first registered in the amygdala) for processing. If the amygdala interprets this information as a perceived danger, then it instantly sends a distress signal to the hypothalamus, which is the primary stress response center in the brain. Within seconds of perceiving danger, the following stress responses are observed:

- The hypothalamus immediately activates the sympathetic-adrenomedullary system (sympathetic nervous system and the adrenal medullary endocrine system) to secrete epinephrine and norepinephrine, which are responsible for the first response to stress. The first norepinephrine is secreted within two to three seconds in response to stress from neurons in the sympathetic nervous system followed by higher amounts of epinephrine and norepinephrine secreted between twenty and thirty seconds from the adrenal medulla.
- The hypothalamus also activates the hypothalamic-pituitary-adrenal axis (HPA axis), which is responsible for the secretion of stress hormones, most importantly cortisol. However, this response takes more time (minutes to hours).
- The hypothalamus produces an antidiuretic hormone (synthesized in the hypothalamus but secreted by the pituitary gland) also known as vasopressin. This hormone is responsible for water retention by the kidneys and also increased blood pressure.
- The hypothalamus secretes thyrotropin releasing hormone, which stimulates the pituitary gland to secrete thyroid stimulating hormone (TSH). TSH stimulates the thyroid gland to secrete thyroxin and triiodothyronine. The purpose of these hormones is to increase metabolism, but this response is a long-term response to stress.

It has been well established in the medical literature that activation of the sympathetic-adrenomedullary system by the hypothalamus provides immediate response to stress while activation of the HPA axis, also by the hypothalamus, provides long-term response to stress. When the hypothalamus activates the sympathetic nervous system, neurons (the locus coeruleus) of the sympathetic nervous system secrete norepinephrine (synthesized from dopamine), and this response is the fastest response to stress (the fight-or-flight response). Then norepinephrine (also known as noradrenaline), which acts as a neurotransmitter, binds with adrenergic receptors (four types of receptors: $alpha_1$, $alpha_2$, $beta_1$, and $beta_2$; many cells throughout the body have these receptors), and this binding further stimulates the sympathetic nervous system. As a result, the adrenal medulla (the inner part of an adrenal gland; adrenal glands are important endocrine organs situated above the kidneys) is also stimulated, secreting epinephrine (synthesized from norepinephrine) and norepinephrine (these hormones are also called catecholamines). Epinephrine is also known as adrenaline. Only a small amount of norepinephrine is secreted by the neurons of the sympathetic nervous system, and the majority of epinephrine and norepinephrine is secreted by the adrenal medulla within twenty to thirty seconds in response to stress. The adrenal medulla secretes more epinephrine than norepinephrine (approximately 80 percent epinephrine and 20 percent norepinephrine). The effects of epinephrine and norepinephrine include the following:

- Heart: increased heart rate due to binding of epinephrine with beta receptors.
- Blood vessels: norepinephrine in particular causes constriction of blood vessels, thus increasing blood pressure.
- Lungs: airways open so that the lungs may take in as much oxygen as possible.
- Pancreas: inhibits beta cells (insulin-producing cells; insulin lowers blood sugar) and activates alpha cells (elevated glucagon levels that increase blood sugar), thus significantly increasing blood glucose levels so that more energy is available for the fight-or-flight response.
- Increased blood glucose: other than effects on the pancreas, adipose tissue is also activated, which leads to higher amounts of lipids in the blood that can also be used for energy. Moreover, glycogenolysis (breakdown of glycogen into glucose) is increased in the liver and skeletal muscles to produce more glucose for energy.
- Overall increase in metabolic rate: oxygen consumption and heat production increases throughout the body due to epinephrine. Sweat glands are also activated, producing more sweat in response to stress.
- Gastrointestinal tract: activity is inhibited, thus slowing down digestion.

Therefore, the first response to stress is mediated by epinephrine and norepinephrine. In response to stress, more blood is pushed through vital organs so that the body is more alert and ready for a fight-or-flight response. Another feature of activation of the sympathetic nervous system in response to stress is increased beta brain wave and decreased alpha wave output, indicating a fear response.

The HPA axis is also essential for the stress response because it completes the fight-or-flight response. When the hypothalamus is stimulated due to stress, corticotropin releasing hormone (CRH) is secreted by the hypothalamic paraventricular nucleus along with another hormone, arginine vasopressin (ARV). CRH and ARV are transported by the bloodstream to the pituitary gland situated just beneath the hypothalamus; as a result, adrenocorticotropic hormone (ACTH) is secreted by the pituitary gland into the bloodstream. ACTH activates the adrenal cortex (outer portion of the adrenal glands), which then secretes cortisol (glucocorticoid), the major stress hormone responsible for the stress response. In response to stress, the adrenal cortex also secretes mineralocorticoid (for example, aldosterone) and androgen (for example, testosterone) hormones. However, unlike epinephrine and norepinephrine, which are secreted immediately, a longer time is needed for cortisol secretion because peak cortisol is observed approximately twenty-five minutes after HPA axis activation.[50] Cortisol, a steroid hormone, is biosynthesized from cholesterol. In addition to glucocorticoid and mineralocorticoid hormones, elevated concentrations of inflammatory cytokines are observed during stress.

After cortisol is released by the adrenal cortex, it travels through the bloodstream and exerts its effect on multiple organs including the brain. Unlike epinephrine and norepinephrine, which does not cross the blood-brain barrier to a significant extent, cortisol crosses the blood-brain barrier to a significant degree, and the brain is a major target for cortisol due to the presence of two receptors that bind with cortisol. Moreover, cortisol increases blood pressure and heart rate so that more blood can flow into muscles for proper response to acute stress. Cortisol increases blood sugar so that more energy is available for the fight-or-flight response. Cortisol also increases oxidative stress and can cause damage to nerve cells (neurons), and it reduces concentrations of antioxidant enzymes.

The HPA axis demonstrates a circadian pattern, with a high level in the morning after waking up and low levels in the late evening hours and the lowest level after midnight in humans. In general, African Americans show flatter morning-to-evening cortisol slopes than Caucasians, and Hispanics exhibit significantly lower evening cortisol levels than Caucasians.[51]

A stressful situation occurs when events exceed an individual's ability to cope. Acute stresses usually have shorter duration (minutes to hours), but chronic stress may last for several hours per day or for weeks or even months. When the stressful situation no longer exists, the body attempts to reestablish its original equilibrium (homeostasis). High cortisol in the blood in response to stress provides negative feedback to the HPA axis; as a result, cortisol secretion is reduced. Moreover, the parasympathetic nervous system, which has a calming effect on the body (reducing heart rate, blood pressure, etc.), is activated, secreting acetylcholine with the goal of reestablishing the original homeostasis. Allostasis is defined as the body's adaptive response to stress (either reestablishing the original homeostasis or achieving a state close to the original equilibrium). However, in people experiencing chronic stress, the original homeostasis may not be reestablished, but the body attempts to maintain the physiological balance as close as possible to original homeostasis; this stage is often referred to as "allostatic load."

> Cortisol is a biomarker of stress.

Altered Activity of the HPA Axis Due to Chronic Stress

In response to acute stress the HPA axis is stimulated, causing secretion of the stress hormone cortisol from the adrenal glands. Cortisol mediates its action by binding with mineralocorticoid receptors (which have a high affinity for cortisol but a limited distribution in the hippocampal region of the brain) and glucocorticoid receptors (which have a low affinity for cortisol but are widely distributed in the hippocampus, amygdala, hypothalamus, brain stem, etc.). Under normal conditions, negative feedback of cortisol to the HPA axis is mediated by the binding of cortisol to mineralocorticoid receptors. Such negative feedback deactivates the HPA axis, and cortisol production is reduced. Acute stress has a short duration, and the HPA axis can easily adapt to such changes. Moreover, positive stress (eustress) always has a shorter duration, and the intensity of such acute stress is mild to moderate. Such stress produces only a transient increase in cortisol levels and is good for one's health. Unfortunately, under severe stress, negative feedback to the HPA axis is mediated through binding of cortisol to low-affinity glucocorticoid receptors. The effects of chronic stress on the HPA axis include the following:

- A hyperactive HPA axis, producing excess cortisol. Higher levels of cortisol have been reported in people experiencing chronic stress and depression.
- The HPA axis may be dysfunctional (dysregulated) and produce a lower amount of cortisol in response to stress compared to healthy people. This may also cause a blunted cortisol response (also known as a flatter cortisol curve) throughout the day.

In general, cortisol levels increase significantly (by more than 50 percent) within the first thirty minutes of waking and then decline significantly through evening, reaching the lowest value around midnight. The cortisol awakening response is measured in saliva within twenty to thirty minutes after waking and also after sixty minutes. Alternatively, salivary cortisol may also be measured at regular intervals throughout the day to establish a daily cortisol response curve. Interestingly, the cortisol awakening response on the weekend is lower than on weekdays in both men and women, indicating less stress during weekends. People experiencing chronic stress or depression may show either a higher cortisol awakening response (hyperactive HPA axis) or a lower cortisol awakening response (dysregulated HPA axis) compared to healthy people. Moreover, if cortisol awakening responses are lower than healthy individuals, cortisol response curves are also flatter (morning awakening cortisol is lower and bedtime cortisol is higher compared to healthy people).

Hyperactivity of the HPA axis is a common finding in depressed patients; as a result, a significant percentage of depressed patients (approximately 50 percent) exhibit hypercortisolemia (high cortisol level in blood, saliva, urine, or cerebrospinal fluid). Increased HPA axis activity has also been reported in patients with melancholic depression, anorexia nervosa, obsessive compulsive disorder, and panic disorder, thus explaining why chronic stress increases the risk of such mental disorders.[52] In one study using twenty unmedicated depressed individuals and forty healthy volunteers, the authors observed a higher cortisol awakening response in depressed patients compared to healthy controls. Patients with depression secreted 25 percent more cortisol within sixty minutes of waking compared to healthy volunteers.[53]

Higher cortisol awakening response has also been reported in healthy young men who showed signs of depression compared to nondepressed healthy men.[54] In another study involving forty-nine young subjects who were not depressed but had a family history of major depression and fifty-five participants with no such family history of depression (the control group), the authors observed a higher cortisol awakening response in individuals with a family history of major depression compared to subjects in the control group. The authors concluded that hypersecretion of cortisol can be observed in asymptomatic individuals with a genetic risk of depression.[55] Significantly increased cortisol awakening responses have been reported in both male and female burnout subjects compared to those who did not report any burnout phenomena.[56] Based on a study of 549 subjects suffering from major depression, the authors observed an increased cortisol awakening response during the recurrence of major depressive events.[57]

However, some studies have reported lower cortisol awakening response in highly stressed-out people. In one study based on 118 healthy women who reported experiencing low or high stress, the authors observed lower cortisol awakening response in highly stressed women compared to the low-stress group.[58] In another report based on 338 police officers, the authors observed lower cortisol awakening response in highly stressed police officers compared to officers experiencing low stress levels.[59]

Although cortisol level can be measured in serum, saliva, or urine, hair cortisol is correlated with long-term cortisol levels in the blood. Elevated hair cortisol levels have been documented in various stressed-out populations, including endurance athletes, shift workers (night-shift workers showed higher hair cortisol levels than day-shift workers), unemployed people, students facing a major life event (death of a close relative or serious illness), people experiencing pain, and stressed-out children. Regarding mental illnesses, higher hair cortisol levels were observed in patients suffering from major depression and posttraumatic stress disorder (PTSD). However, in patients with anxiety disorder, hair cortisol levels were reduced compared to healthy people. Moreover, in PTSD patients, after an initial increase, hair cortisol levels may decrease, indicating less cortisol output due to a dysfunctional HPA axis.[60]

Interestingly, hair cortisol level is reduced following effective stress management. In one study based on thirty-seven stressed-out subjects who attended classes to learn coping skills in response to stress, the authors observed that subjects who completed the program showed significantly lower cortisol levels at the end of the program compared to at the beginning of the program.

> Hair cortisol may be a better biomarker of stress than serum, saliva, or urine cortisol.

However, no difference was observed in salivary cortisol levels in subjects between the first and last sessions. The authors concluded that hair cortisol level is superior to salivary cortisol as a marker of stress.[61]

PSYCHOLOGICAL STRESS INCREASES OXIDATIVE STRESS

Chronic stress increases oxidative stress on the body (the imbalance between free radical production and antioxidant defense in the body), which is very harmful because many physical and mental illnesses are linked to increased oxidative stress. In one study, the authors reported that divorced men showed lower antioxidant defense in the central nervous system (CNS) and were more susceptible to free radical–induced brain injury compared to married men. In addition, posttraumatic stress disorder observed in American soldiers returning from Iraq has been linked to increased oxidative stress in their brains.[62]

In one study, the authors examined the stress levels of fifty-eight healthy premenopausal women who were the biological mother of either a healthy child (nineteen women) or a chronically ill child (thirty-nine women) and observed that women who cared for chronically ill children were stressed out compared to women who cared for healthy children. Moreover, stressed-out women showed higher amounts of oxidative stress.[63] Increased oxidative stress in individuals suffering from chronic psychological stress may also be due to chronically elevated cortisol levels in these subjects. In one study, the authors observed that postmenopausal women who cared for spouses with dementia experienced chronic psychological stress and showed higher oxidative stress and higher cortisol levels in their blood compared to age-matched postmenopausal women who lived with healthy spouses. The authors concluded that chronically elevated blood cortisol is associated with increased oxidative stress.[64]

ACUTE STRESS, EPISODIC ACUTE STRESS, AND CHRONIC STRESS

As mentioned earlier, stress cannot be avoided in life. Acute stress is the most common form of stress, and some types of acute stress (eustress) can be exciting and have positive effects on human performance as well as on achieving desired goals in life. Most people recognize the symptoms of acute stress, and because acute stress has a short duration, its damaging effects on the body are minimal. However, when an individual experiences acute stress frequently, it is defined as episodic acute stress. People with type A personality (excessive competitive drive, aggressive, always in a rush, etc.) are not only prone to heart diseases but also experience episodic acute stress more often. However, people with type B personality are calm and pragmatic, and they have better coping skills for stress. Many people also have a mixed personality, with some traits of type A personality and some traits of type B personality.

Chronic stress occurs when a person does not see any way out of a miserable life situation. Chronic stress is very harmful to the body because chronically elevated cortisol significantly increases oxidative stress. Many stressors have lifelong adverse effects on both physical and mental health. Many situations—such as poverty, a dysfunctional family, being trapped in an unhappy marriage where thoughts about the possibility of divorce induce more stress (cultural stigma, financial distress), an unhappy job situation, prolonged unemployment, caring for a disabled spouse, and chronic health problems—can cause chronic stress. In children, early life stress has devastating effects later in life. Early life stress includes the following:

- Physical abuse
- Sexual abuse
- Physical neglect
- Emotional abuse (verbal aggression affecting the morale of a child or any conduct that humiliates, embarrasses, or threatens the well-being of a child)
- Emotional neglect (failure to provide love and support by parents or caretakers)
- Traumatic experiences in childhood including parental death, severe injury in a motor vehicle accident, and exposure to domestic or community violence
- Bullying in school

Childhood maltreatment is a major social problem, and its psychological consequences can severely affect a child's mental health well into adulthood. Childhood traumas, especially those that are interpersonal, intentional, and chronic, are associated with greater risk of PTSD, depression, anxiety, antisocial behavior, and alcohol and substance abuse when these children become adults.[65]

Individuals with certain personality types are more susceptible to chronic stress. People with type C personality (also known as cancer-prone personality, first described by Linda Temoshol in cancer patients) repress their emotions and are not risk takers. Because people with type C personality deny

Table 1.1. Symptoms of acute stress, episodic acute stress, and chronic stress

Acute Stress	Episodic Acute Stress	Chronic Stress
• Heart palpitation • Increased blood pressure • Stress headache • Stomach upset • Excessive sweating • Anxiety or worries • Irritability • Short-term depression • Reduced libido	• Experiencing symptoms of acute stress more frequently • Recurrent brief periods of depression • More frequent emotional distress • Unnecessary worries • Reduced sex drive	• Frequent headache • Pounding of the heart • Periodic shortness of breath • Dry mouth • Stomachache • Tightening of muscles • Feeling depressed • Frequently tensed up • Difficulty focusing on job • Sleep disturbances • Feeling of fatigue • Lack of interest in sex

their feelings and cannot stand up for their rights, they are at higher risk of feeling chronic stress and even depression compared to people with other types of personality. Individuals with type D personality have a tendency to experience negative emotions, and they often avoid social contact with others often due to an unsubstantiated fear of rejection. People with type D personality experience chronic stress and are prone to major depression. Symptoms of acute stress, episodic acute stress, and chronic stress are listed in table 1.1.

ADVERSE EFFECTS OF STRESS ON MENTAL HEALTH

Stress is a well-known trigger of depression, anxiety, fear, and behavioral disorders.[66] Moreover, early adversity occurring in childhood or adolescence, stressful life events, episodic interpersonal stress, and recent chronic stress are independently associated with increased risk of major depression in life. Approximately 20–25 percent of persons who experience stressful life events develop depression. The most stressful life events are "losses," such as the death of a spouse, family member, or close friend, separation, divorce, or even significant threat of separation. Such negative life events may cause more severe depression in women compared to men. Other significant life stressors include marital conflicts, being fired from a job, prolonged unemployment, chronic illness, and trouble with raising children. Chronic stress, which is defined as ongoing difficulties lasting at least four weeks, is associated with a higher risk of depression. Chronic stress due to absence of social support is also associated with depression.[67]

Chronic stress may be subdivided into interpersonal stress and noninterpersonal stress. Interpersonal chronic stress arises from difficulty in an intimate relationship, a close friendship, one's social life, or family relationships, while noninterpersonal chronic stress is related to achieving academic goals, work-related stress, financial issues, personal health, or the health of a family member. In one study based on 119 previously depressed individuals, who subsequently completed six-month, twelve-month, and eighteen-month follow-up interviews to determine chronic stress and onset of a new major depressive episode, the authors observed that only chronic interpersonal stress was associated with recurrence of another major depressive episode, but no correlation was observed between noninterpersonal stress and recurrence of a major depressive event. Within the interpersonal stress domains, chronic romantic relationship issues, chronic friendship stress, and chronic family conflict all uniquely predicted increased risk for depressive recurrence.[68] In another study, the authors concluded that both chronic stress and episodic interpersonal stress are unique predictors of depression in emerging adults.[69]

> Adverse childhood events, adverse life events, interpersonal episodic stress, and recent chronic stress are associated with significantly increased risk of major depression.

Chronic stress increases the risk of mild cognitive impairment and Alzheimer's disease. Chronic stress is also associated with burnout. Although PTSD may be due to exposure to a life-threatening event such as participating in an active war (veterans are at higher risk of developing PTSD), it may occur after a traumatic life event such as a near fatal accident or exposure to a violent event, including rape or sexual violence. Chronic stress also increases the risk of PTSD.[70] Studies have also indicted a link between manic depressive disorder (bipolar disorder) and stress.[71] Stress and anxiety increase the risk of developing eating disorders.[72] Stress and anxiety moderately increase the risk of suicide in young adults.[73] Moreover, PTSD is frequently associated with suicidal ideation and suicide attempts.[74] The effects of stress on mental health are summarized in table 1.2.

The mechanism between chronic stress and mental disorders is very complex, involving interactions between the HPA axis, cortisol, and various neurotransmitter systems. Depressed patients often show lower serotonin (5-hydroxytryptamine; 5-HT) in the brain, while SSRI (selective serotonin reuptake inhibitor) drugs restore normal serotonin levels in the brain and

Table 1.2. Adverse effects of stress on physical and mental health

Adverse Effects on Physical Health	Adverse Effects on Mental Health
• Increased risk of cardiovascular (heart) diseases • Increased risk of stroke • Increased risk of asthma • Higher susceptibility to colds • Faster progression of AIDS • More joint pain and less mobility in patients suffering from rheumatoid arthritis • May increase risk of cancer • Increased risk of type 2 diabetes • Digestive problems • Sleep disturbances • Sexual dysfunction • Accelerated aging • Increased mortality • Possible weight gain	• Burnout • Increased risk of major depression • Increased risk of melancholic depression • Increased risk of anxiety disorder • Increased risk of panic disorder • Behavioral disorder (irritability, anger, hostile behavior, impulsivity, social withdrawal) • Mild cognitive impairment (problems with memory, learning, work, and difficulty in making decisions) • Increased risk of obsessive-compulsive disorder • Increased risk of Alzheimer's disease • Increased risk of bipolar disorder • Increased risk of violent behavior • Increased risk of suicide • May increase risk of alcohol and or substance abuse • Increased risk of schizophrenia

thus alleviate depression. Elevated cortisol levels due to stressful life events may reduce brain serotonin, causing depression in vulnerable individuals. Polymorphism of the serotonin transporter gene promoter (5-HTTLPR) may increase salivary cortisol secretion and increase the risk of depression in some people (carriers of the shorter allele). Dopamine is called the happy molecule, and the dopaminergic neurotransmitter system is important for the reward mechanism. Both acute and chronic stress may have a detrimental impact on the normal function of the dopaminergic system. A dysfunctional dopaminergic system may increase the risk of mental disorder in vulnerable people. Other neurotransmitter systems such as glutamate and GABA (gamma-hydroxybutyric acid) also play a major role in the central integration of the HPA axis stress response.[75]

Stress Damages Brain Structure and Function

A normal cortisol level has no adverse effect on nerve cells (neurons), but an elevated cortisol level is toxic to neurons (neurotoxic). When the cortisol level is normal, it binds with the high-affinity mineralocorticoid receptors in the brain, but when cortisol concentration is high for a prolonged time due to chronic stress or episodic acute stress, cortisol also binds to low-affinity glucocorticoid receptors because such receptors are stimulated due to stress. Cortisol exerts its neurotoxicity through binding with low-affinity glucocorticoid receptors. Therefore, stress and the activation of glucocorticoid receptors consistently decrease the growth and development of neurons (neurogenesis), especially in the hippocampal area of the brain, causing shrinking of the hippocampal area, which supports learning memory and mood. Other regions of the brain may also be affected.

Reduced Brain Volume in People Suffering from Chronic Stress and Mental Illnesses

Chronic stressful experiences are associated not only with reduced hippocampal volume but also with impaired hippocampal-dependent functions in humans. In one study involving seventy older adult volunteers, the authors showed that stress reduced the volume of the hippocampus in both depressed and nondepressed adults.[76] One major consequence of chronic stress is the development of depression. In another study based on forty-eight healthy postmenopausal women, the authors used an advanced brain scan technique to observe that women who suffered from chronic depression showed decreased gray matter volume in the hippocampus compared to nonstressed women.[77]

More recently, the effect of stress on healthy individuals with no history of depression has been studied using sophisticated brain-imaging techniques. Even in healthy individuals, stressful life situations (death in a family, divorce, ending a relationship, loss of a home, loss of a job) and life trauma (exposure to violence or related trauma) can lead to shrinkages in parts of the brain responsible for regulating emotions and metabolism. In one study, the authors investigated 103 healthy volunteers aged eighteen to forty-eight using brain imaging (whole brain voxel-based morphometry analysis) and observed reduced gray matter volume in the medial prefrontal cortex. The prefrontal cortex is responsible for emotional control as well as vital physiological functions such as maintaining

> Stress and high cortisol levels decrease neurogenesis and trigger neural stem cells to malfunction. Normally these stem cells are converted into neurons, but in response to high cortisol and stress, these cells in the hippocampus are converted into oligodendrocytes (myelin-producing glial cells), causing mild cognitive impairment.[78]

normal glucose levels in the blood. Although recent stressful events were associated with smaller volumes in the prefrontal cortex and right insula (also a part of the cerebral cortex) in healthy subjects, life trauma was associated with small volume in medial prefrontal cortex, anterior cingulate, and subgenual regions. These regions of the brain regulate human mood. Smaller volume in this area is linked to anxiety and mood disorders. Chronic stress also erodes the human brain gradually, causing reduced brain volume.[79]

In one interesting study, the authors performed a multimodal neuroimaging study (a type of magnetic resonance imaging, or MRI) in thirty-six healthy adults who were within 1.5 miles of the World Trade Center on September 11, 2001, during the terrorist attack or were living more than two hundred miles away from New York during the attack but later moved to the New York metropolitan area. More than three years after the 9/11 attack, adults with closer proximity to the World Trade Center during the terrorist attack had a lower volume of gray matter in the hippocampus, the medial prefrontal cortex, and other areas of the brain (the insula, anterior cingulate, and amygdala) compared to people not directly exposed to terrorism.[80]

> Acute stress reduces brain volume in the prefrontal cortex area (although other brain areas may also be damaged), while chronic stress reduces brain volume in the hippocampus, although other areas are also affected.

Reduced brain volume in depressed patients may be related to activation of the GATA1 transcription repressor, which reduces the expression of genes (*CALM2*, *SYN1*, *RAB3A*, *RAB4B*, and *TUBB4*) essential for synaptic connections between neurons in the prefrontal cortex. In addition, when authors stimulated GATA1 in rats, symptoms of depression were observed, along with lower volume of the prefrontal cortex. The authors concluded that activation of GATA1 is responsible for the loss of brain volume in the prefrontal cortex in depressed patients.[81]

Chronic stress results in disrupted neural connectivity between the amygdala and prefrontal cortex. As a result, people suffering from chronic stress may overreact to stress with unnecessary fear and anxiety. Chronic stress also changes the normal neural plasticity of the brain. Neural plasticity refers to the ability of the nervous system to respond and adapt to environmental challenges through interconnections between various parts of the nervous system. Exposure to chronic stress reduces the normal neural plasticity of the brain because the expression of neurotrophic molecules (molecules that promote survival and differentiation of neurons) such as BDNF (brain-derived neurotrophic factor) is reduced. Reduced levels of BDNF have been well documented in depressed subjects. Chronic stress can cause atrophy of the hippocampus and prefrontal cortex, but the amygdala may be hypertrophic. All of these factors increase the risk of anxiety, depression, mood disorders, and other mental health problems in chronically depressed patients.[82]

Chronic Stress Significantly Damages Developing Brains

Stress in young children may be positive, tolerable, or toxic. Positive stress is usually mild to moderate (anxiety before immunization, stress during the first day of school, stress before a final exam, etc.) and has short duration. Tolerable stress has a longer duration and greater magnitude, and it may be associated with parental divorce, death of a family member, and the like, but children can tolerate such stress when parents and other family members buffer it by providing nurturing and affection to the child. However, toxic stress, which is associated with adverse childhood experiences (child neglect and physical or mental abuse, including sexual abuse), damages the developing brain. Toxic stress in early childhood can cause lifelong physical and mental impairment in these children. Childhood maltreatment can reduce hippocampus volume even when these children become adults. In one study, using forty-six adult subjects, the authors observed lower hippocampus volume in adults who were maltreated during childhood.[83] In another study, the authors reviewed data from forty-nine published papers (including 2,720 participants) and concluded that experiences of childhood maltreatment are associated with a reduction in hippocampal volume, and the effects of maltreatment are more pronounced when the maltreatment occurs in middle childhood compared to early childhood.[84]

Childhood emotional maltreatment is also associated with lower brain volume in adulthood. Using high-resolution brain-imaging techniques, the authors in one study observed profound reductions of medial prefrontal cortex volume in adults who reported emotional maltreatment even in the absence of physical or sexual abuse during childhood ($n = 84$, mean age 38.7 years) in both men

> Childhood maltreatment causes significant damage to the developing brain, which can be observed when children reach adulthood.

and women compared to subjects reporting no maltreatment during child-hood (n = 97, mean age 36.6 years).[85]

STRESS INCREASES THE RISK OF PHYSICAL ILLNESS

Cardiovascular diseases (CVDs), including myocardial infarction (heart attack), are one of the leading causes of disability and death worldwide. Many large cohort studies have demonstrated a strong link between stress (psychosocial stress) and increased morbidity and mortality from CVDs in healthy populations. Stress may cause increased sympathetic nervous system activity, which may lead to increased blood pressure and pulse rates. More-over, chronic stress is associated with increased platelet aggregation (which increases the risk of blood clot, a risk factor for CVD) and increased oxida-tive stress (another risk factor for CVD). In one study, the authors followed 73,424 Japanese men and women aged forty to seventy-eight years, who at the time of enrollment were free from CVD, stroke, and cancer, for seven to nine years and concluded that perceived mental stress was associated with increased mortality from stroke for women and with CVD in both men and women. The authors also observed that stress significantly increased the risk of heart attack in men.[86]

In the British Whitehall Cohort study involving 7,268 men and women (mean age 49.5 years) and eighteen years of follow-up, the authors observed that people who reported that perceived stress significantly affected their health at the time of enrollment had a 2.12 times higher risk of heart attack or even death from heart attack compared to people who reported no effect of stress on their health.[87] Even high work-related stress may increase the risk of CVD by 50 percent in healthy people. Moreover, after the first heart attack, work-related stress may increase the subsequent risk of heart attack by 65 percent when compared with people who experience no significant work-related stress.[88]

Beyond chronic stress, significant acute life stress may also increase the risk of CVD. Based on one study involving 95,647 individuals and four to five years of follow-up, the authors observed that the highest relative mor-tality occurred immediately after bereavement, with a greater than twofold higher risk for men and a greater than threefold higher risk for women. After the first month, the mortality rate returned to the normal population level in these subjects.[89] The rate of heart disease also increases in the immediate aftermath of other acute life stressors such as an earthquake or terrorist activity. For example, during the massive earthquake of 1994 in Los Angeles, death due to CVD increased sharply from 4.6 deaths a day in the week preceding the earthquake to 24 deaths on the day of the earthquake. Moreover, anger can trigger a heart attack. In another study involving 1,623 subjects, the authors showed that after an episode of anger, the relative risk of heart attack was increased more than twofold.[90]

> Chronic stress and acute life stressors (e.g., bereavement, earthquake, terrorist attack) may significantly increase the risk of as well as mortality from CVD, including heart attack. An episode of anger may also increase the risk of heart attack more than twofold.

Current research indicates a causal relationship between psychosocial stress and asthma or asthma morbidity.[91] Those individuals with the most stressful life events and higher levels of perceived stress have a higher likelihood of developing cold symptoms. Chronic stress is associated with a faster progression of AIDS. Chronic stress also has proinflammatory effects; as a result, chronic stress is associated with more swelling and reduced mobility in patients with rheumatoid arthritis.[92] Stress increases the risk of various types of cancer. In one study, the authors observed that women with major life events, chronic psychological stress, and depression had a 3.7 times higher risk of breast cancer compared to women who were not stressed. However, job-related stress only increased the risk of breast cancer by 16 percent compared to women with no significant job-related stress, but such a small increase was not statistically significant.[93]

Approximately 220 million people worldwide are living with type 2 diabetes (non-insulin dependent diabetes), the most common type of diabetes. It has been well documented that acute stress is associated with insulin resistance, and people with poor coping skills with regard to psychological stress are at a higher risk of developing type 2 diabetes. Results of longitudinal studies suggest that not only depression but also emotional stress and anxiety, sleeping problems, anger, and hostility are associated

> Major life events, chronic psychological stress, and depression, but not job-related stress, increase the risk of breast cancer in women.

with an increased risk of type 2 diabetes.[94] Certain stressful life events have been associated with onset or symptom exacerbation of common diseases of the digestive system, including gastroesophageal reflux disease (GERD), peptic ulcers, and inflammatory bowel disease.[95]

Sleep disturbance is a common symptom of both acute and chronic stress. Stress may also cause sexual dysfunction as well as have a negative effect on reproduction. In one study based on 193 men, the authors observed that men with a higher level of perceived stress showed lower sperm quality, but job stress had no effect on sperm quality.[96] Chronic stress may lower sexual arousal levels in women.[97] Psychological stress and depression are associated with an accelerated aging process due to excess secretion of cortisol.[98]

Chronic stress may increase the risk of premature death. In one report, the authors linked data from a 1998 National Health Interview Survey with National Death Index mortality data through 2006 and concluded that 33.7 percent of U.S. adults perceived that stress affected their health a lot or to some extent. People who reported a high amount of stress and had the perception that stress significantly affected their health had a 43 percent increased risk of premature death.[99] It has been well documented in the medical literature that stress is associated with eating disorders and a significantly increased risk of weight gain. In a study based on 5,118 participants and a five-year follow-up, the authors concluded that psychosocial stress, including perceived stress and life events stress, is positively associated with weight gain in both men and women.[100] The adverse effects of stress on physical health are listed in table 1.2.

BENEFITS OF STRESS MANAGEMENT

Many ill effects of acute and chronic stress can be reversed by stress management. In one study, the authors showed that mindfulness-based stress management was effective in reducing anxiety and improving health-related quality of life in their study population (inner-city people).[101] Cortisol is elevated in response to stress, but various stress management modalities effectively reduce stress as reflected by lower salivary, urine, and blood cortisol. As mentioned earlier in this chapter, effective stress management also reduces hair cortisol. In one study, the authors observed that stress management for two months reduced cortisol levels and increased social connectedness in seven- to nine-year-old children.[102]

It has been well established that chronic stress and depression can reduce brain volume, especially in the hippocampal area. However, the brain has a great deal of adaptive capability, and, as a result, stress-induced lower brain volume can be restored by proper stress management. Studies have shown that meditation is associated with increased hippocampal volume (see chapter 5). Day-to-day stressors such as misplacing your car keys, traffic jams, and minor arguments with family members or coworkers are called daily hassles, which are less stressful than major negative life events, but even daily hassles increase stress levels. In one study, the authors found that subjects who received four weeks of intervention with biofeedback training showed lower salivary cortisol compared to subjects who did not received biofeedback training. The authors concluded that biofeedback training is effective in reducing stress levels caused by daily hassles. Moreover, subjects who received biofeedback training were calmer and showed positive psychological state compared to subjects in the control group. In addition, using brain scans (MRI), the authors observed more gray matter volume in the hippocampal and other areas of the brain (areas most susceptible to stress) in subjects who received biofeedback training compared to subjects in the control group.[103] Therefore, stress management can protect against and may even reverse loss of brain volume due to exposure to chronic stress.

Many studies have clearly demonstrated smaller hippocampus volume in patients suffering from PTSD. Additional gray matter reductions have been reported in other brain areas, such as the prefrontal cortex, anterior cingulate cortex, and left temporal pole/middle temporal gyrus. These brain areas are involved in fear conditioning and emotional control, which are severely affected in these patients. Moreover, expression of the FKBP5 gene is lower in PTSD patients. In one study, the authors showed that psychotherapy (cognitive behavioral therapy) for twelve weeks significantly reduced symptoms and improved quality of life in PTSD patients. In addition, clinical improvements in these patients were associated with increased hippocampal volume and increased expression of the FKBP5 gene.[104] Therefore, shrinkage in the brain of patients suffering from PTSD can be reversed by psychotherapy.

In patients with social anxiety disorder, the amygdala area of the brain is hyperactive while neural connections with the prefrontal cortex are disrupted. In one study involving patients with social anxiety disorder, the authors observed that after twelve weeks of psychotherapy, these patients showed significant improvements, which were associated with better connection between the amygdala and prefrontal cortex.[105] In another study based on twenty-eight outpatients suffering from treatment-resistant major depression, the authors observed that in twelve patients who sustained remission for six months, the volume of the whole brain as well as gray matter volume in the right orbitofrontal cortex and the right inferior temporal gyrus were significantly increased compared to nonremitters. However, only remission, not use of antidepressant therapy, was associated with increased brain volume.[106]

Shrinkage of the brain due to stress can be reversed by proper stress management. Moreover, reduced brain volume due to major depression or PTSD can be reversed by psychotherapy or, if needed, antidepressant therapy.

Some studies have shown that antidepressants can promote neurogenesis in the hippocampus and other brain areas, thus effectively increasing brain volume, which is also associated with remission of depressive symptoms. In one study, the authors showed that twelve-week treatment with the antidepressant sertraline (an SSRI drug) significantly increased gray matter volume in the prefrontal cortex, which was also correlated with reduced depression levels.[107]

Stress Management Is Essential during Pregnancy

Psychosocial stress during pregnancy increases the risk of preterm birth, a low birth weight infant, or even developmental delays in children. The biological mediators are primarily the stress hormone cortisol and cytokines. Therefore, proper stress management during pregnancy is essential, and primary care physicians may play an important role to help stressed-out pregnant women. It may even be necessary for primary care physicians or gynecologists to refer some women, especially those with preexisting mental disorders such as anxiety or depression, to mental health professionals.[108] Many traditional stress management approaches can also effectively manage stress in pregnant women. Unless placed on complete bed rest, exercise, yoga, and meditation are effective in reducing stress during pregnancy. A prenatal yoga practice has been shown to benefit women who suffer from stress, anxiety, depression, and sleep disturbances.[109] In a study based on 202 pregnant women, the authors showed that both stress management training and standard care reduced perceived stress levels, but reductions were more significant in pregnant women who received stress management training (see chapter 4).[110]

CONCLUSION

Chronic stress reduces gray matter volume in the hippocampal area of the brain, which plays an important role in learning, memory, spatial orientation, navigation, and emotional response. Shrinking of the hippocampal area due to chronic stress may cause mild cognitive impairment, such as difficulty in recalling, and eventually may increase the risk of dementia and Alzheimer's disease. Fortunately, stress management can protect or even reverse such brain damage. For example, meditation can increase the hippocampal gray matter content of the brain, thus reversing damage caused by chronic stress. For severely depressed patients, when remission of the disease is achieved through psychotherapy or antidepressant treatment, some brain damage caused by the depression can be reversed. Moreover, receiving timely treatment can prevent recurrence of such mental disorders. Therefore, seeking professional help is the best approach to getting back into normal life.

Although acute stress can also cause some harm, such as slight damage to the prefrontal cortex area of the brain, such minor damage can be easily reversed by adopting the stress management modality of your choice. However, life trauma that may eventually cause PTSD is associated with significant damage to the prefrontal cortex and other areas of the brain. Nevertheless, proper therapy can reverse some of the damage caused by traumatic experiences.

2

Do Women Have Better Coping Skills in Response to Stress?

Stress is part of everyday life, but men and women cope with stress differently. Throughout human history, men and women have been under divergent pressures of natural selection, which is manifested in physiological and behavioral differences between genders. Men prefer a "fight or flight" approach, which is a traditional aggressive stress response, but women respond to stress with a different approach called "tend and befriend." This is a kinder, nurturing stress response. For example, after a marital argument, the husband may go for a walk alone, while the wife is more likely to call a female friend or a relative for comfort. A woman's approach to stress is probably superior to a man's fight-or-flight approach.

> In response to stress, men prefer an aggressive "fight or flight" approach, while women opt for a "tend and befriend" approach, which is a gentle, nurturing response to stress.

SOCIAL STEREOTYPES AND STRESS IN WOMEN

Considerable attention has been focused during the past two decades on understanding stress in the lives of men and women. Social stereotypes play a role in exposing men and women to different stressors. A girl is sometimes brainwashed into being a good wife and mother, with a primary goal of taking care of her family, where she is responsible for cooking, housecleaning, and child rearing. In contrast, a boy is encouraged to grow up to be a man, having a good income and high social status but little responsibility for household chores. Moreover, parents may encourage a girl to be submissive but may tolerate some degree of aggressive behavior in a boy. If a woman works, it is commonly expected that she will be working as a nurse, not as a doctor, or that she will be a secretary, not the boss. Gender stereotypes emphasize achievement, competency, and competition in men; as a result, men experience a great deal of stress because they are constantly striving to perform well and advance their career in a very competitive world.

In general, women are exposed to more stress than men. Women have less access to power and control at work than men do because women are more likely to be employed in low-prestige, low-paying positions with little opportunity for advancement. Moreover, gender stereotypes for women encourage them to have great concern for the well-being of others, and they are the primary caretakers of children and sometimes the elderly. Therefore, a woman who works full time is expected to perform household duties, which may cause a work-life imbalance, a source of significant stress. As a result, females report more symptoms of anxiety, depression, and psychosomatic problems associated with stress than males.[1]

WOMEN REPORT HIGHER STRESS LEVELS THAN MEN

Women often experience higher levels of stress than men.[2] However, this gender difference in stress exposure is not present in childhood but emerges during adolescence. In general, adolescent boys report school-related problems while girls report interpersonal relationships as the major source of stress. Stress coping approaches also differ significantly between boys and girls. While boys prefer to exercise more in response to stress, girls prefer social support to cope with stress.[3]

Stress levels continue to increase with increasing age. Studies have shown that female students in a university setting experience stress more frequently than male students do. In one study based on a survey of 462 undergraduate students attending a midwestern land-grant university, the authors observed that women reported more stress than men.[4] In another study based on 249 undergraduate university students, the authors reported that despite better time management, female students reported

> Adolescent boys exercise more in response to stress while girls depend on interpersonal relationships for stress relief.

higher academic stress and anxiety compared to male students. As expected, freshmen and sophomore students reported higher overall stress levels than juniors and seniors. Interestingly, male students benefited more from leisure activities than did female students.[5]

According to a report published by the American Psychological Association, women are more likely than men (28 percent vs. 20 percent) to report having a great deal of stress. Moreover, 49 percent of women surveyed said their stress level had increased over the past five years, compared to 39 percent of men. Women are more likely to report physical and emotional symptoms of stress than men. However, men are far more likely than women to cite work as a source of stress. Interestingly, married women report higher levels of stress than single women (33 percent vs. 22 percent). In addition, women are more likely than men to say that having a good relationship with their families is important to them (84 percent vs. 74 percent). A similar trend is observed with friendship.[6]

> Married women experience higher levels of stress than single women.

Women are also more concerned with managing stress than men according to another report of the American Psychological Association. Women adopt multiple strategies to cope with stress, including reading, spending time with family and friends, shopping, praying, attending religious services, getting a massage, or visiting a spa. In contrast, men are more likely to rely on playing sports for stress relief. In addition, it is more likely that a woman will seek help from a mental health professional than a man (5 percent of women vs. 1 percent of men).[7]

WHY WOMEN EXPERIENCE MORE STRESS THAN MEN

There are many reasons why women experience more stress than men. One obvious reason is the traditional perception of masculinity where a man is reluctant to express stress because it may be perceived as a weakness. However, today women are a major part of the labor force in the United States and other countries, as more married women with children have careers. While earning a good salary (paid job) may be the primary goal of a man, a working woman has dual goals: being successful at a paid job and also taking care of her family and household chores (unpaid job). Moreover, single mothers experience more stress than mothers who are married. Single women also experience more stress as new mothers than married new mothers.[8]

Women in the U.S. Labor Force

In the United States, women account for 47 percent of the workforce. According to data from the U.S. Census Bureau and the U.S. Bureau of Labor Statistics, an estimated 56.1 million men and 43.2 million women are in the labor force, but the median income of women ($36,300) is lower than that of men ($47,100). However, the income gap was much wider in 1960, when the median income of women was $20,600 while the median income of men was $34,000. The income gap between women and men is also observed in highly paid professions as reflected in the ratio of women's to men's median earnings (e.g., 0.64 among physicians and surgeons, 0.71 among auditors and accountants). Unfortunately women earn less than men in 99 percent of all professions.

In general, mothers with children (aged six to seventeen years) are more likely to participate in the labor force (71.6 percent) than mothers with children under the age of three (50.8 percent). Also, 81.6 percent of single mothers with children (aged six to seventeen years) work. The percentage of women in the workforce varies widely with profession. For example, only 14 percent of architects and engineers are women, and 34 percent of physicians and surgeons are women, while 82 percent of elementary and middle school teachers are women. Among married-couple families, 54 percent have dual incomes, and women on average contribute 38 percent of family income. However, in 29 percent of households, wives earn more than husbands.[9]

Discrimination-Related Stress in Women Working in a Male-Dominated Workplace

When a woman works in a profession dominated by males, it is a source of additional stress. In one study, the authors observed that female accountants experienced higher anxiety than male accountants in very similar job settings.[10] In another study, the authors reported that during the survey in 2014, only 11.9 percent of women were full professors at medical schools compared to 28.6 percent of men who were full professors. Moreover, women faculty were younger and disproportionately represented in internal medicine and pediatrics, showing gender inequality in medical school faculty members.[11] In a published report involving perfusionists in the United

> When a woman is a token woman in a male-dominated workforce (85 percent or more are men in the profession), she is subjected to psychological stress as reflected by less healthy cortisol levels.

States, the authors reported that even when 33.3 percent of perfusionists were women, there was a significant gender gap, as only 19.3 percent of female perfusionists hold a chief perfusionist position. In addition, the majority of women (50.9 percent) reported discrimination in the workplace.[12] As expected, in one study the authors reported that in occupations where 85 percent or more workers are men, women experienced high stress levels, as evidenced by a less healthy daily pattern of cortisol, a stress hormone.[13]

Sexism, Racism, and Stress in Women

Women may also face sexual discrimination in a male-dominated workplace. Social identity threat is defined as a psychological state that occurs when people are aware that they may be viewed negatively due to their gender, race, or social identity. Social identity threat is associated with psychological distress that activates the hypothalamic-pituitary-adrenal axis, which is associated with release of the stress hormone cortisol. Women may experience this stress during a job interview or in the work environment due to sexism.[14]

Racism and sexism are largely intertwined. Among African American college students, both racism and the interaction of racism with sexism are associated with increased stress. Sexism may be more harmful in the presence of racism. African American women also report higher levels of racial and sexual harassment compared to African American men. Based on a study of 204 African American women residing in a southeastern U.S. city, the authors observed that racism and sexism were a significant source of stress in the lives of these women. Moreover, the authors observed that racism and sexism were strongly correlated and had a substantial influence on the psychological distress experienced by these African American women.[15]

Sexual Harassment and Stress in Women

Women are also subjected to sexual harassment. Sexual harassment is a violation of Title VII of the Civil Rights Act of 1964 and also the Civil Rights Act of 1991. This act also defines a hostile work environment. This occurs when an employee is subjected to "sexual innuendos, remarks and/or physical acts that are so offensive as to create an abusive work environment." Even in a female-dominated medical work environment, approximately 60 percent of registered nurses indicated some form of sexual harassment at work when surveyed.[16] Studies have also shown that rates of sexual harassment were 42 percent among female federal workers, 53 percent among female workers in the general population, and 50 percent among female university students surveyed. Even 40.4 percent of female university faculty reported some sort of sexual harassment.[17]

> Sexual harassment causes significant psychological distress in women but not in men.

Harassment is associated with psychological distress, sleeplessness, anxiety, depression, work loss, and overall worsening of health.[18] In one study, the author reported that in a male-dominated workplace, women who experienced a negative social climate were more prone to drinking alcohol, but no such relationship was found in men.[19] Moreover, sexual harassment is associated with significant psychological distress in women but not in men.[20]

Stereotypes of Good Wives and Mothers: Sources of Additional Stress

Marriage may bring additional stress in a woman's life. Although the husband mostly relies on the wife for emotional support, the wife, in addition to her husband, counts on children, family, and friends for social support. In general, up to age thirty, men and women feel similar marital stress, but after age forty, marital stress is higher for women than men. In addition, older married women experience more stress than their husbands. This may be related to higher spousal support for older men, but unfortunately spousal support for women does not increase significantly with advanced age.[21]

In general, a mother experiences more psychological stress than a father through pregnancy, labor, and delivery, as well as during postpartum care. Infertility affects 10–15 percent of couples worldwide.

> Starting at age forty, women experience higher marital stress than men.

The psychological stress of not having a child affects both men and women and is associated with emotional distress such as anxiety, depression, anger, marital problems, and even feelings of worthlessness when among couples with children. In general, among infertile couples, women show higher levels of distress than men.[22]

Research has shown that even in egalitarian couples, the standard division of household chores still reflects stereotypical male and female role divisions from past generations. In fact, a distinctive paternal style (based on play, recreation, and goal-oriented tasks) and maternal style (based on child care and routine household work) is observed even in families where fathers are highly involved in child care. However, the traditional role of "fatherhood culture" is transforming from the traditional father's role as breadwinner and disciplinarian to a willingness of fathers to get more involved in care of children of all ages. Nevertheless, mothers are still in charge of daily child-care duties, especially for young children. In one study, the authors reported that men's role in parenting is changing due to two factors. The first factor is the current prevalence of families that are geographically separated from their extended families. The second is the growing percentage of postpartum women returning to work. Although men feel stress during the labor and birth of their children, in general, work and social activities tend to remain unchanged during the postnatal period because mothers remain in charge of most daily child-care duties.[23] As a result, compared to fathers, mothers report higher levels of postpartum anxiety, depression, and parenting stress.[24] In another study based on seventy-five couples who were first-time parents, the authors reported that 20.8 percent of mothers, but only 5.7 percent of fathers, experienced high levels of parenting stress.[25]

> Mothers experience more parenting stress than fathers.

Bonding with an infant reduces stress in both parents. In one study, the authors observed that skin-to-skin contact with preterm infants reduced levels of the stress hormone cortisol in both mother and father, indicating stress relief. In addition, maternal and paternal oxytocin levels were significantly increased during skin-to-skin contact with the infant.[26] Oxytocin, a hormone that is synthesized in the hypothalamus but secreted by the pituitary gland, is often called the "love molecule" because it is important in trust building and pair-bonding as well as in bonding between infants and parents.

Gender Inequality in Work-Life Balance

Working women experience more stress than working men due to gender inequality in their work-life balance. Even in couples where the wife earns more than the husband, the wife still spends more time on household chores due to male stereotypes in the society.[27] In general, women with small children who have a full-time job experience more stress and face considerable conflict between marital/parental responsibility and paid work. In one study, the authors concluded that three groups of women in paid employment have been empirically identified as being at relatively high risk for stress: clerical workers, managers, and single (mainly divorced) mothers.[28] In another study, the authors observed that having children and being in a senior position are more strongly related to work-home conflict in women compared to men.[29]

As expected, women living in relationships with a more unequal distribution of responsibility for household duties experience higher levels of stress, fatigue, and work-family conflict compared to women living in more equal relationships.[30] In one report based on a study of 440 males and 529 females who were well-educated white-collar workers in full-time employment (aged thirty-two to fifty-eight years), the authors observed traditional gender differences in the division of responsibilities between men and women. The authors reported that women devoted an average of 5.7 hours more per week than men to performing household duties and 3.6 hours more per week than men on child care. Moreover, women reported having the main responsibility for most of the daily housework (washing dishes, cleaning, grocery shopping, preparing food, laundry, ironing, etc.), while men reported only three main responsibilities: car maintenance, house/apartment maintenance, and household finance. The authors commented that the men in their study were more focused on their paid jobs and had much lower household and child-care responsibilities than women.[31]

In another study, the authors observed that while women spent a little less time commuting to their job and significantly less time at work than men, women reported a higher level of stress due to commuting compared to men. The authors concluded that women's greater responsibility for day-to-day household tasks, including child care and housework, makes them more sensitive to commuting time to work.[32] Examples of some stressors that cause more stress in women than men are listed in table 2.1.

> Even commute time to work is an additional source of stress in women.

"FIGHT OR FLIGHT" VS. "TEND AND BEFRIEND"

Men and women may react differently to the same stressor. For example, a woman may feel more stressed in a long-distance relationship than her male counterpart. In general, men tend to withdraw socially when under stress, but women seek social support. Many decisions we make involve choosing whether to take a risk for potential gain or to select a safer path with no potential reward. Usually men tend to take more risks than women. For example, studies have shown that in the United States, single women have a lower pro-

Table 2.1.   Examples of some stressors that cause more stress in women than men

Stressor	Comments
High school environment	Girls report more stress than boys, but a major source of stress in girls is interpersonal relationships, while for boys it is school-related stress.
University environment	Female students report more stress than male students despite better time management.
Long-distance relationship	Long-distance relationships may cause more stress in women than men.
Marital stress	Married women report more stress than single women. For young couples (age thirty), martial stress is similar in both men and women, but after age forty, marital stress is higher in women than men.
Infertility	Women experience more distress than men in couples that are childless.
Pregnancy and postnatal period	Women are more stressed than men during pregnancy and the postnatal period.
Work-life balance	Women in paid employment are subjected to the double burden of paid work and unpaid housework, including child care. Difficulty in balancing work with life is associated with significant stress in women.
Work-related stress	If a woman works in a male-dominated profession (85 percent or more men), she is subjected to additional stress. Moreover, women usually have a lower-paying job with less control over the work situation and less potential for advancement. This creates stress for women.
Sexism, racial discrimination, and sexual harassment	Even in a work environment with a significant presence of women, sexism is a common stressor. Women face more sexual harassment than men. Sexual harassment causes significant psychological distress in women but not men. Moreover, African American women may experience racism and sexism, which may substantially increase psychological distress.

portion of their wealth held in risky assets than single men. Moreover, acute stress amplifies gender differences in risk-seeking behavior, where men tend to take more risks but women avoid risk when stressed.[33]

Regulation of physiological activities in both humans and animals is crucial for the preservation of homeostasis. Homeostasis refers to the tendency of organisms to maintain fairly stable conditions (equilibrium) for survival. The autonomic nervous system has two divisions: the sympathetic nervous system

> Under stress, men tend to take more risks while women prefer risk avoidance.

and the parasympathetic nervous system. The sympathetic nervous system is responsible for acceleration of heart rate, constriction of blood vessels, and increase in blood pressure due to the secretion of stress hormones. The parasympathetic nervous system has the opposite effect, and activation results in lower blood pressure and heart rate, mediated by acetylcholine, thus reestablishing homeostasis.

In general, both humans and animals react to external threat using the "fight or flight" approach, which was originally described by American physiologist Walter Cannon. The sympathetic nervous system is activated in response to external threat, and neurons (most commonly the locus coeruleus) in this nervous system secrete norepinephrine. In addition, the activated sympathetic nervous system stimulates the adrenal medulla to secrete epinephrine as well as norepinephrine. Moreover, the hypothalamic-pituitary-adrenal axis (HPA axis) is stimulated, and the stress hormone cortisol is secreted by the adrenal cortex, along with other hormones (see chapter 1). These hormones facilitate the immediate physical response to stress, including increased heart rate, higher blood pressure (as a result of constricting blood vessels), and tightening muscles, which prepares the body for a fight-or-flight response.

In 2000, using principles of natural selection, Shelly Taylor and her colleagues proposed that although the fight-or-flight approach may characterize the primary physiological response to stress in both men and women, behaviorally, women respond to stress with a different, more gentle and nurturing approach, which the authors termed "tend and befriend." From a neurological point of view, oxytocin in conjunction with female reproductive hormones and endogenous opioids (endorphins) are responsible for such behavior.[34] The characteristics of the fight-or-flight and tend-and-befriend responses to stress, along with the biochemical bases of the different responses, are given in table 2.2.

From an evolutionary standpoint, it is obvious why women need a different approach to deal with external threat. The fight-or-flight approach would not have been advantageous to the survival of females and their offspring in ancient human groups because most likely a female would be unable to fight or flee during pregnancy or unable to protect her offspring if she would prefer to flee in response to an external threat. Therefore, females may intuitively tend to their offspring during stress and also attempt to develop a social network with other females in the group in order to develop a safety net. As a result, the tend-and-befriend approach is an evolutionary response of females to coping

Table 2.2. Fight-or-flight versus the tend-and-befriend approach in response to stress

Approach	Proposed by	Comments	Biochemical Basis	Genetic Basis
Fight or flight	Walter Cannon in his book *Wisdom of the Body*, published in 1932 by Norton (new edition 1963)	Activation of the sympathetic nervous system and release of stress hormones in response to stress, which increases blood pressure and heart rate, thus preparing a person to fight or flee. This approach is common in males in response to stress.	Stress hormones such as epinephrine, norepinephrine, and cortisol are responsible for the fight-or-flight response to stress. In males, testosterone is also secreted in response to stress, which increases aggressive behavior. In males, vasopressin secreted under stress may further increase aggression.	The *SRY* gene located on the Y chromosome may be associated with the fight-or-flight approach in men. Women do not have a Y chromosome and therefore do not have this gene.
Tend and befriend	Shelly Taylor and her colleagues in a 2000 paper in *Psychological Review*	Although stress hormones including cortisol are also released in females in response to stress, females behave differently under stress due to the release of oxytocin. Under stress, a female first calms her offspring (tends) and then bonds with other females in the group (befriends), thus building a social safety net.	Oxytocin is the biochemical catalyst of the tend-and-befriend response to stress. Oxytocin acts on the parasympathetic nervous system and counteracts the effects of stress. In addition, the female sex hormone estrogen enhances the effect of oxytocin.	No genetic determinant of this approach has been described.

with external threats from ancient times, and such a response to psychological stress is still effective today. The biobehavioral mechanism that underlies the tend-and-befriend approach appears to draw on the attachment-caregiving system, a stress-related system that has largely been explored for its role in maternal bonding and child development.

The tend-and-befriend approach is superior to the fight-or-flight approach because when two adult male rhesus monkeys who never met before are put together in a small cage, they will fight and try to kill each other. In contrast, when two female monkeys not known to each other are put together in a small cage, they will reduce the tension and awkwardness of the situation by exchanging grooming behavior, which reduces stress in both monkeys.[35] Based on a sample of adolescent boys and girls, in one study the authors concluded that adolescent girls rely heavily on their social network during times of stress. In contrast, adolescent boys were more likely to engage in aggressive physical release, similar to the fight-or-flight response to stress.[36]

THE BIOLOGICAL BASIS OF TEND AND BEFRIEND

It has been postulated that testosterone is secreted in response to acute stress and is responsible for aggressive behavior in men. Studies have shown that dominant and aggressive male prisoners have higher levels of testosterone than nonviolent prisoners. In one published report, the authors studied fifty-two rapists and other criminals and observed that rapists who used physical violence had a greater level of circulating testosterone in their blood than those convicted of nonviolent crimes.[37] However, female aggressive behavior is not controlled by testosterone because women have much lower levels of testosterone than men. Females usually do not get involved in "rough and tumble" play like males do. Although female hostility is also known, unlike male hostility, which is linked to sympathetic arousal and is part of the fight-or-flight response to stress, female hostility is not linked to sympathetic nervous system arousal.

In general, men may not be more inherently aggressive than women, but the patterns of aggression between males and females differ. Males are more likely to use physical aggression in the struggle for power within a hierarchy or to defend territory against an external enemy. Females show less physical aggression than males but engage in more indirect aggression patterns in the form of gossip, rumor spreading, and the like. Female aggression may also be more moderate than that of males due to social norms.

Oxytocin, a peptide hormone synthesized in the hypothalamus and stored in the posterior pituitary gland, is secreted under many conditions, including in response to stress. Oxytocin release is enhanced in response to stress in both men and women, but levels are significantly higher in women than men.[38] Oxytocin inhibits the typical fight-or-flight response to stress and acts as the biochemical catalyst for the tend-and-befriend approach in females. Oxytocin also reduces the fear response of stress by acting on the parasympathetic nervous system, thus counteracting activation of the sympathetic nervous system under stress. Human studies have shown that intranasal oxytocin administration reduces stress and increases prosocial behavior. Lower oxytocin levels in males compared to females in response to stress are due to the presence of testosterone, which inhibits the release of more oxytocin under stress.

> Oxytocin is the catalyst for the "tend and befriend" stress response in females.

Oxytocin and Prosocial Behavior

Although oxytocin is present in both males and females, its physiological effects are well established mostly in females. Oxytocin promotes uterine contractions during labor and delivery. Oxytocin (trade name: Pitocin, a synthetic oxytocin) is also used to induce labor and is given by intravenous injection. Although oxytocin levels in pregnant women are low during pregnancy and not different from nonpregnant women, during labor and after delivery, oxytocin levels are increased significantly. Suckling also stimulates secretion of oxytocin, and estrogen enhances this effect. Oxytocin is responsible for maternal bonding with an infant.

Interestingly, there are many similarities between parent-infant bonding and romantic relationships. It has been shown that regions of the brain that are activated during parental bonding with infants are also activated during the initiation of a romantic relationship. Moreover, oxytocin not only facilitates mother-infant bonding but also plays an important role in romantic relationships. In one study, the authors observed that plasma (the aqueous part of the blood) oxytocin levels were significantly elevated in new lovers, both male and female, compared to single men and women.

The elevated oxytocin levels in new lovers stayed elevated even after six months of a continuous romantic relationship, but for couples who broke up, oxytocin levels dropped in both men and women.[39] Oxytocin promotes prosocial behavior and trust building. Oxytocin also plays an important role in sexual arousal and penile erection, promoting sleep, and reducing cravings for drugs and sweets.[40] In one study, the authors reported that when pain was induced in volunteers by asking them to immerse their hand in cold water, intranasal administration of oxytocin reduced the pain intensity and unpleasantness associated with such discomfort.[41] The beneficial effects of oxytocin are summarized in table 2.3.

Table 2.3. Beneficial effects of oxytocin

Beneficial activity	Comments
Labor, delivery, and breastfeeding of infants	Oxytocin concentration in the blood is significantly increased during labor, promoting uterine contraction for delivery. Oxytocin is released during suckling, thus promoting breastfeeding.
Mother-infant bond	Oxytocin is responsible for promoting a strong bond between mother and infant. Oxytocin is also responsible for maternal behavior.
Stress relief and anxiety relief	Oxytocin is released in response to stress, but levels are higher in females than males. In females, oxytocin catalyzes the tend-and-befriend response to stress, which is a gentle and nurturing approach. Oxytocin also reduces fear and cortisol levels in response to stress.
Romantic relationship	Oxytocin plays a similar role in pair-bonding during a romantic relationship, which has a similar mechanism as mother-infant bonding.
Sexual arousal	Animal studies have shown that oxytocin is involved with sexual arousal, including penile erection.
Friendship/prosocial behavior	Oxytocin facilitates friendship and prosocial behavior. When synthetic oxytocin is administered intranasally in male volunteers, their prosocial behavior is increased.
Building trust	Oxytocin affects individuals' willingness to accept social risks arising through interpersonal relationships.
Increases generosity	Intranasal administration of oxytocin is associated with increased generosity in human volunteers.
Brings back fond memories	Oxytocin after nasal administration brings back fond childhood memories with the mother.
Reduces pain perception	Intranasal administration of oxytocin reduces pain intensity and pain perception (induced by asking subjects to put their hand in cold water).
Reduces cravings	Animal studies have shown that administration of oxytocin reduces the craving for cocaine, morphine, and heroin in rodents. Oxytocin may also reduce the craving for sweets and may help with weight reduction.

Oxytocin May Reduce Cortisol Response in Stressed-Out Women

Studies have reported that when the same psychological stressors, such as public speaking or performing arithmetic mentally, were induced in males and females in a laboratory setting, a significantly larger salivary cortisol response to stress was observed in males compared to females, although pretest salivary cortisol levels were comparable. In some studies, the salivary increase of cortisol in men in response to stress was twice as high compared to females under the same stressful conditions. Oxytocin may reduce this cortisol response to stress.[42]

Some studies have shown that intranasal administration of oxytocin may suppress cortisol response to psychological stress. In one study using seventy-three healthy men, the authors demonstrated that both social support and intranasal administration of oxytocin were effective in blunting the response of cortisol under psychological stress. Subjects either came alone or were accompanied by a best friend during a psychological stress experiment. Then a group of subjects received oxytocin intranasally while others received a placebo. Psychological stress was induced by the Trier Social Stress Test, which typically involves a public speaking task and a mental arithmetic task performed in front of an audience. The mean salivary cortisol increase was 15.1 mmol/L (millimoles/liter) in subjects without social support and also without oxytocin but 6.7 mmol/L in subjects without social support but who received oxytocin. In subjects who had social support and received oxytocin, the cortisol increase was only 4.0 mmol/L. The authors concluded that the combination of oxytocin and social support exhibited the lowest cortisol concentrations as well as increased calmness and decreased anxiety during psychological stress in study subjects. The authors further commented that oxytocin seems to enhance the buffering effects of social support on stress responsiveness.[43] In another study based on forty-seven heterosexual couples, the authors reported that intranasal oxytocin was associated with positive communication during marital conflict and decreased salivary cortisol levels after conflict.[44]

> Oxytocin may reduce the cortisol response during stress.

GENETIC ASPECTS OF THE FIGHT-OR-FLIGHT APPROACH

Humans have forty-six chromosomes (except in case of genetic defect) in each cell, including the sex chromosomes (known as X and Y). Females have two X chromosomes while males have one X chromosome and one Y chromosome. The *SRY* gene (the sex-determining region of the Y chromosome gene), present on the Y chromosome, provides instructions for making a protein called the sex-determining region Y protein. This protein causes a fetus to develop male gonads (testes) and prevents the development of female reproductive structures (uterus and fallopian tubes).

Evidence from studies has shown that males exhibit heightened sympathetic nervous system reactivity to stress, which is associated with elevated cardiovascular response (higher heart rate and blood pressure compared to females) and higher plasma levels of catecholamines (epinephrine and norepinephrine). Although the *SRY* gene is expressed in the testes and facilitates testis development and gonadal hormone (testosterone) production, this gene is also expressed in the brain and peripheral tissues, which may be associated with competitiveness, impulsivity, and spatial awareness in males. The *SRY* gene may also be responsible for the lack of estrogen in males. Moreover, the *SRY* gene has a direct effect on the catecholamine-dependent stress reaction in males and may provide a genetic basis for the fight-or-flight approach in response to stress. When humans were hunter-gathers competing with each other for food, resources, and mates, the *SRY* gene may have evolved from that time to influence male-biased behavior.[45]

> The *SRY* gene is probably related to the fight-or-flight response in males in response to stress.

EVOLUTIONARY ADVANTAGE OF THE TEND-AND-BEFRIEND APPROACH

There are many advantages of women's response to stress using the tend-and-befriend approach. Research indicates that under stress, the desire to affiliate with others is substantially higher in females than males. Many studies have also reported a positive impact of social support during stressful moments in life. Interestingly, women's affiliative tendency under stress is to bond with other women. When given a choice to affiliate under stress with an unfamiliar male or be alone, a woman most likely prefers to be alone. Across the entire life cycle, women are most likely to mobilize social support, mostly from other women during stressful times. An adult woman has more female friends than an adult man has male friends. Moreover, a woman is more likely than a man to get involved in helping friends during stress and crisis.

Friendship, or close and prolonged affiliation with non-kin, is characterized by homophily (the tendency of individuals to associate and bond with
others who are similar in age and gender). Typically males are drawn to large
groups, which may be helpful during group defense or war, but females have
a network of close friends who can provide care and emotional support during stressful situations in life.[46] Interestingly, under stress men secrete vasopressin, which is structurally similar to oxytocin, but, unlike oxytocin, which
facilitates calmer behavior under stress, vasopressin increases aggression in
males. Therefore, vasopressin may be another biochemical pathway that explains the aggressive fight-or-flight behavior in males under stress.[47]

GENDER DIFFERENCES IN HPA-AXIS ACTIVATION MAY EXPLAIN
WHY MEN AND WOMEN DIFFER IN STRESS-RELATED ILLNESSES

In general, men show elevated cortisol responses to laboratory-based stressors such as the Trier Social Stress Test (TSST), but not all studies report such
gender differences. Menstrual cycle, pregnancy, and menopause all have
significant effects on stress-related activation of the HPA axis. Studies have
shown that when women were tested using the TSST during the luteal phase
of the menstrual cycle (the last fourteen days of a normal cycle lasting twenty-
eight days, although a menstrual cycle lasting twenty-one to thirty-five days is
also considered regular), they showed a cortisol response similar to men. In
contrast, when women were tested during the follicular phase (the first fourteen days in a twenty-eight-day cycle), increased cortisol levels in response
to stress were lower than observed in men. Interestingly, women on oral
contraceptives also showed lower cortisol response than men when stressed.

In one study based on eighty-one healthy adults (twenty men, nineteen
women in the follicular phase of the menstrual cycle, twenty-one women
in the luteal phase, and twenty-one women on oral contraceptives), the
authors observed that the TSST induced significant increases in ACTH (adrenocorticotropic hormone, which stimulates the adrenal gland to secrete
cortisol), salivary cortisol, plasma cortisol, and heart rate, as well as increased
wakefulness and reduced calmness in all subjects. Although men showed
higher ACTH responses to the TSST compared to each of the three groups
of women, salivary cortisol responses were similar in men and women in the
luteal phase but lower in women who were in the follicular phase or were

receiving oral contraceptives.[48] In another study using 282 healthy volunteers (135 women, all in their follicular phase), the authors observed higher ACTH and cortisol levels in men compared to women. In addition, men had steeper baseline-to-peak and peak-to-end ACTH and cortisol response slopes than women. Moreover, there was a trend for more cortisol responders in men than women. The authors concluded that men show more robust activation of the HPA axis to the TSST than women during their follicular phase.[49] However, there are other published papers in the literature that contradict these findings. Premenstrual syndrome (PMS) is associated with blunted cortisol response under psychological stress.[50] Perceived stress may also increase the severity of premenstrual symptoms, though stress management may reduce these symptoms.

Estrogen levels are reduced after menopause, and sometimes estrogen replacement therapy is needed to reduce the symptoms of menopause. Studies have shown that postmenopausal women have a higher physiological response to stress than premenopausal women. In one study, the authors showed that following exposure to a stressor (math and speech task), significantly higher blood pressure and plasma cortisol levels were observed in postmenopausal women compared to premenopausal women. However, when postmenopausal women were treated with estrogen, such response to stress was blunted.[51] In another study involving eighty-one women, the authors observed that women with low estrogen levels were more vulnerable to posttraumatic stress disorder than women with normal estrogen levels. Low estrogen in women with a normal menstrual cycle was also associated with inability to suppress fear responses even in a safe condition.[52]

Gender Differences in Longevity

Although women experience more stress than men, women also live longer than men. In developed countries, the average life expectancy of women is seven years longer than men. There are many factors that contribute the gender difference in longevity (behavioral factors, environmental factors, and genetic factors). In general, men tend to be employed in jobs with greater risk of mortality, and males also tend to show testosterone-related risky behaviors that promote aggression and competitiveness. Such hormonal effects may increase the odds of reckless behavior, violence, and motor vehicle accidents in men at all ages, a phenomenon known as "testosterone toxicity." Moreover, testosterone increases the blood level of bad cholesterol (low-density lipo-protein cholesterol: LDL cholesterol) and decreases good cholesterol (high-density lipoprotein cholesterol: HDL cholesterol), thus increasing the risk of cardiovascular diseases, including heart attack.

In contrast, the female hormone estrogen increases the blood level of good cholesterol and protects the heart. There may also be genetic factors that contribute to greater longevity in women compared to men. Women have two X chromosomes, one inherited from the mother and one from the father (44, XX), while men have one X chromosome inherited from the mother and one Y chromosome inherited from the father (44, XY). It has been shown that if one X chromosome has defective genes and the other X chromosome is normal in a female, the normal X chromosome can compensate for the defective gene in the other X chromosome (X chromosome inactivation). This benefit is only available in females, not males, because in males if the X chromosome inherited from the mother has a genetic mutation, there is no other X chromosome to compensate for the defective genes. This is why any X chromosome recessive mutation affects males but not females.[53]

> In general, women live approximately seven years longer than men. This may be partly due to testosterone (testosterone toxicity), which promotes risky behaviors in males and also increases the risk of cardiovascular diseases, including heart attack, by increasing blood levels of LDL cholesterol (bad cholesterol) and decreasing levels of HDL cholesterol (good cholesterol). Male sex is a risk factor for cardiovascular diseases.

Gender Differences in Stress-Related Illnesses

There are significant gender differences in stress-related illnesses. In general, men show higher prevalence of cardiovascular diseases, including heart attack, than women in all age groups, although the risk of stroke is comparable in both men and women in the age group forty to fifty-nine, but significantly higher in older men compared to older women (age group sixty to seventy-nine).[54] Currently, an estimated 29.1 million people in the United States are living with type 2 diabetes, according to the Centers for Disease Control (CDC), where 21 million people have the diagnosis while 8.1 million people are undiagnosed. Although the prevalence of diabetes is highest among American Indians (15.2 percent), followed by African Americans (13.2 percent) and

Hispanics (12.8 percent) and lowest among non-Hispanic whites (7.6 percent), overall the prevalence of diabetes is higher in males than females.

The higher prevalence of cardiovascular diseases and diabetes is probably linked to higher HPA axis activity in males in response to stress than females. In general, males have higher total serum cortisol as well as biologically active free cortisol. In one study, the authors reported approximately 18 percent higher total cortisol and 33 percent higher free cortisol in men compared to women.[55] In another study, the authors, based on a study of 283 community-dwelling elderly participants (age range sixty-five to eighty-five years), reported significantly higher hair cortisol levels in men than women (mean value 26.3 pg/mg of hair in men and 21.0 pg/mg in women). Because long-term elevated cortisol levels are associated with increased risk of cardiovascular disease and type 2 diabetes, high cortisol levels in men in response to daily stressors may contribute to the higher risk of cardiovascular diseases compared to women.[56]

> Higher activation of the HPA axis in response to stress and higher cortisol levels in men compared to women may explain the higher risk of cardiovascular diseases and type 2 diabetes in men.

Women are twice as likely as men to develop depression and disorders related to mental health.[57] The prevalences of many stress-related illnesses in men and women are listed in table 2.4. Women are twice as likely to

Table 2.4. Gender differences in prevalence of common stress-related illnesses

Disease	Prevalence in Males	Prevalence in Females
Heart attack (age group: 40–59)	3.3%	1.8%
Heart attack (age group: 60–79)	11.3%	4.2%
Coronary heart disease (age group: 40–59)	6.3%	5.6%
Coronary heart disease (age group: 60–79)	19.9%	9.7%
Stroke (age group: 40–59)	1.9%	2.2%
Stroke (age group: 60–79)	6.1%	5.2%
Diabetes	13.6%	11.2%
Major depression	13.2%	20.2%
Any mood disorder	17.5%	24.9%
Any anxiety disorder	25.4%	36.4%
Panic disorder	3.1%	6.2%
PTSD	3.6%	9.7%
Migraine	6.5%	18.2%
Insomnia	6.2%	12.9%
Irritable bowel disorder	7.7%	14.5%
Alcohol abuse	19.6%	7.5%
Drug abuse	11.6%	4.8%

develop depression compared to men, as well as disorders that are often comorbid with depression and anxiety, such as migraines, insomnia, and irritable bowel disorder. Women are more likely to develop autoimmune diseases (rheumatoid arthritis, lupus, irritable bowel disease, Graves' disease due to an overactive thyroid gland, Hashimoto's disease due to inflammation in the thyroid gland, etc.) and mental disorders linked to underactivity of the HPA axis such as panic disorders and PTSD. Usually patients with panic disorder have normal awakening cortisol, but the HPA axis is unresponsive to stress because cortisol levels do not rise in these people when subjected to stress.[58]

Corticotropin releasing hormone (CRH) orchestrates the stress response by activating the HPA axis as well as modulating the locus coeruleus (LC)–norepinephrine system in the sympathetic nervous system. Hypersecretion of CRH and dysregulation of the HPA axis LC-norepinephrine system are characteristics of many stress-related mental disorders. Sex differences in CRH (1) receptors could render the LC-norepinephrine system more reactive in females, causing hyperarousal (more sensitive to low levels of CRH but less adaptable to high levels) in response to emotional stimuli, a dysregulated state associated with symptoms of depression and PTSD. In addition, sex differences have been observed with glucocorticoid receptors that bind cortisol under stressful conditions. Glucocorticoid receptors are essential for negative feedback to the HPA axis that eventually lowers cortisol secretion. Sex differences in glucocorticoid receptors result in attenuated negative feedback to the HPA axis under chronic stress in females, causing persistently elevated cortisol, an endocrine state associated with depression. Therefore, sex differences in stress-related receptors shift females more easily into a dysregulated state of stress reactivity linked to development of mood and anxiety disorders.[59] Sex hormones such as estrogen and testosterone can also modulate stress-related receptors and HPA-axis activation.

Gender differences in neural response to psychological stress have also been reported. Based on a study of sixteen males and sixteen females, the authors observed increased cerebral blood flow in the right prefrontal cortex (using brain MRI) and reduced blood flow in the left orbitofrontal cortex in males in response to stress (mental arithmetic task). In contrast, stress-induced increased blood flow in the limbic system of the brain was observed in women. The prefrontal activation in males showed good correlation with salivary cortisol, but limbic activation in females showed a lower degree of correlation with salivary cortisol. These results indicate that in males, the HPA axis and cortisol are the major stress response, which is fight or flight, but in females the limbic system, which is involved in reward systems and has receptors for oxytocin, vasopressin, dopamine, and endorphin, is activated, indicating a more tend-and-befriend response to stress. Activation of the limbic reward system in response to stress may also regulate the fight-or-flight approach in women. However, these findings indicate a blunt acute stress response between low- and high-stress tasks in female subjects. It is also possible that female subjects were more stressed than men during the low-stress task. The female sex hormones, while attenuating HPA-axis responsiveness, could lead to sluggish cortisol feedback in the brain and reduced or delayed containment of the stress response. Compared to the male group, the authors observed fewer correlations between cerebral blood flow and cortisol variations in females, indicating compromised cortisol feedback during stress responses in females. Compromised cortisol feedback to HPA-axis activation in females has been proposed as a major neurobiological pathway mediating the tendency of women to develop depression.[60]

Gender differences in stress levels and negative life events also increase the prevalence of depression in women compared to men. In general, negative life events affect women more than men. It has been estimated that 7–19 percent of girls (compared to 2–7 percent of boys) suffer from childhood sexual abuse, which is associated with depression in adulthood. In one study, the authors estimated that 35 percent of gender differences in adulthood depression could be accounted for by the higher incidence of sexual abuse of girls compared to boys. Moreover, women face a number of chronic stress burdens in everyday life as a result of social status and roles relative to men. In general, women are paid less than men for similar work, but at the same time they have major household responsibilities compared to men. A woman may also face sexual discrimination or sexual harassment at work. All of these chronic stresses may explain why women are more vulnerable to stress-related depression and anxiety.[61] Based on a study of 1,100 adults aged twenty-five to seventy-five, the authors in one study showed that women are more vulnerable to depressive symptoms than men because they are more likely to experience chronic stress, to have a low sense of mastery, and to engage in ruminative coping.[62]

CONCLUSION

Men in general prefer the fight-or-flight approach in response to stress, but such an approach is maladaptive for females because they are primary caretakers of offspring. Therefore, a mother cannot flee in response to an external threat, leaving her offspring unprotected. As a result, from an evolutionary standpoint, women must have a different approach to stress. In contrast to men, women prefer the tend-and-befriend approach in response to stress. A woman in response to stress first protects her offspring and then forms bonds with other females in the group (befriend) so that group members can protect each other from external threats.

This ancient approach in response to stress in women when hunter-gatherers started living in groups is also applicable today. Women form close networks with other women so that under stress they can help each other, and this approach in response to stress is facilitated by the hormone oxytocin. In one published report, the authors commented that sometimes during a couple counseling session the wife might say that her husband has no friends and that they do not communicate much. The authors further commented that while men express a desire for close friendships with other males, they often avoid pursuing them. Emotional restraint, homophobia, and traditional masculine stereotypes reduce the possibility of a man to form close relationships with other men.[63] In another report, the author commented that females invest more heavily in a few high-quality, time-consuming friendships, while males prefer groups with less investment per member. Based on a sample of approximately 112,000 profiles in nine countries, the authors concluded that women favor dyadic relationships, whereas men favor large, all-male cliques such as clubs. These apparently different solutions to quality-quantity trade-offs suggest a universal and fundamental difference in the function of close friendships for men and women.[64]

3

Pets Are Natural Stress Busters

Pets do not pay rent or buy their own food. Cats do not even clean their litter boxes. Pet owners take care of them and pay for everything, including the veterinarian bill. So what do humans get in return? Studies have shown that pets offer unconditional love and companionship, and they reduce stress. Many health benefits of pet ownership—for example, protection against cardiovascular diseases (diseases related to the heart and blood vessels supplying blood to the heart)—are directly related to the natural stress-busting effect of pets.

PET OWNERSHIP IN U.S. HOUSEHOLDS

Pet ownership is very popular, not only in the United States but in all developed countries. It has been estimated that approximately 60 percent of American households and 50 percent of people in all developed countries own at least one pet.[1] Cats and dogs are more popular than horses, birds, and reptiles. According to the American Veterinary Association's *U.S. Pet Ownership and Demographics Sourcebook* published in 2012 (latest available), 36.5 percent of American households (43.3 million) have pet dogs, 30.4 percent have cats (36.1 million), and only 3.1 percent have birds (3.7 million) and 1.5 percent have horses (1.8 million). There are approximately 70 million pet dogs and 74.1 million pet cats in the United States, and 62.3 percent of pet owners consider their pets family members.

Interestingly, in New England and the Pacific Northwest, cat ownership is favored over dog ownership, but in southern states, dogs are more popular than cats as pets. However, neither dogs nor cats are popular in Washington, D.C., as only 13 percent of households own dogs and just 12 percent own cats—the lowest numbers in the nation.

> A majority of pet owners, including children, consider their pets as family members and spend money for care of sick pets rather than putting them to sleep and then acquiring new pets.

Other than dogs, cats, birds, and horses, people also have fish, ferrets, rabbits, hamsters, guinea pigs, turtles, lizards, snakes, and other species as pets. In 2015, Americans spent $60.3 billion on pet care, with the highest expenditure being for food ($23.05 billion), followed by veterinary care ($15.42 billion). In 2016, Americans are expected to spend approximately $62.75 billion for their pets.[2] This data explains why Americans prefer to spend money on their very sick pets to keep them alive as long as possible rather than putting them to sleep and acquiring new pets. Moreover, pet health insurance helps more pet owners afford optimal pet care.[3] Children also perceive their pets as special friends, important family members, and providers of social interaction, affection, and emotional support.[4]

In one study, the authors reported that Native Americans are most likely to have companion animals (73.5 percent), followed by Caucasians (65 percent). People of Hispanic/Spanish heritage (56.9 percent), African Americans (40.9 percent), and Asians (37.5 percent) are less likely to have companion animals. However, all pet owners, regardless of ethnic background, consider their pet a part of the family, providing unconditional love, companionship, and emotional support. Hispanics are less likely to have cats than dogs.[5]

Although dogs are usually not allowed to roam outdoors freely, owners may allow a cat to spend some time outdoors unsupervised. In general, most

> Indoor cats live longer than outdoor cats.

cat owners limit their cats' outdoor access to the daytime only, and few owners allow cats to remain outside at night. Cats acquired from shelters are more likely to be kept exclusively as indoor cats than those acquired as strays. However, cats allowed outdoor access are more likely to have been bitten by other cats and may live shorter lives than indoor cats.[6]

ANTHROZOOLOGY

Human-animal interaction (also known as anthrozoology) can take various forms, including simple pet ownership, interacting with pets, animal-assisted activities where pets casually interact with humans for potential therapeutic benefits, or animal-assisted therapy (pet therapy) where trained pets and their handlers interact with a select group of people or patients with a therapeutic goal in mind. In 1860, Florence Nightingale, the founder of the nursing profession, commented that "a small pet animal is often an excellent companion for the sick, for long chronic cases especially. A pet bird in a cage is sometimes the only pleasure of an invalid confined for years to the same room."[7] In the 1940s, the American Red Cross brought dogs into the Pawling Air Force Convalescent Center in New York and found that the veterans working with dogs felt less stressed and more relaxed. In the 1960s, child psychologist Dr. Levinson used pets as an adjunct to traditional psychotherapy and proposed that relationships with companion animals may significantly improve the mental health of humans.[8]

HISTORY OF DOMESTICATION OF DOGS AND CATS

Human relationships with companion animals can be traced back to half a million years ago, as fossil evidence indicates an association between *Homo erectus* (meaning upright man; early ancestors of humans) and a canine-like species. More recently, scientists have discovered a twelve-thousand-year-old tomb in modern Israel where a person was buried with one arm around a puppy, indicating an affectionate relationship between early humans and companion animals.[9]

Dogs and cats are two of the most common pets today, but they are very different in temperament and evolutionary origin. The molecular biological evidence indicates that the wolf is the ancestor of all breeds of domestic dog. Wolf domestication originated more than fourteen thousand years ago when humans were hunter-gatherers (the nomadic period). Once ancient humans started interacting with these wolves, they were tamed, and from that point a wolf in all respects became a dog. However, the wide phenotype variation of modern breeds of dogs (approximately four hundred breeds) began approximately three thousand to four thousand years ago.

The domestication of cats took a different trajectory because, unlike wolves, which are pack animals, cats live solitary lives and defend their exclusive territories. The domestication of cats started much later than the domestication of dogs because there was almost no reason for ancient humans to domesticate a cat, even when humans started agriculture, because terrier dogs and ferrets are more effective than cats at killing mice. Most likely, wild cats exploited human environments, and ancient humans simply tolerated cats. With time these wild cats were tamed and became human companions. It has been estimated that the domestication of cats probably dates back to about 9,500 years ago.[10]

WHY HUMANS LOVE PETS

Edward O. Wilson described the biophilia hypothesis, explaining humans' desire to love other life-forms, including pet animals.[11] In ancient times, human-animal interactions provided support to humans—for example, participation of wolves in hunting. Therefore, love for nature and animals may have an evolutionary link. In today's urban lifestyle, many people find little time to spend in nature and few opportunities to interact with animals. Having a companion animal at home may provide a link to human evolutionary history that enhances feelings of well-being in the presence of companion animals.

Another hypothesis explaining human interactions with animals is the human attraction for baby faces. An accumulation of behavioral and neurophysiological studies indicates that an infantile face is an effective stimulus that rapidly and unconsciously captures human attention and facilitates the desire to care for a baby (baby schema), an instinct essential for the survival of the species. Konrad Lorenz proposed that the baby schema (*kindchenschema*) is a set of physical features, such as a large head, round face, and big eyes, that is perceived by humans as "cute" and motivates caretaking behavior. Interestingly, baby-faced adults are considered more likeable, warm, and friendly than adults without a baby face. It has been hypothesized that the presence of infantile physical and behavioral features in pets might form the basis of human attraction for these animals. The bond between owners and companion animals has remarkable similarities between human parents (typically the mother) and their children (attachment theory). Moreover, the ability of companion animals to bond with humans and fulfill the needs for attention and emotional intimacy has similar functions as human-human friendship.[12]

Another interesting observation is that the language used in talking to a pet often mimics motherese. Motherese, also known as infant-directed speech or baby talk, refers to the spontaneous way in which mothers, fathers, and caregivers speak with infants and young children. In one study using dog owners and their dogs, the authors observed a striking similarity between motherese and the language of communication of owners with their pet dogs.[13] Another study reported that although men and women were equally attached to their pet dogs, women talked more than men to their dogs, and their communication closely resembled motherese during the study. Moreover, dogs petted by women showed lower levels of the stress hormone cortisol in their plasma as well as more relaxed behavior compared to when petted by men. Studies in different cultures also showed that more women than men considered their pets as equals.[14]

> People (women more often than men) spontaneously talk to their pets using a language similar to motherese, indicating that love for pets is similar to love for children.

The social support hypothesis of human-animal bonding speculates that companion animals are social support by themselves and also facilitate social interactions with other humans. Animal companionship reduces loneliness, stress, anxiety, and depression. Pets provide very important social support because of their constant availability, nonjudgmental support, and unconditional love. As a result, people form strong emotional bonds with their pets, and such bonding is similar to human-human bonds.

The Neurobiological Basis of Human-Pet Bonding

Oxytocin is a peptide hormone secreted by the hypothalamus of the brain in response to touch, warmth, and trust, as well as during breastfeeding and sex. Oxytocin is often called the "love molecule" because it helps in bond formation between two human beings, including mother-child bonding, but oxytocin may also play a role in human-animal bonding. In one study, the authors showed that when female dog owners petted and talked to their dogs for only three minutes, significantly increased oxytocin levels were observed in both owners and dogs.[15] In another study, the authors observed that after interacting

> Oxytocin and other neurochemicals associated with positive emotion, happiness, and human-human bonding are also responsible for human-pet bonding.

Table 3.1.   Hypotheses explaining human-animal relationships

Hypothesis	Comments
Biophilia	Biophilia indicates human affinity for the living world and the human tendency to interact and form bonds with other living beings—for example, a pet. Biophilia is considered innate, felt by all humans. However, an opposite effect is biophobia, which may also be an effect of natural selection, where humans fear and thus avoid large carnivorous animals, snakes, and spiders.
Baby schema (*kindchenschema*)	Baby schema indicates the affectionate feeling of humans toward infants due to their infantile facial features. It has been hypothesized that the presence of infantile physical and behavioral features in cats and dogs (which they retain lifelong) might form the basis of human attraction for cats and dogs. A pet may act as a baby substitute.
Motherese in communicating with pets	People often talk to their pets using a language very similar to motherese or baby talk, indicating that love for a pet is similar to love for an infant or child.
Attachment theory	The bond between pets and humans has many similarities with the bond between parents and their children. The shared features of these two relationships include dependency, proximity seeking, caregiving, and feelings of affection, which ultimately ensure security, comfort, and protection for the child as well as for the pet.
Neurobiological hypothesis	Interaction with dogs is associated with secretion of oxytocin, prolactin, dopamine, phenylethylamine, and beta-endorphins. These neurochemicals are associated with positive emotion and bond formation between humans and pets.
Social support hypothesis	Human-pet relationships often lead to a bond that serves a similar emotional function as human-human friendships. Pets are available constantly, are nonjudgmental, and offer unconditional love.

with dogs, serum levels of oxytocin, beta-endorphin, dopamine, prolactin, and phenylacetic acid (a metabolite of phenylethylamine) were significantly increased, while the concentration of cortisol, a stress hormone, was decreased. Moreover, after interacting with dogs, blood pressure was also reduced in humans.[16] Hypotheses explaining human-animal relationships are summarized in table 3.1.

THE IMPORTANCE OF PETS IN HOUSEHOLDS

A poll of more than one thousand pet owners conducted by the Associated Press in 2009 and 2010 showed that 50 percent of respondents considered their pets as much a part of the family as any other person in the household, 30 percent reported sleeping with their pets in the same bed, and 35 percent included their pet in a family portrait. Interestingly, 25 percent of married couples (or those living with a significant other) with pets reported that their pets were better listeners than their spouses or significant others. In general, pet owners enjoy greater self-esteem, more physical fitness, and less loneliness, and they are more conscientious than non–pet owners. In addition, pets can offset negativity from a rejection.[17]

Pets provide three important benefits to humans:

- Pets facilitate social networking and social support, which are associated with stress release.
- Pets provide many mental health benefits, including protection against depression.
- Pets provide many physical health benefits.

Pets Improve Social Network and Social Support of Owners

One reason why people benefit from pet ownership is that their pets represent an important source of social support. Greater social support improves functions of the heart, endocrine glands, and immune system. In one study, the authors reported that pet owners were significantly more likely to get to know people in their neighborhood than non–pet owners. In addition, around 40 percent of pet owners reported receiving one or more types of social support, including emotional support via people they met through pets. Given growing evidence for social isolation as a risk factor for mental health problems and, conversely, friendships and social support as enhancers of individual and community well-being, pets may be an important factor in developing healthy neighborhoods.[18] Another study involving 273 individuals responding to a survey revealed that participants with greater childhood attachment to a pet are more likely to avoid eating meat as adults.[19]

A pet acts as a "social catalyst" and facilitates interpersonal interactions. For example, walking with a dog is associated with increased social interaction with strangers compared to walking without a dog.[20] In one study based on the behavior of 1,800 pedestrians who were strangers toward a female experimenter, the author observed that when the experimenter was alone or with a teddy bear or a plant, pedestrians ignored her, but when she was in the company of a dog, she got the most attention from these strangers. Moreover, when the experimenter was with a puppy or a Labrador retriever, she had more conversations with strangers than when she was accompanied by a Rottweiler. These results indicate that a pet acts as a facilitator of social interaction.[21]

In another report, the authors conducted different studies to evaluate the role of domestic dogs as facilitators in social interactions. In the first experiment, a twenty-two-year-old male subject (accompanied or not by a dog) asked people for money in the street. When the subject was not accompanied by a dog, only 11.3 percent (nine out of eighty people) donated money, but when the same subject was accompanied by a dog, 35 percent (twenty-eight out of eighty people) donated money, indicating that the presence of the dog was associated with higher compliance with the subject's request. In the second experiment, a female subject was used instead of a male subject. Again, in the presence of a dog, 51 percent of people donated money, while in the absence of a dog, only 26 percent donated money. In another interesting experiment, a male accompanied by a dog or alone asked females for their telephone number. In the presence of a dog, 28.3 percent of women provided their phone number, while in the absence of a dog only 9.2 percent of women complied with the request.[22] Having a pet may also help in dating situations, as a woman may consider a man more responsible if he has a pet.

Many families buy holiday gifts for their pets and often celebrate their birthday. All family members bond with their pets, including children. However, child-pet bonding is especially important in children living in single-parent families and those without siblings. Children often consider their relationship with their pets more important than some human relationships. Pets contribute positively in the psychosocial development of children. Children with pets often show enhanced empathy, self-esteem, and cognitive development, as well as greater participation in social and athletic activities. These children also demonstrate increased trust, community feelings, sense of safety, and self-confidence. People in general are deeply attached to their pets, and the loss of a pet can resemble the loss of a human family member or companion.[23] The social, mental, and physical health benefits of pet ownership are summarized in table 3.2.

Pets and Homeless People

Pets are sometimes the only support and lifeline of a homeless person. Based on a survey of 105 homeless men and women in the San Francisco Bay area,

Table 3.2. Social health, mental health, and physical benefits of pet ownership

Social health benefits	• Dogs offer the opportunity for socialization with other dog owners, thus building social connections in the neighborhood, especially during dog walking. • Children with pets have more friends visiting them than children with no pets. • Pet owners can interact with other pet owners regarding pet issues, such as recommendations for a veterinarian, thus forming a friendship. • Pets can facilitate bonding among members of the family and also with extended family members and friends.
Mental health benefits	• Interaction with a pet reduces stress. • Unconditional love offered by pets improves feelings of well-being and self-esteem. Moreover, a survey of married couples indicates that it is easier to talk to a pet than a spouse because pets don't talk back. • Pet ownership significantly decreases anxiety, depression, and loneliness in both young and older people. • AIDS patients who own pets report less depression than AIDS patients with no pets. • Children who grow up with pets have better self-esteem, self-confidence, and empathy, and they participate more in social and athletic activities.
Physical health benefits	• Higher level of physical activities, especially in dog owners who also walk their dogs. • Reduced secretion of stress hormones in response to stress. • Better lipid profile (lower cholesterol and triglycerides). • Fewer doctor's office visits than non–pet owners. • Lower risk of mortality from cardiovascular diseases (including heart attack) in healthy people. • Lesser probability of dying after first heart attack in pet owners compared to non–pet owners. • Children with type 1 diabetes who care for a pet have better control of their blood sugar than children with no pet. • Exposure to a pet lowers the likelihood of developing allergies in children.

the authors reported that 50 percent of homeless people owned pets and were extremely attached to their pets. The authors concluded that pets provide very important mental and physical health benefits to homeless people.[24] Homeless pet owners often feed their animals first.[25] In another study based on 398 homeless youth in the Los Angeles area, the authors reported that 23 percent of youth owned pets. Pets contributed positively to the mental health of these youths, as pet owners had fewer symptoms of depression and feelings of loneliness. Interestingly, 85 percent of respondents reported that their pets kept them company, and 80 percent reported receiving unconditional love from their pets.[26]

STRESS RELIEF AND OTHER MENTAL HEALTH BENEFITS OF PETS

As mentioned earlier, stress reduction is a major benefit of human-pet inter-action. Companion animals can decrease anxiety and sympathetic nervous system arousal associated with psychological stress by providing compan-ionship, unconditional love, and attention, as well as by creating a pleasant environment. Pets can also reduce the feeling of loneliness and depression, thus significantly increasing overall feelings of well-being. Many studies have investigated the effect of interacting with pets on stress reduction. Stress can be measured using the Perceived Stress Scale or other psychological measure-ment scales based on various questions. However, stress can also be measured using various biochemical parameters, including blood levels of the stress hormone cortisol and other stress-related hormones (see chapter 1).

Pets Reduce Loneliness, Stress, Anxiety, and Depression

Loneliness is an unpleasant experience that occurs as a result of social or emotional isolation. Loneliness is often associated with negative feelings such as depression, anxiety, and low self-esteem and may provoke negative behav-ior such as alcohol or drug abuse and, in the extreme case, suicidal thoughts. Loneliness is also associated with heart diseases. The prevalence of loneliness increases with advanced age, as 40 percent of adults aged sixty-five years and older report being lonely at least sometimes. Several studies have indicated that pets may be a source of social connectedness that buffers people from feelings of loneliness. In one study, older persons who were strongly attached to their pets reported greater happiness and lower depression than those who were not pet owners. In addition, subjects aged sixty years and older reported less loneliness, anxiety, and depression one year after adopting a cat com-pared to non–cat owners.[27]

Pet ownership can also diminish feelings of loneliness by compensating for the absence of human companionship in younger women (mean age 28.4 years) living alone.[28] In one study, the authors observed that older pet owners (sixty years of age or older) living alone were 36 percent less likely than non–pet owners to report loneliness.[29] In another study using fifty-eight subjects, the au-thors reported that when anxiety was initiated in subjects by telling them they may have to hold a tarantula spider, petting animals reduced anxiety.[30]

Pets can reduce feelings of loneliness and depression not only in older people but also in younger people.

People are motivated to maintain social connections with other humans, and those who lack social connections may try to compensate such desire by creating a sense of human connection with a nonhuman agent (for example, a pet). When a person is chronically lonely, it may induce stress, and at such a moment a pet owner may anthropomorphize (attribute human traits and emotions to a nonhuman entity such as a pet) his or her pet to alleviate stress. In one study, when people were experimentally induced to feel lonely, anthropomorphism was observed in all subjects.[31]

Patients with AIDS experience depression. Based on a study of 1,872 men, the authors observed that AIDS patients who were also pet owners reported less depression than AIDS patients who did not have pets.[32]

Parenting children with developmental disorders such as autism spectrum disorders (ASD: persistent difficulties in social interaction in a range of contexts and showing restricted, repetitive behaviors) is associated with higher levels of stress, anxiety, and depression compared to parenting children with normal development. In one study based on thirty-eight primary caregivers for children with ASD who also acquired dogs and twenty-four control caregivers who did not acquire dogs, the authors observed that acquiring dogs was associated with significant stress reduction in primary caregivers for children with ASD.[33] Moreover, children with ASD have deficits in social skills, but these children also bond with dogs, and such bonding is associated with increased social skills in these children.[34]

Interactions with Pets Reduce Cortisol: Biological Evidence of Stress Relief

Several studies have reported reduced secretion of cortisol under stress in subjects during experimental settings when pets are present. In one study using twenty health-care professionals where each participant rested for twenty minutes followed by a five- or twenty-minute interaction with a therapy dog, the authors reported significant reductions in serum and salivary cortisol after interacting with a dog, indicating stress relief. The maximum decline in cortisol was observed forty-five minutes after the interaction.[35] In another study using thirty-three adults (sixteen pet owners and seventeen non–pet owners), the authors reported that interaction with dogs reduced stress levels in both pet owners and non–pet owners. Interestingly, pet owners had lower levels of salivary cortisol than non–pet owners at the baseline. When pet owners interacted with a five-year-old female Labrador for twenty minutes, the mean cortisol level was decreased by 12 percent, but in non–pet owners, the mean cortisol level was also reduced by 14 percent after interacting with the same dog.[36]

In one published report, the authors measured salivary cortisol levels in forty-two children with ASD in three experimental conditions: prior to and during the introduction of a service dog to their family and a short period after removing the dog. The authors observed that before the introduction of the dog, salivary cortisol level was increased by 58 percent in the morning after awakening (morning cortisol increases after awakening and then diminishes in the evening), but cortisol increased by only 10 percent when the dog was present. When the dog was removed, morning cortisol again increased by 48 percent after awakening in the morning.[37] Therefore, the presence of a service dog reduced stress levels in these children. One of the physiological responses of stress is elevation of blood pressure. Interestingly, studies have shown that when stress was induced in subjects by asking them to perform stressful tasks such as mental arithmetic or public speaking, the presence of companion animals could blunt the effect of stress as reflected by a lower than expected increase in blood pressure.

> Pets reduce the secretion of the stress hormone cortisol and also attenuate increased blood pressure and heart rate in response to stress.

In a study with forty-five women, the authors reported that relative to the support of friends or spouses, the presence of a pet elicited significantly lower blood pressure and heart rate reactivity during mental stress.[38] In another study, the authors investigated cardiovascular reactivity to psychological and physical stress in 240 married couples, half of whom owned a pet. The experiment took place in the participant's home, where, after a resting period, participants were exposed to psychological stress by asking them to perform mental arithmetic (rapid serial subtraction, five-minute duration). Then participants were allowed to rest for fifteen minutes and were exposed to physical stress (cold pressor, asking participants to immerse their hand for two minutes in ice water). The authors reported that relative to people without pets, people with pets showed lower heart rate and blood pressure during the resting baseline and significantly smaller increases from baseline values during the mental arithmetic task and the cold pressor task. In addition, pet owners showed faster recovery after stress than non–pet owners. Among pet owners, the lowest reactivity to stress and the fastest recovery were observed when pets were present during the experiment instead of a spouse or friend. In fact, cardiovascular reactivity during the mental arithmetic task was increased in the presence of a spouse compared to when a pet was present. However, reactivity was reduced if both spouse and pet were present. No difference in reactivity to stress was observed between cat owners and dog owners.[39]

Studies have shown that the support of friends and family can buffer the physiological response to stress. However, pets can also offer such valuable support by blunting the physiological response to stress. In one study based on forty-eight subjects, the authors demonstrated that pet ownership, not blood pressure–lowering medicine (lisinopril), was associated with the blunting of blood pressure increase during mental stress (induced by arithmetic task and public speaking).[40]

> Pets are more effective than the blood pressure–lowering medicine lisinopril in blunting blood pressure increases due to mental stress.

PHYSICAL HEALTH BENEFITS OF PET OWNERSHIP

There is no dispute in the medical literature that pet ownership protects against cardiovascular diseases, including heart attack (myocardial infarction), not only in healthy pet owners but also in pet owners with health issues. Pet ownership also reduces mortality after a first heart attack. Cardiovascular diseases include a range of conditions that ultimately affect the heart. These diseases include coronary artery disease (narrowing of the coronary arteries due to atherosclerosis, which may eventually cause a heart attack if not treated), heart rhythm problems (arrhythmias), heart failure, and related disorders. Cardiovascular diseases are the number-one killers in the United States and developed countries.

> In the opinion of a panel of experts from the American Heart Association, pet ownership, particularly dog ownership, is probably associated with reduced risk of cardiovascular diseases.

In 2013, the expert panel of the American Heart Association, based on a review of many related studies involving pet ownership, concluded that pet ownership, particularly dog ownership, is probably associated with decreased risk of cardiovascular diseases.[41] In general, there is evidence that dog owners are less sedentary and have lower blood pressure, plasma cholesterol, and triglycerides; attenuated response to mental stress; and better survival after heart attack compared to non–pet owners. These benefits are probably due to improved mood and reduced stress in pet owners, which is associated with improved endothelial function that reduces blood pressure as well as the risk of developing cardiac arrhythmia. Overall ownership of a pet, particularly a dog, is associated with positive health benefits.[42]

Social support and dog ownership have been associated with better coronary artery disease survival. Based on a study of 369 patients who suffered from myocardial infarction (heart attack), the authors observed that dog owners were significantly less likely to die within one year of a heart attack (only one died out of eighty-seven dog owners) compared to non–dog owners (19 deaths out of 282 patients). The authors concluded that both dog ownership and social support are significant predictors of survival after a heart attack regardless of physiological status.[43] In another study based on ninety-two patients (sixty-four men and twenty-eight women) who were admitted to a cardiac care unit or intensive care unit with myocardial infarction or angina pectoris (chest pain due to reduced blood flow to heart muscles as a result of blocked coronary arteries), the authors observed that eleven (28 percent) of thirty-nine non–pet owners died in a one-year period but only three (6 percent) of fifty-three pet owners died during the same one-year period. The authors concluded that pet ownership has a beneficial effect on survival in patients with cardiovascular diseases that is independent of age and the severity of the disease.[44]

> Pet owners have a better chance of survival after a first heart attack than non–pet owners.

Benefits of Dog Walking

Common sense tells us that dog owners who walk their dogs benefit from regular exercise. The American Heart Association recommends 150 minutes of moderate exercise per week for improving overall health, and walking is a simple form of exercise that anyone can easily adopt in their daily routines. Physical inactivity explains more than 20 percent of risk factors associated with cardiovascular diseases.[45] In one study based on a review and meta-analysis of thirty-two published reports, the authors concluded that walking reduces systolic and diastolic blood pressure. In addition, regular walking is associated with reduced body weight, waist circumference, percentage body mass index, and percentage body fat. The authors concluded that walking reduces many risk factors for cardiovascular diseases.[46] In another study, the authors observed that 80 percent of dog owners who walked their dogs regularly fulfilled the recommendation of 150 minutes of physical activity per week.[47]

In one published report, the authors observed that dog owners who walked their dogs had a significantly lower incidence of high blood pressure, diabetes, and depression than non–dog owners or those who did not walk their dogs. In addition, dog owners in general had lower body mass index and lower blood cholesterol than non–dog owners. The authors concluded that owning and walking a dog is a good way of living a healthy lifestyle.[48] In another study based on 11,466 pregnant women, the authors reported that dog owners were 50 percent more likely to achieve the recommended three hours of activity per week, equivalent to thirty minutes of walking per day, most days of the week.[49] In addition, dog ownership is associated with more physical activity among adolescents.[50]

Cat Ownership and Protection from Cardiovascular Diseases

Although many studies show that dog ownership is associated with re-duced risk of cardiovascular diseases, some studies also clearly document the health benefits of cat ownership. In one study based on German and Austra-lian surveys of nine thousand pet owners (dogs, cats, fish, birds, or other pets), the authors ob-served that pet owners were the healthiest group, and people who cease to have a pet or never had a pet were less healthy. In both Australia and Germany, pet owners had about 15 percent fewer annual doctor visits than non–pet owners.[51] In another study based on 938 elderly Medicare enrollees in a health maintenance program and a one-year follow-up, the authors reported that pet owners had fewer doctor con-tacts over the one-year period compared to non–pet owners. Furthermore, pets seemed to help their owners during stressful situations.[52]

> In general, pet owners are healthier and have fewer annual doctor's office visits than non–pet owners.

Pet ownership in general, including cat ownership, is associated with significant stress reduction and overall improvement of health. In one study based on 3,964 adults over the age of fifty who were free from major physical illness and eighteen years of follow-up, the authors reported that pet owner-ship was associated with low rates of death from cardiovascular diseases or stroke. The authors estimated that among pet owners, the overall risk of dying from a cardiovascular event was 31 percent lower, and the risk of dying from a stroke was 46 percent lower compared to non–pet owners. Interestingly, the risk of dying from a cardiovascular disease was 18 percent lower, and the risk of dying from a stroke was 24 percent lower among dog owners compared to non–dog owners. In contrast, for cat owners, there was a 38 percent lower risk of death from cardiovascular disease and a 78 percent lower risk of death from stroke compared to non–cat owners.[53]

Cat ownership is also associated with a lower risk of dying from cardiovascular diseases or stroke.

In another study based on 4,435 participants and twenty years of follow-up, the authors reported that the risk of death from a heart attack was reduced by 37 percent among current cat owners. However, the risk of death was also reduced by 26 percent among past cat owners compared to non–cat owners. In contrast, dog ownership was not associated with reduced risk of death from cardiovascular diseases. The authors concluded that acquisition of cats as domestic pets may represent a novel strategy for reducing the risk of cardiovascular diseases in high-risk individuals.[54] Mechanisms by which pets protect against cardiovascular diseases are summarized in table 3.3.

Other Health Benefits of Pet Ownership

Some trained dogs can smell the onset of low sugar (hypoglycemia) in human companions and may alert them when their owners have no idea such an event is occurring. Hypoglycemia, if not detected and treated in a timely fashion (drinking orange juice or taking another form of sugar), may be life threatening. However, in one study the authors observed a significant false positive rate.[55]

Although common sense tells us that having a cat or dog at home may increase the risk of asthma or allergy in children, scientific evidence shows that pets may protect children against developing asthma and allergies. In one study, based on 224 schoolchildren, the authors observed that having a cat in the household protected children against atopy of outdoor allergen, wheeze, and asthma. However, the cat must be acquired before the age of eighteen.[56] In another study, the authors reported that the prevalence of respiratory allergies and symptoms was lower in children of current pet owners than children of parents who owned no pet.[57] However, pets such as rabbits and rodents

Table 3.3. Mechanisms by which a pet reduces the risk of cardiovascular diseases

Mechanisms	Comments
Lower stress in pet owners	Work-related stress may increase the risk of cardiovascular diseases by 50 percent. Pet ownership not only reduces work-related stress but also other emotional stress.
Less feelings of loneliness in pet owners	Loneliness is associated with increased risk of cardiovascular diseases, Alzheimer's disease, reduced cognitive function, and poor health. Pet ownership reduces the feeling of loneliness.
More physical activity in pet owners	Dog owners who walk their dogs get daily physical exercise. However, in general, pet ownership is associated with more physical activity.
Improved lipid profile in pet owners	High cholesterol increases the risk of cardiovascular diseases while high triglycerides may also increase the risk. In general, pet owners have lower blood cholesterol and triglycerides than non–pet owners.
Lower blood pressure in pet owners	Pet ownership may reduce blood pressure, which also reduces the risk of cardiovascular diseases.
Improved endothelial function in pet owners	Improved mood and emotional state in pet owners may decrease central and regional autonomic nervous system activity, thus improving endothelial function and reducing the risk of cardiac arrhythmia.
Overall good health in pet owners	Pet owners have fewer visits to the doctor's office and report overall good health, which may also be associated with a reduced risk of cardiovascular diseases.

may increase the risk of allergy rather than protecting against allergy. This author suggests that if you have a child with chronic health issues, you should consult with a physician before owning a pet.

PET THERAPY

Pet therapy is an accepted complementary and alternative medicine therapy that is virtually risk free. Most commonly, dogs are used in pet therapy, but cats, rabbits, birds, and even fish in an aquarium may be used for therapy. Other animals may also be used. Although the benefits of pet therapy are usually described in a pediatric and geriatric context, people of any age can benefit from pet therapy. The benefits of pet therapy are summarized in table 3.4.

One of the most common benefits of pet therapy is improved mood and diminished overall anxiety in hospitalized children. Children are often distressed during physical examination by doctors. The presence of a dog is associated with less distress in children as evidenced by lower blood pressure and heart rate. Studies have shown that for hospitalized children, interaction with a therapy dog is associated with lower perception of pain,

Table 3.4. Benefits of pet therapy

Population	Benefits
Pediatric patients	• One of the most common benefits of pet therapy is overall improvement of mood and reduced anxiety in hospitalized pediatric patients. • Lower salivary cortisol, lower perception of pain, and less stress in hospitalized children after interaction with therapy dogs. • Lower blood pressure and heart rate in children after interacting with therapy dogs before examination by physicians.
Adult patients	• Decreased perception of pain and anxiety in adult hospitalized patients after interacting with therapy dogs. • Reduced anxiety and better cardiopulmonary function in patients hospitalized for heart failure. • Reduced anxiety and depression in critically ill patients. • Pet therapy is very useful in reducing anxiety and depression in patients with a wide variety of psychiatric illnesses. • Pet therapy may reduce pain, anxiety, depression, and fatigue in patients coping with terminal illnesses.
Nursing home population	• Reduced depression and improved quality of life. • Lesser use of pain medication. • Improvement in patients with dementia. • More socialization in patients with Alzheimer's disease. Moreover, pet therapy dogs may be used in conjunction with other approaches to calm an Alzheimer's patient.

better mood, and lower stress (as evidenced by decreased salivary cortisol), and such positive effects are better than child life activity interventions, such as playing games or watching videos.[58]

Pet therapy is also useful for adults. In one study based on fifty-nine inpatients (mean age 59.6 years), interaction with a therapy dog was associated with decreased perception of pain, tension, and anxiety, as well as increased energy. Pet therapy using a dog was also associated with reduced perception of pain in cancer patients undergoing chemotherapy. Therapy with a dog can improve cardiopulmonary pressure and reduce anxiety in patients hospitalized with heart failure. Pet therapy is useful in reducing anxiety and depression among critically ill patients. However, one of the most studied areas of pet therapy in the adult population is patients with psychiatric illnesses. Pet therapy can help patients with bipolar disorder. Therapy with a dog can also reduce anxiety levels in patients with schizophrenia. Pet therapy is more useful in reducing anxiety and depression in patients with a wide range of psychiatric disorders. Pet therapy is also useful in a palliative care setting where such therapy may reduce pain, anxiety, depression, and fatigue in patients coping with terminal illnesses.[59]

Pet therapy is very useful for elderly people. In one published report, the authors studied the effect of six weeks of pet therapy with a cat (three one-hour visits per week) in twenty-eight subjects suffering from chronic age-related disability and living in a nursing home. The authors observed significant improvement of mood (less depressive symptoms) and reduced blood pressure in residents who received pet therapy compared to residents who were undergoing the usual recreational activity programs.[60]

A published report has demonstrated that the presence of a therapy dog may reduce medication usage (most commonly analgesic medicines) in nursing home patients receiving long-term care.[61] Moretti and colleagues commented that pet therapy is effective in improving cognitive function and reducing depression in elderly patients with mental illnesses.[62] The presence of a therapy dog can increase socialization in patients suffering from Alzheimer's disease. Moreover, a therapy dog can be used as an adjunct to other calming interventions in patients with Alzheimer's disease.[63] In a review article on pet therapy, the authors concluded that a therapy dog reduces aggression and agitation as well as promotes social behavior in people with dementia. Interestingly, having an aquarium in the dining rooms of dementia units stimulates residents to eat more of their meal and to gain weight.[64]

CONCLUSION

Pet ownership has many benefits, but most benefits can be related to the stress-relieving effect of pets. Pets are nonjudgmental and offer unconditional love. Pets are very useful in reducing feelings of loneliness and depression in elderly people. Pet ownership may reduce the risk of cardiovascular diseases and protect against mortality after a first heart attack. Pets also have beneficial effects on children. Pet therapy is very useful in reducing anxiety and depression, not only for hospitalized children but also for adults. However, some people are allergic to pets, and having a pet may not be a good option for them. If you are allergic to pets, please consult with your physician before you acquire a pet. Some breeds of pets are less allergy-inducing than others. Although the risk of spreading an infection from pets to people is relatively low, if you have a sick child or elderly person at home requiring long-term medical care, it will be best to talk to your physician before acquiring a pet.

4

Child Development and Social Influences on Stress

Relief through Social Networking, Volunteering, Laughter, and Taking a Vacation

Social support is very effective in reducing stress in both men and women. Volunteering is associated with positive emotion and is a natural stress buster. Natural laughter is an effective stress buster. Taking a vacation is not only relaxing but also associated with positive emotions, happiness, and physical well-being. Taking a family vacation is very useful for strengthening the bonds among family members.

Even children in elementary school and adolescents in high school report significant stress. As expected, all adults are also exposed to stress, but men and women respond differently to stress (see chapter 2). Men prefer a "fight or flight" approach while women prefer a "tend and befriend" approach. Women effectively use their female friends and relatives to cope with stress, while a man may prefer physical activities for stress relief. Married men are healthier and live longer than never-married or divorced men living alone. One of the reasons that married men are healthier and live longer is the stress-buffering effect of marriage.

EFFECT OF PARENTAL DISTRESS ON OFFSPRING

Maternal stress is common, but excessive maternal stress may be associated with preterm birth. In one study based on 203 pregnant women, the authors reported that women who delivered preterm babies showed higher concentrations of cortisol, the stress hormone, in plasma (the aqueous part of the blood) during the fifteenth and nineteenth weeks of pregnancy. The authors also observed that elevated cortisol at the fifteenth week predicted the surge of placental corticotropin releasing hormone (CRH) at the thirty-first week of gestation that primed the placental clock for earlier delivery than expected.[1] Although a moderate amount of stress during pregnancy has no adverse effect on the fetus because stress hormones including cortisol are required for normal fetal maturation and birth process, highly increased levels of stress hormones due to maternal distress, particularly early in the pregnancy, may affect the fetus's own stress response system. Maternal anxiety is associated with reduced blood flow to the fetus.[2] Moreover, a higher maternal cortisol awakening response (morning cortisol is higher than bedtime cortisol due to diurnal variation) late in pregnancy is correlated with an elevated cortisol level in the infant.

Prenatal stress is predictive of restlessness and disruptive temperament in infants and small children. In general, crying and fussing begins in infants during the first two weeks after birth, peaks around six weeks, and subsides around the age of three months. In one study, the authors investigated whether prenatal stress could impact behavioral and emotional regulation problems (crying/fussing) in infants using data from 120 pregnant women. The authors observed that at six weeks of age, infants of mothers reporting more emotional distress in late gestation cried and fussed more than infants of mothers who experienced less stress. Elevated maternal cortisol has been associated with maternal reports of negative reactivity in infants, which is in accord with Baker's fetal origins hypothesis, which proposes that high cortisol may have some effect on the developing brain of the fetus. However, according to the social-interactive hypothesis proposed by Papousek, excessive infant crying may be due to a dysfunctional mother-infant interaction. Interestingly, the authors also observed that even when mothers were highly stressed during the late gestational period, the mother's self-efficacy (a person's belief in her ability to complete a task, bringing about a positive outcome) can reduce the crying/fussing behavior of infants. Overall, infant boys fussed more than infant girls.[3] However, a well-adapted parent-infant relationship may reduce the crying/fussing of an infant.[4]

> In general, infant boys cry/fuss more than infant girls.

Maternal stress during pregnancy may have adverse effects on offspring when they reach young adulthood. In one study based on 167 persons whose fathers died before the birth of the child and 168 fathers who died during the first year of the child's life, with follow-up at thirty-two years, the authors observed that the incidence of schizophrenia was significantly higher in adults whose father died before their birth. However, the prevalence of alcoholism and personality disorders was relatively high in both groups.[5] In another study, the authors concluded that maternal bereavement during pregnancy may increase the risk of overweight or obesity in male offspring, and this may be related to severe stress exposure early in life in these male subjects.[6]

OXYTOCIN FACILITATES PARENT-CHILD BONDING

Oxytocin, a peptide hormone, is secreted in both men and women, but the beneficial effect of oxytocin is more clearly documented in women. Oxytocin concentration is increased significantly during birth and afterward as a result of suckling the infant. Oxytocin is responsible for strong mother-infant bonding. In addition, oxytocin plays an important role during romantic relationships as parts of the brain that are activated during parent-infant bonding are also activated during the initiation of a romantic relationship.

Studies have shown that a strong bond between parent and infant is the best way to alleviate stress in infants. Currently, there is compelling evidence that links oxytocin with sensitive caregiving in both men and women. Testosterone, on the other hand, decreases in men who become involved fathers because testosterone may interfere with paternal care.[7] In one study based on 112 parents, the authors reported that baseline oxytocin plasma levels were similar in both parents. However, when mothers interacted affectionately with infants, plasma oxytocin levels were significantly increased. For fathers, oxytocin levels were only increased after a high level of stimulatory contact with infants.[8]

> Oxytocin in fathers is increased after childbirth, but testosterone is decreased only in fathers who are involved with infants.

A significant increase in maternal oxytocin levels from early pregnancy to postpartum is associated with higher maternal responsiveness, lower maternal stress, and more optimal mother-infant bonding. Moreover, higher levels of plasma oxytocin during the first trimester are associated with more positive maternal behavior in the postpartum period, including gazing at the infant's face, affectionate touching, motherese, singing a song, and treating the infant as a very special person. Oxytocin levels are also stable over a six-month period after childbirth.[9]

In one study involving plasma oxytocin and cortisol levels in sixty-two women during the first trimester, third trimester, and one month postpartum, the authors observed that higher oxytocin levels and lower cortisol levels in the postpartum period were uniquely predictive of superior mother-infant bonding as reflected by the mother's frequent checking of the infant, talking to the infant, affectionate touch, and attachment-related thoughts. Moreover, high oxytocin levels in the first trimester

> Higher oxytocin levels in the first trimester are associated with superior mother-infant bonding during the postpartum period.

were associated with positive maternal behavior, a finding that is in agreement with other studies. Such positive maternal behavior facilitates infant care not only by sustaining protection and nurturing but also by permitting a longer period of brain development, a prerequisite for higher intelligence.[10]

Postpartum depression is known to affect 10–15 percent of all mothers. Postpartum depression may occur within four weeks after delivery but may also develop three to six months after childbirth. Risk factors for developing postpartum depression include lack of social support, low self-esteem, partnership problems, previous history of mental illness, and insecure attachment style. Postpartum depression is associated with deficits in child development because mothers with postpartum depression show impaired mother-infant bonding. It has been postulated that dysregulation of the oxytocin system may be the biological cause of postpartum depression. Postpartum oxytocin release also initiates lactation in the mother. Therefore, postnatal stress and failed lactation may dysregulate the

> Low plasma oxytocin concentration during mid-pregnancy is predictive of postpartum depression.

oxytocin system in mothers with postpartum depression. It has been reported that the birth-related stress of an emergent Caesarean birth was associated with diminished oxytocin production during suckling compared to a vaginal birth, and this association was stronger in anxiety-prone women. In one study based on seventy-four healthy pregnant women, the authors reported that compared to women with no postpartum depression, women who had postpartum depression (fourteen out of the seventy-four women) at two weeks after delivery showed significantly lower concentrations of oxytocin in their plasma during mid-pregnancy.[11] It has been postulated that intranasal administration of oxytocin may alleviate some symptoms of postpartum depression and may also improve mother-infant bonding. However, more research is needed to establish the therapeutic value of oxytocin in treating the symptoms of postpartum depression.[12]

A POSITIVE PARENT-INFANT BOND BUFFERS INFANTS FROM STRESS

The word "infant" is derived from the Latin word *infans*, meaning "unable to speak." Usually infancy lasts up to one year of age, while young children between age one and three are considered toddlers. Parent-infant bonding is very important for proper development of infants and children. When couples expecting babies attend a prenatal lecture series regarding infant care, the mother's sensitivity to cues and responsiveness to the infant's needs are significantly enhanced. In addition, attending such classes fosters a couple's social and emotional growth, as well as their response to the infant's distress and the overall quality of parent-infant bonding.[13] Research has shown that the human nervous system reacts to early stress, and such stress can also increase oxidative stress in the brain of an infant. Similarly, chronic stress during childhood or adolescence may increase the risk of anxiety, depression, and other psychiatric illnesses during early adulthood.[14]

John's Bowlby's Attachment Theory

Attachment is a deep and enduring emotional bond that connects one person to another over a long period of time and is evolutionary in nature. Attachment is a behavior that characterizes a human from cradle to grave, and such behavior initiates during infancy but continues across the life span.[15] Attachment theory, first proposed by John Bowlby and then further developed by Mary Ainsworth, suggests that infants have a universal need to seek closeness with their caregivers under stressful or fearful situations and that this is an evolutionary phenomenon essential for the survival of the species. The four stages of attachment of infants to their mother and other members of the family are summarized in table 4.1.

Table 4.1. Various stages of attachment of newborns, infants, and young children with their family members and caregivers

Age	Comments
Birth to six weeks (asocial/ pre-attachment stage)	This is also known as undiscriminating social responsiveness stress, where infants react to their basic needs but have no preference for any person.
Six weeks to six months (attachment in progress)	This stage is also known as discriminating social responsiveness, where infants start forming bonds with other humans, especially the mother or caregiver. An infant may smile more often in the presence of the mother than a stranger but may not protest if the mother leaves the infant.
Six months to up to two years (specific attachment stage)	This is a stage where a baby wants to be close to his or her mother (active proximity seeking) and develops a true attachment with the mother. A baby will cry if the mother leaves the room (separation anxiety).
Two years and beyond (goal-directed attachment)	Toddlers can form multiple attachments with family members and close friends of the family. At this stage a toddler also believes that if parents leave, they will return. Moreover, they have more impulse control, as they may wait for an adult to come and feed them without crying.

It is also important that the mother should create a safe nurturing and emotional haven for the infant. The caregiving system of the mother is to promote proximity and comfort when she receives a cue from her infant indicating stress. In women this system remains immature during puberty but slowly matures during the transition to adulthood. The maternal caregiving system undergoes its greatest development during pregnancy, and oxytocin plays an important role in the development of the caregiving system to maturity.[16] An impaired caregiving system may be one of the reasons that teenage pregnancy is associated with many complications for offspring. In one study, the authors reported that the depression risk was 18.2 times greater in adolescent mothers (aged less than seventeen years) compared to mothers over eighteen years of age. In adolescent mothers (105 mothers studied), 39.0 percent reported mild depression, 37.1 percent moderate depression, and 10.5 severe depression. In contrast, among adult mothers (105 women studied), only 4.8 percent reported any depression.[17]

> Risk of depression is 18.2 times higher in teenage mothers compared to adult mothers.

Mary Ainsworth's Various Types of Attachment Theory

Mary Ainsworth also described three types of attachment that an infant could possibly demonstrate. These behaviors are based on the observation of infants during the "Strange Situation" experiment, which is based on the be-havior of an infant in the presence of a stranger when the mother is present or absent (eight different experimental situations in each experiment lasting for approximately three minutes). In "secure attachment," the infant is distressed when the mother leaves (separation anxiety) but is happy when she returns (reunion behavior). This is the most common as well as the best type of attachment, where an infant is experiencing a safe and nurturing environment for normal growth. Mary Ainsworth also described two types of insecure attachment behavior known as "avoidant attachment" behavior and "ambivalent attach-ment" behavior.[18] Later, a fourth type of attachment known as "disorganized/disoriented attachment" was described by Martin and Solomon.[19] Various types of infant behavior are summarized in table 4.2.

> Maternal depression is a risk factor for insecure attachment behavior of infants.

The secure attachment pattern provides the best protection from stress in infants. The prevalence of secure attachment between infants and their moth-ers is higher than attachment between infants and their fathers.[20] In general,

Table 4.2. Various types of attachment as described by Mary Ainsworth and Mary Martin

Attachment Style	Type of Attachment	Comments
Secure attachment*	Secure	Most common type of attachment (prevalence: 65 to 70 percent), where the infant is distressed when the mother leaves (separation anxiety) but is happy when she returns (reunion behavior). The infant also avoids strangers but is happy with a stranger when the mother is present. The infant uses only the mother as a safe base from which to explore his or her environment.
Avoidant attachment*	Insecure	In this type of attachment, the infant shows no sign of distress when the mother leaves and shows little interest when she returns. The infant can play normally when a stranger is present, and anyone can comfort the stressed infant.
Ambivalent attachment*	Insecure	In this type of attachment, an infant shows significant distress when the mother leaves, avoids strangers, and, when the mother comes back, resists physical contact. Moreover, the infant cries more.
Disoriented/ disorganized attachment**	Insecure	In this type of attachment, an infant does not know how to be attached with a caregiver. This may be associated with infant maltreatment.

*Described by Mary Ainsworth.
**Described by Mary Martin.

disorganized/disoriented association behavior is associated with a higher stress response as reflected by cortisol reactivity. Moreover, relative to infants with secure attachment, infants with insecure attachment, and particularly disorganized attachment, showed higher salivary cortisol levels following interaction with a stranger.[21]

A disorganized/disoriented attachment pattern in infants is a predictor of hostile and aggressive behavior in the preschool classroom. In one study involving sixty-two low-income families (disorganized/disoriented attachment is more prevalent in low-income families compared to middle-income families), the authors examined the relation between attachment types of infants at age eighteen months and the child's behavior problems at age five years as rated by preschool teachers. The authors observed a significant correlation between a disorganized/disoriented pattern of attachment at age eighteen months and hostile behavior toward peers in the classroom at age five years (71 percent of hostile preschoolers were identified as having a disorganized/disoriented attachment in infancy). Moreover, maternal psychosocial problems independently predicted hostile behavior of children in the preschool classroom.[22] An infant's insecure attachment and behavioral inhibition in early childhood also predicts social anxiety symptoms during the adolescent years, but only for males.[23] In another study based on 6,650 children, the authors concluded that the odds of obesity are 30 percent higher among children (aged 4.5 years) who have insecure attachment at age twenty-four months compared to children who have secure attachment at that age.[24]

Lower socioeconomic status may be associated with higher stress as reflected by higher salivary cortisol levels in both mothers and infants (six to twelve months old) compared to salivary cortisol levels in mothers and infants belonging to high socioeconomic status. Children and adolescents from families with lower socioeconomic status also demonstrate higher salivary cortisol levels compared to children and adolescents from families with higher socioeconomic status. Studies have shown that a child's salivary cortisol level is negatively correlated with the family's income. Living in poverty for a long time since birth is associated with higher salivary cortisol level even at age thirteen.[25]

STRESS IN SCHOOLCHILDREN: THE BUFFERING EFFECT OF PARENTS
Studies have shown that even children attending elementary school are subjected to worries and stress. In general, in children from second to sixth grade

(aged seven to twelve years), girls report more worries than boys. Moreover, African American children report more worries than white or Hispanic children. The three most common areas of worry are school-related issues, health, and personal harm. Anxiety observed in these children is significantly associated with worries.[26] Insecure attachment during infancy is also associated with anxiety in preschool children (aged three to four years). In addition, the highest levels of anxiety were reported by children who had anxious mothers as well as insecure attachment during infancy.[27]

Positive parent-child relationships lead to better adjustment and fewer behavioral problems among children. This is in accordance with the stress-buffering model, which indicates that social support or a positive relationship with others protects people from the harmful physiological effect of stress. Unfortunately, negative parent-child interactions are associated with significant stress. In one study based on 101 five-year-old children, the author showed that salivary cortisol levels were increased twenty minutes after a negative parent-child interaction, but no cortisol increase was observed in children after a positive interaction with parents.[28] A good relationship between teacher and child can also protect a child from stress.

Reactive attachment disorder (RAD) is described as a markedly disturbed and developmentally inappropriate social relatedness in young children that usually develops before age five. Children who have been neglected or abandoned by their mother or parents early in life are at risk of developing RAD. Children of alcoholics, drug abusers, and mentally ill parents, as well as children of incarcerated mothers/parents, are also at risk of developing RAD. These children are not attached to their mother/caregiver, do not smile, have a sad appearance, and usually hold back their emotions. Physically abused and sexually abused children are at the highest risk of developing RAD. Proper treatment of these children is essential to prevent further damage.[29]

Corporal Punishment and Aggressive Behavior in Children

When parents discipline their children, they do it to correct their children's inappropriate behavior and have good intentions. In a survey, 72 percent of Americans overall considered that spanking was OK, with the highest approval rating in the South and the lowest in the Northeast. However, many scientific organizations, including the American Academy of Pediatrics, encourage parents to avoid spanking or any other form of corporal punishment and to develop nonviolent methods for disciplining children. Studies have shown that spanking or corporal punishment may correct the unwanted behavior for the time being, but in the long run it may predispose children to aggressive behavior. In one report, the authors found that mothers' use of spanking more than twice over the previous month when the child was three years of age was associated with increased levels of child aggression when the child was five years of age.[30] Any type of corporal punishment also increases the anxiety of children.

> Spanking at age three is associated with aggressive behavior of a child at age five.

Orphanages, Foster Care, and Divorce Are Associated with Significant Stress in Children

Children living in orphanages or removed from birth parents due to child abuse and then placed into foster homes by Child Protective Service (CPS) may experience much higher levels of stress than children living with their birth parents. It has been estimated that more than half a million children in the United States live in foster care. Foster children are also at high risk of developing psychiatric problems later in life. An estimated 27 percent of foster children at age seventeen suffer from depression. In one study, five out of twenty-one children (24 percent) with a mean age of 9.6 years showed an atypical salivary cortisol pattern indicating significant stress.[31] In another study based on 55 young children living in foster care and 104 children living with their birth parents, the authors observed that children living with foster parents showed atypical salivary cortisol indicative of higher stress levels compared to children who were living with their birth parents.[32]

In one published report, the authors studied salivary cortisol levels in children six and a half years after adoption from Romanian orphanages by Canadian parents and compared their salivary cortisol levels with Canadian-born children living with their birth parents. The authors observed no difference between daily cortisol patterns in children adopted from orphanages before the age of four months and Canadian-born children living with their birth parents. In contrast, children who were adopted after spending eight months or more in orphanages showed higher morning cortisol levels.[33]

As expected, parental unemployment, divorce, and separation can significantly increase stress in children. Before reaching the age of eighteen, more than 55 percent of American children spend some time living in a single-parent family, typically headed by the mother. In addition, more than one million American children experience parental divorce each year. Fifty percent of divorced adults in America remarry within four years, and one-third of American children eventually become a member of stepfamilies, with the majority of stepfamilies composed of a biological mother and a step-father. Although in the immediate aftermath of a parental divorce or remarriage, most children experience emotional distress as they are coping with changing relationships, within two to three years following divorce or three to five years af-

> A warm mother-child relation after divorce can protect a child from divorce-related stress.

ter remarriage, the majority of children recover fully from the initial stress.[34] However, maternal warmth may reduce stress induced by divorce in children. In one report, the authors concluded that for children from divorced families, a warm mother-child relationship after divorce and across development as perceived by the child may promote efficient stress management capabilities later in life as reflected by lower cortisol increases after performing a social stress task in a laboratory setting.[35] In another study, the authors concluded that stress experienced by children due to parental divorce may not necessarily lead to negative later life outcomes. For example, the higher mortality risk associated with experiencing parental divorce is ameliorated among individuals (especially men) who achieve a sense of personal satisfaction by midlife.[36]

PARENTAL SUPPORT IS EFFECTIVE IN BUFFERING STRESS IN ADOLESCENTS

It has been well documented in the medical literature that a strong bond with a mother or father has stress-buffering effects for young children. In one study, the authors recruited sixty-two girls (aged seven to twelve years) and their mothers for a stress study where, after experiencing a social stressor, girls were randomly selected to have complete contact with their mothers, no physical contact but allowed to call and talk to their mothers, or no contact at all. The authors reported that both the presence of mothers or talking to mothers was associated with higher salivary oxytocin levels and the swiftest return of salivary cortisol to the baseline. However, girls who received no support (physical or vocal) from their mothers showed lower salivary oxytocin levels, indicating more stress. Moreover, longer times were needed for salivary cortisol to return to normal, indicating a longer duration of stress in absence of any support from their mothers.[37]

Adolescence is a time when children begin to shift their reliance on parents as their sources of security toward friends and later romantic partners. Nevertheless, parental support can still buffer stress in adolescents because poor parental support is associated with significantly more stress in these boys and girls. In one study based on 1,004 school students (aged nine to thirteen years), the authors observed that boys worried more about the future whereas girls worried more about being liked or being overweight. Adolescents who preferred talking to their parents when worried reported more comfort compared to those who talked to friends or teachers.[38] In another study based on fifty-four children (aged nine to ten years) and adolescents (aged fifteen to sixteen years), the authors concluded that parents have better stress-buffering effects than friends in adolescence.[39]

> Parents are still effective in buffering stress in fifteen- to sixteen-year-old adolescents.

At what point the support system of adolescents switches primarily from parents to friends is debated in the medical literature. Some studies indicate that puberty is the switching point, but parental support is still valuable for coping with stress. However, as adolescents transit to young adulthood and leave home for college, friends and peers become important support systems for coping with stress. At this point a romantic partner can be very effective in buffering stress. Nevertheless, parental support is valuable throughout life, as most adults introduce their romantic partners to their parents and seek their approval before getting married.

STRESS-BUFFERING EFFECTS OF SOCIAL SUPPORT IN THE ADULT POPULATION

Adult human beings are subjected to various stressful life events. It is essential for everyone to develop adequate coping mechanisms to deal with stress because chronic stress is harmful to both the physical and the mental well-being of a person (see chapter 1). Chronic stress and lack of social support may increase the possibility of alcohol and drug addiction. Terrorist attacks may also increase alcohol use among people, as studies have shown that following the terrorist attack that destroyed the World Trade Center in New York in 2001, alcohol consumption increased in New York City and elsewhere for a

Table 4.3. Commonly encountered life stressors

Common life stressors	• Being fired from a job/prolonged unemployment • Serious financial hardship • Foreclosure • Death of a family member/close friend/spouse • Divorce or separation • Breaking up a relationship • Changing job/relocation (alone or with family) • Serious health problem/health problem with spouse • Child with chronic health issue • Being a single mother • Living alone/social isolation • Victim of violence/crime/terrorist attack • Difficulty with coworker/boss • Difficulty with spouse/family member • Problem with children's behavior/school performance • Living in a neighborhood with a high crime rate • Facing legal trouble
Special stressors for women	• Working in a male-dominated workplace • Potential sexual harassment/abuse • Discrimination based on sexism • Lower pay than men for the same job
Special stressors for minorities	• Potential racial discrimination • African American women and other minority women may face both racial and sexual discrimination
Natural disasters	• Flooding, hurricanes, earthquakes, etc., can cause significant stress in all people affected by such disaster

short time after the attack. Long-term studies also showed increased alcohol consumption one and two years later among New Yorkers who had higher exposure to the attack.[40] Various life stressors are summarized in table 4.3.

Long-lasting positive social bonds between spouses (pair-bond formation), parents, children, peers, and friends can effectively buffer against stress, depression, anxiety, and even alcohol and drug abuse. Furthermore, such social bonding also lowers the risk for cardiovascular diseases, asthma, and infection. On the other hand, the inability to form and maintain such positive bonding is a characteristic of many psychological problems, including anxiety and depression. Neurobiological studies have shown that bonds between spouses as well as between parents and their children involve similar neurobiological mechanisms, where oxytocin and dopamine (a neurotransmitter involved with the reward system) play an important role.[41] Whether the positive association between social support and the well-being of a person is attributable to an overall beneficial effect of support (main or direct effect model) or is related to protection of an individual from the potentially adverse effects of stress (buffering model) is an open question because studies have provided supporting evidence for both models.[42]

Social support, although needed throughout the life span, is salient during times of intense social change, such as during the transition to adulthood, a divorce, the death of a family member, or other adverse negative life experiences. Family, romantic partners, and friends are good and dependable sources of social support. Loneliness should be avoided at all costs because loneliness is a risk factor for a number of physical and psychological health problems, including elevated blood pressure, reduced immunity, depressive symptoms, alcoholism, and even suicidal thoughts. Loneliness is

> For college students, friends but not family members can buffer the stress associated with loneliness.

also associated with early mortality. Studies have shown that late adolescence and early adulthood are the two stages of life where loneliness is arguably most prevalent. As individuals transit to adulthood, support from friends and a romantic partner becomes very effective in reducing stress. In one study based on 636 college students (aged eighteen to twenty-five years), the authors reported that only support from friends buffered the association between stress and loneliness. In addition, females were more susceptible to stress associated with loneliness than males when perceived social support was poor.[43]

A romantic partner can effectively buffer stress in adolescents and young adults, but breaking up is associated with substantial stress. Interestingly, involvement with a much older romantic partner is associated with the risk of a poor emotional outcome in adolescent girls but not in adolescent boys.[44] Moreover, adolescent girls are more affected emotionally if caught in a bad relationship than adolescent boys are. Bad romantic relationships may also cause severe depression and even suicidal thoughts in adolescent girls.[45]

Injury is associated with significant stress in college athletes, but social support from trainers has a buffering effect. In one report based on a study of 387 collegiate athletes (256 males, 131 females) who suffered from various injuries, the authors observed that 84.3 percent of athletes received social support from their trainers during injury recovery. However, compared with athletes who were dissatisfied with the social support they received from their trainers, athletes who were very satisfied or satisfied with such social support were less likely to report symptoms of depression at return to play.[46]

Good workplace networks (social capital) can buffer stress associated with job insecurity. Generally, social capital includes bonding with coworkers, bridging with immediate supervisors/managers, and linking with higher authorities. However, bonding with coworkers is probably the most common. In one study based on 2,971 employees at two factories, the authors observed that workers who had poor workplace social capital suffered the most from job-related stress.[47] Based on a study of 84,263 respondents, in one study the authors concluded that social support has its strongest effect in buffering psychological stress associated with financial difficulties.[48]

> Social support can effectively reduce stress due to financial difficulties.

Elderly people often experience significant stress due to various factors, including health issues, living alone, death of close friends and family members, and potential financial distress. Social support is very effective in buffering stress in the elderly. Even getting a pet is associated with significant improvement in perceptions of well-being (see chapter 3). In one study based on seventy-eight older people, the authors concluded that elderly persons who spent more time and effort in developing and strengthening their social ties showed healthy cortisol patterns throughout the day compared to people with fewer social ties.[49] In another study based on 1,047 older adults (mean age 71.7 years), the authors showed that social support in these subjects was independently associated with lower blood pressure, indicating a stress-buffering effect of social support in the elderly.[50]

MARRIAGE REDUCES STRESS AND IMPROVES HEALTH

Currently, approximately 56 percent of adults in the United States are married and living with their spouses. A good marriage not only acts as a buffer to stress but also improves overall quality of life. Surveys have indicated that married individuals report greater happiness and life satisfaction and have a lower risk of depression than their unmarried counterparts. Marriage can lower the risk of various diseases, including hypertension, cardiovascular diseases (heart diseases), cancer, infectious diseases, influenza, and liver diseases. Marriage also improves immune function and blunts cortisol response under stress. Caring spouses often facilitate a healthy lifestyle in each other, including eating a balanced diet, exercising, and partaking in pleasurable leisure activities, including taking a vacation together.

Moreover, in terms of economic well-being, married people have a higher median household income than unmarried people. Interestingly, marriage can increase life expectancies in both genders, but this benefit is five times stronger in men than women.[51] In addition, lovemaking is a great way to release stress in both husband and wife (see chapter 7).

In one study based on a survey of 127,545 American adults aged eighteen and older, the authors reported that married adults are healthier than divorced or single adults. Moreover, a married man living with his wife lives longer than a man without a spouse. Interestingly, for men, being married after the age of twenty-five is associated with great physical and mental health benefits from marriage compared to men who get married at a younger age. However, married adults, particularly men, have a greater tendency to be overweight or obese. Never-married adults are less likely to develop obesity.[52]

> Married men live longer than single or divorced men.

Studies have shown that unmarried adults have a higher probability of early death than those who are married. Based on a survey of 80,018 adults, the authors reported that using married people as their reference group, those who were widowed had a 39 percent higher chance of mortality, and those who were divorced or separated had a 27 percent higher chance of mortality. For never-married people, the risk was 58 percent higher.[53] Although widowhood in general is associated with increased mortality, men have shown greater mortality risk in widowhood than women, perhaps because marriage represents a primary source of social support in men while women generally have a network of close friends who can support them during stressful times in life. Good socioeconomic status during widowhood also has protective effects in women.

> Widowed men have a higher mortality risk than widowed women.

In one published study based on 26,366 men and a twelve-year follow-up, the authors observed that the higher the level of education of wives, the lower the prevalence of men's sedentary behavior, being overweight, having high blood pressure requiring treatment, having high cholesterol, and having a smoking habit. In addition, men's age-adjusted mortality from cardiovascular diseases decreased with the increasing level of the wife's education.[54] Marriage also has protective health effects on women. Women in high-quality marriages are at a lower risk of developing atherosclerosis (narrowing of coronary arteries due to plaque formation that may cause heart attack). Based on a study of 393 postmenopausal women (the risk of atherosclerosis increases significantly after menopause), the authors reported that women in satisfying marriages had the least atherosclerosis in the arteries compared to those in low-satisfaction marriages.[55]

Approximately 65 percent of married women are also working women. Interestingly, employed women of all ages and occupations have a lower mortality rate and better reported and perceived health than housewives. Moreover, working does not worsen women's health during pregnancy, whereas perinatal outcomes may be improved for employed married women. Employment seems to have a beneficial effect on women's family as well because more employed women confide in their husbands and report helpful and support-ive responses from them. In addition, studies have found no difference in the psychological and educational characteristics of children of working versus nonworking mothers. Interestingly, children of working mothers are less likely to believe in traditional gender stereotypes. Employment is also associated with better maternal well-being, which is a definite gain for the children.[56]

> Employment seems to have a beneficial effect on women's physical and mental well-being and is also positively associated with maternal well-being, which benefits children.

The prevailing explanatory framework for the protective benefits of mar-riage is the stress/social support hypothesis. This model also explains why a bad marriage is associated with a higher amount of stress and negative health outcomes. In one study based on married couples and single men and women, the authors observed that high marital quality was associated with lower blood pressure, lower stress, less depression, and greater satisfaction with life compared to unmarried people as well as couples in low-quality marriages. Interestingly, single

> A bad marriage/ relationship increases the risk of heart disease.

individuals fared better than their unhappily married counterparts for overall perception of well-being.[57] In another study based on a prospective cohort study of 9,011 British government workers (6,114 men and 2,897 women), mostly married (4,987 men and 1,771 women), with 12.2 years of follow-up, the authors reported that those with the worst close relationships (spouse, close relatives, and friends) were 34 percent more likely to have a heart attack or heart disease than those with good relationships.[58]

In summary, the benefits of a good marriage include the following:

- Higher life expectancy, although the benefit is more significant in men than women.
- Lower risk of heart diseases, cancer, infection, and liver disease and better immune function.
- Lovemaking reduces stress in both husband and wife.
- Better financial situation and lower financial stress, although women worry more than men about finances and savings.
- Lower stress, a healthier lifestyle, and greater satisfaction with life.
- Working women in a good relationship get effective work-related stress relief after coming home due to spousal support.
- Marriage increases social networks, which buffers stress.
- In general, working married women are happier and have lower mortality than nonworking married women.
- Working women also report better maternal well-being, which has a positive impact on children.
- Children of working mothers are less likely to believe in traditional gender stereotypes.

VOLUNTEERING FOR STRESS RELIEF

The United States has long been known for its rich tradition of volunteer service, as American adults are more than twice as likely as European adults to have contributed time and energy in voluntary community work in the past year. More than 50 percent of American adults participate in some voluntary service, including church, charity, educational group, care of older citizens, political groups, and others. The person most likely to volunteer is a middle-aged, middle-class, married woman with more than a high school education and with school-age children. Married women are more likely to volunteer for religious, educational, and senior citizen organizations, while unmarried women prefer to volunteer more often for an education group. Older people prefer to volunteer for religious and senior citizen groups.

Beyond benefiting the community, volunteer work also benefits volunteers. Volunteer work reduces stress, improves overall physical health, and lowers mortality. Compared to elderly nonvolunteers, elderly volunteers have significantly higher life satisfaction, a stronger will to live, greater feelings of self-respect, and fewer symptoms of depression and anxiety. Moreover, in one study, the authors observed that elderly volunteers serving with two or more organizations (high volunteering) had a 44 percent lower mortality rate than elderly nonvolunteers over a five-year follow-up period. Volunteering was also very protective (60 percent lower mortality) for those with high religious involvement (weekly attenders of religious service) and high perceived social support.[59] In another study based on 2,681 subjects, the authors concluded that volunteer work increases happiness, life satisfaction, self-esteem, sense of control over life, and overall physical health while reducing depression and anxiety.[60]

LAUGHTER FOR STRESS RELIEF

Humor and laughter have long been recognized as central to the human condition and probably existed before language was developed. From an evolutionary point of view, laughter, like all traits that are passed though natural selection, must have survival value. Laughter serves many functions, including a bonding function, a peacemaking function, and a health-boosting function. Laughter and humor may also be considered as instinctive coping mechanisms that help people deal with disappointment and stressful situations in life. In one study based on 176 university students, the authors observed that having a sense of humor was associated with a lower perception of stress and higher levels of optimism, hope, and happiness. Laughter is comparable to mild aerobic exercise and is capable of improving mood, probably through the release of the neurotransmitter serotonin. In another study involving twenty healthy women, the authors observed that humor (watching a humorous video) had the greatest effect in reducing anxiety and improving mood compared to cycling, listening to music, or sitting quietly.[61] There are many theories that may explain the mechanisms of laughter, but three commonly cited theories are summarized in table 4.4.

In one study, the authors commented that a good sense of humor and laughter are associated with good health and stress reduction. Laughter provides a physical release for accumulated tension. Laughter can effectively reduce stress and also has a positive effect on the immune system.[62] Laughter has physiological, psychological, and social benefits. The therapeutic efficacy of laughter is mainly derived from spontaneous laughter (triggered by external stimuli or positive emotion) and self-induced laughter (triggered by

Table 4.4. **Three theories that attempt to explain the physical and mental health benefits of laughter**

Theory	Comments
Relief theory	Relief theory proposes that laughter is a physiological compensatory mechanism by which stress is relieved. Most people engage in laughter at something humorous with a feeling of mirth, and laughter has health benefits.
Incongruity theory	The incongruity theory proposes that people laugh at something that surprises them or at something that violates an accepted pattern and is different enough from the norm but nonthreatening. Neuroimaging research has shown that the part of the brain involved in resolving incongruities is also activated while processing cartoons.
Superiority theory	The superiority theory suggests that a person laughs at someone's faulty behavior because it makes them feel superior. This theory also explains why some people may laugh at other people's misfortunes.

the person at will), both occurring with or without humor. The brain is not able to distinguish between these two types of laughter, and benefits may be derived from each type.[63] In another study based on ten healthy male subjects who viewed a sixty-minute humor video, the authors observed that mirthful laughter can reduce stress by reducing blood levels of cortisol and other stress hormones.[64] In one Japanese study based on 20,934 individuals (10,206 men and 10,728 women) aged sixty-five and older, the authors observed that the prevalence of heart diseases among those who never or almost never laughed was 21 percent higher than those who reported laughing every day. The authors concluded that daily laughter is associated with a lower prevalence of cardiovascular diseases.[65]

Laughing may lower the risk of heart disease.

VACATION FOR STRESS RELIEF

Leisurely activities and taking a vacation can reduce stress at least on a short-term basis. In one study based on fifty-three subjects, the authors observed that vacation may improve people's feelings of well-being on a short-term basis. Three days after vacation, subjects reported better mood and sleep quality compared to pre-vacation days. Such positive effects of vacations lasted even after five weeks of being back at work.[66] In another study based on 12,338 middle-aged men with high risk from cardiovascular disease and nine years of follow-up, the authors observed that the frequency of annual vacations was associated with a reduced risk of all-cause mortality, and more specifically mortality associated with cardiovascular diseases. The authors concluded that vacationing is good for your health.[67]

Stress relief from vacation is facilitated by free time for oneself, a warmer and sunnier vacation location, exercise during the vacation, a good night's sleep, and making new acquaintances. How-ever, larger time zone differences from home and health problems during the vacation may have adverse effects.[68] In one study, the authors investigated the effect of an eight-day stay at a hot springs spa for stress relief and overall health benefits using fifteen married couples and thirteen women staying at the spa with a female companion. The authors observed that the spa vacation was more beneficial for stress release and positive health benefits for married women staying with their husbands compared to married men staying with their wives or women staying with a female companion.[69]

> Married women staying at a spa resort with their husbands derive more health benefits than married men staying with their wives or women staying with their women companions.

CONCLUSION

Effective management of stress is essential for both psychological and physi-ological well-being because chronic stress adversely affects physical as well as mental health. Social support is very effective in buffering stress. Married couples enjoying a good martial relationship also report overall better health and less stress. Overall life satisfaction is also greater in happily married couples. However, a bad marriage is associated with significant stress and also has negative health outcomes. Probably single men and women are better off than couples in a poor-quality marriage. Humor and laughter can effectively reduce stress and facilitates social bonding. People who laugh every day may get some protection against heart diseases compared to people who do not laugh on a regular basis. Vacationing is also effective in reducing stress and improving both physical and mental well-being.

5

Exercise, Yoga, and Meditation for Stress Management

Physical activity is essential for good physical and mental health. Lack of physical activity is the fourth leading risk factor for global mortality, accounting for 6 percent of deaths worldwide.[1] As a result, the World Health Organization (WHO) in 2010 published a global call for physical activity with the following recommendations:

- Adults (aged eighteen to sixty-four years) should engage in at least 150 minutes (two hours and thirty minutes) of moderate-intensity physical exercise every week or seventy-five minutes of vigorous exercise per week or a combination of both. Each session of activity should last at least ten minutes. For additional health benefits, up to 300 minutes (five hours) of moderate physical activity or 150 minutes of vigorous physical activity may be performed each week. Muscle-strengthening activities at least twice a day are also beneficial. People sixty-five years or older should follow the same guidelines unless physical mobility is compromised.
- Children aged five to seventeen years should accumulate sixty minutes of moderate- to vigorous-intensity physical activity daily. Engaging in physical activity over sixty minutes per day may provide additional benefits. Vigorous-intensity exercise, including that which strengthens muscle and bone, is beneficial and should be incorporated at least three times a week.

In November 2007, the American College of Sports Medicine, with the support and endorsement of the American Medical Association and the Office of the Surgeon General, launched a global initiative to educate physicians and health-care professionals on the value of exercise in everyday life. The recommendation is a minimum of 150 minutes (two hours and thirty minutes) of moderate dynamic exercise per week for healthy individuals to prevent many diseases, including cardiovascular diseases.[2] The *2008 Physical Activity Guidelines for Americans* from the Centers for Disease Control and Prevention (CDC) also recommend that adults and children engage in physical activity.[3] These guidelines are very similar to the 2010 WHO guidelines, which recommend that adults engage in 150 minutes (two hours and thirty minutes) of moderate-intensity physical activity per week or 75 minutes (one hour and fifteen minutes) of vigorous-intensity or aerobic exercise per week, or an equivalent combination of moderate and vigorous exercise.

The American Heart Association also recommends exercise for good cardiovascular health. The guidelines recommend the following:

- At least 150 minutes of moderate exercise, which may include thirty minutes of exercise at least five days a week. Walking is an acceptable form of moderate exercise.
- Instead of moderate exercise, vigorous exercise can also fulfill the requirement for regular exercise. This may include twenty-five minutes of vigorous exercise at least three times a week and moderate- to high-intensity muscle-strengthening activity at least two days per week for additional benefits.

For lowering blood pressure and cholesterol, the American Heart Association guidelines recommend an average of forty minutes of moderate- to vigorous-intensity aerobic activity three to four times per week. Aerobic exercises include playing sports, climbing stairs or any physical activity in a gym, and even simply walking. Interestingly, the various guidelines for optimal physical activities are very similar.

WALKING AS EXERCISE

Physical activities include walking, cycling, playing games, planned exercise, or sports. Even walking to perform chores, walking at the workplace, and the like can be included in physical activities. Interestingly, walking is the most common moderate-intensity aerobic exercise in the United States and is the preferred form of exercise for sedentary individuals who begin exercising. The energy expended by walking or other physical activity is often expressed as MET (metabolic equivalents), which represents an x-fold increase in energy expenditure relative to sitting at rest (1 MET). Walking at a speed of three miles an hour is equivalent to approximately 3.0 MET, and walking at this speed for thirty minutes per day for five days a week (150 minutes of moderate-intensity aerobic exercise) is equivalent to 7.5 MET hours per week. However, the number of calories burned during walking depends on the body weight (more calories burned with increasing body weight) and walking speed (more calories burned with a faster walking pace). For example, a 160-pound man walking at a speed of three miles per hour (normal walking speed) may burn around 130 calories during a thirty-minute walk, but the same person may burn around 160 calories during a thirty-minute walk if the walking speed is 3.5 miles per hour (brisk walking). However, the distance walked per day may provide better guidance for exercise than time spent during the walk because more calories are burned during brisk walking than normal walking.[4]

> Any exercise is better than a sedentary lifestyle. Simply walking or brisk walking for thirty minutes at least five times a week provides significant health benefits.

Although running is considered more effective than walking, in one study involving the National Runners (33,060 subjects) and Walkers (15,945 subjects) Heath Study Cohort, the authors observed that moderate walking and running are equally effective in lowering the risk of hypertension, diabetes, and high cholesterol. The authors concluded that walking and running are equally effective in improving cardiac health and reducing the risk of coronary heart diseases, including heart attack.[5]

Ten Thousand Steps Recommendation

There is a general recommendation of walking ten thousand steps per day, and this corresponds to walking approximately five miles per day. Moreover, walking ten thousand steps per day is more demanding than the recommended 150 minutes of weekly exercise. Although this goal per day may not be applicable to everyone, it is a good goal for healthy individuals to maintain a healthy body weight and for a selected group of obese people to lose weight because studies have shown that walking ten thousand steps per day can effectively reduce body mass index. Moreover, such an exercise protocol can lower blood glucose as well as blood pressure.[6] Pedometers or fitness trackers, which are low cost and commercially available, can be used to integrate walking into one's daily life.

In general, walking one hundred steps per minute for at least ten minutes is considered an acceptable form of aerobic exercise. In one study, the authors observed that an average of 6,574 steps per day is associated with most health benefits of aerobic exercise, such as lowering blood pressure, body mass index, percentage of body fat, waist circumference, blood cholesterol, and blood glucose.[7] Another study based on older Australians indicates that most of the benefits of exercise can be achieved with eight thousand steps per day.[8]

PHYSICAL HEALTH BENEFITS OF EXERCISE

As discussed earlier, the exercise recommended by the *2008 Physical Activity Guidelines for Americans* published by the CDC (150 minutes of moderate-intensity exercise or 75 minutes of vigorous-intensity exercise per week) is equivalent to 7.5 MET hours per week. In one study, the authors observed that even people who are engaged in less than the recommend physical activity by the CDC (less than 7.5 MET hours per week) have a 20 percent lower mortality risk compared to people with no leisure-time physical activity (sedentary lifestyle). However, people who are engaged in the recommended minimum physical activity of 7.5 MET hours per week or more

> Physical activity reduces the risk of mortality. Even physical activity lower than the minimum recommendation of physical activity per week (7.5 MET hours per week) is associated with a 20 percent reduced risk of mortality compared to people who do not engage in any physical activity at all.

(one to two times the recommended minimum) have a 31 percent lower mortality risk than people with a sedentary lifestyle. An upper threshold for mortality benefits was observed with three to five times the recommended physical activity (39 percent reduction in mortality risk). Interestingly, no harm was observed in the study for people performing even ten times more than the recommended minimum physical activity per week.[9]

Another study based on a meta-analysis of nine cohort studies with 122,417 participants sixty years of age or older also showed that people who were involved in physical activities below the minimum recommended guidelines had a 22 percent lower mortality risk compared to sedentary people.

However, people who followed the recommended minimum physical activity guidelines each week had a 28 percent lower risk of mortality, and people who exercised more than 16.7 MET hours per week had a 35 percent lower risk of mortality compared to people with a sedentary lifestyle.[10] Regular exercise also reduces the risk of premature death. Other health benefits of exercise include the following:[11]

- Lower risk of cardiovascular diseases, including heart attack
- Lower risk of type 2 diabetes (non–insulin dependent diabetes, the most common form of diabetes with late onset, which accounts for approximately 90 percent of all patients with diabetes)
- Lower risk of hypertension
- Lower risk of weight gain
- Lower risk of colon and breast cancer
- Weight-bearing exercise may improve bone density, thus reducing the risk of osteoporosis. The risk of fractures is also lower in physically active people.

EXERCISE FOR STRESS RELIEF

Exercise is an effective approach for stress management. Studies have shown that physically active people are less prone to depression than people with a sedentary lifestyle. In one study based on 19,842 subjects, both men and women, the authors observed that any form of daily physical activity was associated with lower risk of psychological distress after adjustment for age, gender, socioeconomic group, marital status, body mass index, and other variables in these subjects. Different types of activities, including domestic housework, gardening, walking, and sports were all associated with lower risk of psychological distress, but sports showed the strongest effect in enhancing mental well-being. Moreover, the authors observed mental health benefits even at a minimal level of at least twenty minutes of physical activity per week. However, more physical activity provided better mental health benefits.[12]

> Mental health benefits can be derived from at least twenty minutes of any physical activity per week.

Walking is the most popular form of physical activity in the United States and United Kingdom. Walking not only reduces the risk of cardiovascular disease and obesity but also reduces stress and the risk of developing depression. Although walking alone or with a spouse or friend is very beneficial, the CDC recommends walking with a group because the social environment in such a walking group may augment adherence to walking. Research has shown that people prefer and enjoy outdoor walking with others more than walking outdoors alone. Walking in a natural environment provides additional benefits of emotional well-being. Studies have shown that even walking alone in a natural environment provides stress relief, improves attention, and increases positive emotion. Moreover, group walking in a natural environment is very beneficial in improving mood and self-esteem along with releasing stress. The greenness of the natural environment enhances the mental health benefits of walking. Exercising in a park such as jogging is more beneficial for stress release than exercising indoors. Beach or river environments can also enhance the mental health benefits of walking in such an environment.

"Green prescription" is an outdoor physical activity prescription from a health-care practitioner, and such prescriptions are issued in the United States, New Zealand, and Scotland. Outdoor walking group programs could be endorsed through "green prescription" to improve the physical, mental, and emotional well-being of people.[13] In one study involving 331 participants, the authors concluded that green exercise (physical activity in nature) was associated with significant stress reduction as well as enhancement of mood in these study participants, but no significant difference was observed between walking on the beach, riverside, or grassland.[14] Even exercising outdoors may have added benefits over exercising indoors.

> Walking with a group may provide more stress release than walking alone. Moreover, walking in nature (green physical activity) alone or with a group may provide additional stress release and mood enhancement. Exercising outdoors may provide greater mental health benefits than exercising indoors.

Based on a systematic review of eleven trials, the authors in one review article concluded that compared with exercising indoors, exercising in natural environments is associated with greater feelings of revitalization, increased energy, and positive engagement, as well as reduced tension, confusion, anger, and depression. Therefore, exercising outdoors in a natural environment may provide greater effects on physical and mental well-being compared to exercising indoors.[15]

Walking during lunchtime can improve mental well-being of physically inactive employees. In one study based on fifty-six employees (92.9 percent females), the authors observed that a thirty-minute walk during lunch three times a week was associated with relaxation, stress release, reduced nervousness at work, and also increased enthusiasm.[16] Walking is effective in reducing depression in inactive postmenopausal women. In one study based on 121 postmenopausal women, the authors divided the women into two groups, with one group of women walking for forty minutes three times a week for six months and the other group of women not walking. At the end of the study, the authors observed that women who walked had much less depression compared to women who did not walk.[17]

Walking is also very effective in reducing depression among older people. In one Canadian study, the authors reported that older individuals who did not walk outside their homes reported more depressive symptoms or a greater likelihood of developing clinical depression compared to individuals who regularly walked outside their homes.[18] In addition to stress release, walking is effective in preserving cognitive function in older people. Walking a few times a week, as well as brisk walking, is effective in reducing the risk of developing age-related dementia. Walking in a park is more effective in preserving cognitive function in older populations compared to indoor walking or walking in shopping malls.[19]

Mechanism of Stress Release Due to Physical Activity

Physical fitness and physical activity blunt the response to stress by reducing the activity of the hypothalamic-pituitary-adrenal axis (HPA axis) responsible for the secretion of the stress hormone cortisol. Many positive physical health effects, such as reduced risk of cardiovascular diseases and reduced risk of developing type 2 diabetes, are related to the stress-releasing effects of various physical activities, including walking. Chronic stress is associated with low-grade inflammatory response. However, regular physical activity has an anti-inflammatory effect as evidenced by lower blood levels of C-reactive proteins and other markers of inflammation in physically active people. Moreover, exercise may benefit the brain by enhancing growth factor expression and neural plasticity, thereby contributing to improved mood and cognition.[20]

Endorphins are the endogenous equivalent of opioids produced by the pituitary gland and the hypothalamus in vertebrates, including humans, during strenuous exercise, moderate exercise, pain, or excitement. Similar to opioids, endorphins can produce analgesia because endorphins bind with opioid receptors present in the brain, mainly mu-receptors. Endorphins also improve mood and the sense of well-being. Exercise leads to an increased secretion of endorphins, which in turn reduces stress and improves mood. The secretion of endorphins during exercise of sufficient intensity is one of the factors explaining why physical activities can reduce the risk of depression. It has been postulated that exercise can be used as an adjunct therapy to treat patients with depression.[21]

> Endorphins, especially beta-endorphins, are secreted during exercise of sufficient intensity. Endorphins have an analgesic and mood-elevating effect and can also counteract depression.

Exercise Increases Gray Matter Volume, Brain Volume, and Plasticity

Significant acute stress, chronic stress, depression, and other mental disorders linked to chronic stress can reduce brain volume and impair brain plasticity. Brain damage due to mild to moderate acute stress is insignificant and can easily be prevented by proper stress management. However, significant acute stress associated with negative life events (e.g., death of a spouse, divorce, being fired from a job with prolonged unemployment) can damage the prefrontal cortex and other areas of the brain, while chronic stress mostly damages the hippocampal area of the brain. Fortunately, reduction in brain volume due to stress and depression can be reversed through stress management, psychotherapy, and, if necessary, antidepressant treatment (see chapter 1). Exercise is an effective stress management modality, and increased brain volume as well as improved brain plasticity has been reported in people who exercise on a regular basis. Even mild to moderate exercise increases brain volume in the hippocampus and prefrontal cortex area of the brain, which are affected by acute and chronic stress, respectively.

Studies have shown that an appropriate level of exercise can promote neurogenesis (growth and development of neurons) in the adult human brain, including in the hippocampal area, thus increasing brain volume and brain plasticity. Exercise, even mild exercise, also improves brain function by increasing blood flow to the brain and increasing oxygenation of the blood.

Physical exercise increases gray matter volume in healthy adults (aged eighteen to forty-five years), and such increases correlate with the total minutes of the weekly exercise protocol.[22] In one study based on 299 older adults, the authors recorded brain images at the time of enrollment and nine years later. The authors observed that greater physical activity predicted greater volumes of the frontal cortex, hippocampus, and other brain areas nine years later. Walking seven to nine miles per week was necessary to detect increased gray matter volume, but walking more than that did not cause any further volume increase.[23] In another study based on fifty-nine healthy older sedentary subjects, the authors observed significantly increased brain volume in both gray and white matter regions in subjects who participated in aerobic exercise.[24]

> Exercise, including walking, can significantly increase brain volume as well as gray matter volume.

The hippocampal area of the brain shrinks in late adulthood, causing impaired memory. However, exercise can reverse such age-related brain loss, thus improving memory in elderly people. In one study based on 120 older adults (mean age 67.6 years), the authors observed that aerobic exercise training was associated with a 2 percent overall increase in hippocampal brain volume in one to two years ($n = 60$), while hippocampal volume declined in the control group ($n = 60$), who did not participate in aerobic exercise training. Increased hippocampal area was also associated with increased serum levels of BDNF (brain-derived neurotrophic factor), and these people also showed improved memory. BDNF is an important growth factor that promotes neurogenesis and supports survival of existing neurons, thus playing an important role in improving memory. The authors concluded that aerobic exercise training is effective at reversing hippocampal volume loss in late adulthood, which is accompanied by improved memory function.[25]

> Exercise reverses age-related volume loss in the hippocampus and also improves memory function in the elderly.

POSSIBLE HEALTH RISKS OF STRENUOUS EXERCISE

Although physical activities have many health benefits, parents should be concerned about health problems associated with physical activities in children and adolescents. The prevalence of self-reported exercise-induced respiratory problems such as wheezing among twelve- to fourteen-year-old adolescents is approximately 19 percent. In general, adolescents with undiagnosed exercise-induced respiratory problems should be checked by a physician because such problems may be related to asthma, other respiratory illnesses, congenital heart issues, or other factors. Moreover, girls are at a higher risk for such exercise-induced respiratory problems compared to boys.[26]

Strenuous exercise and long-distance running such as marathon running may have some potential health hazards, but such hazard rates are low in healthy athletes. The relative risk of sudden cardiac death is only 1.5 out of 100,000 participants for triathlons and 0.75 per 100,000 runners of marathons. Middle-aged men, especially poorly trained runners, are at the highest risk. In addition to sudden death, serious cardiovascular complications may arise due to participation in strenuous exercise.[27] Therefore, it is advisable to undergo a health screening, which also includes a detailed family history, prior to participation in strenuous exercise, bodybuilding, or marathon running. Moreover, proper training with a coach is recommended to gradually build physical endurance.

> Although the risk is low, serious cardiovascular complications and even sudden death may occur due to strenuous exercise and marathon running. Proper pre-participation health screening is recommended to avoid such incidences.

YOGA AND MEDITATION: AN INTRODUCTION

"Yoga" is a Sanskrit word meaning connection or union. The goal of yoga is to integrate body and mind through postures (*asana*) and breathing methods (*pranayama*). Pranayama is derived from two Sanskrit words: "prana" (life energy) and "ayama" (prolonging). Therefore, pranayama means prolonging life's energy. The practice of yoga was originated in ancient India during the Vedic period. The practice of meditation was also originated at the same time, and on many occasions yoga was combined with meditation to achieve spiritual growth in ancient India. The classic book *Yoga Sutra of Patanjali* is considered a spiritual guide for practicing yoga. It was written during the late Vedic period, but it is also relevant today for people practicing yoga. The English version of this book is available in the United States. The National Center for Complementary and Integrated Health, part of the National Institutes of Health, considers yoga to be part of a complementary and integrated health approach used by many Americans.

There are different types of yoga, but in the United States hatha yoga is the most commonly practiced form. Hatha yoga is also suitable for beginners because it is relatively easy to learn. It is estimated that approximately 7.4 million Americans practice hatha yoga.[28] Vinyasa yoga is a practice similar to hatha yoga where postures are synchronized with breathing. Iyengar yoga (founded by B. K. S. Iyengar), which is also widely practiced in the United States, has some similarity to hatha yoga but may be slightly more intense. Bikram yoga (founded by Bikram Choudhury) is practiced in a hot room where the temperature may be as high as 105°F. The idea is that such elevated temperature results in more muscle relaxation and sweating, which eventually detoxes the body. Ashtanga yoga (founded by Pattabhi Jois, where principles were derived from Ashtanga yoga according to the *Yoga Sutra of Patanjali*) is a more aggressive form of yoga involving various postures where an individual may move quickly from one posture to another.

In kundalini yoga, postures and breathing exercises are practiced at the same time. The goal of kundalini yoga is to energize the "kundalini energy" (female energy) located at the base of the spine so that such energy can move through the spine and eventually reunite with the male energy located at the head (crown chakra). When such union takes place, a practitioner achieves total enlightenment, and nothing in the universe is unknown to the person. In reality, this does not happen for most practitioners, but it is a good practice to derive health benefits and spiritual growth at the same time. Although kundalini yoga has its origins in the ancient texts of Tantra, in 1968 Yogi Bhajan introduced his own version of kundalini yoga combining his teachings with yogic postures, Tantric theories, and mantras (chanting). This is also a popular form of yoga practiced in the United States. Other types of yoga practiced in the United States include Sivananda yoga (founded by Swami Sivananda), Kripula yoga (founded by Swami Kripalu), integral yoga (founded by Swami Satchidananda), and Viniyoga (founded by T. K. V. Desikachar).

Yoga has many physical and mental health benefits regardless of the type of yoga practiced. In one systematic review of 306 trials published on yoga, the authors observed that fifty-two different yoga styles were practiced, with the most common being hatha yoga (thirty-six trials), Iyengar yoga (thirty-one trials), pranayama (twenty-six trials), and an integrated approach to yoga therapy (fifteen trials). Interestingly, positive health benefits of yoga were reported in 277 trials (91 percent of all trials), and such positive health benefits were observed regardless of the yoga style practiced.[29]

Meditation is a mind-body healing practice where a meditator trains his or her mind to suspend the stream of various thoughts that normally occupy one's mind. Meditation should be practiced on a regular basis in order to get health benefits. In general, a meditator needs to select a quiet place, and meditation can be done sitting on the floor using a floor mat or even sitting comfortably in a chair. There are several approaches, including focusing the mind on a breathing pattern, focusing on a word or phrase with spiritual meaning (mantra), or focusing on a particular part of the body, feeling the sensation of each part in a sequential manner starting from the toes to the head. During meditation, one may also focus on a picture of an individual and direct his or her love toward that person. Meditation can be learned from a teacher, a health-care professional, or by reading an instructional book or watching a video. Although many types of meditation are practiced today, the major meditation techniques practiced in the United States include the following:

> The physical health and mental health benefits of yoga can be derived from any type of yoga practice. Therefore, the choice of an individual yoga style should be based on personal preferences and availability.

- Mantra or sound meditation: in this type of meditation, one may repeat a mantra such as "om," or, during spiritual initiation (Sanskrit: *Diksha*), a teacher may repeat a mantra specific for the student secretly in his or her ear. However, any holy word can be repeated during this type of meditation depending on one's religious belief because meditation is a nondenominational practice.
- Zen meditation: this type of meditation is practiced by many Buddhist monks. In this meditation, both breathing and mind control are practiced, and the emphasis is on achieving enlightenment through the teachings of the Buddha.
- Mindfulness-based stress reduction (MBSR) meditation: Dr. Jon Kabat-Zinn in 1979 developed the mindfulness-based stress reduction program at the University of Massachusetts Medical Center. MBSR is an eight-week training course where participants meet for about ninety minutes once a week, and then they can practice this meditation at home. The goal of

MBSR practice is to focus attention on moment-by-moment experiences with an attitude of curiosity, openness, and acceptance. Various practices, such as body scanning (paying attention to parts of the body and bodily sensations in sequence, starting from the feet to the head), breathing (focusing on the rise and fall of the abdomen), and even hatha yoga, may be a part of MBSR-type meditation. Currently MBSR is offered in more than two hundred hospitals in the United States.

- Vipassana meditation: this form of meditation has its roots in the ancient Zen meditation practice where a person develops present-moment awareness without being judgmental. This type of meditation has similarities to MBSR, although Vipassana meditation may be linked to Buddhist religious practice, whereas MBSR is a totally secular practice.
- Loving-kindness meditation: in this meditation practice, a person during meditation cherishes all living beings on the earth. This type of meditation is based on Buddhist philosophy but can easily be practiced in a secular way.
- Transcendental meditation: taught by Maharishi Mahesh Yogi in the West, where a mantra or a series of mantras is repeated during meditation to achieve mental calmness and eventually a transcendental state of mind similar to the fourth level of consciousness. Usually transcendental meditation is learned from a teacher who may select a mantra specific for the student.

YOGA FOR STRESS MANAGEMENT AND MENTAL HEALTH

Stress is linked with many physical and mental diseases, and effective stress reduction significantly reduces the risks of such illnesses, including cardiovascular diseases, diabetes mellitus, cancer, anxiety, and depression (see chapter 1). Yoga is very effective for stress management, but at the same time yoga fosters spiritual growth. In one study, the authors surveyed 360 yoga students and 156 yoga teachers and reported that the majority of yoga students and teachers practice yoga for stress relief and exercise, but for many students and teachers, spirituality is the primary reason for practicing yoga.[30]

Many studies have shown the stress-reducing and antidepressant effects of yoga. Yoga practice is effective in reducing serum levels of the stress hormone cortisol, thus confirming the effectiveness of yoga in stress management.[31] Yoga is also effective in reducing salivary cortisol and twenty-four-hour urine norepinephrine and epinephrine (stress-related molecules) levels, as well as decreasing heart rate and blood pressure, indicating significant stress relief.

Yoga likewise reverses the negative impact of stress on the immune system by increasing levels of immunoglobulin A and natural killer cells. Stress is associated with low-grade inflammation, but yoga can also reverse such effects by its anti-inflammatory effects, as evidenced by lower serum levels of markers of inflammation such as C-reactive protein and inflammatory cytokines, including interleukin-6 and lymphocyte-1B. Therefore, yoga has immediate quieting effects on the sympathetic nervous system/HPA-axis response to stress. Yoga is more effective than exercise in releasing stress as well as in improving mood and sleep quality in healthy people as well as individuals with chronic illnesses.[32]

Although both yoga and walking have health benefits and stress-reducing effects, in one study based on nineteen subjects practicing yoga and fifteen subjects who walked, with a twelve-week follow-up, the authors observed greater improvement of mood and significantly reduced anxiety among subjects who practiced yoga compared to subjects who walked. Moreover, subjects in the yoga group showed higher brain levels of gamma-aminobutyric acid (GABA) compared to subjects in the walking group, and positive mood in people in the yoga group was also correlated with brain GABA levels. It has been well documented in the medical literature that people suffering from mood and anxiety disorders have lower concentrations of brain GABA.[33] In another study, the authors divided eighty-one undergraduate students who experienced moderate depression, anxiety, or stress into three groups: integrated yoga, exercise, and control. Although participants in both the integrated yoga group and the exercise group reported reduced stress levels and lower depression levels compared to the control group, only participants in the integrated yoga group experienced decreased anxiety and decreased salivary cortisol from the beginning to the end of the study. The authors concluded that yoga, which has ethical and spiritual elements, may provide additional benefits over exercise for stress reduction.[34]

Practice of hatha yoga is very effective in relieving stress in middle-aged women (aged forty to sixty years). Stress relief was observed even after one ninety-minute session of hatha yoga.[35] Nursing is a stressful profession, but

> The practice of yoga reduces serum and salivary cortisol levels, thus confirming stress relief. In addition, yoga reverses the negative effects of stress on the immune system and also promotes good sleep quality. Yoga may provide more mental health benefits than exercise.

regular yoga practice (fifty- to sixty-minute sessions more than two times a week) can improve sleep quality and reduce work-related stress in staff nurses.[36] In another study, the authors divided sixty mental health care professionals into two groups, with one group participating in a weekly sixty-minute practice of yoga and another group relaxing one hour during tea time (control group). After twelve weeks of intervention, the authors reported significant reduction in work-related stress in the yoga group compared to the control group. The authors concluded that offering regular yoga classes is a viable strategy for work-related stress reduction in health-care professionals.[37] In a similar study involving twenty-four women who perceived themselves as emotionally stressed, the authors observed that women who participated in two weekly ninety-minute Iyengar yoga classes for three months showed significant improvements on measures of stress and psychological outcomes compared to women who did not participate in yoga classes (control group).[38] A study involving inner-city children's well-being also demonstrated that children who participated in yoga (one hour per week for twelve weeks) reported fewer negative reactions in response to stress compared to children who did not participate in yoga. Yoga also improved overall well-being in these children.[39]

> Yoga is also effective for reducing stress in children.

In addition to stress relief and improving overall feelings of positive emotion, yoga can significantly reduce anxiety, depression, and panic disorder. Emotional eating is often associated with chronic stress, but yoga is effective in reducing emotional eating. In one study, a group of fifty-two females with this disorder were randomly assigned to an eight-week (twice weekly) hatha yoga group or a waiting-list control. The authors observed that women in the yoga group showed significant reduction in emotional eating as well as improved distress tolerance.[40]

YOGA REDUCES OXIDATIVE STRESS

Psychological stress increases oxidative stress in the human body, and many ill effects of stress are related to increased oxidative stress (see chapter 1). However, yoga is very effective in reducing oxidative stress, thus counteracting the physiological effects of stress. In one study based on 104 subjects (59 males and 45 females) who participated in a yoga-based lifestyle-modification program (a nine-day outpatient program consisting of one hour of practicing yoga a day and educational videos on yoga), the authors demonstrated that serum concentrations of malondialdehyde (a biomarker of oxidative stress), as measured by thiobarbituric acid reactive substances (TBARS), decreased significantly after nine days of yoga practice. The mean initial concentration of TBARS in these subjects was 1.72 nmol/mL, but after participation in the yoga program, the mean TBARS value decreased to 1.57 nmol/mL. The authors concluded that yoga reduces oxidative stress by boosting the antioxidant defense of the body.[41] In another study, the authors divided fifty-one healthy male volunteers into two groups: one group ($n = 30$) participated in a six-month yoga program, while the volunteers of the control group ($n = 21$) were engaged in exercise for the same six-month period. After six months, the authors observed a significantly increased total antioxidant capacity of the blood in volunteers who participated in the yoga program compared to the control group. In addition, the blood level of reduced glutathione, an antioxidant, was increased significantly in volunteers who participated in the yoga program compared to volunteers in the control group, indicating that yoga improves the antioxidant defense of the body.[42]

Yoga is superior to exercise in increasing the antioxidant defense of the body. In one study, the authors observed that after three months of practicing yoga, serum levels of vitamin C, vitamin E, and reduced glutathione (all antioxidants) were increased in volunteers who participated in the yoga program compared to volunteers who participated in physical training. The total antioxidant capacity of the blood was also significantly increased in volunteers who participated in the yoga training compared to volunteers who were engaged in physical training. The authors concluded that yoga improves the antioxidant defense of the body and is superior to exercise.[43]

> Yoga is superior to exercise in increasing the antioxidant defense of the body.

PHYSICAL HEALTH BENEFITS OF YOGA

Cardiovascular diseases are the number-one killer in developed countries. Yoga is very effective in reducing the risk of cardiovascular diseases, including heart attack (myocardial infarction), because yoga reduces serum cholesterol, triglycerides, and low-density lipoprotein cholesterol (LDL cholesterol: bad cholesterol) but increases high-density lipoprotein cholesterol (HDL cholesterol: good cholesterol). An improved lipid profile is associated with cardio-protection in people who practice yoga on a regular basis. Moreover, yoga is effective in reducing blood pressure, thus providing additional protection. In one study, the author reviewed thirty-seven clinical trials enrolling 2,768 subjects and observed that the mean systolic blood pressure was reduced by 5.21 mm Hg (millimeters of mercury), LDL cholesterol was reduced by 12.14 mg/dL, and HDL cholesterol was increased by 3.2 mg/dL in subjects who practiced yoga compared to subjects who did not participate in any yoga program.[44] Increased oxidative stress is also associated with a higher risk of cardiovascular diseases. Yoga significantly reduces oxidative stress, thus lowering the risk of cardiovascular diseases, including heart attack.

Yoga is helpful for individuals with type 2 diabetes because yoga improves glucose control in diabetic patients by lowering body weight and decreasing insulin resistance. In one study, the authors recruited thirty diabetic patients (age range: thirty to fifty-five years) and thirty nondiabetic patients who participated in daily yoga training every day for six months. Before the initiation of yoga practice, the mean fasting glucose in type 2 diabetic patients was 154.1 mg/dL. After six months, the mean fasting glucose value was reduced to 141.42 mg/dL. In nondiabetic patients, the mean fasting glucose value was 84.38 mg/dL before the initiation of yoga and 82.14 mg/dL after six months. The authors concluded that yoga is effective in reducing blood sugar in patients with type 2 diabetes.[45] Yoga is also effective in reducing blood pressure in people suffering from pre-hypertension or hypertension. Yoga can reduce symptoms of arthritis, osteoarthritis, lower back pain, and other types of pain. Yoga is effective in improving balance in older people.[46] The physical health benefits of yoga are summarized in table 5.1.

Yoga Increases Gray Matter Volume in the Hippocampus

Yoga increases the volume of the hippocampus in elderly people. In one study based on seven healthy elderly subjects who practiced yoga for six months, the authors observed an increased hippocampal area of the brain using a magnetic resonance imaging technique (voxel-based morphometric analysis).[47] Yoga also protects the brain from stress-related damage.

Table 5.1. Physical health benefits of yoga

Physical Health Benefit	Comments
Yoga reduces the risk of cardiovascular (heart) diseases, including heart attack.	Stress relief and reduced oxidative stress protects the heart. In addition, yoga reduces blood levels of total cholesterol, triglycerides, and LDL cholesterol (bad cholesterol) while increasing the level of HDL cholesterol (good cholesterol). A better blood lipid profile in people practicing yoga provides protection against heart diseases and heart attack.
Yoga is helpful in patients with type 2 diabetes.	Increased oxidative stress increases the risk of developing type 2 diabetes. Yoga reduces oxidative stress and also lowers blood glucose levels and insulin resistance, thus helping patients with sugar control. Moreover, yoga promotes weight loss, which may lower insulin resistance.
Yoga is useful for people suffering from pre-hypertension or hypertension.	Yoga is effective in lowering blood pressure through activation of the parasympathetic nervous system, thus reducing both stress and blood pressure. Yoga also increases brain levels of GABA, which may produce mental calmness and reduce blood pressure.
Yoga reduces the perception of pain in various musculoskeletal diseases (lower back pain, rheumatoid arthritis, osteoarthritis, fibromyalgia, and carpal tunnel syndrome).	Lower back pain is the most commonly reported pain. Yoga-based movements are very effective in reducing such pain because yoga improves posture. Rheumatoid arthritis is an autoimmune disease. Yoga reduces the progression of rheumatoid arthritis, probably by improving the immune system. In general, reduced perception of pain in people practicing yoga may also be related to stress reduction and the calming effect of yoga.
Yoga is effective in improving quality of life in some cancer patients.	This may be related to stress relief due to practicing yoga. In addition, yoga improves sleep quality and fosters spiritual growth, which may help people cope with cancer.
Yoga is associated with positive outcome in pregnancy.	Maternal stress and anxiety during pregnancy may negatively affect the outcome of pregnancy by affecting the intrauterine environment by altering blood flow and oxygen to the fetus and also by releasing stress hormones from the placenta. Yoga, a mind-body approach, is more effective than exercise in reducing maternal stress, anxiety, and depression. Yoga can improve intrauterine fetal growth and the utero-fetal placental circulation in women with high-risk pregnancies.
Yoga reduces premenstrual syndrome.	Yoga reduces premenstrual syndrome probably due to reduction in the perception of pain by the brain. Alpha brain waves increase after yoga, which may be associated with the perception of pain reduction.
Yoga reduces symptoms of menopause.	Yoga is effective in reducing the frequency and intensity of hot flashes in postmenopausal women.

Physical Health Benefit	Comments
Yoga reduces symptoms in asthma patients.	In asthma patients, chronic inflammation causes blockage of airways, leading to symptoms such as wheezing, breathlessness, chest tightness, and coughing at night or in the early morning. Yoga has anti-inflammatory effects, thus reducing symptoms of asthma. Eosinophils play a crucial role in asthma attacks, but yoga reduces the percentage of eosinophils in the blood, thus protecting from asthma attack.
Yoga improves sleep quality and reduces the incidence of insomnia.	Yoga improves sleep quality due to stress release and reduction of cortisol in the blood.
Yoga improves balance and reduces the risk of falling in the elderly.	Yoga improves posture and balance in older people.
Yoga may reduce tobacco, alcohol, and drug abuse and help with drug/alcohol rehabilitation.	This may be related to both reduced depression and anxiety in patients undergoing alcohol/drug rehabilitation as well as spiritual growth associated with yoga practice.
Yoga reduces symptoms in patients with multiple sclerosis.	Yoga's focus on movement, breathing, and stretching is helpful in managing symptoms of multiple sclerosis. Yoga also alleviates symptoms such as pain, fatigue, spasticity, balance, bladder control, and sexual function in patients suffering from multiple sclerosis.

MEDITATION FOR STRESS MANAGEMENT

Many scientific investigations have demonstrated that meditation is very effective in stress management. In one study, the authors reviewed seventeen published papers dealing with the stress reduction capacity of mindfulness-based stress reduction (MBSR) meditation in healthy individuals. The authors reported that sixteen out of seventeen studies demonstrated positive outcomes related to the reduction of stress or anxiety and concluded that MBSR

> Even ten to fifteen minutes of meditation per day is very effective in stress management.

meditation is an effective approach toward stress management in healthy individuals.[48] In another report based on a review of forty-seven clinical trials involving 3,515 participants, the authors concluded that the practice of meditation is associated with stress reduction. Moreover, eight weeks of meditation can effectively reduce anxiety, depression, and the perception of pain.[49]

Loving-kindness meditation is also very effective at reducing stress. In one study, the authors observed seven inexperienced and five experienced healthy meditators in one sitting who participated in twenty minutes of loving-kindness meditation. The authors observed significant stress reduction after meditation even in inexperienced meditators.[50] In another report based on a review of the medical literature, the authors concluded that loving-kindness meditation is effective in reducing depression, social anxiety, marital conflict, and anger and in coping with long-term caregiving.[51]

Silent repetition of a word or a phrase (mantra) with spiritual significance, an ancient form of meditative prayer, is also very effective in reducing stress. The mantra can be repeated any time of a day and also in response to stress. In one study based on sixty-two outpatient veterans, the authors concluded that mantra repetition significantly reduced stress and anxiety in these subjects and also improved their quality of life and spiritual well-being.[52] In another study, thirty veterans, mostly male (97 percent), and thirty-six hospital employees, mostly female (86 percent), with a mean age of fifty-six years, participated in a five-week study where subjects were instructed to participate in meditation involving mantra repetition when they were subjected to stressful situations. Each subject selected a mantra based on his or her religious belief, but each mantra had spiritual significance. The authors observed that mantra repetition was helpful in reducing stress, unwanted thoughts, insomnia, and negative emotions such as anger.[53] Common mantras chanted during meditation are listed in table 5.2.

Table 5.2.   Common mantras that may be chanted during meditation

Religion	Common Mantra
Hinduism	• Om (sacred sound of Hinduism) • Om shanti (Peace be everywhere) • Om namah Shivaya (Adoration to Lord Shiva) • Ram Ram sri Ram (Ram is a mythological person of the epic *Ramayana*)
Christianity	• Jesus or Lord Jesus Christ • Hail Mary or Ave Maria
Buddhism	• Om mani padme hum (an invocation of self) • Namo Amitabha (homage to Lord Buddha) • Sabhe sotta sukhi hontu (let all living beings be happy)

Meditation Lowers Cortisol

Cortisol is the main hormone secreted in response to stress. Persistently elevated blood cortisol in response to chronic stress has many adverse health effects including reducing brain volume (see chapter 1). Meditation can effectively reduce cortisol levels, indicating that meditation is an effective approach for stress relief. In one study using thirty second-year medical students, the authors demonstrated that after four days of mindfulness meditation, the average serum cortisol level was reduced from a premeditation level (collected at 8 a.m.) of 381.93 nmol/L (13.8 microgram/dL) to 306.39 nmol/L (11.1 microgram/dL; normal range at 8 a.m.: 5–23 microgram/dL) postmeditation.[54] In another study using nine experienced meditators and eleven novices who underwent eight weeks of meditation training, the authors observed significantly lower morning serum cortisol levels in meditators compared to novices, indicating that meditators were calmer than novices at the beginning of the study. Interestingly, even in novices, serum cortisol levels were decreased from pretraining levels after eight weeks of meditation training.

> The stress-relieving effects of meditation are reflected in reduced cortisol levels in people who regularly meditate. Meditation can also reverse HPA-axis activation in response to stress.

Moreover, sleep quality was improved in novices after receiving meditation training.[55] Basal cortisol levels also decreased significantly in subjects who meditate for two to four weeks compared to subjects who participated in a relaxation exercise.[56] One study has shown that cortisol levels were usually lower in people who had practiced transcendental meditation for three to five years, and cortisol levels were further decreased after completion of a meditation session. The authors concluded that long-term practice of meditation acutely blunts the HPA-axis response to psychological stress.[57]

Meditation Improves the Antioxidant Status of the Body

Psychological stress increases the oxidative stress of the body, but, like yoga, meditation is effective in reducing oxidative stress. Long-term transcendental and Zen meditators usually show diminished oxidative stress, as evidenced by reduced lipid peroxidation products in the blood. Moreover, the practice of meditation increases serum glutathione levels (a potent antioxidant) and the activity of several antioxidant enzymes, including catalase, superoxide dismutase, glutathione peroxidase, and glutathione reductase.[58] In one study using twenty subjects who practiced Zen meditation and twenty control subjects who did not meditate, the authors showed significantly lower serum levels of malondialdehyde, a marker for lipid peroxidation and oxidative stress in meditators compared to nonmeditations. The authors concluded that Zen meditation is effective in reducing oxidative stress and improving the antioxidant defense of the body.[59]

MEDITATION INCREASES GRAY MATTER VOLUME

Acute stress associated with negative life events as well as chronic stress may damage various areas of the brain, shrink overall brain volume, and reduce plasticity of the brain, but meditation may reverse such damage to the brain. In one study involving forty-four subjects, the authors used high-resolution magnetic resonance imaging (MRI) of the brain and observed increased gray matter volumes in the orbitofrontal cortex and hippocampus in long-term meditators compared to nonmeditators. In addition, the increased gray matter volume in these long-term meditators was independent of the specific style and practice of meditation. In general, stress damages these brain areas.[60] In another study, using brain MRI, the authors observed increased overall brain volume in older adults who participated in meditation compared to nonmeditators.[61]

> Meditation, irrespective of style, increases gray matter in the prefrontal cortex, hippocampus, and other brain areas. Acute stress damages the prefrontal cortex, while chronic stress damages the hippocampal area of the brain along with various other areas, but meditation can reverse such damages.

Even short-term meditation can increase brain volume in certain areas. In one study, the authors recorded MRI scans of sixteen healthy individuals who never meditated. The authors also used seventeen healthy individuals as controls who did not meditate during the study period. The authors reported that only eight weeks of practicing MBSR was associated with increased regional brain gray matter density (mostly in the left hippocampus), confirming that even just eight weeks of MBSR can increase brain gray matter density. Moreover, whole brain analysis identified volume increases in four regions of the brain (the posterior cingulate cortex, the temporo-parietal junctions, and two areas of the cerebellum) after eight weeks of practicing MBSR. These results suggest that participation in MBSR is associated with increased volume of gray matter in the brain regions involved in learning, memory, emotion regulation, self-referential processing, and perspective taking.[62] In another study, the authors observed that an eight-week MBSR course was associated with increased gray matter concentration in several brain areas in healthy subjects as observed by advanced echo MRI scans. Such areas of the brain are involved in the synthesis and release of neurotransmitters including serotonin, which may explain improved perception of psychological well-being due to participation in an MBSR course.[63] The neurotransmitter serotonin is associated with positive emotion and mood because reduced serotonin levels in the brain are associated with depression.

In a review article, the authors commented that eight weeks of MBSR practice can induce positive changes in the brain similar to long-term meditation practice. Overall, the prefrontal cortex shows increased activity after MBSR. Moreover, increased gray matter volume and increased activity in the hippocampal area of the brain has been confirmed by multiple studies. The amygdala is involved in the processing of emotion and the fear response, and this area is highly activated in patients with generalized anxiety disorder. This disorder affects approximately 6.8 million Americans and is characterized by persistent and excessive worries that may not have a rational basis. Studies have reported lower activity of the amygdala in meditators, which may explain why meditators are calmer and more rational during stressful events. More volume or activity in relation to MBSR has also been reported in other brain areas, including the parietal cortex, temporal cortex, occipital cortex, cerebellum, and basal ganglia.[64]

MENTAL HEALTH BENEFITS OF MEDITATION

In addition to stress management, meditation has many mental health benefits. Studies have shown that meditation improves cognitive function, processing of information, concentration, and memory, which may be related to increased gray matter volume in various regions of the brain as well as to increased plasticity of the brain. In one study, the authors compared brain images from fifty adult meditators and fifty adult nonmeditators and observed that people who practiced meditation for many years had more folds (gyrification) in the cortical structure of the brain, indicating better mental focus and intelligence.[65] In general, gyrification is reduced with aging. Therefore, increased gyrification in meditators indicates that meditation may slow and even stall the normal aging of the brain. Moreover, meditation increases the bridging between the left hemisphere and the right hemisphere of the brain (through the corpus callosum), thus enhancing mental strength. Meditation also increases levels of gamma-aminobutyric acid (GABA), a neurotransmitter that reduces anxiety and depression. In addition, activation of the parasympathetic nervous system during meditation decreases heart rate, blood pressure, and consumption of oxygen. Meditation increases melatonin production by the pineal gland of the brain, which contributes to a good night's sleep, mental calmness, and decreased awareness of pain.[66]

Age-related dementia and cognitive decline are sometimes associated with advanced age. However, regular practice of meditation is effective in slowing the rate of neural degeneration. Moreover, meditation may slow or stall many psychiatric illnesses related to neurodegeneration, such as age-related dementia, Alzheimer's disease, Parkinson's disease, and Huntington's disease. In general, after the age of forty, the human brain decreases by volume and weight at a rate of approximately 5 percent every decade; as a result, the elderly population is more vulnerable to diseases that are related to brain degeneration. Meditation has a brain-preserving effect, thus reducing the risk of developing neurodegenerative diseases.[67] The mental health benefits of meditation are summarized in table 5.3.

> The regular practice of meditation not only increases mental focus and memory but also protects the brain from age-related shrinkage and neurodegeneration (progressive loss of structure or function of neurons, including death of neurons). As a result, meditation lowers the risk of age-related dementia, Alzheimer's disease, Parkinson's disease, and Huntington's disease.

Posttraumatic stress disorder is a serious psychological issue that often affects veterans. In one study, the authors reported that loving-kindness meditation is very effective in reducing symptoms of posttraumatic stress disorder among veterans.[68] Psychiatric illness is common among prisoners. In one study, the authors reviewed reports dealing with the effect of meditation programs on prisoners and concluded that meditation-based programs in prisons provide enhancement of psychological well-being, a decrease in substance abuse, and reduced recidivism.[69]

Meditation and Spiritual Bliss

Although most people practice meditation for stress management, the ultimate goal of meditation according to the Hindu and Buddhist religions is to achieve the fourth state of consciousness, called *turiya chetana* in Sanskrit. When a meditator achieves this state of mind, the person directly feels divine bliss and is enlightened. The highest stage, known as *nirvikalpa samadhi*, is the ultimate state of fourth consciousness where a human soul

Table 5.3. Mental health benefits of meditation

Mental health benefits	Comments
Meditation is very effective in stress management. People who meditate are in general happier in life due to positive mood, emotional stability, and capacity to cope with negative life events.	Meditation reduces levels of the stress hormone cortisol in serum and saliva, which is associated with stress release. Meditation may also release serotonin, which has a calming effect on the brain. In addition, during meditation, the brain produces theta waves, which are associated with a very relaxed state of mind and may also foster spiritual growth.
Meditation improves the brain's structure and function, thus improving concentration, memory, and other brain functions.	Meditation increases cortical gyrification in the brain, cortical thickness, as well as gray matter in the areas of the brain responsible for learning, memory, and emotional balance. Meditation increases the plasticity of the brain, thus increasing mental capacity. Meditation not only protects the brain from chronic stress-induced brain damage but also reverses reduced brain volume caused by stress.
Meditation reduces anxiety, depression, and symptoms of posttraumatic stress disorder.	Such effects may be related to the stress-releasing effects of meditation.
Meditation reduces the addiction for nicotine, alcohol, and drugs.	This may be related to stress release and spiritual growth due to the practice of meditation.
Meditation reduces the risk of developing age-related dementia, Alzheimer's disease, Parkinson's disease, and Huntington's disease.	Meditation reduces aging of the brain by increasing cortical gyrification (gyrification reduces with advanced age), thus preventing various age-related neurodegenerative diseases. MRI studies also show less age-related degeneration in brains of meditators compared to nonmeditators.
Meditation may reduce emotional eating disorders.	This effect may also be related to the stress-relieving effect of meditation.

is flooded with divine consciousness. However, many years of dedicated practice are needed for achieving such a state of mind, and for most of us this goal is unachievable. Nevertheless, practicing meditation even for a short time on a regular basis can provide some spiritual bliss, as evidenced by changes in brain waves during meditation.

Four types of brain waves are observed in an EEG (electroencephalogram). The beta wave (fifteen to forty cycles per second) is the fastest brain wave and is the major brain wave when we are awake and engaged in various tasks. The alpha wave (nine to fourteen cycles per second), which is slower than beta waves, represents a more relaxed state of mind, and this wave is observed when a person takes a break after completion of a task. The theta wave (five to eight cycle per second), which is slower than alpha waves, represents deep relaxation, and delta waves, which are the slowest brain waves (1.4–4 cycle per second) are observed during deep sleep. In one study, the authors observed that during meditation, theta waves were the most abundant brain waves in the frontal and temporal central region of the brain. Theta waves represent a very relaxed state of mind where attention is focused on our inner self. Theta waves also unlock the door to the unconscious mind and may produce spiritual bliss during meditation. In addition, authors have observed significantly greater alpha waves in the posterior of the brain compared to the frontal part. Alpha waves are associated with a relaxed state of mind.[70] In another study, the authors observed that the frequency of weekly meditation was associated with increased theta waves in the EEGs.[71]

Neurotransmitters may also play an important role in the experience of spiritual bliss during meditation. Serotonin is an important neurotransmitter that controls mood, behavior, and appetite. An increased level of serotonin is associated with mood elevation, while a decreased level may cause depression. Increased concentrations of serotonin metabolites are observed in the urine of meditators, indicating that meditation may increase brain serotonin levels. Dopamine, another neurotransmitter associated with the reward system of the brain, is also increased during meditation.[72]

PHYSICAL HEALTH BENEFITS OF MEDITATION

Like yoga, meditation has many physical health benefits, which are listed in table 5.4. Yoga breathing (pranayama) and meditation can improve longevity.

> Meditation on a regular basis can increase longevity. Meditation for fifteen to twenty minutes per day is also associated with a lower rate of hospital admission and a lower rate of doctor's office visits.

The major physical health benefits of meditation are derived mostly from its stress-reducing effect and from improving the antioxidant defense of the body.[73] In one study, the authors investigated the effect of transcendental meditation on longevity using seventy-three residents of eight homes for the elderly with a mean age of eighty-one years. The authors randomly assigned these subjects to three groups, where subjects in one group practiced transcendental meditation, the second group received mindfulness meditation training,

Table 5.4. Physical health benefits of meditation

Physical Health Benefits	Comments
People who meditate have fewer doctor's office visits and hospital admissions.	Practice of transcendental meditation for fifteen to twenty minutes twice a day on a regular basis is associated with good health, as evidenced by lower rate of hospitalization and lower rate of doctor's office visits among meditators compared to nonmeditators.
Meditation increases longevity.	In general, meditators may live longer than nonmeditators. This may be related to lower stress levels, better antioxidant status, and slowing of the aging process of the brain in meditators.
Meditation reduces the risk of cardiovascular diseases, including heart attack.	Meditation reduces oxidative stress and improves the blood lipid profile (reduced levels of cholesterol, triglycerides, low-density lipoprotein cholesterol and increased levels of high-density lipoprotein cholesterol), thus reducing the risks of cardiovascular diseases. In addition, meditation is effective in lowering blood pressure, which has a positive impact on heart function.
Meditation reduces the risk of stroke.	Studies have shown that the practice of transcendental meditation alone for one year reduces the likelihood of a heart attack or stroke by 33 percent.
Meditation reduces blood sugar and may help patients with type 2 diabetes.	Meditation helps lower blood sugar and improves the antioxidant defense of the body. Higher oxidative stress is a risk factor for type 2 diabetes.
Meditation may lower blood pressure.	Meditation has a profound relaxing effect on the human body, and meditation also activates the parasympathetic nervous system, which results in lower blood pressure.
Meditation improves quality of life in cancer patients.	Meditation reduces stress and the perception of pain, thus improving quality of life in cancer survivors. Moreover, meditation improves the antioxidant defense of the body and may reduce the risk of certain types of cancer because oxidative stress increases the risk of cancer.
Meditation is effective in chronic pain management.	Meditation can reduce the frequency of migraine attack and also reduce back pain. Pain relief may be related to stress release associated with meditation.
Meditation improves sleep quality and reduces insomnia.	Meditation increases melatonin concentration and also causes profound relaxation, which explains improved sleep quality in meditators.
Meditation may boost the immune system.	Meditation boosts the immune system as reflected by lower blood levels of C-reactive protein and interleukin-6 in meditators. Meditation also has anti-inflammatory effects.

and the third group did not participate in any kind of meditation. After three years of follow-up, the survival rate was 100 percent in subjects who practiced transcendental meditation and 87.5 percent in people who practiced mindfulness meditation, in contrast to a low survival rate among those who did not practice meditation. The authors concluded that meditation may increase longevity.[74] The practice of transcendental meditation for fifteen to twenty minutes twice a day on a regular basis is associated with good health as evidenced by a lower rate of hospitalization and a lower rate of doctor's office visits among meditators as compared to nonmeditators.[75]

Meditation also lowers the risk of cardiovascular diseases, including heart attack. The practice of meditation is associated with a better lipid profile (reduced total cholesterol, triglycerides, and LDL cholesterol). Studies have shown that the practice of transcendental meditation alone for one year reduces the likelihood of heart attack or stroke by 33 percent.[76] In another report, the authors concluded that all types of meditation are associated with blood pressure control, reductions in lipid peroxidation (reduced oxidative stress), and reduced cellular senescence, and all such mechanisms contribute to better cardiovascular health. Therefore, all types of meditation are effective in reducing the risk of heart diseases.[77] Meditation is also effective in improving blood sugar control and reducing blood pressure.

> Meditation reduces the risk of cardiovascular diseases and stroke. Meditation is also beneficial to patients with type 2 diabetes because meditation improves blood sugar control and reduces blood pressure.

Based on a study of 117 cancer survivors who practiced meditation, the authors observed reduced cancer-related symptoms, including fatigue, pain, insomnia, constipation, anxiety, and depression, in these patients. The authors concluded that meditation is an effective way of improving the physical and mental health of cancer survivors.[78] In another study using teachers who teach meditation, the authors showed that long-term meditation is associated with lower incidences of cancer. The authors commented that stress reduction and reduced oxidative stress in meditation teachers may be responsible for lowering the risk of cancer in these subjects.[79] Several studies have indicated that meditation is effective in lowering the perception of chronic pain and reducing the frequency of migraine attack. Meditation is also effective in improving sleep quality and reducing symptoms of insomnia among older people.

CONCLUSION

Regular exercise is recommended for everyone, not only for stress relief but also for the many other physical benefits of regular exercise. Yoga also has many physical and mental health benefits. One notable difference between yoga and exercise is that during yoga the parasympathetic nervous system is activated, but during exercise the sympathetic nervous system is activated. Moreover, yoga reduces the oxidative stress of the body, while strenuous exercise may increase oxidative stress. For mental health benefits, meditation is probably superior to yoga and exercise because the regular practice of meditation increases the gray matter volume in various areas of the brain, which improves mental focus and memory. Meditation can also prevent age-related neurodegeneration, thus providing protective effects against the development of age-related dementia, Alzheimer's disease, and Parkinson's disease. Moreover, both yoga and meditation are nondenominational practices. Nevertheless, exercise, yoga, and meditation are very effective in stress management, and the selection of one of these practices for stress management is a personal choice.

6

Aromatherapy, Massage, Reiki, and Music for Stress Management

Aromatherapy is defined as the use of essential oils extracted from herbs, flowers, or other plant materials for healing purposes. Essential oils have been used for therapeutic purposes for more than six thousand years. The ancient Indians (Indian ayurvedic massage incorporates essential oils), Egyptians, Greeks, and Romans used essential oils for healing. The word "aroma" means pleasant smell, but instead of inhaling essential oil, sometimes these oils are incorporated during massage therapy by blending essential oils with massage oil. More recently, the French chemist Rene-Maurice Gattefosse discovered the healing properties of lavender oil when he applied it to heal a burn caused by an explosion in his laboratory. Then he researched the composition of various essential oils and also the application of such oils to heal wounded soldiers during World War I. In 1928 he founded the science of aroma-therapy.[1] The benefits of aromatherapy can be achieved when essential oil is inhaled. When applied topically or through massage, rapid absorption of such oil through the skin is achieved within ten to thirty minutes.[2]

Some form of massage has been practiced from prehistoric times. Physical touch with the goal of reducing physical or emotional pain is common in all cultures. Massage was mentioned as an important component of ancient Indian ayurvedic medicine. The ancient Chinese book *The Yellow Emperor's Classic of Internal Medicine* (*Huangdi Neijing*), written between the first and second century BC, recommended massage as a form of treatment.

The founder of medicine, the Greek physician Hippocrates, was a proponent of massage. The Roman dictator Julius Caesar received daily massages for treating chronic headaches. In the sixteenth century, massage was widespread in France due to the use of massage therapy for healing by the royal court physician Ambroise Pare. The most common form of massage practiced today in the West, "Swedish massage," was initially introduced by Swedish physician Per-Henrik Ling when he founded the Royal Central Institute for Gymnastics in Stockholm in 1813. Then, in 1878, Dutch massage practitioner Johan Georg Mezger compiled the various massage strokes that are practiced in Swedish massage today.[3] The various strokes of Swedish massage include effleurage (a gliding massage technique covering different areas of the body), petrissage (kneading), tapotement (rhythmic tapping of muscle), friction, and vibration.

Reiki is a vibrational or subtle energy therapy most commonly facilitated by light touch, which is believed to balance the biofield and strengthen the body's ability for self-healing. Miko Usui (1865–1926), a lifelong practitioner of Buddhism and a dedicated spiritual aspirant, formulated the basic practice of Reiki, a spiritual healing practice where any physical, emotional, or mental health benefits from a Reiki session were viewed as natural by-products. Later, Chujiro Hayashi (1878–1940), a retired naval officer and a disciple of Usui, transformed Reiki into a practical healing modality without the encumbrance of spiritual practice. The word "Reiki" is derived from the words "Rei," meaning universal, and "ki," meaning subtle energy.

> Miko Usui formulated the principles of Reiki, while his disciple Chujiro Hayashi transformed Reiki into a healing practice without spiritual content. Mrs. Hawayo Takata, an American from Hawaii and a student of Chujiro Hayashi, introduced the healing practice of Reiki in the United States.

Hayashi opened a small eight-bed clinic in Tokyo where sixteen practitioners provided Reiki treatment in pairs. Mrs. Hawayo Takata (1900–1980), an American, came to Hayashi's clinic in 1936 because she was suffering from respiratory and abdominal complaints. After receiving treatment for four months and recovering from her illness, she became Hayashi's student and also practiced in Hayashi's clinic. Mrs. Takata returned to Hawaii in 1938 and introduced Reiki in the West. When she died in December 1980, she had initiated twenty-two Reiki masters.[4] Aromatherapy, massage, and Reiki are all considered complementary and alternative therapies.

Music is an integral part of all cultures and probably has a prehistoric origin. Although arguments have been made for a Neanderthal (closely related to modern humans; extinct forty thousand years ago) musical tradition and the presence of musical instruments in Middle Paleolithic assemblages (Middle Stone Age; three hundred thousand to thirty thousand years ago), concrete evidence of a musical tradition came from the discovery of bone and ivory flutes at excavation sites in Germany, where early humans lived more than thirty-five thousand years ago. Other archaeological evidence of music in prehistoric times, approximately thirty thousand years ago, came from sites in France and Austria.[5] Charles Darwin described the human capability for carrying out musical behavior as among the most mysterious gifts with which humans are endowed. At a fundamental level, music and dance can be considered as deliberate, metrically organized gestures that constitute a specialized system dedicated to the expression and comprehension of social and emotional information between members of a society. Musical abilities are not only a ubiquitous feature of humanity today but also a fundamental component of what makes human societies possible.[6]

> Archeological evidence indicates that a musical tradition was present among ancient humans living in Europe at least thirty-five thousand years ago.

AROMATHERAPY

Aromatherapy uses essential oils, which are highly concentrated substances extracted from flowers, leaves, and other plant parts. Essential oils contain various saturated fatty acids, unsaturated fatty acids, aldehydes, ketones, esters, higher alcohols (containing more carbon atoms than ethyl alcohol), phenols, and terpenes. The characteristic odors of essential oils are due to volatile components, including various esters. Essential oils can be directly inhaled from a bottle, or a few drops may be applied on the palm or a cotton ball/handkerchief and inhaled. A blend of essential oils may be put in an inhaler for sniffing. In addition, essential oils (or a blend of several essential oils) can be added to a cream for application on affected areas for pain relief. Blending essential oils with regular massage oil or massage cream is also very popular (aromatherapy massage). There are many essential oils, but the commonly used essential oils, their sources, and their application in aromatherapy are summarized in table 6.1. Major applications of aromatherapy include the following:

- Reducing stress and anxiety
- Reducing depression
- Relief from fatigue
- Relief for insomnia
- Pain relief
- Treating dementia
- Boosting immunity
- Improving quality of life in cancer patients
- Skin care

How Aromatherapy Works

The human perception of smell is due to the presence of olfactory cells (neurons) in the nasal cavity. Interestingly, human beings have more than one thousand different genes that regulate specific receptors capable of detecting only a few odor molecules. However, human beings can differentiate up to ten thousand odors due to the presence of approximately six million olfactory cells. The response to an odor—for example, the inhalation of an essential oil—triggers the response of olfactory cells, and the signal is neurologically transmitted to the olfactory bulb in the brain. Then information from several olfactory receptors is combined in the olfactory bulb, thus forming a pattern that is then perceived as a distinct odor in multiple areas of the cerebral cortex and the limbic area of the brain. As a result, the autonomic nervous system is instantaneously activated through the amygdala and limbic structure of the brain. Thus, inhaled odors activate the release of neurotransmitters such as serotonin, endorphin, norepinephrine, and others, providing the benefits of aromatherapy such as elevating mood, reducing stress and anxiety, and relaxing the mind after inhalation of the essential oil. The effect is immediate and works beyond the level of conscious awareness.[7]

As mentioned earlier, when essential oil is applied to the skin or blended in massage oil, the active ingredients due to their small molecular weight can diffuse through the skin and enter the bloodstream. In one study, the authors showed that following application of lavender oil on the abdomen of male volunteers during gentle massage for ten minutes, trace amounts of linalool and linalyl acetate were detected in the blood after five minutes; both active compounds disappeared from the blood within ninety minutes.[8] The clinical efficacy of essential oil when applied topically or during massage is also

Table 6.1. Commonly used essential oils in aromatherapy, their sources, and their application

Essential Oil	Source	Application in Aromatherapy
Bergamot	Bergamot orange fruit	Stress, depression, and anxiety relief.
Cedarwood	*Juniperus virginiana* (red ceder) tree	Calming agent.
Chamomile (also known as Roman chamomile)	Leaves of the flowering plant Roman chamomile	Stress, depression, and anxiety relief. Also a great sleeping aid.
Eucalyptus	Leaves of the eucalyptus tree	Relief of headache, treatment of skin problems such as cuts, treatment of joint pain due to rheumatoid arthritis by local application.
Geranium	Extracted from the geranium plant, a perennial shrub	A natural perfume used for reducing stress and anxiety and as a sleeping aid. The oil may also have antibacterial properties.
Jasmine	Extracted from the jasmine flower	A sweet-smelling essential oil with antidepressant, antiseptic, and aphrodisiac properties. It elevates mood and is a great sleeping aid. Also improves skin health.
Lavender	Extracted from the lavender plant	A popular essential oil in aromatherapy used for reducing stress, stress headache, pain relief, anxiety, and depression. It is also an effective sleeping aid.
Lemon	Extracted from the lemon fruit	Used for boosting the immune system, controlling nausea and vomiting, and elevating mood. May rejuvenate dull skin. It is also used to reduce labor pain.
Marjoram	Leaves of the marjoram plant	Stress, anxiety, and depression relief; may also combat fatigue.
Orange	Peel of the orange fruit	Stress and pain relief, sedative.
Peppermint	Peppermint herb	Relief of headache and sinus congestion and for elevating mood. Also has antibacterial and antifungal activity.
Rose	Fresh rose petals	A popular essential oil for women due to its fragrance. Rose oil reduces anxiety and depression, and it has an aphrodisiac property. Also good for the skin.
Rosemary	Extracted mostly from leaves of the rosemary plant	Used for skin care, boosting the immune system, pain relief, and stress relief. Also used to improve mental activity and reduce fatigue.
Sandalwood	Wood chips of the sandalwood tree	Calming and spiritual effect, very popular in India and east Asia for spiritual growth. Often used by yoga teachers to boost spirituality.
Tea tree	Extracted from leaves of the tea tree, which grows in Australia	Widely used to treat skin problems.
Ylang-ylang	Flowers of the tropical tree ylang-ylang	Recognized for its strong fragrance and sweet aroma, it is used for reducing stress, headache, and nausea. May also be used as a sleeping aid.

evidenced by significant changes in metabolite profiles in human urine after aromatherapy.[9] When applied topically, certain essential oils can improve skin health. In general, lavender, chamomile, rose, sandalwood, and ylang-ylang essential oils are used for skin care, but other essential oils may also be used. Certain essential oils have antibacterial and antifungal activity. Tea tree oil is useful in treating certain skin problems including skin infection. Although taking essential oil orally is sometimes recommended, it is important to note that essential oils are highly concentrated and may be toxic if ingested. A good example is tea tree oil, which is very toxic if ingested.

> Essential oils should be used for inhalation, topical application, or blending with base massage oil for aromatherapy massage. This author recommends not ingesting any essential oil.

AROMATHERAPY FOR STRESS RELIEF

Both aromatherapy and aromatherapy massage are very effective in reducing stress. Sometimes stress can cause anxiety, but aromatherapy can also reduce anxiety. Inhalation of lavender oil (four drops of essential oil diluted with 20 mL of hot water) for thirty minutes by thirty young healthy volunteers (mean age thirty-four years) resulted in significant stress relief, as evidenced by significant reduction in serum cortisol (a major stress hormone) after aromatherapy. Moreover, noninvasive transthoracic Doppler echocardiography indicated better blood flow to the heart after aromatherapy due to stress relief.[10] In another study involving twenty-two healthy volunteers who sniffed lavender or rosemary oil for five minutes, the authors showed that cortisol levels in the saliva were significantly reduced after aromatherapy. Interestingly, the free radical scavenging capacity (antioxidant capacity) of saliva was also increased after sniffing lavender or rosemary oil, indicating that aromatherapy not only reduces stress but also improves the antioxidant defense of the human body.[11] Aromatherapy using lavender essential oil can also reduce stress in healthy students ($n = 30$) after performing a serial arithmetic task.[12] However, peppermint aroma may be more effective (causing a more significant decrease in salivary cortisol after inhalation) than lavender in providing stress relief.[13]

Lavender oil inhalation can decrease blood pressure, heart rate, and skin temperature, indicating stress relief and decreased autonomic nervous system arousal (stress increases autonomic nervous system arousal). The subjects who inhaled lavender oil also reported better mood and a more relaxed state of mind compared to volunteers who inhaled base oil (control). An electroencephalogram (EEG) study showed increased power of theta (4–8 Hz) and alpha (8–13 Hz) brain activity. This increased power of theta waves is indicative of deep relaxation after the inhalation of lavender oil.[14] In another study involving forty-one healthy females, the authors demonstrated that aromatherapy involving inhalation of bergamot essential oil along with water vapor was associated with significant stress release as evidenced by significant reductions in salivary cortisol levels. Moreover, mood was improved and fatigue reduced following aromatherapy in all female subjects.[15]

Nursing is a stressful profession, but aromatherapy can significantly reduce stress in nurses. In one study, fifty-three nurses pinned small bottles containing 3 percent lavender oil on the right chest of their clothes, while fifty-seven participants pinned a bottle with no lavender oil (control group) on their clothes. The authors observed that work-related stress levels of nurses were significantly reduced three to four days after use of lavender oil compared to nurses in the control group. In fact, stress levels were increased in the nurses of the control group.[16] In another study involving twenty-nine elementary school teachers in Taiwan, the authors showed that aromatherapy with natural bergamot oil relieved work-related stress in these teachers.[17]

> Aromatherapy is very effective for stress management. Commonly used essential oils for stress reduction include lavender, rosemary, peppermint, bergamot (these four essential oils are most commonly used), clary sage, chamomile, marjoram, germanium, orange (also known as sweet orange), rose, jasmine, sandalwood, and ylang-ylang.

Aromatherapy is very effective in reducing stress, anxiety, depression, and pain in community-dwelling older people. In one study involving eighty-two participants, the authors assigned forty-four subjects (thirty-seven females, seven males) to receive aromatherapy for four weeks while thirty-eight participants (thirty females, eight males) were assigned to the control group receiving no aromatherapy. The aromatherapy containing lavender and bergamot essential oils as well as lavender hydrolat was formulated by an aromatherapist. The authors observed significant reduction in anxiety, stress, and depression (based on scores on anxiety, depression, and stress scales) in subjects who received aromatherapy compared to the subjects in the control group. Some reduction in perception of pain was also reported by subjects who received aromatherapy.[18]

The aroma of lemongrass oil can reduce anxiety, stress, and tension immediately after inhalation in human subjects.[19] In one study based on forty male
volunteers, the authors showed that inhalation of sweet orange essential oil
reduced anxiety in human volunteers. The authors concluded that the aroma
of sweet orange essential oil has an anxiolytic effect.[20] Based on a study of
two hundred subjects aged eighteen to seventy-seven years waiting for dental
treatment, the authors observed that inhalation of lavender or orange essential oil significantly reduced anxiety and improved mood in these people.[21]

Postpartum depression affects approximately 15 percent of women after
childbirth. In another study based on twenty-eight postpartum women with
high risk of anxiety and depression, the authors observed that fifteen minutes
of aromatherapy involving inhalation though a cotton pad containing a 2
percent blend of rose and lavender essential oil twice a week for four weeks
caused significant reductions in anxiety and depression in these women.
There was no adverse effect of aromatherapy.[22] Inhalation of only lavender
scent for four weeks can also prevent stress, anxiety, and depression in the
postpartum period as observed by authors in one study involving 140 women
who delivered babies in the author's hospital.[23] Based on a study of one hundred women during labor (divided into two groups, one group of women who
were exposed to orange essential oil and the control group who were exposed
to water vapor), the authors showed that exposure to orange essential oil significantly reduced anxiety during labor.[24]

In one study, very young infants were given a bath with or without lavender-
scented bath oil. The mothers in the lavender bath oil group were more relaxed and smiled and touched the infants more during the bath. The infants also cried less and slept well after the bath. Salivary cortisol levels in both mothers and infants were significantly reduced after the lavender-scented oil bath. The authors concluded that lavender scent reduces stress in mothers and infants, and it also promotes deep sleep in infants.[25]

Lavender bath oil reduces stress and crying in infants (aged one week to four and a half months) and promotes deep sleep. Lavender scent also reduces stress in mothers.

Although inhalation of essential oils can reduce stress, anxiety, and depression, topical application of essential oils or blending essential oils with massage oil for aromatherapy massage has a similar stress-reducing effect. When
healthy volunteers applied blended lavender and bergamot essential oil to

their abdomens, their pulse rate and blood pressure were reduced, indicating decreased autonomic nervous system arousal compared to volunteers who applied a placebo on their abdomens (control group). At the emotional level, subjects in the aromatherapy group rated themselves as calmer and more relaxed compared to subjects in the control group. The authors concluded that a mixture of lavender and bergamot oil has relaxing effects on humans and may be used for treating depression or anxiety.[26] Topical application of rose oil (on the abdomen) was also associated with lowering of blood pressure and stress relief in human subjects.[27] Studies have shown that transdermal application of ylang-ylang oil[28] and jasmine oil[29] not only reduces stress and depression but also improves mood. In another study, the authors observed that emergency room nurses were more anxious in winter than summer months, but aromatherapy massage with music significantly reduced the level of anxiety in emergency room nurses during both seasons. The higher level of anxiety in winter months may be related to the fact that, in general, emergency rooms are busier in winter months due to admission of patients with cardiac and respiratory dysfunctions.[30]

Healthy first-time mothers are often stressed after childbirth, but aromatherapy massage is an effective way to reduce stress in these mothers. In one study, the authors recruited thirty-six healthy first-time mothers, where sixteen mothers received a thirty-minute aromatherapy massage with neroli (extracted from a citrus fruit) and lavender oil on the second day after delivery, while twenty mothers did not receive any aromatherapy massage. The authors observed a significant reduction in stress and anxiety as well as better mood in mothers who received aromatherapy massage compared to mothers in the control group.[31] Another study reported that aromatherapy massage with a combination of lavender, chamomile, rosemary, and lemon essential oil significantly reduced stress and anxiety and increased self-esteem in Korean elderly women.[32]

> Instead of inhalation, topical application of essential oil as well as aromatherapy massage is also very effective in reducing stress, depression, and anxiety.

Aromatherapy for Insomnia

Aromatherapy can reduce symptoms of insomnia and improve sleep quality. Based on a review of twelve studies and meta-analysis, the authors concluded that aromatherapy is very effective in treating insomnia.[33] In another study involving sixty-seven women aged forty-five to fifty-five years who were suffering from insomnia, the authors demonstrated that the women in

> Inhalation of lavender may significantly improve sleep quality.

the experimental group ($n = 34$) who inhaled lavender oil for twenty minutes twice per week for twelve weeks, with a total of twenty-four sessions, reported significant improvement in sleep quality compared to women ($n = 33$) who received a health education program for sleep hygiene but did not inhale lavender.[34]

Other Applications of Aromatherapy

Aromatherapy may reduce pain perception in healthy people. In one study based on thirty volunteers who were randomly assigned to receive oxygen with a face mask coated with lavender or oxygen with a face mask but no aromatherapy, the authors observed that aromatherapy with lavender reduced not only stress levels in these volunteers but also the perception of pain

> Aromatherapy massage alleviates menstrual pain and its duration and may also prevent excessive bleeding.

during needle insertion. The authors concluded that aromatherapy with lavender is effective in reducing both stress and the pain intensity of needle insertion.[35] In another study, the authors assigned forty-eight nursing students to receive aromatherapy abdominal massage where a base

almond massage oil was blended with cinnamon, clove, rose, and lavender essential oils once daily for seven days prior to menstruation. Another forty-seven nursing students received similar abdominal massage with almond oil only (control group). The authors observed that the duration of menstrual pain and the amount of menstrual bleeding were significantly lower in the aromatherapy massage group compared to women in the control group.[36]

Hot flashes are generally considered to be the primary symptom of menopause and are typically the most common complaint in menopausal women.

> Inhalation of lavender aroma may reduce the number of hot flashes in menopausal women.

Based on a study utilizing one hundred menopausal women who were divided into two groups, where women in the aromatherapy group inhaled lavender aroma for twenty minutes twice a day over a twelve-week period while women in the control group did not receive any aromatherapy, the authors observed that women in the aromatherapy group reported significantly fewer hot flashes compared to women in the control group. The authors concluded that aromatherapy with lavender may reduce the frequency of hot flashes in menopausal women.[37]

The Benefits of Aromatherapy in Various Patient Populations

Many studies reported in the medical literature deal with the effectiveness of aromatherapy in treating various symptoms in patients, most commonly anxiety, depression, and pain perception. In a large study involving 10,262 hospital admissions in acute care settings where nurses delivered aromatherapy, significant reductions in anxiety and pain perception were observed among these patients following the aromatherapy. Overall, 75 percent of all aromatherapy sessions were administered by inhalation, but some patients received aromatherapy through topical administration or through both inhalation and topical administration. Aromatherapy using lavender essential oil was the most common (49.5 percent), followed by ginger (21.2 percent), sweet marjoram (12.3 percent), mandarin (9.4 percent), and combination oils (6.7 percent). The authors observed that lavender and sweet marjoram oil were equally effective in reducing anxiety in these patients, while aromatherapy with sweet marjoram oil was most effective in reducing pain. Ginger oil was very effective in reducing symptoms of nausea.[38]

Based on a study of forty-six hemodialysis patients, the authors observed that inhalation of rosewater for four weeks significantly reduced anxiety in these patients.[39] In another study based on sixty inpatients who were admitted to the coronary intensive care unit, the authors reported that inhalation of 2 percent lavender essential oil for fifteen days was very effective in reducing anxiety and improving sleep quality in these critically ill patients.[40] Aromatherapy massage is also effective in alleviating anxiety, depression, and the severity of emotional symptoms in psychiatric patients. In general, lavender, rose, orange, bergamot, lemon, sandalwood, clary sage, chamomile, and rose-scented geranium essential oils are effective as anxiolytic agents.[41]

The effectiveness of aromatherapy and aromatherapy massage for stress, anxiety, and pain relief in various patients has also been studied. In one study involving forty burn patients, the authors observed that both inhalation aromatherapy with a blend of rose and lavender aroma and aromatherapy massage with a blend of lavender and almond oil effectively reduced anxiety and the perception of pain in these patients.[42] Aromatherapy massage for thirty minutes twice a week for four weeks also relieved anxiety in breast cancer patients.[43] However, the utility of aromatherapy or aromatherapy massage in reducing pain and anxiety in cancer patients is not clear. For example, in one study involving 313 cancer patients, the authors observed no benefit of aromatherapy in reducing anxiety, but another study involving malignant brain tumor patients showed that aromatherapy massage with chamomile or lavender essential oil was effective in reducing blood pressure and stress levels in these patients. In another study involving 288 cancer patients, the authors showed that aromatherapy massage had short-term benefits (up to two weeks after massage), including reducing stress and depression in cancer patients, but the authors did not observe any long-term benefits.[44]

Eucalyptus, rosemary, lavender, and cardamom essential oils contain 1, 8-cineole, which has an analgesic effect. Lavender essential oil was most frequently used in studies evaluating the effectiveness of aromatherapy in pain management. In one study, the authors showed that a ten-minute upper neck and shoulder aromatherapy massage with lavender oil reduced the use of analgesic medicine in patients suffering from rheumatoid arthritis. Moreover, patients reported better sleep quality after receiving aromatherapy massage. In another study involving one hundred patients admitted to a critical care unit, the authors reported an approximately 50 percent reduction in perception of pain after aromatherapy massage with lavender oil. Studies have also shown that peppermint oil is effective in reducing headache.[45] Aromatherapy massage with lavender oil is effective in reducing knee pain in patients with osteoarthritis.[46] Aromatherapy massage with lavender oil is also effective in reducing colic pain in infants (measured as changes in length of time infants cried per week).[47]

> Abdomen massage with lavender oil reduces colic pain in infants.

Aromatherapy is beneficial for patients with dementia. Agitated behavior (in 18–65 percent of patients) and restless behavior are common in patients with dementia. The behavioral and psychological problems of dementia are hard to control, but in one study involving seventy-two patients with dementia, the authors showed a significant reduction in aggression and restless behavior after topical application of Melissa essential oil on the face or arm twice per day for four weeks. In another study, the authors showed that a footbath with a combination of lavender, chamomile, rosemary, and marjoram essential oils reduced aggression and challenging behavior in some dementia patients. However, some studies showed no improvement of symptoms after aromatherapy in patients with dementia. Therefore, further studies are needed to demonstrate the clinical utility of aromatherapy in improving the quality of life in patients with dementia.[48] The benefits of aromatherapy in various patient populations are summarized in table 6.2.

MASSAGE THERAPY FOR STRESS RELEASE

Massage therapy is an ancient healing practice of which Hippocrates in 400 BC said, "Medicine being the art of rubbing, physicians must be experienced in many things, most especially rubbing." In ancient times, medicine was effectively the art of rubbing because few medicines were available for therapy. In certain countries, such as China, Japan, Russia, and Germany, massage therapy is considered part of medical treatment, as the cost is covered by national health insurance. In the United States, massage therapy is considered a complementary and alternative therapy. Nevertheless, massage therapy is very popular in the United States, and 42 percent of Americans pay out of their pockets for massage therapy because most health insurance does not cover such treatment. Swedish massage is the most popular in the United States, but other forms of massage such as the Trager method (gentle holding and rocking of different body parts), reflexology, Thai massage, ayurvedic massage, and others are also practiced. Massage therapy, in addition to feeling good, releases muscle tension, facilitates the removal of toxic metabolite waste products, and allows more oxygen and nutrients to reach tissues.[49]

Although aromatherapy massage as well as massage with regular massage oil such as almond oil can effectively reduce stress, aromatherapy massage may have some added advantages. In one study using seven female and six male volunteers, the authors observed that both aromatherapy massage and massage therapy were effective in reducing stress levels and fatigue in these volunteers. Moreover, volunteers reported better mood after receiving massage. Compared to massage alone, the aromatherapy massage provided a stronger continuous relief from fatigue, especially mental fatigue.[50] However, massage therapy without essential oil can also significantly reduce stress. Although a twenty-minute foot massage (ten minutes per foot) can slightly reduce blood pressure, a twenty-minute facial massage is more effective in reducing blood pressure, indicating significant stress relief. In one study based on 263 volunteers, the authors observed that a forty-five- to

Table 6.2. Application of aromatherapy in various patient populations

Patient Group	Type of Aromatherapy	Commonly Used Essential Oils	Improvement
Acute care patients	Inhalation, topical application, or both	Lavender (most common), ginger, sweet marjoram, mandarin orange, combination blend	Reduced anxiety, pain, and nausea in acute care patients. Sweet marjoram is most effective in reducing pain, while both lavender and sweet marjoram have equivalent effect in reducing anxiety. Ginger oil is very effective in reducing nausea.
Breast cancer	Aromatherapy massage	Sweet orange, lavender, sandalwood	Reduced anxiety.
Burn patients	Inhalation or aromatherapy massage	Lavender, rose	Reduced anxiety and pain perception.
Cancer patients	Inhalation or aromatherapy massage	Chamomile, lavender, bergamot, cedarwood	Conflicting reports, with some studies showing reduced anxiety but other studies reporting no benefit.
Coronary intensive care unit patients	Inhalation	Lavender	Reduced anxiety and improved sleep quality.
Dementia patients	Inhalation/bath	Melissa, lavender, chamomile, rosemary, marjoram	Some studies report reduction in aggressive behavior and improvement after aromatherapy, while other studies report no significant benefit.
Hemodialysis patients	Inhalation	Rosewater	Reduced anxiety.
Pain management	Aromatherapy massage	Lavender (most common), eucalyptus, rosemary, cardamom, peppermint (headache relief)	Reduced use of analgesics or reduced perception of pain. Lavender aromatherapy massage reduces knee pain due to osteoarthritis.
Colic in infants	Aromatherapy massage in the abdomen	Lavender	Reduced crying, indicating some pain relief.
Psychiatric patients	Aromatherapy massage	Lavender, rose, orange, bergamot, lemon, sandalwood, clary sage, chamomile, and rose-scented geranium essential oils	Reduced anxiety, depression, and severity of emotional symptoms.

sixty-minute full-body deep-tissue massage was associated with a significant reduction in blood pressure and heart rate, indicating a significant stress-reducing effect of the massage. In another study, a simple twenty-minute massage utilizing gentle kneading and long gliding strokes of the head, neck, back, arms, and feet was taught to spouses of pregnant women in their second trimester. The authors observed significant reductions in anxiety, depression, anger, and pain (leg and back) in pregnant women who received regular massages from their spouses compared to pregnant women who did not receive any massage. Moreover, pregnant women who received massages reported significant improvement in their relationships with their spouses. Massage can also lower stress, anxiety, and the perception of pain in laboring women.[51] In another study, the authors observed that after back, neck, and chest massage, diastolic blood pressure was reduced by 11 percent. The authors concluded that massage can be tried as a complementary therapy in individuals suffering from increased blood pressure due to stress.[52]

> Massage therapy alone without the use of essential oils is very effective in reducing stress and lowering blood pressure.

Massage Reduces Cortisol and Increases Dopamine and Serotonin

Serum and salivary cortisol concentrations are increased in response to stress. Therefore, a decrease in cortisol levels is considered a biochemical marker of stress relief. Moreover, epinephrine and norepinephrine are increased in response to stress. In one study based on thirty-four female office workers, the authors showed that both fifteen-minute and twenty-five-minute scalp massage was effective in reducing blood pressure and serum stress hormone levels (cortisol and norepinephrine). In addition, after twenty-five minutes of scalp massage, serum levels of epinephrine, another stress hormone, were reduced in addition to reductions of cortisol and norepinephrine. The relaxing effect of massage is due to a decrease in sympathetic nervous system activity as evidenced by reduction in cortisol and norepinephrine levels in plasma. Moreover, peripheral cutaneous stimulation during massage promotes circulation through the activation of the parasympathetic nervous system, causing further stress release. The authors concluded that scalp massage at the workplace is very effective in reducing stress.[53] In another study based on one hundred health-care workers in a major public hospital, the authors showed that a fifteen-minute chair massage on-site was associated with significantly reduced job-related stress, anxiety, and depression. In addition, urinary cortisol levels were decreased by 24 percent, indicating significant stress relief.[54] A study based on thirty university dance students showed that although both a thirty-minute massage twice a week for five weeks and relaxation therapy reduced shoulder and back pain in these students, only massage therapy was associated with significant stress release, as demonstrated by a 35 percent reduction in salivary cortisol levels. No such decline in salivary cortisol was observed in dance students who received relaxation therapy.[55]

> Massage therapy provides stress relief by activating the parasympathetic nervous system and reducing the arousal of the sympathetic nervous system. Moreover, reductions in salivary cortisol after massage provide further biochemical evidence of the stress-releasing effect of massage therapy.

Serotonin is a neurotransmitter associated with human mood because reduced serotonin concentration may cause depression. Some antidepressants such as SSRIs (selective serotonin reuptake inhibitors) increase serotonin levels in the nervous system to counteract depression. Serotonin level is usually measured in urine as its metabolite (5-hydroxyindoleacetic acid). Dopamine is also a neurotransmitter associated with the reward system of the brain. Serotonin interacts with dopamine in a complex way. Dopamine, like serotonin, is also involved in reducing depression and stress. Studies have shown that massage therapy increases serotonin and dopamine levels, thus producing further stress relief. In one study involving eighty-four depressed pregnant women in their second trimester, the authors reported that sixteen weeks of massage (once per week) by significant others was associated with significantly reduced saliva cortisol levels (23 percent reduction), indicating significant stress relief, compared to women who received a muscle relaxation session or standard care. Moreover, urine dopamine (25 percent increase) and serotonin levels (23 percent increase) were increased in women who received massage, further demonstrating the stress-releasing and mood-elevating effects of massage.[56]

> The mood-elevating effect of massage may be related to increases in dopamine and serotonin levels.

The Benefits of Massage Therapy in Different Patient Populations

Similar to aromatherapy, massage therapy is beneficial to various patient populations. In a study involving fifty-three acute care hospital patients, the authors demonstrated that after thirty minutes of massage, the average pain score in these patients was reduced from 5.18 to 2.33, a statistically significant decrease. Moreover, patients reported less stress and anxiety as well as better quality of sleep after massage.[57] In another study involving ninety patients admitted to a coronary care unit, the authors observed that when patients received massage from a specialist nurse, the median blood cortisol level decreased from 281.9 nmol/L to 197.0 nmol/L, a significant decrease indicating stress release. However, no reduction of cortisol was observed in patients who received massage from their relatives or received no massage. The authors concluded that the beneficial stress-reducing effect of massage can only be observed when given by trained professionals.[58]

> The benefits of massage in patients admitted to a coronary care unit were observed when provided by specialized nurses as reflected by a significant reduction in blood cortisol levels. When relatives of patients provided such massage, no reduction in cortisol was observed.

Massage therapy is effective in reducing stress and anxiety in cancer patients (and possibly pain perception as well). However, oncologists should discuss massage therapy benefits with cancer patients, and massage must be provided by a qualified massage therapist.[59] Massage can reduce the perception of pain in patients suffering from knee osteoarthritis.[60] Massage therapy is also effective in reducing resting heart rate, salivary cortisol, anxiety, and depression in young adult psychiatry patients admitted to hospitals.[61] In addition, the benefits of massage therapy have been documented in burn patients, breast cancer patients, children with asthma, people suffering from chronic fatigue syndrome, depressed children and adolescents, people with eating disorders, people with migraine headaches, patients with HIV, mothers with postpartum depression, and female victims of sexual abuse.[62] The benefits of massage therapy in various patient populations are summarized in table 6.3.

Table 6.3. Benefits of massage in various patient groups (sources of data, notes 57–62)

Patient Group	Parameters	Comments
Acute care patients	Significant reduction in pain	Patients also reported more relaxation and better sleep quality and healing process due to massage.
Burn patients	Salivary cortisol reduced by 20 percent	Lesser anxiety and perception of pain.
Breast cancer patients	Urine dopamine and serotonin levels increased by 26 percent and 38 percent, respectively, after massage	Massage therapy has immediate effect of reducing anxiety, depression, and anger.
Cancer patients	Pain reduction	Reduced anxiety and stress in cancer patients after receiving massage.
Children with asthma	Significant reduction in salivary cortisol	Massage therapy can reduce anxiety in children with asthma.
Chronic fatigue syndrome	Salivary cortisol reduced by 32 percent and urine cortisol reduced by 41 percent; urine dopamine concentration increased by 21 percent	The massage therapy group reported fewer depressive symptoms, lower anxiety, and less pain after each massage. Moreover, overall symptoms of chronic fatigue syndrome were reduced after massage.
Coronary care unit patients	Significant reduction in blood cortisol levels	Stress reduction as reflected by reduced cortisol levels can be observed only when specialist nurses provide the massage.
Depressed children and adolescents	Lower salivary cortisol after massage	A thirty-minute daily back massage for five days reduced anxiety and depression in children and adolescents hospitalized due to depression. Children and adolescents were more cooperative after massage, as reported by nurses.
Eating disorders	Lower salivary cortisol in people suffering from anorexia (10 percent reduction) and bulimia (29 percent reduction)	Lower stress, depression, and anxiety levels in people suffering from both anorexia and bulimia after massage therapy.
Migraine headache	Serotonin increased by 13 percent	Following two thirty-minute massages per week for five weeks, the number of migraine headaches was lower and sleep quality was better in subjects suffering from migraine headache.
Patients with HIV	Urinary cortisol reduced by 45 percent	Decreased anxiety and depression with improvement of immunological function.
Pregnancy depression	Salivary cortisol reduced by 23 percent and urinary dopamine increased by 25 percent	Lower levels of anxiety and depression after massage.
Postpartum depression	Salivary cortisol decreased by 28 percent	Lower stress after receiving massage over a five-week period.
Osteoarthritis	Reduced pain	Reduced stiffness and significant improvement in mood after massage in patients with knee osteoarthritis.
Psychiatry patients	Significant reduction in resting heart rate and salivary cortisol	Significant improvement in mental status and reduced anxiety and stress in young adult psychiatry patients after twenty-minute massage therapy daily during hospitalization.
Victims of sex abuse	Salivary cortisol reduced by 25 percent	A thirty-minute twice-a-week massage for one month reduced anxiety and depression in women who experienced sexual abuse.

REIKI FOR STRESS MANAGEMENT

Reiki is an energy-based touch therapy that provides a means for the life force to recharge and rebalance the human energy field. In a typical Reiki session, which may last twenty to thirty minutes or more, the therapist lightly touches a person or works with the energy field of the person by moving his or her hands just over the physical body. Reiki can be practiced at the first or second level, but the highest level, the third level, of practice skill is usually achieved only by Reiki masters. Reiki therapy is a cost-effective, noninvasive therapy without any side effect, and such holistic therapy can be easily adopted for stress relief in clinical situations. Although the benefits of aromatherapy and massage have been clearly documented in the medical literature, the benefits of Reiki have not been clearly established by scientific research. This may be because relatively fewer scientific reports have been published on Reiki healing compared to extensive scientific literature on stress relief and many other health benefits of aromatherapy, aromatherapy massage, and massage therapy. Another reason is conflicting reports, with some studies showing benefits but other studies failing to confirm such benefits. Therefore, more scientific research is needed to establish the health benefits of Reiki.

In one study based on twenty-three healthy subjects, the authors observed that thirty minutes of Reiki session were associated with significant relaxation and reduced anxiety. The salivary immunoglobulin A (IgA) level was also increased, indicating stress relief, but no significant change was observed in salivary cortisol level after Reiki treatment.[63] Burnout is a common phenomenon among health-care physicians working at mental health clinics. In one study, the authors showed that Reiki intervention for thirty minutes was very effective in reducing the burnout phenomenon among community mental health clinicians.[64] In another study involving a nine-year-old female child with a history of perinatal stroke, seizures, and type 1 diabetes (insulin dependent diabetes), six weeks of Reiki treatment by a Reiki master resulted in positive changes in sleep patterns (better sleep during 33.3 percent of nights) and no report of seizures during the Reiki treatment. The Reiki master reported that the child was relaxed within five to seven minutes of the Reiki treatment. The authors concluded that Reiki is a helpful adjunct therapy for children with increased stress levels and sleep disturbances.[65]

Reiki may be effective in pain management in various patient groups. In one study involving twenty-four cancer patients, the authors observed that patients who received pain medication along with Reiki showed significantly lower perception of pain, lower diastolic blood pressure, and decreased heart rates on days they received Reiki treatment compared to patients who received pain medication alone.[66] Reiki is effective in reducing pain due to diabetic neuropathy (severe nerve pain associated with complications of diabetes).[67] In another study, the authors reported that after abdominal hysterotomy, women who received Reiki intervention reported less pain and requested smaller amounts of pain medication compared to women who did not received Reiki therapy.[68]

However, there are also published reports indicating no benefit of Reiki. In one report based on a systematic review of three studies, the authors found no effect of Reiki in reducing depression and anxiety.[69] In another study based on clinical trials involving Reiki, the authors concluded that currently the evidence is insufficient to suggest that Reiki is an effective treatment for any condition. Thus the value of Reiki remains unproven.[70]

MUSIC FOR STRESS REDUCTION

Music has been used from ancient times to reduce stress, enhance well-being, and reduce pain and suffering. Music is very effective in reducing stress. In one study based on fifty-three volunteers, the authors observed that listening to music in the company of others is more effective in reducing stress than listening to music alone. However, solitary music listening can also reduce stress when a person specifically listens to music for relaxation.[71] Based on a study of sixty healthy female volunteers, the authors observed that listening to relaxing music before exposure to a psychosocial stress test resulted in faster return of salivary cortisol to baseline, indicating the stress-reducing effect of music.[72] When undergraduate students (forty-three females and forty-four males) were exposed to a cognitive stressor task involving preparation for an oral presentation either in the presence of music (Pachelbel's Canon in D Major) or in silence, stress-induced changes in subjective anxiety, heart rate, blood pressure, cortisol, and immunoglobulin A (IgA) were observed only in students who did not listen to music. The authors concluded that music can blunt the physiological effect of stress.[73] In another study, eighty-eight healthy college students (forty-four males and forty-four

> Music is effective in reducing stress as evidence by reduced cortisol levels in the saliva.

females) were randomly assigned to four different conditions: (1) thirty minutes listening to music, (2) thirty minutes listening to music with visual stress (a documentary film without sound including violent scenes), (3) thirty minutes of visual stress without music, and (4) thirty minutes in silence. Saliva specimens were collected before and after the intervention. Interestingly, salivary cortisol decreased in students who were exposed to music but increased in other groups. The authors concluded that music can reduce stress.[74]

Reuscher and Shaw first proposed the "Mozart effect," which is an enhancement of reasoning skill and solving spatial problems in normal subjects after listening to Mozart's Piano Sonata k448. Whether improvement in reasoning skill is due to listening to a specific Mozart sonata or listening to any calming music is debatable. Positron emission tomography (PET) and functional magnetic resonance imaging (fMRI) of the brain have revealed that listening to pleasurable music activates cortical and subcortical cerebral areas of the brain responsible for processing emotions. Such auditory stimulation evokes emotions that may cause relaxation and release of stress and anxiety, as well as diverting attention away from pain or an unpleasant experience. As a result, music therapy is clinically useful in cancer patients, patients with cardiovascular diseases, epilepsy, dementia, and psychiatric illnesses. Interestingly, music may also boost the immune system, as evidenced by increased activity of natural killer cells, lymphocytes, and interferon. Therefore, music helps to decrease the burden of a disease and enhances the immune system by reducing stress.[75] Based on a systematic review of twenty-six clinical trials, the authors concluded that listening to music has beneficial effects such as stress and anxiety reduction in patients with coronary heart diseases, especially in those patients who have suffered from a heart attack.[76] In one review article, the authors commented that music therapy is useful in a wide range of clinical settings with patients experiencing health problems as diverse as hypertension, cardiovascular diseases, migraine headache, and gastrointestinal ulcers. Music therapy is thus a beneficial complementary and alternative therapy in a diverse patient population which is virtually risk free.[77] However, it is more beneficial to let patients select their own music choice for maximum effects.

CONCLUSION

Aromatherapy, aromatherapy massage, and massage therapy are very effective in reducing stress and elevating mood, not only in healthy subjects but also in diverse patient populations. Reductions of salivary and blood cortisol levels after aromatherapy, aromatherapy massage, and massage therapy have been well documented in the medical literature, thus confirming their stress-relieving effects. Blood pressure and resting heart rates are also reduced after such therapies, providing further evidence of the relaxing effects of aromatherapy, aromatherapy massage, and massage therapy. Although several publications have shown stress relief following Reiki as well as the healing benefits of Reiki in diverse patient populations, further studies are needed to confirm scientifically the medical benefits of Reiki.

Although aromatherapy through inhalation and topical application can be easily adopted in clinical practice or hospital settings, aromatherapy massage as well as massage therapy is more personal in nature. Often massage is provided in hospital settings by specialized nurses, but the intimacy of massage therapy may present some problems for professional nurses. There may be a risk for misinterpretation by the patient that a professional female nurse providing a professional massage is interested in a more intimate person relationship rather than providing compassionate caregiving. If a patient is unsure or uncomfortable, massage therapy should not be administered, but inhalation aromatherapy may be considered. Moreover, if a patient is taking a blood thinner, massage may cause bruising. Therefore, evaluating the medical condition of a patient is important prior to the administration of massage therapy. For a healthy person to get the benefit of massage therapy, this author recommends going to a licensed massage therapist who is trained to determine whether massage therapy will benefit an individual.

Making Love to Your Spouse/Romantic Partner— A Great Stress Buster

As mentioned in detail in chapter 4, marriage has both physical health and mental health benefits. Making love to your spouse or romantic partner is a great way to release stress, and many benefits of marriage are due to stress relief. A good sex life is associated with longevity, reduced risk of heart diseases, better immunity, better sleep quality, lower risk of depression, and many other benefits. The health benefits of sex are summarized in table 7.1. Other than intercourse, hugging your spouse/romantic partner and even holding hands can also reduce stress. Oxytocin, a neuropeptide containing nine amino acids, is secreted not only during childbirth and breastfeeding (see chapter 4) but also during physical contact, hugging, and lovemaking. This is the reason oxytocin is often called the "love molecule," as it promotes mother-infant bonding as well as romantic love.

In general, humans are usually engaged in monogamous sexual relations with one romantic partner at a time (serial monogamy) or for life (happy marriages lasting lifelong). Interestingly, only 3–5 percent of four thousand mammalian species are monogamous, but monogamy is common in bird species, as approximately 90 percent of all birds are monogamous.[1] In order to understand the many benefits of warm physical contact between partners as well as sex, it is relevant to discuss the basis of marriage and monogamy in humans. Waite and Gallagher, in their book *The Case for Marriage: Why Married People Are Happier, Healthier, and Better Off Financially*, conclude that

Table 7.1. Health benefits of sex

Health Benefit of Sex	Comment
Sex is associated with stress relief and better mood.	Sexually active people have better response to stress than people not sexually active, but people who have intercourse derive the most stress-releasing effect from sex. However, warm partner contact such as holding hands and hugs can also significantly reduce stress. Warm partner contact at the beginning of a day protects individuals from daily stress and improves mood.
Sex promotes healthy heart.	People engaged in sexual activities at least two times a week have a lower risk of heart attack compared with people having sex less than once a month. Sex lowers blood pressure and relieves stress, thus further promoting healthy hearts.
Sex increases longevity.	More frequent sex (two or more times per week) as well as orgasms are associated with longevity in men, but frequency of sex is not predictive of longevity in women. However, women who reported past enjoyment from sex may live longer.
Sex boosts the immune system.	Sex increases salivary IgA levels, indicating boosting of the immune system.
Sex is a form of exercise.	Men burn more calories during sex compared with women.
Sex helps with weight loss.	Regular intercourse may help with weight loss.
Sex improves sleep quality.	Sex stimulates release of oxytocin, which may induce sleep due to the calming effects of these molecules.
Sex may act as an analgesic.	Oxytocin and other calming molecules secreted during sex can reduce the perception of pain, including migraine headache.
Sex may be associated with regular menstrual cycle in women.	Women who have penile-vaginal intercourse at least once a week in every nonmenstruating week show more regularity in their menstrual cycles compared with women with no sexual activity.
Sex reduces the risk of prostate cancer in men.	Men who have twenty-one or more ejaculations per month have a significantly reduced risk of prostate cancer compared with men who had four to seven ejaculations per month.
Sex reduces the risk of breast cancer in women.	More frequent sex is associated with a lower risk of breast cancer, which may be related to the secretion of oxytocin.
Sex promotes better skin health and younger appearance.	Sex improves skin health due to the secretion of DHEA, a steroid hormone. Sexual activity also improves penile health and reduces the risk of insufficient vaginal lubrication in women after menopause.
Sex improves memory in the elderly.	Sexual activity increases cognitive function in the elderly.
Sex reduces depression.	Sex reduces depression, probably due to release of oxytocin, dopamine, and endogenous opioids.

"science tends to confirm Grandma's wisdom: On the whole, man was not meant to live alone, and neither was woman. Marriage makes people happier." Based on data from the National Sex Survey, the authors report that 48.9 percent of married men were extremely emotionally satisfied with their sex lives compared to 37 percent of men who were not married but cohabiting with their

> Married women and men enjoy sex more than unmarried people cohabiting with partners.

partners. Similarly, 42 percent of married women reported being extremely emotionally satisfied with their sex lives compared to 31 percent of unmarried women and 27 percent of divorced women, both living with sex partners.[2]

It is interesting to note that ancient humanoids were polygamous, and even today polygamy is practiced in some societies. The human journey from polygamy to monogamy is very interesting, and there are many hypotheses that attempt to explain the transition.

MONOGAMY VERSUS POLYGAMY IN THE MODERN WORLD

When humans shifted from polygamy to monogamy is an open question. Nevertheless, polygamy is currently legal in fifty-seven out of two hundred sovereign countries in the world; the vast majority of these countries are Muslim nations. Polygamy is most commonly practiced as polygyny, where a man has two or more wives. Polyandry, where a woman may have multiple husbands, is not allowed by law in any nation. Currently most countries that allow polygyny are located in Africa, the Middle East, and some Asian countries. No country in West-

> Fifty-seven out of two hundred sovereign countries in the world allow polygyny; the vast majority of these countries are Muslim nations.

ern Europe, North or South America, or Oceania allows polygamy legally.[3] In addition to Muslim countries, many tribal societies allow polygamy. Anthropological research indicates that 850 societies allow polygamy. However, in countries where polygyny is legally allowed, only a minority population adopts such a practice. For example, in Kuwait, where polygyny is legal, only 8–13 percent of marriages are polygynous marriages.[4]

The United Nations strongly encouraged monogamy as the preferred form of marriage when the General Assembly in 1979 adopted the Convention on the Elimination of All Forms of Discrimination against Women as an international treaty that was ratified by 189 nations. Although polygamy is permitted in 80–85 percent of traditional human societies, this figure is based on cultural norms, not on individual behavior. Closer scrutiny of the data indicates that the majority of individuals within such societies are currently married monogamously. In a monogamous relationship, fathering a child outside of marriage is not common. The rate may vary from 1.7 to 9 percent depending on the survey sample.[5]

WHY MONOGAMY?

Men and women derive the most benefits of sex when engaged in a monogamous relationship. There are several hypotheses that attempt to explain monogamy in humans. Mate guarding, where a male guards a female partner from predatory males, is one of the factors associated with monogamy among mammals, and such a phenomenon is also observed in humans. Another hypothesis proposes that male infanticide (murder of young offspring by a rival male) is responsible for monogamy in primates. A monogamous relation has an added advantage where a male is present during the rearing of offspring and counteracts the threat of rival males killing his offspring.[6] However, other investigators have disputed that this model may not be applicable to human monogamy. It has been postulated that humans are cooperative breeders because human mothers routinely rely on others to help raise their infants and children. Moreover, another interesting observation in human relation is kin selection and kin discrimination. In general, helpers choose to help family members and close relatives (kin preference) over distant relatives or unrelated individuals (kin discrimination) with infant and child care.[7]

In humans, parental care of infants has been established. Although mothers may bear the majority of the burden of child care, fathers are also involved as providers of resources required for successful child rearing. In ancient hunter-gatherer societies, the father was responsible for feeding offspring and mothers. Even in ancient hunter-gatherer societies, it took almost eighteen years before a male could produce more food than he consumed. Moreover, in hunter-gatherer societies, the time period between pregnancies for a woman was three to four years. Therefore, high male investment in offspring (protecting offspring and their mother) and gender-based division of labor in acquiring food (including hunting for meat) could be responsible for monogamy in early humans.[8]

Economic game theory can also be applied to understanding the basis of monogamy in human marriage. In general, in a monogamous environment, a man protects his paternity by guarding and giving food to the same woman during his entire adulthood. In the serial monogamous relation, where a man does not keep the same partner lifelong, in a given period he has to support children he fathered with other women. This reduces the support for individual families headed by mothers. Moreover, if a woman receives support from two different men with whom she has children, there is a free-rider problem whereby each man realizes that his contribution to his children will be shared with other children who are most likely not his. Therefore, lifelong monogamy is more efficient because it prevents such wasteful activities by men. This is in agreement with the Nash equilibrium in economic game theory because, in equilibrium, altruistic ties (for example, food transfer among siblings and proper use of all resources for education) occur only in the context of monogamy but not in polygamy. Monogamy is thus a most desirable family structure where an adult man values his children because they provide him with the assurance that some of his genes will survive into future generations.[9]

Monogamous marriage prevailed among the historical societies of Eurasia, where intensive agricultural development led to scarcity of land with continued population growth due to irrigation and plowing. One of the approaches to avoid depleting the land was to adopt socially imposed monogamous marriage. Norms promoting high paternity were common among ancient societies in this region, and this may be the reason for the societal adoption of monogamous marriage.[10] Therefore, ownership of agricultural land where ownership automatically transferred to offspring in monogamous marriages was associated with avoiding the depletion of land and thus optimizing farming. Moreover, in ancient times there was no cure for sexually transmitted diseases, so even syphilis and gonorrhea could easily be epidemic. Therefore, the burden of sexually transmitted diseases may have forced our ancestors to impose monogamy.[11] Hypotheses explaining monogamy are summarized in table 7.2.

BIOLOGICAL BASIS OF LOVE
Human romantic love is universal as it is observed in all cultures and is associated with certain distinct physiological, psychological, and behavioral

Table 7.2. Hypotheses attempting to explain human monogamy

Hypothesis	Comments
Mate guarding	In monogamous mammal species, a male guards his female partner from rival males. Such a hypothesis may also explain monogamy in humans.
Male infanticide	In some animal species, a rival male may kill offspring in order to mate with a female. The presence of a male partner prevents such killing. Although this hypothesis may be applicable to explain human monogamy, there are critics who disagree with this model.
Partner scarcity	If a female partner is not readily available, it is advisable to have a monogamous relationship so that a male does not need to look for a mate. However, even in this model, male mate guarding, which secures a partner and ensures paternity in the face of more promiscuous competition, emerged as a major factor for human monogamy.
Cooperative breeder	Humans are cooperative breeders because mothers routinely rely on others to help raise their infants and children. In a monogamous relation, where all siblings live with the parents, the siblings can help the mother in rearing young siblings. Moreover, men in monogamous relationships know that their genes will survive many generations.
Parental care	Human fathers are also involved in caring for children, and thus males invest a lot in the mother and offspring. This is due to the extended time needed for an infant to develop into a mature adult. In ancient societies, high male investment in offspring (protecting offspring and their mother) and gender-based divisions in labor in acquiring food (including hunting for meat) may have contributed to monogamy in early humans.
Economic game theory	When a man invests in a monogamous relationship, all of his resources go to the family members, thus rendering maximum benefit to his offspring.
Society-imposed monogamy	When humans switched from hunter-gatherers to agriculturalists, society may have imposed monogamous marriages so that limited farmland was not depleted between different offspring belonging to different mothers. Paternal inheritance was effective in preventing the depletion of farmland.
Sexually transmitted diseases	In ancient societies where many humans lived together, society may have imposed monogamy to prevent the spread of sexually transmitted diseases, which might have caused epidemics because there was no treatment for diseases like syphilis and gonorrhea.

traits. Functional magnetic resonance imaging (fMRI) studies have shown that areas of the brain associated with motivation and goal-oriented behavior are also activated during romantic relations. In addition, different parts of the brain play important roles in the perception of romantic love. For example, the ventral pallidum area is involved in people who have been madly in love for the past twenty years, but the ventral tegmental area is active during new love. In contrast, the nucleus accumbens area of the brain is activated when a person who is madly in love is dumped by the partner.[12] Therefore, romantic love can be viewed as a motivation and goal-oriented approach in humans rather than as a purely emotional endeavor.

Several psychologists have attempted to define romantic love from a different standpoint. In general, romantic love has three components: attachment, caregiving, and sex.[13] Sternberg postulated a triangular theory of love. According to this theory, love has three components: intimacy, passion, and decision/commitment. In the first stage of love, sex appeal initially attracts partners to each other, which may lead to intimacy (connectedness and bonding with each other in a loving relationship). The next step is passion, which encompasses the drive that leads to romance and sexual consummation. In the last step, a decision may be made by both partners to continue the romantic relation, or it may be a commitment in which both partners are committed to each other and to continuing the love for a long time.[14]

Large Brain and Monogamy

One of the biological bases of human monogamy may be related to the large brain size of humans compared to the body. A big brain requires a large head, which complicates childbirth in humans. The human brain requires 20 percent of total energy from food at rest compared to just 13 percent for chimpanzees. The large human brain may be responsible for the long life span of humans compared to apes.[15] Romantic love is a gift of the large brain size. Studies have shown that larger brains are associated with a monogamous mating system in both primates and birds. In line with Dunbar's "social brain hypothesis," it can be concluded that monogamy and pair-bonding are cognitively more difficult because higher intelligence is needed to detect deception and cheating.[16]

The relatively larger brain size of humans compared to their body size may be the reason for romantic love and monogamy in humans.

Decrease in Sexual Dimorphisms in Humans Related to Monogamy

Sexual dimorphism refers to differences in body characteristics between males and females. Sexual dimorphisms, especially body size, are correlated with sexual practice. A large male has an advantage in competing with other males for a female mate, and in polygamous animals, males are usually much bigger than females. However, in monogamous animals, males are not in intense competition with other males for a mate; as a result, the body size differences between males and females are much less. Decreased sexual dimorphism is an indication of pair-bonding and the trend toward monogamy.

Based on fossil evidence, it has been postulated that in early humanoid species—for example, *Australopithecus afarensis* (*A. afarensis*)—males weighed 60–100 percent more than females, indicating that our very distant prehistoric ancestors approximately four million years ago were polygamous. However, around one and a half to two million years ago, *Homo erectus* (meaning upright man; probably migrated out of Africa and survived until twenty-six thousand years ago) emerged where sexual dimorphism was significantly reduced, as males were approximately 20 percent heavier than females—a difference similar to what is observed today. In addition to this substantial decrease in sexual dimorphism, the brain size was increased significantly. With the emergence of early *Homo sapiens* approximately one hundred thousand years ago, the brain size increased further to approximately 1,300 cc (compared to only 400 cc in *A. afarensis*). This brain size is comparable to the brain size of modern humans. Therefore, as early as one and a half to two million years ago, early human ancestors may have started the transition from polygamy to monogamy. Another factor related to monogamy is the long infancy and childhood of humans. It requires approximately eighteen to twenty years for a human baby to reach full maturity, while early humanoids matured in ten years.[17] The long infancy of humans is another factor that requires committed parents, thus promoting the concept of marriage.

Other Factors Associated with Monogamy

In general, larger testes size compared to the body size is observed in polygamous mammals. This is due to sperm competition where males with larger testes produce more sperm and can impregnate females. However, testes size is moderate compared to body size in monogamous mammals. Humans have moderately sized testes, indicating a preference for monogamous relations.[18] Concealed ovulation in females is associated with monogamous behavior in mammals. It has been considered that ovulation signs have been lost under monogamy because, in the absence of visual signs of ovulation, a male must always be with his female partner in order to increase paternity confidence. This also improves paternal care for offspring.[19]

The Institution of Marriage

There are conflicting reports regarding the time frame when the institution of monogamous marriage was established. Probably when humans started an agricultural society, some form of monogamy may have emerged due to rapid population growth and limited land for cultivation. Some type of inheritance pattern probably prevented the depletion of farmland. In one study based on comparative phylogenetic analysis of the data, the authors commented that arranged marriages probably have an evolutionary history going back at least fifty thousand years. The authors also commented that the level of polygyny was low in ancient humans.[20]

However, in another phylogenetic study, the author reconstructed the history of marriage in Indo-European-speaking societies and commented that monogamous marriage was possibly initiated during the prehistoric period, well before the earliest documented history. Based on genetic analysis, the relatedness of one adult male and one adult female with two children recovered in one burial at the site of Eulau, Germany, indicated that the institution of monogamous marriage could be traced back to 2600 BC. However, large-scale analysis of male Y chromosome data indicates that early human society was polygamous, but the shift from polygamy to monogamy may have been initiated much later, between ten thousand and five thousand years ago in Europe and Asia, and more recently elsewhere in the world.[21]

OXYTOCIN, VASOPRESSIN, AND PAIR-BONDING

Most of our knowledge about the neurobiological basis of monogamy is derived from research on the prairie vole, a monogamous rodent found in the grasslands of the central United States. After mating, prairie voles form monogamous pairs and stay together for a lifetime. In the event of the death of a partner, the prairie vole does not find another mate. However, prairie voles are closely related to the promiscuous montane voles, and these species are often compared in studies on the biological basis of monogamy and pair-bonding. In general it is recognized that oxytocin, arginine vasopressin (also known as vasopressin), and dopamine play an important role in pair-bonding, parental care, and mate guarding. However, for biological action, oxytocin and vasopressin need to bind to specific receptors. While oxytocin has only one receptor, vasopressin has three receptors (V1a, V1b, and V2). The differences in mating systems between these voles can be linked to oxytocin and vasopressin receptor expression differences in various parts of the brain. Studies have shown that prairie voles have higher densities of oxytocin receptors in the brain than montane voles. Prairie voles also have higher vasopressin V1a receptor densities in the lateral amygdala and ventral pallidum of the brain.

The ventral pallidum of the brain is a part of the dopamine reward system and plays a role in motivation. When prairie voles mate, oxytocin and vasopressin are released, where oxytocin is mainly responsible for pair-bonding of females and vasopressin facilitates pair-bonding in males. When oxytocin and vasopressin release are blocked by drugs, prairie voles become promiscuous. Therefore, oxytocin and vasopressin, along with the higher density of oxytocin receptors and vasopressin receptors in the prairie vole, form the neurobiological basis of monogamy. Moreover, oxytocin and vasopressin interact with the dopamine reward system in the brain causing the release of dopamine (the reward molecule), thus making lovemaking a rewarding experience. Studies have shown that the release of dopamine in the brain after lovemaking plays a central role in the formation of pair-bonding in prairie voles.[22]

The Role of Oxytocin, Vasopressin, and Other Neurochemicals in Human Romantic Love

It has been postulated that oxytocin, vasopressin, and related receptors, along with the dopamine reward pathway, form the neurobiological basis of pair-bonding in humans as well.[23] Studies have suggested that a mutation of the gene encoding arginine vasopressin V1a receptors plays an important role in the pair-bonding of humans, but other investigators have commented that human monogamy may not be controlled by a single gene.[24] Interestingly, oxytocin may also play some role in romantic bond formation in males. In one study, the authors recruited forty heterosexual young men, all of whom had been in a passionate romantic relationship over six months. While in a brain scanner, subjects received either oxytocin through a nasal spray or a placebo while they viewed pictures of their women partners, women they knew but were not involved with romantically, and women they had never met. The pictures were matched by independent observers so that all women appeared equally attractive. The brain centers responsible for pleasure and desire (the dopaminergic pathway) were activated only in men who received oxytocin when they viewed photographs of the women they loved. Viewing pictures of equally attractive unfamiliar women did not trigger such a strong response. The authors concluded that oxytocin potentially contributes to the romantic bond in men by enhancing their partner's attractiveness compared to other equally attractive women.[25]

Oxytocin is secreted during interacting, hugging, and kissing of a romantic partner. Therefore, in men, oxytocin is responsible for unconsciously making a romantic partner more attractive than an equally attractive unfamiliar woman. Although oxytocin is a molecule associated with stress reduction and calmness, oxytocin may also trigger some aggressive behavior in men to protect their mates when approached by another man with romantic interests. This feature, known as "mate guarding," is observed in other monogamous mammals.

Another study also indicates that oxytocin may be responsible for male monogamy. The authors used fifty-seven heterosexual male volunteers (mean age 25.1 years) who were either single ($n = 27$) or in a stable monogamous relationship ($n = 30$). These volunteers received an intranasal spray of oxytocin forty-five minutes before the experiment. In the first experiment, all male volunteers stood on one side of the room with their toes on a marked line, and an attractive female experimenter unknown to volunteers approached them. In the first half of the experiment, the volunteers were instructed to say "stop" when they felt that the female experimenter was at the ideal social distance in terms of physical distance between them. In the second half of the experiment, the attractive female experimenter was standing while each male volunteer approached her and stopped at what he considered an appropriate social distance between them. The authors observed that intranasal administration of oxytocin stimulated men in a monogamous relationship to keep a much greater distance (twenty-eight to thirty inches) between themselves and an attractive woman during a first encounter compared to single men (twenty to twenty-four inches). The personal space was greater if the female experimenter made eye contact with a male participant involved in a monogamous romantic relationship. The authors concluded that oxytocin may promote fidelity in men.[26]

Oxytocin is also released after orgasm. In one study using twelve women, the authors showed that levels of oxytocin were significantly increased one minute after sexual stimulation but then decreased to the baseline value after five minutes. The authors concluded that in women oxytocin increases immediately after orgasm.[27] Therefore, vasopressin and oxytocin are a neuroendocrinological basis for why humans prefer the stability of a monogamous relation.[28] Interestingly, a PET (positron emission tomography) scanning study showed that blood flow in the pituitary gland was increased following female sexual orgasm but not during male ejaculation. Higher blood supply in the pituitary gland was associated with increased oxytocin and prolactin secretion.[29] A neurophysiological study on erection and ejaculation in males indicates that erection is not a prerequisite for ejaculation, as sexual responses can exist without each other. However, the neurotransmitters dopamine and serotonin have a central role in modulating erection and ejaculation.[30]

> Oxytocin may promote fidelity in men.

Another hormone, prolactin, which is also secreted during orgasm, plays an important role in sexual pleasure, stress release, and pair-bonding. In one study, the authors observed that after intercourse, prolactin concentrations were increased more than 400 percent in both male and female subjects compared to values after masturbation, indicating that intercourse is more physiologically and emotionally satisfying than masturbation. The authors concluded that prolactin increase is a neurohormonal index of sexual satiety.[31]

> Oxytocin, vasopressin, and the specific distributions of oxytocin and vasopressin receptors in various regions of the brain, as well as the interaction of these hormones with the dopaminergic system in the brain reward pathway that secretes the reward molecule dopamine, are responsible for the motivation to form a romantic relation and the joy derived from such a relationship.

Another interesting feature in human pair-bonding is reduced testosterone levels in both men and women who are in a committed relationship compared to single men and women. However, testosterone levels in partnered males who have a strong desire to participate in uncommitted sex are comparable to

Table 7.3. **Biological basis of romantic love and monogamy**

Biological Basis	Comments
Larger brain size in humans compared to body size	Romantic love and monogamy are a gift of the large brain size in humans. Research has indicated that birds that prefer to live in pairs have relatively larger brain size compared to body weight than other birds.
Neurobiological basis	Hormones such as oxytocin and vasopressin and receptors of these hormones in the brain are mostly responsible for human monogamy. Dopamine may also be involved in the reward circuit so that humans get pleasure from sex and romantic relation. In addition, oxytocin may promote fidelity in men.
Decreased sexual dimorphism	Decreased sexual dimorphism indicates monogamy. Approximately four million years ago, humanoid males weighed 60–100 percent more than females, but around one and a half to two million years ago *Homo erectus* (early humans) emerged, in which sexual dimorphism was significantly reduced, as males were approximately 20 percent heavier than females—a difference that is similar to what is observed today.
Testis size	Large testis size compared to body size is observed in polygamous mammals, but moderate testis size is observed in monogamous mammals. Humans have moderate testis size, which is associated with monogamy.
Testosterone level	Testosterone levels in both men and women are reduced when they are in a committed relationship. This also reduces male aggression because a male is no longer competing with other males for a mate.
Concealed ovulation	Visual signs of ovulation in female mammals are lost in monogamy. This is also applicable to humans.

testosterone levels of single men. A similar trend is also observed in women.[32] Testosterone is associated with libido in both men and women, but in general men have much higher levels of testosterone than women. Biological factors that contribute to monogamy are listed in table 7.3.

SEX FOR STRESS RELIEF

Making love to your spouse or soul mate is a great way to reduce stress. A rewarding sex life is considered an important contributor to satisfaction with life. Sex also elevates positive emotion and mood. In one large study involving 1,600 adult women, the authors reported that sexual activity is positively correlated with happiness. Moreover, married people reported having more sex than single, divorced, widowed, or separated people. Higher income does not buy happiness or more sexual partners. The other striking features of the study include the following:[33]

- A single sexual partner in the past year is associated with the most happiness.
- The median American has sexual intercourse two to three times a month (the median frequency is once a week in people below forty years of age). Approximately 7 percent of people surveyed report having sex at least four times a week.
- Some evidence indicates that sex has a disproportionately strong effect on the happiness of highly educated people.
- Highly educated females have fewer sex partners.

A rewarding sex life is considered an important contributor to positive mood and satisfaction with life. In one study based on fifty-eight middle-aged women (mean age 47.6 years) who recorded physical affection, different sexual behaviors, stressful events, and mood ratings every morning for thirty-six weeks, the authors demonstrated that physical affection, genital stimulation, and sex with a partner on a particular day correlated with higher positive mood the following morning, indicating that physical intimacy in these women correlated with stress relief. Such a positive effect was also observed in lesbian couples after genital stimulation or orgasm. However, this effect was not observed when a woman achieved orgasm without a partner. In fact, orgasm without a partner was associated with higher anxiety and negative mood the following day. The authors proposed that orgasm causes oxytocin release, which is associated with stress relief and positive social interaction. Moreover, positive touch and physical intimacy are associated with oxytocin release.[34]

> A single partner is associated with maximum happiness, indicating the rewarding effect of a monogamous relationship.

Being married or living with a significant other appears to be one of the most powerful supports in humans. Affectionate touch during a couple's interaction has a protective effect from physiological responses to stress. In one study, the authors exposed sixty-seven women (aged twenty to thirty-seven) who had been married or cohabiting with a male partner for at least twelve months at the time of the study to a standardized psychosocial laboratory stressor (the Trier Social Stress Test). Participants were randomly assigned to three groups differing in the type of a ten-minute period of social interaction they had with their partners prior to the laboratory-induced stressor. In one group (n = 25), women had no partner interaction, while in the second group (n = 22) women received verbal support from their partners, and in the third group (n = 20) women received positive physical contact (a neck and shoulder massage) from their partners. The authors measured salivary cortisol, blood oxytocin level, and heart rate in these women before and after exposure to the stressor. The authors observed that women with positive physical contact from their partners before exposure to stress showed significantly lower cortisol levels and heart rate response to stress compared to women who received verbal support or no support from their partners before exposure to the stressor. The authors concluded that positive physical affection from a husband/partner is associated with stress release.[35]

> Affection and sex reduce stress and improve mood due to oxytocin release.

Penile-vaginal intercourse frequency is associated with better physical and psychological health. Freud conjectured that noncoital sexual activity is incomplete. Intercourse is more of a synchronized sensorimotor and emotional interaction compared to other sexual behavior. Therefore, individuals who may not want to get emotionally involved with their partners may avoid intercourse while engaging in other sexual activities with their partners. In addition, intercourse requires more complex brain activity compared to other sexual behavior. Manual or oral stimulation of the clitoris stimulates the pudendal nerve, but the vagina-cervical stimulation during intercourse additionally stimulates pelvic, hypogastric, and vagal nerves. Based on a study of twenty-four women and twenty-two men who recorded their daily penile-vaginal intercourse (PVI) activity for two weeks, the author demonstrated that both men and women who reported PVI activities had a better stress response (lower blood pressure under stress) when exposed to a laboratory-induced stressor (public speaking and verbal arithmetic challenge) compared to men and women who reported other sexual activities or no intercourse. Persons who masturbated or had sexual activities with partners but no intercourse showed higher systolic blood pressure reactivity (average 14 mm of mercury increase) in response to stress compared to subjects who had PVI.[36]

> Intercourse is associated with more stress relief than any other type of partnered sex or masturbation.

Based on a large population study involving 1,570 people aged thirty-five to sixty-five years, the authors observed that simultaneous orgasm produced by penile-vaginal intercourse as well as vaginal orgasm for women was associated with greater sexual satisfaction, life satisfaction, intimacy, and mental health satisfaction. Moreover, statistical analyses indicated that frequency of intercourse as well as orgasm consistency were independently associated with life satisfaction and stress reduction in both men and women.[37] In a more recent study based on eighty-five Czech long-term couples (aged twenty to forty years, mean relationship length 5.4 years), the authors also observed that frequency of intercourse and vaginal orgasm in women were correlated with better intimate relationship, life satisfaction, and stress relief. In contrast, masturbation in women was inversely correlated with life satisfaction and personal satisfaction.[38] However, there are other studies that indicate the stress-releasing effects of masturbation. In one study, the authors showed that following masturbation, oxytocin concentration in the saliva increased rapidly (peak value ten to fifteen minutes after initiation of sexual stimulation) and then declined to a baseline value after thirty minutes in both men and women. Because oxytocin has a remarkable stress-releasing effect, it can be concluded that self-stimulation such as masturbation can also release some stress.[39]

Hugs and even holding hands have health benefits and are effective in reducing stress. In one study, couples who were married or long-term cohabiting partners were divided into two groups: group 1 consisted of one hundred adults with a long-term spouse or partner who were instructed to hold hands while watching a ten-minute pleasant video and then to hug each other for twenty seconds; group 2 consisted of eighty-five adults without their spouse or partner, and they were instructed to rest quietly for some time. Both groups were then asked to give a brief speech discussing what factors stressed or angered them. Heart rate and blood pressure of all subjects were also measured. The authors observed that blood pressure and heart rate following giving speeches were increased more significantly in subjects who did not receive hugs. Because public speaking is associated with stress, the authors concluded that holding hands and hugs are effective

> A twenty-second hug from a spouse or romantic partner is associated with stress release. African Americans may get more benefit from hugging compared with Caucasians.

in lowering stress.[40] In another study involving 68 African American and 117 Caucasian healthy adults, the authors observed that subjects who held hands with their partners for ten minutes and hugged their partners for twenty seconds showed a much lower increase of heart rate and blood pressure when exposed to the stress of public speaking compared to subjects who rested quietly before public speaking but were not allowed to hold hands or hug their partners. The effect of warm partner contact was comparable in men and women, with a greater effect observed for African Americans compared with Caucasians. The authors concluded that affectionate relationships with a supportive partner may contribute to lower reactivity to stressful life events and may also promote healthy hearts.[41]

Frequent and positive partner contact is associated with higher oxytocin levels in both men and women. In one study involving seventy-six adults who were either married or engaged in a long-term cohabiting relationship, the authors observed that spouses or partners who described their relationship as happy showed higher levels of oxytocin in their plasma (both men and women) compared with subjects who described themselves as unhappy. Moreover, warm partner contact including hugs resulted in higher oxytocin levels, lower blood pressure, and lower norepinephrine (a stress hormone) in women. The authors concluded that oxytocin triggers physiological changes that protect women's hearts and at the same time improve their relationship quality, benefiting both their husbands and their offspring.[42] In another study based on fifty-nine premenopausal women, the authors observed that warm contact with their husbands/partners ending with hugs resulted in significant stress release, as evidenced by lower blood pressure, lower heart rate, and higher plasma oxytocin levels. Menstrual cycle phase did not influence oxytocin levels.[43] Therefore, any form of warm contact with a partner is associated with stress release and better health, as evidenced by lower blood pressure and lower heart rate.

OTHER HEALTH BENEFITS OF SEX

Stress is one of the major causes of increased risk of cardiovascular diseases, including heart attack. Therefore, it can be assumed that warm partner contact and sex have protective effects against cardiovascular diseases. Many studies have shown that sex promotes healthy hearts. In one study involving 1,165 men, the authors reported that having sex twice or more a week reduced the risk of fatal heart attack by approximately 50 percent compared to men who reported having sex once a month or less.[44] However, older people may worry about being sexually active due to the anticipated risk of heart disease or stroke. Contrary to popular belief, sex in older age does not increase the risk of heart disease or stroke. In one study based on 914 men aged forty-five to fifty-nine years during the time of recruitment and a twenty-year follow-up, the authors concluded that frequency of sex was not associated with increased risk of stroke in these men. In contrast, sex may offer some protection against fatal heart disease.[45] It is important to note that older people with significant health issues must consult with their physician before engaging in sexual activity or taking medication such as Viagra. For certain health conditions, taking Viagra or similar medication may be dangerous.

An active sex life also increases longevity. In one study with a ten-year follow-up, the authors concluded that mortality risk was 50 percent lower in the group with high orgasmic frequency (sex two to three times per week) compared to men experiencing infrequent orgasms (less than once a month). The authors concluded that sexual activity seems to have a protective effect on men's health.[46] In another study based on 252 subjects and a twenty-five-year follow-up, the author observed that frequency of intercourse was a predictor for longevity in men but not in women. However, women who reported past enjoyment of sex lived longer.[47] Sex also boosts the immune system. In one study involving 112 college students, the authors observed that subjects who reported having sex once or twice a week showed 30 percent higher levels of immunoglobulin A (IgA) in their saliva specimens, indicating a boost in their immune systems.[48]

Sexual activity is associated with burning calories, and people who are sexually active also exercise more often and have better dietary habits than people who are sexually less active. Based on a study of twenty-one heterosexual couples aged eighteen to thirty-five years, the authors demonstrated that approximately twenty-five minutes of sexual activity was associated with burning of 101 calories (4.2 calories per minute) in men and 69 calories (3.1 calories per minute) in women. Although thirty minutes of exercise in men in the same study was associated with burning 276 calories, while in women it was associated with burning 213 calories, study subjects all agreed that sexual activities were more enjoyable than exercise. The authors concluded that sexual activity can be considered a form of exercise.[49] In addition, sexual intercourse on a regular basis may help with weight loss.[50]

Sexual release is associated with the release of oxytocin and other neuro-chemicals, which may work as a sleep aid. Sex also has an analgesic effect. In one study, the authors reported the case of a man who was suffering from restless leg syndrome (uncomfortable sensations in the legs with the urge to move the legs while falling asleep, also considered a sleep disorder because it interferes with sleep) and had difficulty sleeping but could easily go to sleep after intercourse or masturbation.[51] In another study, the authors reported that sexual activity was associated with significant reduction in the perception of migraine and cluster headache pain.[52] Women who have penile-vaginal intercourse at least once a week in every nonmenstruating week show more regularity in their menstrual cycles compared to women not engaged in any type of sexual activity.[53]

Based on a study of 29,342 men, the authors observed that men who experienced twenty-one or more ejaculations per month had a significantly reduced risk of prostate cancer compared to men who had four to seven ejaculations per month.[54] Sex is associated with the release of oxytocin, which may protect women against breast cancer. The secretion of oxytocin due to nipple stimulation would cause contraction of specific cells in the breast that may eliminate carcinogenic compounds from the breast.[55] In one study involving nulliparous women aged twenty-five to forty-five years, the authors observed that increased sexual activity was correlated with reduced incidence of breast cancer. A higher incidence of breast cancer was observed in women who had sex less than once a month. The risk was also reduced when women were directly exposed to semen (using oral contraceptives, IUD, safe period, or no contraceptive) during intercourse.[56]

Sex may promote healthy skin and younger appearance because sex induces secretion of a hormone known as DHEA (dehydroepiandrosterone). Maintaining sexual activity or having regular erections keeps penile tissue healthy. Women who continue to be sexually active after menopause through sexual partners or through masturbation are more likely to report sufficient vaginal lubrication.[57] Regular sex may also strengthen the pelvic muscle in women, which may aid in bladder control. Sex also increases self-esteem.[58] Based on a large study involving 6,833 subjects aged fifty to eighty-nine years, the author concluded that sexual activity increases cognitive function in older age, thus reducing the risk of dementia.[59] Sex also reduces depression and improves mental health.[60]

CONCLUSION

Monogamous sexual relationships have many health benefits, including significant stress release. However, sexual misadventure is not a rewarding experience because the neurochemicals secreted during sex in sexually active people, such as oxytocin and vasopressin, are associated with pair-bonding and trust building. Romantic relationships are an evolutionary gift to mankind associated with happiness and higher self-esteem. Sexual misadventure should be avoided because it not only increases stress but also increases the risk of sexually transmitted diseases and unwanted pregnancies.

Balanced Diet for Prevention of Chronic Diseases and Stress Management

Psychological stress increases oxidative stress in the human body due to the excess production of free radicals, and many chronic illnesses related to chronic stress are linked to increased oxidative stress. The human brain is also exposed to chronic oxidative stress, which increases the risk of depression, anxiety, and other mental illnesses (see chapter 1). Antioxidant phytochemicals present in many fruits and vegetables are very effective in neutralizing these free radicals, thus significantly reducing oxidative stress. Therefore, daily consumption of fruits and vegetables is effective in preventing many chronic diseases related to chronic stress. In addition, antioxidants present in fruits, vegetables, tea, and coffee can reduce the oxidative stress experienced by the brain, thus providing protection against depression, anxiety, mood swings, and age-related neuro-degenerative diseases such as age-related dementia, Alzheimer's disease, and Parkinson's disease. Moreover, deficiency of certain vitamins and minerals may increase the risk of anxiety and depression. A balanced diet can alleviate these vitamin and mineral deficiencies, thus helping to reduce stress, anxiety, and depression. One apple a day probably keeps doctors away because apples are very rich in antioxidants and multiple vitamins.

DIETARY GUIDELINES FOR AMERICANS

The United States Department of Agriculture (USDA) and the Department of Health and Human Services jointly publish the *Dietary Guidelines for Americans* every five years, suggesting to Americans what constitutes a balanced

Table 8.1. Major dietary recommendations according to the latest published *Dietary Guidelines for Americans* (2015–2020) based on a diet of two thousand calories per day

Food Group	Amount in the 2,000-Calorie Diet Each Day	Comments
Vegetables	2.5 cups each day	Vegetables include dark green (broccoli, spinach, etc.; 1.5 cups per week), red and orange (tomatoes, carrots, pumpkins, red peppers, sweet potatoes, etc.; 5.5 cups per week), legumes (beans and peas; 1.5 cups per week), starchy (white potatoes, corn, etc.; 5 cups per week), and others (iceberg lettuce, onions, etc.; 4 cups per week).
Fruits	2 cups each day	It is preferable to eat whole fruits rather than fruit juice because whole fruits contain fiber.
Grains	6 ounces each day	It is preferable to eat whole grains (three ounces or more per day) over refined grains (three ounces or less per day).
Protein food	5.5 ounces each day	Recommended seafood consumption, eight ounces per week; meats, poultry, and eggs, twenty-six ounces per week; nuts, seeds, and soy products, five ounces per week.
Dairy products	3 cups each day	Fat-free or low-fat dairy products (milk, yogurt, cheese, etc.) are recommended.
Oil	27 grams each day	Cooking oil should be vegetable oils that are rich in unsaturated fatty acids.

diet. The latest guidelines (2015–2020) strongly recommend that people eat fruits and vegetables every day and encourage eating whole grains. It also recommends eating nuts and consuming fat-free or low-fat dairy products. Moreover, the guidelines advise people to use less cooking oil (27 grams per day, or five tablespoons), consume less than 2,300 mg of sodium (salt) per day, and get less than 10 percent of calories per day from sugar and less than 10 percent of calories per day from eating saturated fats. If alcohol is consumed, it must be consumed in moderation (up to one drink per day for women and up to two drinks per day for men). The major dietary guidelines are summarized in table 8.1. In general, it is recommended that half of the plate should contain vegetables and fruits.

Scientific research has shown that eating a balanced diet every day and participating in physical activities prevents many chronic diseases. These diseases are the leading cause of morbidity and mortality, not only in the United States but globally. In the United States, an estimated 117 million men and women, representing approximately 50 percent of the total U.S. population, suffer from one or more chronic conditions, including hypertension, coronary heart disease, stroke, diabetes, cancer, arthritis, hepatitis, weak or failing kidneys, current asthma, or COPD (chronic obstructive pulmonary disease). Furthermore, one in four adults (26 percent) suffers from multiple chronic conditions.[1] These chronic diseases are partly due to poor-quality diets.[2]

The 2015 Dietary Guidelines Advisory Committee found that vitamins A, D, E, and C, as well as folate, calcium, magnesium, fiber, and potassium, are shortfall nutrients in the general population, while iron is a shortfall nutrient among adolescents and premenopausal women. In general, most Americans have a low intake of key food groups, which are important sources of these shortfall nutrients, such as vegetables, fruits, whole grain, and dairy. In addition, foods that should be consumed less, such as saturated fats, sodium (salt), added sugar, and refined grains, are in fact overconsumed by Americans. As a result, overall dietary quality remains generally poor among many Americans.

> Approximately 50 percent of Americans suffer from one or more chronic diseases, partly due to poor dietary choices.

According to U.S. Behavioral Risk Factor Surveillance data, only 7.7 percent of U.S. adults have a low-risk lifestyle, defined as consuming adequate of amounts of fruits and vegetables every day, not smoking, engaging in physical activities, and having a normal weight as well as body mass index (body mass index less than 25 kg/m²).[3] Unfortunately, fewer than one in ten Americans meets their calorie-specific fruit or vegetable recommendations in their diet.[4] Obesity is also related to poor diet. In one study, the authors observed that the prevalence of obesity was higher in rural than urban residents (35.6 percent vs. 30.4 percent) among both men and women because rural adults had a lower intake of fiber and fruits and a higher intake of sweetened beverages. Moreover, compared to urban adults, more rural adults reported no leisure time for physical activity.[5]

> Fewer than one in ten Americans eat recommended amounts of fruits and vegetables.

A healthy diet as defined by the *U.S. Dietary Guidelines for Americans* has been associated with lower morbidity and mortality from major chronic diseases, not only in non-Hispanic whites but also in other ethnic groups, including low-income populations.[6] In one study based on 215,782 adults,

> Eating a balanced diet and following the U.S. dietary guidelines may increase longevity in all ethnic groups.

including Caucasians, African Americans, Native Hawaiians, Japanese Americans, and Latino adults, the authors concluded that consuming a balanced diet and following key recommendations of the dietary guidelines is associated with a lower risk of mortality from all causes, including cardiovascular diseases and cancer in both men and women.[7]

THE HEALING POWER OF FRUITS AND VEGETABLES

Eating fruits and vegetables is associated with lower risk of mortality. The physical health benefits of eating sufficient quantities of fruits and vegetables each day include the following:

- Lower mortality
- Lower risk of cardiovascular diseases
- Lower risk of stroke
- Lower risk of cancer
- Lower risk of type 2 diabetes
- Lower risk of inflammatory diseases
- Improved bone health
- Better weight stability
- Possible reduction in risk of age-related macular degeneration and cataracts
- Youthful appearance

In 1990, the World Health Organization (WHO) issued recommendations for a minimum daily intake of 400 grams of fruits and vegetables. Consumption of fruits and vegetables can reduce mortality

> Vegetables, salads, and fresh and dried fruits are most effective at reducing the risk of all-cause mortality, including mortality from cardiovascular diseases and cancer.

from all causes. In one study based on 451,151 subjects from ten European countries, the authors observed a 10 percent lower mortality rate among subjects consuming 569 grams (20 ounces) or more of combined fruits and vegetables each day compared to less than 249 grams (8.8 ounces) per day. The authors concluded that consuming sufficient amounts of fruits and vegetables each day is associated with a lower risk of death.[8] In another study based on 65,226 participants, with 7.7 years of median follow-up, the authors observed that people who ate at least one but less than three servings of fruits and vegetables every day showed a 12 percent lower mortality risk than people who ate less than one serving of fruits and vegetables each day. People who consumed more fruits and vegetables showed a lower risk of mortality, with the best reduction of 33 percent observed among people who consumed seven or more servings of fruits and vegetables each day. Consumption of fruits and vegetables was also associated with reduction in mortality from cardiovascular diseases and cancer, with the best benefits observed with seven or more servings of fruits and vegetables per day. Vegetables, salads, and fresh and dried fruits showed a significant association with lower mortality, although consumption of fresh vegetables appeared to be better than fruits. However, frozen/canned fruit consumption was apparently associated with a higher risk of mortality.[9]

Cardiovascular diseases are the major cause of mortality in the United States and many other developed countries, but daily intake of fruits and vegetables in sufficient quantities may significantly reduce the risk of such diseases. The latest U.S. dietary guidelines recommend consuming at least two and a half cups of vegetables and two cups of fruits every day. In a study based on 15,220 men without any heart disease, stroke, or cancer during enrollment and six-year follow-up, the authors observed that men who consumed at least two and a half servings of fruits and vegetables per day showed a 23 percent lower risk of coronary heart diseases compared to men who consumed one or fewer servings of fruits and vegetables each day. The authors concluded that eating fruits and vegetables in sufficient quantities can protect a person against heart diseases.[10] In another study based on 84,251 women (age thirty-four to fifty-nine years) with fourteen years of follow-up as well as 42,148 men (aged forty to seventy-five years) with eight years of follow-up, the authors concluded that consumption of at least four servings a day of fruits and vegetables, particularly green leafy vegetables, cruciferous vegetables, and fruits rich in vitamin C, was associated with lower risk of cardiovascular diseases in both men and women. Moreover, for subjects who did not eat enough fruits and vegetables, even eating one additional serving of fruits and vegetables was associated with a 4 percent risk reduction.[11]

Eating adequate amounts of fruits and vegetables can reduce the risk of stroke. In one report, the authors reviewed data from eight studies involving 257,551 individuals and after a meta-analysis of the data concluded that

the relative risk of stroke was 11 percent lower in individuals who consumed three to five servings of vegetables per day and 26 percent lower for
individuals who consumed more than five servings of fruits and vegetables
per day, compared to individuals who had less than three servings of fruits
and vegetables per day.[12] It may be assumed
that the reduced risk of cardiovascular diseases
and strokes in people who consume the recommended amounts of fruits and vegetables may
partly be due to the blood pressure–lowering
effects of fruits and vegetables. Lower blood pressure is more often observed
in vegetarians than in the total population. Some reduction of blood pressure may also be observed in individuals when they switch from a traditional to a totally vegetarian diet.

> Vegetarians may show lower blood pressure than nonvegetarians.

As mentioned earlier, eating fruits and vegetables is also associated
with a reduced risk of various types of cancer, including prostate cancer
(35 percent reduced risk with twenty-eight or more servings of fruits and
vegetables per week compared to intake of less than fourteen servings),
pancreatic cancer, colon cancer, and cancer of oral cavities. Moreover, all-
cause cancer mortality is reduced in individuals
who consume sufficient servings of fruits and
vegetables every day. Many beneficial antioxidants are present in fruits and vegetables that
are responsible for reducing the risk of cancer.[13]

> Apples, tomatoes, and citrus fruits are effective in reducing the risk of digestive tract cancer.

In another study, the authors commented that a high intake of fruits and
vegetables reduces the risk of many common types of cancer, including
cancer of the digestive tract. High consumption of apples and tomatoes may
reduce the risk of digestive tract cancer. Eating citrus fruits is also useful in
reducing the risk of digestive tract cancer.[14]

Eating fruits and vegetables may provide protection against type 2 diabetes (non-insulin dependent diabetes), the most common type of diabetes
with adult onset. Type 1 diabetes has early onset during childhood. This
type of diabetes accounts for 5–10 percent of all diabetes and is due to a
lack of production of insulin by pancreatic beta cells. In one report, the
authors reviewed studies published up to June 2014 in medical journals,
and based on their meta-analysis of the data, they concluded that two to
three servings of vegetables and two servings of fruits per day conferred a

lower risk of type 2 diabetes. These findings are consistent with the general recommendation of five servings of fruits and vegetables per day (3 servings of vegetables and 2 servings of fruits per day).[15] Lifestyle interventions such as increased intake of vegetables, fruits, and whole-grain cereals and increased physical activities may lower the risk of type 2 diabetes because all of these interventions contribute to weight loss, a key factor to lower the risk. In addition, higher intake of green leafy vegetables (such as cabbage, brussels sprouts, broccoli, cauliflower, and spinach) lowers the risk of type 2 diabetes by approximately 14 percent independent of any effect on weight loss.[16]

> Eating two to three servings of vegetables and two servings of fruits every day is associated with reduced risk of type 2 diabetes. Eating green leafy vegetables also lowers the risk of diabetes independent of weight loss.

Inflammatory bowel diseases, such as Crohn's disease and ulcerative colitis, are examples of chronic recurrent diseases of the gastrointestinal tract. High intake of fruits but not vegetables is associated with reduced risk of Crohn's disease. A higher intake of cooked vegetables (2.9 servings per day) may lower the risk of rheumatoid arthritis, but raw vegetables have no protective effect. Although vegetable intake has no effect, an increase of fruit intake of 100 grams per day reduces the risk of COPD (chronic obstructive pulmonary disease) by 24 percent. Eating apples is associated with reduced risk of asthma.

Consuming fruits and vegetables may also promote bone health by increasing bone density. High consumption of dark green and deep yellow vegetables is associated with higher bone mass in children. Although consumption of vegetables and fruits does not result in weight loss, fruits and vegetables consumed in sufficient amounts may provide weight stability (i.e., no weight gain). Age-related eye diseases such as macular degeneration and cataracts are common, but intake of fruits and vegetables may protect against such eye diseases. High intake

> Eating apples may reduce the risk of asthma attack.

(more than five times per week) of food rich in lutein, such as spinach and collard greens, significantly reduces the risk (86 percent reduction) of age-related macular degeneration. High intake of vitamin C, especially from fruit juices, reduces the risk of cataracts. The combined intake of vitamin C and other antioxidants (beta-carotene, vitamin E, zinc, etc.) from foods and or supplements may reduce the risk of cataracts by 38–49 percent.[17]

Fruits and vegetables contain carotenoid pigments that accumulate in the human skin after eating such foods and contribute to normal yellowness of the skin, especially in Caucasians and light-skinned Asians. Carotenoid pigmentation of the human skin is perceived as healthy and attractive by others. Moreover, such coloration makes a person look younger. Yellowness of the skin is related to diet, and people who consume more fruits and vegetables appear to look more attractive and younger. In one study based on thirty-five Caucasians, the authors concluded that modest dietary changes are required to enhance health (2.9 servings of fruits and vegetables per day) and attractiveness (3.3 servings of fruits and vegetables per day). The minimum color change required to confer perceptibly healthier and more attractive skin coloration can be achieved with the recommended consumption of fruits and vegetables within six weeks.[18] In another study involving ninety-one Caucasian women (aged 18.1–29.1 years), the authors also concluded that increased fruit and vegetable consumption was associated with higher overall skin yellowness, which contributed to overall increased attractiveness.[19]

FOOD FOR STRESS MANAGEMENT AND EMOTIONAL WELL-BEING

Emotions influence the food choices people make. Negative emotions can act as a trigger to consume snacks high in fat and sugar over healthy meals containing fruits and vegetables.[20] Studies have shown that healthy dietary patterns characterized by vegetables, fruit, meat, fish, and whole grains have a protective effect against depression and anxiety, while an unhealthy diet consisting of processed or fried foods, foods containing high amounts of sugar, and refined grains increases the risk of depression.[21] In one study based on a review of data from sixteen published papers, the authors concluded that both a traditional healthy diet and the Mediterranean diet have a protective effect against depression and anxiety.[22] In another study, the authors performed a meta-analysis on data obtained from thirteen observational studies and observed that a high intake of fruits, vegetables, fish, poultry, low- or no-fat dairy products, and whole grains has a protective effect against depression and anxiety.[23]

In general, people are in a better mood during the weekend than on weekdays, but studies have shown that eating fruits and vegetables is associated with overall better mood regardless of the particular day of the week. Exercise and sleeping well are also associated with better mood.[24] In one large study involving eighty thousand British individuals, the authors observed a positive correlation between emotional well-being and consumption of fruits and vegetables. Although consuming five servings of fruits and vegetables per day was associated with positive mood and emotional well-being, the maximum effect was observed when people consumed a total of seven servings per day.[25]

Fruit and vegetable consumption also promotes emotional well-being among healthy young adults. In one study involving 281 undergraduate students (mean age 19.9 years) who kept a diary of their food intake for twenty-one days, the authors observed that on days when young adults ate more fruits and vegetables, they reported feeling calmer, happier, and more energetic. They also felt a more positive attitude the next day. The association between fruit consumption and better mood was more significant in men than woman, but men and women benefited equally from vegetable consumption.[26] In another study involving 405 young adults who completed an Internet diary of food intake for thirteen consecutive days, the authors observed that young adults who ate more fruits and vegetables reported higher eudaemonic well-being, more intense feelings of curiosity, and greater creativity compared to young adults who ate less fruits and vegetables. Moreover, on a given day, when an individual consumed more fruits and vegetables, he or she reported a more positive mood compared to other days when the same individual consumed less fruits and vegetables.

The positive effect of fruits and vegetables on mood and emotional well-being may be related to nutrients present in the fruits and vegetables. Consuming more fruits and vegetables improves overall physical health, which may have a positive effect on emotional well-being. Vitamin C, vitamin B complex, and antioxidants present in fruits and vegetables may increase the synthesis of the neurotransmitters dopamine and serotonin, which are associated with the neurochemistry of eudaemonia. Increased dopamine concentrations in the brain are also associated with increased positive emotion, goal-oriented behavior, motivation, creativity, and curiosity. The carbohydrate content of fruits and vegetables increases the brain level of tryptophan and tyrosine, which are precursors of serotonin and dopamine.[27] Nutritional factors related to mental health issues and foods rich in such nutrients are summarized in table 8.2.

> Eating fruits and vegetables in sufficient amounts daily (at least four to five servings a day) is associated with not only better physical health but also emotional well-being and happiness.

Table 8.2. Nutritional factors related to mental health issues and foods rich in such nutrients

Nutritional Factor	Mental Health Issues	Foods Rich in Such Nutrients
Antioxidants in foods	Increased oxidative stress in the brain is associated with mood disorder and depression.	Many antioxidants present in fruits, vegetables, tea, coffee, and nuts can reduce oxidative stress in the brain, thus elevating mood and reducing the risk of depression.
Folate	Low folate intake is associated with depression and melancholic depression.	Folate is found in a wide variety of vegetables (especially dark green leafy vegetables such as spinach, asparagus, and brussels sprouts), avocados, fruits (oranges, papayas, grapes, grapefruits, cantaloupes, bananas, strawberries, etc.), nuts, beans, peas, dairy products, poultry and meat, eggs, seafood, grains, and cereals fortified with folate.
Vitamin B_{12}	Vitamin B_{12} deficiency may increase the risk of depression. Other vitamin Bs may be good for mental health, but studies are limited.	Vitamin B_{12} is found in animal products, including fish, meat, poultry, eggs, milk, and dairy products, but not in fruits and vegetables. However, fortified breakfast cereals are a good source of vitamin B_{12}.
Vitamin C	Lower than normal serum vitamin C levels are associated with mood disorders.	Although fruits and vegetables are a good source of vitamin C, citrus fruits, tomatoes and tomato juice, and potatoes are rich in vitamin C. Other good food sources are red and green peppers, kiwifruits, broccoli, strawberries, brussels sprouts, and cantaloupes.
Vitamin D	Low intake of vitamin D may be associated with depression, low mood, and poor cognitive function in the elderly.	Few foods are a good source of vitamin D, and this is the reason milk and some breakfast cereals and other foods are fortified with vitamin D. The flesh of fatty fish (such as salmon, tuna, and mackerel) and fish liver oils are among the best food sources of vitamin D. Small amounts of vitamin D are found in beef liver, cheese, and egg yolks.
Magnesium	Low dietary intake of magnesium may cause depression.	Magnesium is widely distributed in plant and animal foods, including green leafy vegetables such as spinach, legumes, nuts, seeds, and whole grains.
Selenium	Low dietary intake of selenium is associated with poor mood.	The major food sources of selenium in the American diet are breads, grains, meat, poultry, fish, and eggs. Seafoods are particularly rich in selenium.

Nutritional Factor	Mental Health Issues	Foods Rich in Such Nutrients
Omega-3 fatty acid	Omega-3 fatty acids stabilize mood. Therefore, deficiency increases the risk of depression.	Fish, especially fatty fish (salmon, tuna, sardine, trout, mackerel, etc.), are a good source of omega-3 fatty acids (eicosapentaenoic acid and docosahexanoic acid). Vegetarians should get alpha-linolenic acid from a plant source because this fatty acid is converted into eicosapentaenoic acid.
Tryptophan	Tryptophan is a precursor of the neurotransmitter serotonin, which plays an important role in mood and depression. Tryptophan depletion in the blood may cause mood disorders.	Nuts, seeds, soybeans, turkey, poultry, meat, milk, cheese, yogurt, fish, shellfish, eggs, and whole grains contain tryptophan.

There are many reasons why fruits and vegetables are associated with both physical and mental well-being. Fruits and vegetables are rich in antioxidants, which are effective not only in reducing oxidative stress linked to many chronic illnesses but also in alleviating oxidative stress in the brain. Increased oxidative stress in the brain is associated with mood disturbances, anxiety, and depression. In addition, chronic oxidative stress in the brain increases the risk of many neurodegenerative diseases, including age-related dementia, Alzheimer's disease, and Parkinson's disease. Antioxidants present in fruits and vegetables are effective in lowering the risk of such degenerative diseases. Moreover, fruits and vegetables are rich in vitamins and micronutrients, which have physical as well as mental health benefits.

Folate, Vitamin B$_{12}$, and Mood

Folate, a water-soluble B vitamin (B$_9$), is important for the synthesis of neurotransmitters, including dopamine and serotonin, which are associated with emotional well-being. A deficiency of serotonin may cause depression, and many antidepressants (SSRIs: selective serotonin reuptake inhibitors) act by restoring healthy serotonin levels in the brain. Several studies have shown that low serum or red blood cell folate levels (erythrocyte folate levels) are associated with depression. In one study based on the determination of serum and erythrocyte folate levels of 2,526 nondepressed, 301 depressed, and 121 dysthymic (characterized by persistent depression) subjects, the authors concluded that serum and erythrocyte folate levels were significantly lower in depressed subjects compared to nondepressed subjects. The authors concluded that low folate status was detectable in depressed members of the general U.S. population.[28] In a Finnish population study based on 2,806 participants (1,328 men and 1,478 women, aged forty-five to seventy-four), the authors also concluded that people who consumed the most folate had a 55 percent lower chance of developing melancholic depressive symptoms than those who consumed the least amount of folate.[29]

The best way to prevent folate deficiency is to eat a balanced diet. Many fruits, vegetables (especially green leafy vegetables), nuts, poultry, meat, seafood, rice, grains, and cereals (fortified with folate) are a good dietary source of folate. The recommended daily allowance for folate is 400 micrograms per day for adults and 600 micrograms per day for pregnant women. Meeting this dietary guideline is sufficient to avoid depression due to folate deficiency. In one study based on 141 Japanese women (aged eighteen to twenty-eight years), the authors concluded that the risk of depression was higher in women who consumed less than 240 micrograms of folate per day.[30] Just eating one cup of cooked spinach will provide approximately 250 micrograms of folate. Therefore, the dietary requirement of folate can be easily fulfilled by eating a balanced diet.

Although the relation between low folate and higher risk of depression is well reported in the medical literature, the relationship between other B vitamins and depression is not well established. In one study based on hemodialysis patients, the authors observed low serum folate and low vitamin B_{12} in depressed subjects.[31] In another study based on 669 older Chinese adults (aged fifty-five years and older), the authors observed lower serum folate levels (mean: 21.5 nmol/L) in depressed subjects compared to subjects with no depression (mean: 24.0 nmol/L). In addition, vitamin B_{12} deficiency increased the risk of depression in these older Chinese subjects.[32] However,

> Low serum or erythrocyte folate levels are found more in depressed people than in the normal population.

there are other studies reporting no correlation between lower serum vitamin B_{12} levels and depression. The daily recommended intake of this vitamin is 2.4 micrograms, but a slightly higher level is recommended for pregnant women (2.6 micrograms) and lactating mothers (2.8 micrograms). Although vitamin

B_{12} deficiency may not cause depression, folate and/or vitamin B_{12} deficiency is associated with megaloblastic anemia. Fruits and vegetables do not contain vitamin B_{12}, except cereals fortified with both folate and vitamin B_{12}. However, meat, poultry, and dairy products are rich in vitamin B_{12}. Like folate, vitamin B_{12} is water soluble.

Vitamin C and Mood

Vitamin C is the major water-soluble antioxidant present in the blood, and the recommended daily allowance is 90 mg for males and 75 mg for females who are nonsmokers. Smokers need higher amounts of vitamin C. Vitamin C deficiency is classically associated with scurvy, but today vitamin C deficiency is rare among the healthy U.S. population. The normal range of vitamin C is 28.4–84 micromoles/L in serum, but lower than normal levels may be observed in elderly and hospitalized patients. Smokers may have lower than normal serum levels of vitamin C. In general, values below 11.4 micromoles/L are indicative of significant vitamin C deficiency. Low serum vitamin C levels may be associated with mood disorders because vitamin C is involved in neuronal transmission and neurotransmitter metabolism, and its cerebrospinal fluid concentration is approximately three times higher than serum concentrations. Subnormal concentrations of vitamin C in the cerebrospinal fluid and brain adversely affect mood, but normalizing serum vitamin C concentrations restores mood. In one study, the authors reported that when hospitalized patients with subnormal vitamin C serum levels (mean: 16.3 micromoles/L) were supplemented with a 500 mg vitamin C tablet twice a day for seven days, the mean serum level of vitamin C was increased to normal levels (mean: 71.0 micromoles/L), which was also associated with significant mood improvement in these patients.[33] In another study based on 322 older patients, the authors observed that patients with vitamin C deficiency (serum vitamin C concentrations below 11 micromoles/L) had significantly increased symptoms of depression compared to those with normal concentrations. Older age, smoking, male gender, and tissue inflammation were associated with lower vitamin C concentrations.[34]

Although vitamin C deficiency is associated with mood disorders, vitamin D has no effect on mood. In one study, the authors observed that administration of a 500 mg vitamin C tablet twice a day was associated with improved mood in acutely hospitalized patients with below-normal concentrations of vitamin C, but supplementing vitamin D in patients with low vitamin D status had no significant effect on mood.[35] In another study involving eighty subjects, the authors observed that individuals with generalized anxiety disorder had significantly lower blood levels of not only vitamin C but also other antioxidant vitamins (vitamins A and E) in comparison to healthy subjects. After dietary supplement of these vitamins for six weeks, a significant reduction in anxiety and depression was observed in these subjects. The authors concluded that supplementing antioxidant vitamins may be useful in patients with stress-induced psychiatric disorders.[36] Vitamin C may also act as an antidepressant. Vitamin C supplement may be an effective adjuvant agent in treating pediatric major depression along with the antidepressant fluoxetine.[37]

Vitamin D and Depression

As mentioned earlier, the role of dietary vitamin D deficiency in causing depression is controversial. In one study based on 81,189 women (aged fifty to seventy-nine) and three years of follow-up, the authors observed that women who reported a total intake of 800 IU or more of vitamin D (estimated from dietary history) per day had a much lower prevalence of depression compared to women who reported a total intake of less than 100 IU of vitamin D daily. In further analysis limited to women without evidence of depression at the beginning of the study, the authors observed that women with an intake of 400 IU or more of vitamin D per day had a 20 percent lower risk of depression symptoms at year 3 compared to women who consumed less than 100 IU of vitamin D per day from diet.[38] In another study based on eighty elderly subjects, the authors reported that low vitamin D levels in serum (20 ng/mL or less) were associated with low mood and some impairment in cognitive function.[39] However, other studies did not report any direct association between vitamin D and depression. It is best to get adequate vitamin D (daily recommended intake: 600 IU per day for both males and females and 800 IU per day for people over seventy years of age) from diet because studies indicate that taking vitamin D supplements may not be useful. Moreover, unlike vitamin C and vitamin B complex, which are water soluble, vitamin D is fat soluble. Therefore, high vitamin D levels are associated with adverse effects, and vitamin D supplements should be taken only under medical advice. Dietary sources of vitamin D are listed in table 8.2.

Both vitamin D and calcium are needed for healthy bones. However, in one study based on Korean woman, the authors observed an association between low dietary calcium intake and self-reported depression.[40] In another study based on 1,057 women, the authors observed that women with a median dietary vitamin D intake of 706 IU per day had a much lower risk of suffering from premenstrual syndrome (PMS; symptoms include mood swings, depression, irritability, headache, and abdominal cramping) than women with a daily vitamin D intake of 112 IU, which was well below the recommended daily intake of vitamin D. Moreover, adequate intake of calcium from dietary sources (median: 1,283 mg/day) showed a 30 percent lower chance of getting PMS compared to women with low dietary intake of calcium (median: 529 mg/day). Intake of skim or low-fat milk may also reduce the risk of PMS. Because calcium and vitamin D may also reduce the risk of osteoporosis and certain cancers, women should get adequate amount of calcium from their diet.[41] The daily recommended intake of calcium is 1,000 mg for both men and women, and 1,200 mg for men and women over seventy years of age. Milk, cheese, and yogurt are a good source of calcium, but a few vegetables such as broccoli and kale also have calcium.

> Adequate intake of vitamin D and calcium from food sources (1,200 mg of calcium and 400 IU of vitamin D per day) significantly reduces the risk of incidence of PMS.

Magnesium and Depression

Magnesium is one of the most essential minerals in the human body which plays a vital role in many physiological processes. Dietary magnesium deficiency is associated with depression. In one study based on 2,320 Finnish men (aged forty-two to sixty-one years), the authors observed that participants with adequate dietary magnesium intake had a 51 percent lower risk of depression than people with low dietary magnesium intake. The authors concluded that low dietary intake of magnesium may increase the risk of depression.

The mechanism by which magnesium may cause depression is very complex. Magnesium interacts with the hypothalamic-pituitary-adrenal axis (HPA axis) and may reduce the release of the stress hormone cortisol. Magnesium is associated with the synthesis of gamma-aminobutyric acid (GABA), which has a calming effect on the brain. Moreover, magnesium interacts with the glutamate neurotransmitter receptor N-methyl-D-aspartic acid (NMDA receptor).[42] In another study involving 8,894 U.S. adults, the authors observed that low dietary intake of magnesium (less than 184 mg/day) was associated with depression only in subjects younger than sixty-five years of age.[43] The daily recommended intake of magnesium is 420 mg for males (age thirty-one years or more) and 320 mg for non-pregnant females. Diet is a good source of magnesium (see table 8.2).

> Low dietary intake of magnesium may be associated with depression only in subjects younger than sixty-five years of age.

Selenium and Mood

Selenium is a micronutrient (daily recommended intake: 55 micrograms) required for the optimal functioning of several selenoproteins (such as glutathione peroxidase) involved in antioxidant defense within the brain and the nervous system. Lower selenium levels may be a risk factor for depression because adequate activity of glutathione peroxidase is needed for proper antioxidant status of the brain. To date, mood is the clearest example of psychological functioning that is affected by selenium. Several studies have reported poorer mood in people due to low dietary intake of selenium.[44] In one study, the authors reported a higher risk of major depression in women with a low daily intake of selenium.[45] In another study based on 978 young adults (aged seventeen to twenty-five), the authors observed that participants with the lowest serum selenium concentrations (62.0 ng/mL) and, to a lesser extent, those with the highest serum selenium concentrations (110.0 ng/mL) had significantly greater adjusted depressive symptoms than people with mid-range serum selenium concentrations (82–85 ng/mL). The authors concluded that in young adults, the optimal serum selenium levels are 82–85 ng/mL for the best positive mood, but too much selenium may cause mood disorders.[46]

Omega-3 Fatty Acids for Physical and Mental Health Well-Being

Omega-3 fatty acids are polyunsaturated fatty acids that are found in abundance in fish and seafood. These fatty acids have many health benefits. The American Heart Association recommends consumption of fish at least twice a week for the general population for good health. The World Health Organization recommends regular fish consumption (one to two servings per week, providing 200–500 mg of omega-3 fatty acids per serving) for the general population. The two major omega-3 fatty acids are eicosapentaenoic acid (20-carbon fatty acid with five double bonds) and docosahexaenoic acid (22-carbon fatty acid with six double bonds). Vegetarians are recommended to get alpha-linolenic acid from plant sources because a small amount of this fatty acid is metabolized into eicosapentaenoic acid. Many studies have shown that eating fish on a regular basis has protective effects against cardio-vascular diseases, including heart attack. Eating fish also produces a better blood lipid profile and reduces inflammation, thus having a protective effect against rheumatoid arthritis. Moreover, intake of omega-3 fatty acid reduces the risk of cancer and various psychiatric illnesses, including depression, and improves cognitive function in the elderly. Eating fish may also provide protection against Alzheimer's disease.[47]

Although fish is very good for health, some fish living in contaminated rivers and lakes may be high in mercury (organic methyl mercury because bacteria converts inorganic mercury into this form) and polychlorinated biphenyls (PCB), which are industrial pollutants. Predator fish are also high in mercury because they eat small fish contaminated with mercury. Therefore, people should avoid or consume fish high in mercury infrequently (once a week or less). However, omega-3 fatty acids have positive effects on fetal growth and overall development. As a result, the Food and Drug Administration (FDA) recommends that pregnant women eat two to three servings of fish per week, but they should completely avoid fish high in mercury (see table 8.3).

The Environmental Protection Agency (EPA) has determined that a safe methyl mercury intake level for a pregnant woman is 6–8 micrograms per day or up to 64 micrograms per week. However, eating one serving of orange roughy has approximately 80 micrograms of mercury, and one serving of yellowfin tuna may contain 49 micrograms of mercury. One serving of lobster has 47 micrograms of mercury. However, scallops (8 micrograms), shrimp (less than 1 microgram), clams (13 micrograms), and squid (11 micrograms) are a decent source of omega-3 fatty acids and low in mercury.[48] The FDA recommends eating a variety of fish, and children can also eat one to two servings of fish starting at age two. However, eating too much fish, especially fish high in mercury, may increase the risk of mercury toxicity. Studies have shown that ethnic

> Eating two to three servings of fish is good for your health, but it is advisable to avoid fish high in mercury or consume such fish infrequently.

Table 8.3. Omega-3 fatty acid content and mercury content of some popular fish and seafoods

Fish/Seafood High to Moderate in Omega-3 Fatty Acid and Also Low in-Mercury	Fish/Seafood with Adequate Omega-3 Fatty Acid and Low to Moderate Mercury	Fish/Seafood with Adequate Omega-3 Fatty Acid but Elevated Mercury (above 30 micrograms/ 4 oz. serving)	Fish High in Mercury (above 100 micrograms/serving): Pregnant Women, Lactating Mothers, and Children Should Avoid
• Anchovies, herring, shad • Salmon (Atlantic, king, pink, coho, and sockeye) • Sardines: Atlantic and Pacific • Mackerel (Atlantic and Pacific, but not king) • Flounder • Pollock (Atlantic) • Tuna (light, canned) • Oysters (Pacific) • Clams • Halibut	• Grouper • Snapper • Cod (Atlantic and Pacific) • Plaice • Sole • Seabass • Catfish • Tilapia • Scallop • Haddock • Hake • Crayfish • Shrimp • Trout (freshwater) • Red snapper • Crabs (blue, king, snow, queen, and Dungeness)	• Tuna (bluefin, yellowfin, and albacore) • Tuna (white, canned) • Lobster • Marlin • Orange roughy*	• King mackerel • Swordfish • Tilefish (Gulf of Mexico) • Shark

*Although orange roughy is not on the FDA list to avoid by pregnant woman, lactating mothers, and children, this fish has high mercury content (approximately 80 micrograms per four ounces of cooked fish), and this author recommends avoiding this fish during pregnancy/lactation.

populations such as Asians who eat fish more frequently than others tend to have higher blood mercury levels. In one study involving Brazilian Amazon subjects, who eat fish very frequently (average of 7.4 fish meals per week), 19.9 percent of subjects showed mercury levels in their urine that were higher than the highest acceptable level.[49]

Eating adequate amounts of fish is good for mental health. Studies have shown that the prevalence of depression is lower in countries where people eat more fish. In one study, the authors performed a meta-analysis of data collected from twenty-six reports and concluded that eating fish on a regular basis can reduce the risk of depression.[50] In another study based on 2,124 men and women who were undergraduate students, the authors observed that subjects who ate fish more frequently had lower risk of depression than people who almost never ate fish. Compared to subjects who almost never ate fish, subjects who ate fish one to two times per month showed a 22 percent lower risk of depression, and people who ate fish two to three times per week had a 30 percent lower risk of depression. The association between eating fish and a lower risk of depression was stronger in women than men. The mechanism by which omega-3 fatty acids lower the risk of depression is not completely understood. However, omega-3 fatty acids may increase serotonergic neuro-transmission, modulate dopaminergic functions, and regulate corticotropin releasing factor, which is directly related to response of the HPA axis to stress. Moreover, low blood eicosapentaenoic acid is associated with poor mood because eicosapentaenoic acid is positively associated with cerebral blood flow in the prefrontal cortex, suggesting an increased oxygenation level, thereby improving mood.[51]

Eating fish is also beneficial to both children and the elderly. In a study based on 584 children (seven to nine years old), the authors observed that children who consumed two fish meals per week, including one fatty fish meal, were less likely to have emotional-behavioral problems including social problems, attention problems, rule-breaking problems, and aggressive behavior problems than children who did not consume any fish.[52] Mood disorders are associated with low levels of eicosapentaenoic acid and docosa-hexanoic acid. In adolescents, lower red blood cell eicosapentaenoic acid and docosahexanoic acid may increase the risk of developing bipolar disorder.[53] Eating fish is also beneficial to older people (3,718 subjects studied, aged sixty-five years and older) because eating fish has protec-tive effects against age-related dementia and Alzheimer's disease. Eating fish once a week reduced the risk of dementia by 10 percent compared to not eating fish at all. Eating fish twice a week further reduced the risk by 13 percent.[54]

> Eating fish even once a week significantly reduces the risk of depression, but eating two to three servings of fish as recommended by dietary guidelines reduces the risk of depression further. Women get more mental health benefits from eating fish than men. Eating fish also reduces the risk of age-related dementia and Alzheimer's disease in elderly people.

Tryptophan and Mood

Tryptophan is an essential amino acid that is a precursor of serotonin, an important neurotransmitter associated with mood. Tryptophan must be obtained from the diet because the human body cannot synthesize this essential amino acid. Reduced brain serotonin levels cause depression, irritability, impulsive behavior, aggression, poor judgment, and poor sleep quality. In humans, serotonin is synthesized from tryptophan by the action of two enzymes. In the first step, tryptophan is converted into 5-hydroxy tryptophan by the action of the enzyme tryptophan hydroxylase. Then another enzyme, aromatic amino acid decarboxylase, converts 5-hydroxy tryptophan into serotonin. Therefore, low blood levels of tryptophan due to inadequate dietary intake may be associated with low brain tryptophan levels, which eventually result in lower brain serotonin levels. As a result, adequate intake of tryptophan is essential for emotional well-being and good sleep quality. In general, eating a balanced diet is sufficient to maintain a healthy blood tryptophan level.

Studies have shown that a tryptophan-rich diet is associated with emotional well-being. In one study based on thirty-eight subjects (twenty-eight women and ten men), the authors observed that a tryptophan-rich hydrolyzed protein diet was associated with mood improvement and reduced secretion of salivary cortisol in response to stress in study subjects, indicating both stress relief and mood improvement following a tryptophan-rich diet.[55] In another study based on twenty-five healthy young adults, the authors observed that subjects who consumed more dietary tryptophan showed a much lower risk of depression and anxiety.[56] However, in one study, the authors did not observe any association between dietary tryptophan intake and mood.[57]

The conflicting results between a tryptophan-rich diet and mood is due to the fact that the transport of tryptophan from blood to brain depends not only on blood concentrations of tryptophan but also on blood concentrations of six other large neutral amino acids (LNAAs; tyrosine, phenylalanine, leucine, isoleucine, valine, and methionine), which compete with tryptophan for the blood-brain barrier for transport into the brain. Dietary carbohydrate intake is associated with increased insulin production, which results in insulin-mediated decreases in blood LNAA concentrations because insulin facilitates uptake of LNAA by tissues but not tryptophan. As a result, blood tryptophan levels remain unchanged, but the tryptophan-to-LNAA ratio in the blood is increased. This phenomenon facilitates transport of tryptophan to the brain, which eventually increases brain serotonin synthesis. In contrast, after eating a high-protein diet, LNAA concentrations in the blood are increased because protein diets contain significantly more LNAA compared to tryptophan. Therefore, the tryptophan-to-LNAA ratio in the blood is decreased, which results in lower tryptophan uptake by the brain. In one study, the authors showed that after eating an American breakfast high in carbohydrates (waffles, maple syrup, orange juice, brewed coffee, granulated sugar), the plasma tryptophan-to-LNAA ratio was increased, but when the same subjects on a different day ate an American breakfast high in protein (turkey, ham, eggs, cheese, butter, and grapefruit), a significantly lower serum tryptophan-to-LNAA ratio was observed. The median differences were 54 percent, indicating a significant effect of diet on the plasma tryptophan-to-LNAA ratio.[58]

Foods rich in tryptophan include nuts (cashews, peanuts, walnuts, almonds), seeds (sesame, pumpkin, sunflower), soybeans, chicken, turkey breast, other meats, fish (salmon, cod, tuna, haddock), shellfish, milk, yogurt, eggs, and grains such as wheat, rice, and corn. In general, healthy people maintain adequate blood levels of tryptophan and desire snacks rich in carbohydrates for mood improvement due to increases in the blood tryptophan-to-LNAA ratio that facilitate tryptophan uptake by the brain. As a result, the brain synthesizes more serotonin from tryptophan, which results in mood improvement. This phenomenon is called "carbohydrate craving," which may also be observed more frequently in subjects suffering from seasonal affective disorder (winter blues or winter depression), premenstrual syndrome, obesity associated with carbohydrate snacking (such as potato chips or pastries), and smoking withdrawal. In addition, decreases in brain tryptophan, and hence serotonin, caused by a low-carbohydrate weight loss diet may be responsible for binge eating in female dieters. Eating carbohydrate-rich snack foods restores brain serotonin levels and improves mood. In one study based on thirty-seven healthy subjects, the authors observed that consuming a carbohydrate drink rich in sugar was associated with a higher plasma tryptophan-to-LNAA ratio and lower cortisol response during stress compared to subjects who did not consume a sugary carbohydrate drink. The authors concluded that consuming a carbohydrate-rich drink can significantly lower stress by boosting serotonin levels in the brain due to increased tryptophan uptake from the blood.[59]

Although the easiest way to increase brain serotonin levels is to eat candy high in sugar or drink a sugar-containing beverage, it is better to eat snacks containing complex carbohydrates such as a breakfast cereal bar, oatmeal, whole grain crackers, biscuits, bread, low-fat cake, fruits, and so forth for

In general, a high-carbohydrate, low-protein diet is effective for stress release, but a diet high in carbohydrates is also associated with weight gain. Therefore, it is best to eat snacks high in complex carbohydrates rather than eating candy, which is high in sugar, or drinking a sugary beverage for boosting mood. Eating dark chocolate also improves mood.

mood boosting. It is also important to know that excess carbohydrates (most commonly simple carbohydrates) and sugar are converted into fat; as a result, eating foods high in carbohydrates may increase the risk of weight gain. Snacking on chocolate, especially dark chocolate, also improves mood (see chapter 10).

Overall, many reports in the medical literature indicate the beneficial effects of adequate dietary intake of tryptophan for emotional well-being. Although certain foods such as cheese, meat, fruits, and vegetables contain serotonin, such dietary serotonin is not available to the central nervous system because dietary serotonin cannot cross the blood-brain barrier. In contrast, dietary tryptophan, the precursor of serotonin, can cross the blood-brain barrier and is then converted into serotonin. Therefore, a diet poor in tryptophan may induce depression. A tryptophan-rich diet is important not only for healthy people but also for people who are susceptible to depression, as well as people with posttraumatic stress disorder, attention deficit disorder, Parkinson's disease, Alzheimer's disease, and schizophrenia. Moreover, tryptophan helps one to feel satisfied after eating and promotes relaxation as well as restful sleep. However, in addition to a tryptophan-rich diet, it is very important to get adequate vitamin B_6 from the diet because this vitamin is helpful in boosting the serotonergic neurotransmission system. Therefore, adequate intake of both tryptophan and vitamin B_6 is important for physical and mental well-being.[60]

Bananas contain serotonin, but such dietary serotonin cannot cross the blood-brain barrier. However, bananas are a good snack food because they are rich in B vitamins, including vitamin B_6, which improves mood indirectly by boosting serotonergic neurotransmission. Moreover, bananas are rich in carbohydrates, which promote the uptake of tryptophan by the brain. Serotonin is also effective in promoting good sleep quality, along with melatonin, a neurohormone. Tryptophan is a precursor of serotonin, and serotonin is converted into melatonin by the action of two enzymes: N-acetyl cysteine and hydroxy indole-O-methyltransferase. Serotonin is also metabolized by the monoamine oxidase enzyme and alcohol dehydrogenase enzyme into 5-hydroxyindole acetic acid. Conventional wisdom suggests that drinking milk at night improves sleep quality. Milk is a good source of tryptophan, but another milk protein, alpha-lactalbumin, boosts uptake of tryptophan by the brain. Moreover, the body breaks down alpha-lactalbumin into tryptophan and cysteine. Therefore, scientific research confirms the conventional wisdom that consuming milk or milk products such as cheese at night promotes good sleep quality.[61]

Tryptophan depletion increases aggression in women during the premenstrual phase. In one study based on thirty-seven women who were treated with tryptophan supplements and thirty-four women who did not receive such supplements, the authors observed that mood swings, tension, and irritability during premenstrual dysphoria (severe symptoms of premenstrual symptoms affecting 3–8 percent of women) were significantly reduced in women who received tryptophan supplements, indicating usefulness of tryptophan in reducing symptoms of premenstrual syndrome.[62] Aggressive men are more prone to plasma tryptophan depletion. In one study, tryptophan supplements (3 grams per day) were associated with decreased quarrelsome behavior and increased agreeableness more significantly in men than women. The authors concluded that tryptophan supplements enhance socially constructive behaviors among quarrelsome people.[63] However, it is important to note that tryptophan supplements may cause severe side effects, including heartburn, severe stomach pain, diarrhea, loss of appetite, drowsiness, lightheadedness, visual problems, sexual dysfunction, and others. Therefore, do not take tryptophan supplements unless advised by a physician.

> Getting adequate tryptophan from diet is the best approach for physical and emotional well-being. Tryptophan supplements may cause serious side effects. Do not take tryptophan supplements unless advised by your physician.

TEA AND COFFEE FOR STRESS MANAGEMENT

Drinking tea is good for stress management. In one study based on seventy-five healthy volunteers divided between two groups (subjects in one group drank four cups of black tea per day while subjects in another group consumed the same amount of caffeinated drinks, the placebo), the authors observed that subjects who drank black tea every day for six weeks had better subjective mood and lower salivary cortisol levels in response to stress compared to people who consumed the placebo drink. The authors concluded that drinking black tea reduces stress.[64] Drinking coffee can also reduce stress. In another study, the authors observed that job demand influenced the association between coffee consumption and anxious mood in men, and those who experienced high job demand drank more coffee on days when they felt highly stressed and anxious. In contrast, women (but not men) who enjoyed high social support at work felt more relaxed on days when they drank more tea.[65]

In a paper based on a meta-analysis of seventeen studies, the authors concluded that both tea and coffee are effective for stress management. Moreover, drinking tea or coffee reduces the risk of depression. The main active components of tea are L-theanine and caffeine, which (either alone or in combination) improve attention span, alertness, and mood. Tea is also rich in many polyphenolic antioxidants, and one such compound, epigallocatechin, not only is a powerful antioxidant that protects the brain from neurodegenerative diseases but also may modulate GABA-A receptors (receptors to which benzodiazepine drugs bind and produce an anxiolytic effect), thus reducing anxiety levels after drinking tea. Though tea contains many polyphenolic antioxidant compounds, the precise role of the individual polyphenols in improving mood is not well understood. Caffeine, which is also found in abundance in coffee, can reduce depression and elevate mood. However, drinking decaffeinated coffee is not associated with lower risk of depression.[66]

> Both tea and coffee drinking can reduce stress. Men drink more coffee in response to higher job-related stress, while women with good social support at work report better mood when they drink more tea.

Although drinking coffee in moderation (two to three cups daily) improves mood, emotional well-being, and alertness and also reduces the risk of depression (15 percent reduced risk of depression based on a study of 50,730 women) and suicide (45 percent lower risk of suicide based on a study of 73,820 women), consuming a high amount of coffee is associated with feelings of anxiety, increased blood pressure, sleeplessness, insomnia, and tachycardia. Usually consuming 200–300 mg of caffeine per day is considered safe (the upper limit is probably 400 mg daily, which is four to five cups of coffee), but pregnant women should drink less coffee or switch to decaffeinated coffee.

Coffee drinking in moderation protects from neurodegenerative diseases such as cognitive decline, Alzheimer's disease, and Parkinson's disease. Moreover, coffee drinking in moderation reduces all-cause mortality and protects against cardiovascular diseases, type 2 diabetes, and stroke.[67] However, drinking coffee in excess may be harmful. In one study based on 43,727 participants and a seventeen-year median follow-up, the authors observed a higher mortality rate in men and women younger than fifty-five years who consumed more than twenty-eight cups of coffee per week (more than four cups a day). However, no such effect was observed in men and women older than fifty-five years. The authors concluded that younger men and women should avoid heavy coffee consumption.[68] Tea also has many physical health benefits. The health benefits of tea and coffee are summarized in table 8.4. The major health benefits of tea and coffee are due to the presence of many antioxidants in both drinks. Interestingly, one cup of coffee contains more antioxidants than one cup of tea. However, the amount of caffeine is much lower in tea than coffee.

Although there are no established guidelines for drinking tea, daily consumption of coffee should be restricted to two or three cups per day. Drinking up to four cups daily may be safe, but drinking more than four cups per day (more than twenty-eight cups per week) may be harmful for men and women younger than fifty-five years of age. Pregnant women should drink less coffee or drink decaffeinated coffee. It is better to drink filtered coffee over instant coffee or espresso because filtered coffee contains only negligible amounts of kahweol and cafestol (these compounds bind to the coffee filter), which may increase serum cholesterol levels.

Table 8.4. Physical health benefits of tea and coffee

Health Benefits of Tea	Health Benefits of Coffee
• Reduced risk of cardiovascular diseases, including heart attack • Reduced risk of stroke • Reduced risk of type 2 diabetes • Reduced risk of cancer • Boosted immune system • Reduced risk of neurodegenerative diseases, including age-related dementia, Alzheimer's disease, and Parkinson's disease • Green tea may be effective in reducing obesity • Green tea may help with bone health	• Reduced risk of type 2 diabetes • Reduced risk of cardiovascular diseases • Reduced risk of cancer • Prevention of gallstones and diseases of the gallbladder • Reduced chance of gout • Laxative effect of coffee • Reduced risk of neurodegenerative diseases, including age-related dementia, Alzheimer's disease, and Parkinson's disease

HEALTH BENEFITS OF NUTS

Eating nuts is good for your health. Based on a study involving 120,852 men and women aged fifty-five to sixty-nine years and ten years of follow-up, the authors observed that total nut intake was associated with a low mortality rate from cardiovascular diseases, respiratory diseases, cancer, diabetes, neurodegenerative diseases, and other causes. When comparing those consuming 0.1 to less than 5 grams of nuts daily, the all-cause mortality risk was lowered by 12 percent compared to subjects who did not consume any nuts. The mortality risk was further reduced by 26 percent in people who consumed 5–10 grams of nuts per day. However, peanut butter did not reduce the mortality rate.[69]

Various nuts such as hazelnuts, peanuts, pistachios, kola nuts, cashew, and walnuts are energy-dense foods associated with high calories. Nevertheless, nuts have high nutritional value due to the presence of polyphenolic antioxidants, protein, vitamins (vitamin E, folic acid, vitamin B$_6$, and niacin), magnesium, potassium, copper, and phytosterols (stigmasterol, campesterol, and sitosterol). Therefore, consuming nuts is associated with many health benefits, including lowering cholesterol and protecting against cardiovascular diseases, diabetes, inflammation, and cancer. Although high in nutrients and high in calories, nuts are rich in unsaturated fats; as a result, eating a handful of nuts even daily does not cause weight gain.[70]

> Eating a handful of nuts even a few times a week has many health benefits, including reduced risk of cardiovascular diseases and lower blood cholesterol. Although nuts are high in calories, eating nuts on a regular basis is not associated with weight gain.

Eating nuts may indirectly boost mood. Walnuts are rich in alpha-linolenic acid, and eating walnuts reduces blood pressure during stress.[71] Cashew nuts are a good source of tryptophan and magnesium. Therefore, eating cashew nuts may improve mood and reduce anxiety levels. Studies have shown that adherence to the Mediterranean dietary pattern, with adequate intake of fruits, nuts, vegetables, cereals, legumes, and fish, is useful in reducing stress and preventing depression.[72]

ANTIOXIDANTS PRESENT IN FOODS

In general fruits, vegetables, nuts, tea, coffee, and spices contain many useful antioxidants that have many health benefits. Although spices have the highest amounts of antioxidants, spices are not a major source of antioxidants in the diet because relatively small amounts of spices are used in cooking. Moreover, vitamin C, vitamin E, and beta-carotenes found abundantly in fruits and vegetables have antioxidant properties. Vitamin C is the only water-soluble antioxidant vitamin, which is the first defense of the body against oxidative stress. Certain alcoholic beverages such as beer and wine also contain useful antioxidants (see chapter 9), as does chocolate (see chapter 10).

More than twenty-five thousand bioactive compounds are present in human diet, and many of these compounds have antioxidant properties. Most bioactive compounds present in the typical diet are derived from fruits, vegetables, and nuts (plant foods); these chemicals are collectively called "phytochemicals" and can be broadly classified as phenolic compounds, nitrogen-containing compounds, organosulfur compounds, phytosterols, and carotenoids. The majority of phytochemicals are also antioxidants, but phenolic compounds, including phenolic acid, flavonoids, stilbene, coumarin, and tannins, have especially excellent antioxidant properties. In general, berry fruits (blackberries, strawberries, cranberries, blueberries, raspberries, etc.) are very high in antioxidants. Other fruits rich in antioxidants include grapes, apples, mangoes, prunes, oranges, plums, guavas, pineapples, bananas, kiwifruit, and many more, because all fruits commonly consumed in the United States are rich in antioxidants. In general, eating whole fruits is healthier than drinking fruit juices because fresh fruits also contain dietary fibers, which have many health benefits. If you prefer fruit juices over fruit, it is better to drink freshly squeezed fruit juices, as opposed to commercially available fruit juices, because sugars are often added to commercial fruit juices.

> Eating whole fruit has more health benefits than drinking fruit juices because fruits are also a good source of dietary fibers.

Vegetables are also a good source of antioxidants. Interestingly, cooking vegetables in many instances increases the antioxidant value of food. This may be due to softening of the matrix and increased extractability of antioxidants after cooking. Therefore, cooked vegetables often have higher antioxidant capacity than raw vegetables. The antioxidant capacity of carrots, spinach, mushrooms, broccoli, potatoes, cabbage, tomatoes, and

> Cooking vegetables (steaming, boiling, or microwave cooking) increases their antioxidant capacity.

sweet potatoes is increased after cooking. In general, boiling or steaming is more effective in increasing the antioxidant capacity of vegetables than frying. Toasting wheat bread and bagels also increases their antioxidant capacity. Eating fruits and vegetables likewise reduces the oxidative stress in the body.[73]

The major antioxidants present in coffee include caffeic acid, chlorogenic acid, and dihydro-caffeic acid. The major antioxidants present in green tea include various catechins, such as epigallocatechin gallate, epigallocatechin, epicatechin gallate, and epicatechin, as well as quercetin, kaempferol, and myristicin. The major antioxidants present in black tea include theaflavins and thearubigins, which are produced from catechins during the fermentation process by which black tea is prepared from green tea leaves. However, black tea also contains some catechins, although much lower in quantity than in green tea. Polyphenolic antioxidants such as catechins and resveratrol are present in nuts. Red wine is also a good source of resveratrol.

CONCLUSION

Fruits, vegetables, tea, coffee, and nuts are full of antioxidants. In addition to many physical health benefits, these foods have mental health benefits because increased oxidative stress in the body is associated with depression, anxiety, and neurodegenerative diseases. Studies have shown that depression is associated with increased oxidative stress as reflected by higher concentrations of markers of oxidative stress such as F2 isoprostanes (a marker of lipid oxidation) and 8'-hydroxy-2'deoxyguanosine (a marker of DNA damage due to oxidation) in the blood and urine of depressed individuals. Many antioxidants present in food are absorbed from the gastrointestinal tract and reduce the oxidative stress of the body.[74] Moreover, vitamins and micronutrients present in fruits and vegetables are beneficial for both physical and mental health. In general, eating balanced meals every day containing adequate amounts of fruits and vegetables, whole grains, fish, poultry, meat, and low-fat or fat-free dairy products is good for physical and mental health.

9

Drinking in Moderation for Stress Relief

Fermentation of sugar by yeast, a process that produces a colorless liquid known as ethyl alcohol, or simply alcohol, was known to humans in prehistoric times. The first historical evidence of alcoholic beverages came from the archeological discovery of Stone Age beer jugs dating approximately ten thousand years ago. Egyptians probably consumed wine and beer approximately six thousand years ago and the Chinese around 5000 BC. In ancient India, an alcoholic beverage known as *sura* was mentioned in ancient ayurvedic texts written between 3000 and 2000 BC. In ancient Greece, wine making was common practice in 1700 BC. Hippocrates identified numerous medicinal properties of wine but was critical of drunkenness.[1] In ancient civilization, alcohol was used primarily to quench thirst because water was contaminated with bacteria. Beer was a drink for common people, while wine was the preferred drink of elites. However, in ancient Eastern civilization, drinking tea was more common for quenching thirst.

Professor Robert Dudley of the University of California, Berkeley, proposed a rationale for why humans drink in his "drunken monkey hypothesis." Primates, our ancestors several million years ago, used fruits as their major source of diet. Primates capable of detecting the smell of alcohol in ripe fruits (during the ripening of fruit, alcohol is produced from sugar by yeast present on the fruit skin) survived better due to natural selection. As a result, when humans evolved from primates one to two million years ago, a keen taste for alcohol probably became a part of their genetic makeup. Interestingly, even today, most humans consume alcohol with their evening meals.[2]

Alcohol is a double-edged sword, with many health benefits (including stress release) if consumed in moderation but a health hazard if consumed in excess. According to the U.S. National Survey, 57.1 percent of males and 47.5 percent of females are current drinkers. Unfortunately, an estimated 16.3 million Americans are heavy alcohol users (drinking five or more drinks on one occasion during five or more days in the past thirty days), and an estimated 60.9 million Americans are binge drinkers. The World Health Organization (WHO) estimates that 5.1 percent of the global burden of diseases and injuries are related to alcohol abuse. There is also a gender difference in alcohol consumption. Compared to men, more women are lifetime abstainers, they drink less, and they are less likely to engage in problem drinking. However, women, if drinking heavily, are more susceptible to alcohol-related adverse effects than men.[3]

GUIDELINES FOR CONSUMING ALCOHOL IN MODERATION

In order to derive the health benefits of alcohol, it is very important to consume alcohol in moderation following accepted guidelines. The United States Department of Agriculture (USDA) and the Department of Health and Human Services (DHS) jointly publish the *Dietary Guidelines for Americans* every five years, suggesting to Americans what constitutes a balanced diet. These guidelines also include the suggestion for drinking in moderation. However, alcohol is not a component in the USDA food pattern. The latest *Dietary Guidelines for Americans, 2015–2020*, the eighth edition, suggests that if alcohol is consumed, it should be consumed in moderation: up to one drink per day for women and up to two drinks per day for men—and only by adults of legal drinking age (twenty-one years or older).

Regardless of the nature of the drink, one standard alcoholic beverage contains approximately 14 grams (0.6 fluid ounces) of pure alcohol. Therefore, blood alcohol level can be calculated from the number of drinks consumed and the time spent consuming the alcohol.

One drink is defined by the guidelines as containing approximately 14 grams (0.6 fluid ounces) of pure alcohol. Although the alcohol content of alcoholic beverages varies widely, so does the serving size. Therefore, one alcoholic drink is equivalent to twelve fluid ounces of regular beer (5 percent alcohol), five fluid ounces of wine (12 percent alcohol), or 1.5 fluid ounces of 80 proof distilled spirits (40 percent alcohol). If light beer is consumed (4.2 percent alcohol), it should be considered 0.8 of a drink. Mixed drinks (including fruit drinks mixed with sprits) with more than 1.5 fluid ounces of alcohol should be considered as more than one drink. Here is the formula for calculating the drink equivalent: drink equivalent = volume of alcoholic beverage × alcohol content/0.6.

Energy drinks are gaining popularity among young adults as well as among underage drinkers. Studies have indicated that energy drinks may increase cravings for alcohol and the potential for binge drinking. When an energy drink, which often contains caffeine, is combined with alcohol, the desire to drink alcohol is more pronounced. Moreover, the pleasurable experience of drinking alcohol is enhanced by consuming energy drinks due to the presence of caffeine.[4] The Food and Drug Administration (FDA) recommends not mixing alcohol with caffeine—for example, not mixing rum with Coca-Cola. People who mix alcohol and caffeine may drink more alcohol and become more intoxicated than they realize, increasing the risk of adverse alcohol-related events.

> Combining alcohol with caffeine is not a safe practice. Therefore, it is strongly recommended not to mix rum with Coca-Cola.

High-Risk Drinking and Binge Drinking

The National Institute of Alcohol Abuse and Alcoholism (NIAAA) considers high-risk drinking as consuming four or more drinks in any day or eight or more drinks per week for women and five or more drinks in any day or fifteen or more drinks per week for men. Binge drinking is defined by the NIAAA as the consumption of five drinks in two hours for men and four drinks in the same time period for women. Binge drinking always produces a blood alcohol level exceeding the legal limit of driving (0.08 percent; 80 mg/dL).

A person's blood alcohol level can be estimated by the number of drinks consumed and the time spent during the drinking episode using the modified "Widmark formula" first developed by Swedish scientist Eric P. Widmark in 1932. The modified formula used in the United States to calculate blood alcohol is as follows: blood alcohol = (number of drinks × 3.1/weight in pounds × r)/0.015 × t, where r is 0.7 for men and 0.6 for women, and t is the number of hours elapsed during the drinking episode.

Using this formula, if a 160-pound man drinks two drinks in a one-hour period, his blood alcohol should be 0.04 percent. However, if the person is involved in binge drinking (five drinks in two hours), his estimated blood alcohol should be 0.11 percent (110 mg/dL), which exceeds the legal limit. For a woman weighing 140 pounds, binge drinking (four drinks in two hours) should produce a blood alcohol content of 0.12 percent (120 mg/dL). Binge drinking is both a health hazard and a safety hazard. Binge drinking is responsible for more than 50 percent of eighty thousand annual deaths caused by alcohol each year in the United States. A study found that 39 percent of full-time college students (aged eighteen to twenty-two) had engaged in binge drinking on at least one occasion in the past thirty days. The authors commented that binge drinking is a leading culprit in preventable deaths on college campuses.[5]

DRINKING IN MODERATION FOR STRESS RELIEF

It has been well documented in the medical literature that alcohol, if consumed in moderate amounts, is very effective in reducing stress and increasing happiness, conviviality, and pleasant carefree feelings. Low to moderate blood alcohol levels are also associated with euphoria. In addition, moderate drinking is effective in reducing tension and depression. Interestingly, abstainers have a higher rate of depression than moderate drinkers.[6] In general, the pleasant experience after drinking starts within ten to fifteen minutes of drinking and is associated with a blood alcohol level as low as 0.01–0.02 percent (10–20 mg/dL) and as high as 0.05 percent (50 mg/dL). Alcohol is known to cause a reduction in social inhibition, and such loss of inhibition after drinking is more significant in females compared to males.[7] However, alcohol consumption has also been implicated in sexual disinhibition and sexual risk taking.

> Moderate consumption of alcohol results in positive and prosocial behavior by improving decoding of positive emotions but impairing decoding of negative emotions. Moreover, alcohol enhances perceptions of the attractiveness of faces of the opposite sex.

Alcohol, when consumed in moderation, not only induces subjective relaxation, positive mood, and prosocial behavior but also facilitates recognition of happy faces. In one study, the authors observed that alcoholic beer produced positive subjective effects, including being talkative, open, and desiring to be with others rather than being alone. The positive effects of alcohol were more significant in women compared to men despite women showing lower blood alcohol levels than men (the maximal blood alcohol level was 35 mg/dL, 0.035 percent, in women versus 41 mg/dL, 0.041 percent, in men). In addition, the authors reported that low to moderate alcohol consumption improved decoding of positive emotion but impaired decoding of negative emotion. Moreover, pictures of explicit sexual content were rated more pleasant by study subjects after consuming beer but not after consuming nonalcoholic beer. Interestingly, women reported more pleasure in viewing sexual images compared to men, indicating that alcohol may decrease the inhibition of women with regard to sexual content.[8] However, another study reported more significant sexual disinhibition in men than women after drinking. Studies have also shown that alcohol consumption increases the attractiveness of faces of the opposite sex.[9]

However, all pleasurable effects of alcohol disappear with heavy drinking. At lower blood concentrations (10–40 mg/dL; 0.01–0.04 percent), alcohol acts as a stimulant and produces pleasurable effects, but at blood alcohol levels of 0.08 percent and above (80–125 mg/dL; 0.08–0.125 percent), people experience the negative effects of alcohol such as significant sedation and impairment.[10] This effect is known as the biphasic effect of alcohol or the biphasic blood alcohol curve.

Usually at a blood alcohol concentration above 0.06 percent, people start feeling the negative effects of alcohol such as mild impairment. This point is called the "point of diminished returns." The legal limit of driving is 0.08 percent because at any level above the legal limit, alcohol-induced impairment, including impaired driving skill, is well documented in the medical literature. Usually at a level of 0.15 percent (150 mg/dL), most people are severely impaired, and some people may experience a blackout. At a blood alcohol level of 0.3 percent, most people may lose consciousness, and a level of 0.4 percent or more may be fatal, but fatality may also be associated with a much lower blood alcohol level. Even drinking excessive alcohol on one occasion may cause alcohol poisoning, which, if not treated promptly, may be fatal. In one study, the authors reported that postmortem blood alcohol levels ranged from 136 to 608 mg/dL (0.14–0.61 percent) in thirty-nine individuals who died due to alcohol overdose. Most of those deceased were male.[11] The mechanism of death from alcohol poisoning is usually attributed to paralysis of the respiratory and circulatory centers in the brain, causing asphyxiation.

The effect of the number of alcoholic drinks consumed on blood alcohol levels and overall mood is summarized in table 9.1. In general, for an average man weighing 160 pounds, consuming one drink quickly should produce a blood alcohol level of 0.028, which is sufficient to enjoy the pleasurable effects of drinking. Alcohol is metabolized by the liver into acetaldehyde by the action of the enzyme alcohol dehydrogenase, and then acetaldehyde is further metabolized into acetate (which finally breaks down into carbon dioxide and water) by the action of another liver enzyme, aldehyde dehydrogenase. The metabolism of alcohol is initiated as soon as alcohol enters the bloodstream, and alcohol is eliminated at a rate of 0.015 percent per hour. Therefore, if a person consumes two alcoholic drinks in one hour, the estimated blood alcohol level should be 0.04 percent, which is also associated with stress relief and the pleasurable effects of alcohol. According to USDA guidelines, a man should consume up to two drinks per day. Interestingly, even one drink for a man weighing 160 pounds should cause relaxation and euphoria, and if he consumes two drinks in one hour, the blood alcohol level should still remain in the pleasurable zone.

> Just one drink can produce relaxation and the pleasurable effects of alcohol in a man, but if he wants to consume two drinks in one hour, the blood alcohol level will still remain in the pleasurable range.

For an average woman weighing 140 pounds, consuming one alcoholic drink rapidly should produce a blood alcohol level of 0.036. After drinking the same amount of alcohol and with the same body weight, women usually show a higher blood alcohol content than men because women have a lower amount of body water than men. According to the USDA guidelines, a woman should consume only one drink per day. Therefore, if a woman weighing 140 pounds drinks one alcoholic beverage quickly, her blood alcohol level should be 0.036 percent and then decline to 0.021 percent after one hour due to metabolism of alcohol by the liver. Even for a woman weighing 175 pounds, consuming one drink, with a projected blood alcohol level of 0.03 percent, should be associated with the pleasurable effects of alcohol.

> For women, consuming one drink is associated with the pleasurable effect of alcohol.

Food usually slows down the absorption of alcohol. In one study, ten healthy male volunteers consumed a moderate dosage of alcohol in the morning either on an empty stomach or immediately after breakfast (two cheese

Table 9.1. Effect of number of alcoholic drinks consumed on blood alcohol content and overall mood

Blood Alcohol Content	Mood	Approximate Number of Drinks (Male) Based on Body Weight	Approximate Number of Drinks (Female) Based on Body Weight
0.01% (10 mg/dL)	Initiation of stimulatory effect of alcohol, which is pleasurable.	125 lb.: 0.28 drink 150 lb.: 0.34 drink 175 lb.: 0.40 drink 200 lb.: 0.46 drink 250 lb.: 0.50 drink	100 lb.: 0.19 drink 125 lb.: 0.24 drink 150 lb.: 0.29 drink 175 lb.: 0.32 drink 200 lb.: 0.39 drink
0.02% (20 mg/dL)	Relaxation and mild euphoria.	125 lb.: 0.56 drink 150 lb.: 0.68 drink 175 lb.: 0.80 drink 200 lb.: 0.92 drink 250 lb.: 1.10 drinks	100 lb.: 0.38 drink 125 lb.: 0.48 drink 150 lb.: 0.58 drink 175 lb.: 0.64 drink 200 lb.: 0.78 drink
0.03% (30 mg/dl)	Relaxation, euphoria, buzz, and great social interaction.	125 lb.: 0.84 drink 150 lb.: 1.0 drink 175 lb.: 1.2 drinks 200 lb.: 1.4 drinks 250 lb.: 1.6 drinks	100 lb.: 0.57 drink 125 lb.: 0.72 drink 150 lb.: 0.87 drink 175 lb.: 1.0 drink 200 lb.: 1.2 drinks
0.04% (40 mg/dL)	Highest alcohol level associated with buzz. Such effects may be observed up to the 0.045% level in males.	125 lb.: 1.1 drinks 150 lb.: 1.4 drinks 175 lb.: 1.6 drinks 200 lb.: 1.8 drinks 250 lb.: 2.2 drinks	100 lb.: 0.92 drink 125 lb.: 1.1 drinks 150 lb.: 1.4 drinks 175 lb.: 1.6 drinks 200 lb.: 1.8 drinks
0.05% (50 mg/dl)	Mild impairment may be seen more in females than males.	125 lb.: 1.4 drinks 150 lb.: 1.7 drinks 175 lb.: 2.0 drinks 200 lb.: 2.3 drinks 250 lb.: 2.8 drinks	100 lb.: 1.2 drinks 125 lb.: 1.4 drinks 150 lb.: 1.7 drinks 175 lb.: 2.0 drinks 200 lb.: 2.3 drinks
0.06% (60 mg/dL)	At this point, the stimulatory effect of alcohol may disappear and a depressant effect may start.	125 lb.: 1.7 drinks 150 lb.: 2.0 drinks 175 lb.: 2.4 drinks 200 lb.: 2.8 drinks 250 lb.: 3.4 drinks	100 lb.: 1.4 drinks 125 lb.: 1.7 drinks 150 lb.: 2.0 drinks 175 lb.: 2.4 drinks 200 lb.: 2.8 drinks
0.07% (70 mg/dL)	More impairment and depressed feeling.	125 lb.: 2.0 drinks 150 lb.: 2.4 drinks 175 lb.: 2.8 drinks 200 lb.: 3.2 drinks 250 lb.: 3.9 drinks	100 lb.: 1.6 drinks 125 lb.: 2.0 drinks 150 lb.: 2.4 drinks 175 lb.: 2.8 drinks 200 lb.: 3.2 drinks
0.08% (80 mg/dL)	Legally drunk. At this blood alcohol level, alcohol clearly acts as a depressant, causing sedation.	125 lb.: 2.2 drinks 150 lb.: 2.7 drinks 175 lb.: 3.2 drinks 200 lb.: 3.7 drinks 250 lb.: 4.5 drinks	100 lb.: 1.8 drinks 125 lb.: 2.2 drinks 150 lb.: 2.7 drinks 175 lb.: 3.2 drinks 200 lb.: 3.7 drinks
0.10% (100 mg/dL)	Severe impairment and sedation as alcohol works as a depressant.	125 lb.: 2.8 drinks 150 lb.: 3.4 drinks 175 lb.: 4.0 drinks 200 lb.: 4.6 drinks 250 lb.: 5.6 drinks	100 lb.: 2.3 drinks 125 lb.: 2.8 drinks 150 lb.: 3.4 drinks 175 lb.: 4.0 drinks 200 lb.: 4.6 drinks

sandwiches, one boiled egg, orange juice, and fruit yogurt). Subjects who consumed alcohol on an empty stomach felt more intoxicated and showed higher blood alcohol levels (mean: 104 mg/dL) than subjects who consumed the same amount of alcohol after breakfast (mean: 67 mg/dL). Moreover, the metabolism of alcohol was faster in volunteers who consumed alcohol after breakfast compared to volunteers who consumed alcohol on an empty stomach. The authors concluded that food in the stomach before drinking not only reduces the peak blood alcohol concentration but also increases the elimination of alcohol from the body.[12] Interestingly, sipping instead of drinking also slows down absorption of alcohol.

> Consuming alcohol along with food reduces the peak blood alcohol level. For getting maximum pleasure out of drinking, it is advisable to drink alcohol with food and to sip rather than drink it.

If a person follows the guidelines of drinking in moderation, blood alcohol levels should be well below the legal limit for driving. This author suggests consuming one drink with food per hour, not exceeding two drinks in two hours, for males, but only one drink with food for females to avoid a DWI.

When Not to Drink

Certain populations should not drink at all. A woman planning to conceive as well as any pregnant woman should not drink at all because drinking during pregnancy may be associated with a poor outcome in pregnancy, including miscarriage, stillbirth, or significant birth defect (fetal alcohol syndrome). There is no safe amount of alcohol to consume during pregnancy. Moreover, there is no treatment for fetal alcohol syndrome.[13] In addition, during breastfeeding, a woman should refrain from drinking because alcohol is excreted in the breast milk and may harm a newborn baby.

> A pregnant woman or a woman who plans to get pregnant should not consume any amount of alcohol.

People who respond impulsively to negative emotions or have sensation-seeking behavior may exhibit greater willingness to consume alcohol in excess.[14] In one study based on 818 college students, the authors observed that shy individuals may drink more to fit in with others in a social situation, which may eventually contribute to greater risk for subsequent alcohol-related problems.[15] Although family studies have shown that the risk for alcohol abuse is four to ten times higher in the offspring of an alcoholic parent, it is important to remember that alcohol abuse is not an inheritable genetic disorder because no single gene related to alcohol abuse has been found. In fact, many genes contribute small amounts in making a person susceptible to alcohol abuse, and alcoholism is a result of complex interactions between genes and environment. Therefore, the offspring of an alcoholic may get more pleasure out of drinking, and such individuals should exercise caution when drinking. Alcohol also interacts with certain drugs, and usually warning labels are printed on drug bottles cautioning users not to consume any alcohol while taking the medication. Elderly individuals taking prescription medications must consult with their physician or pharmacist before consuming any amount of alcohol. Situations when drinking should be completely avoided are summarized in table 9.2.

Genetic Factors and Alcohol Intolerance

Alcohol is metabolized by the alcohol dehydrogenase enzyme into acetaldehyde, and then another liver enzyme, aldehyde dehydrogenase, converts acetaldehyde into acetate. Usually acetaldehyde is not detected in the blood due to very low concentrations, but in individuals with alcohol intolerance, acetaldehyde may be detected in the blood. An unpleasant reaction after consuming alcohol, such as facial flushing, nausea, headache, and rapid heartbeat, known as alcohol flushing or alcohol intolerance, is mostly due to acetaldehyde. Alcohol intolerance is not an allergic reaction but is related to a specific genetic mutation. Therefore, alcohol intolerance can only be avoided by not consuming alcohol. Usually this is observed more commonly in Asian populations, but individuals belonging to other racial groups may also have alcohol intolerance. Alcohol intolerance deters a person from drinking.

Alcohol intolerance may be related to a defective gene (*ALDH2*) encoding a poorly active or inactive aldehyde dehydrogenase enzyme. As a result, acetaldehyde produced after drinking is not metabolized, and acetaldehyde buildup in the blood causes an unpleasant reaction. The most common genetic mutation (single nucleotide polymorphism; SNP) is the *ALDH2*2* genetic allele that encodes a poorly active enzyme. This mutation is found among 45 percent of East Asians, including Han Chinese, Japanese, and Koreans, but rarely in other ethnic groups. It has been estimated that 540 million people worldwide (8 percent of the world population) carry this genetic mutation. If homozygous, this genetic mutation produces an inactive enzyme, but if heterozygous, it

Table 9.2. **When not to drink at all**

Population/Condition	Reason
Pregnant women	Alcohol crosses the placenta and harms the fetus (miscarriage, stillbirth, premature birth, and birth defects). Alcohol severely damages the brain of a developing fetus. No amount of alcohol is safe during pregnancy.
During breastfeeding	Alcohol is present in the breast milk and may cause harm to a newborn.
When taking certain medications	Certain antibiotics (erythromycin, metronidazole, sulfonamides, ornidazole, etc.), antihistamines (Benadryl, hydroxyzine, chlorpheniramine), pain medications (ibuprofen, naproxen, indomethacin, etc.), narcotic pain medications (codeine, oxycodone, hydrocodone, hydromorphone, tramadol, propoxyphene, etc.), sedatives (alprazolam, lorazepam, temazepam, diazepam, etc.), the blood pressure medicine felodipine, and other medications interact with alcohol causing toxicity. These medications also include some over-the-counter medications (especially cold medications).
Offspring of alcoholic parents	The risk for alcohol abuse is four to ten times higher in the offspring of an alcoholic parent. Although no single gene has been identified as related to alcohol abuse (susceptibility to alcohol abuse is due to complex interactions between multiple genes and the environment), the offspring of alcoholic parents may have a higher susceptibility to alcohol abuse, and these people should exercise caution during drinking.
Individuals with impulse control problems	Some people cannot control drinking behavior, and these people should avoid drinking.
Shy individuals	Shy individuals may drink more to overcome their shyness during social drinking and should be careful about their drinking habit.
Elderly people	Alcohol metabolism may be reduced in elderly people. Moreover, elderly people often take multiple medications. Therefore, elderly individuals are advised to talk to their physician before dinking in moderation.
People who do not drink for various reasons	Approximately 40 percent of Americans are abstainers. Current guidelines discourage these individuals from starting drinking in moderation for health reasons.

may have partial enzymatic activity. Genetic and epidemiological studies have shown that homozygous individuals have significant intolerance to alcohol, while heterozygous individuals have partial intolerance.[16]

Acetaldehyde buildup may also be due to a superactive alcohol dehydrogenase enzyme, where acetaldehyde is produced so fast after drinking that even a normally active aldehyde dehydrogenase enzyme cannot remove the acetaldehyde from the blood fast enough to avoid unpleasant reactions after drinking. The class I alcohol dehydrogenase enzymes responsible for the majority of the metabolism of alcohol into acetaldehyde are encoded by the *ADH1A*, *ADH1B*, and *ADH1C* genes. There are two superactive alcohol dehydrogenase enzymes due to polymorphisms of the genes encoding such enzymes. One such polymorphisms is the *ADH1B*2* gene, which is found commonly among East Asians (Han Chinese, Japanese, Koreans, Filipinos, Malays, etc., and aborigines of Australia and New Zealand) and among approximately 25 percent of people of Jewish origin. This genetic mutation is also encountered in small frequencies among Caucasians. The enzyme encoded by this mutated gene is superactive, causing rapid metabolism of alcohol into acetaldehyde and producing acetaldehyde buildup in the blood. This genetic mutation is associated with alcohol intolerance.[17] Another polymorphism, *ADH1B*3*, found primarily in people of African descent and Native Americans also encodes superactive alcohol dehydrogenase. As a result, this genetic mutation causes alcohol intolerance. Sometimes both the *ALDH2*2* and the *ADH1B*2* genetic mutation are present in the same person. These individuals are totally intolerant to any amount of alcohol and are usually teetotalers.[18] Although these genetic mutations deter a person from drinking alcohol, thus protecting them from potential alcohol abuse, there is no evidence that people with normally functioning alcohol dehydrogenase and aldehyde dehydrogenase enzymes are particularly susceptible to consuming too much alcohol.

> Inactive aldehyde dehydrogenase enzymes encoded by the *ALDH2*2* gene cause alcohol intolerance due to acetaldehyde buildup in the blood. A superactive alcohol dehydrogenase enzyme (thirty to forty times more active than the normal enzyme) encoded by the *ADH1B*2* or *ADH1B*3* gene is also associated with alcohol intolerance, also due to acetaldehyde buildup in the blood.

OTHER MENTAL HEALTH BENEFITS OF MODERATE DRINKING

In addition to stress relief, there are other mental health benefits of moderate drinking, which include the following:

- Perception of overall good health and psychological well-being
- Reduced inhibition and more prosocial behavior
- Reduced risk of anxiety disorders
- Reduced risk of depression

- Improved psychological well-being during the transition through menopause
- Reduced risk of age-related dementia and Alzheimer's disease

Studies have shown that moderate alcohol consumption (three to nine drinks per week) is very effective not only in reducing stress but also in developing self-perception of good health and psychological well-being. Subjective health may simply be an indicator of actual health status, and moderate consumption of alcohol may provide a rewarding sense of well-being in association with good physical health. Moderate drinking is also effective in enhancing mood, social integration, and improvement of cognitive function. Moderate drinkers have better psychosocial adjustment at work. Moreover, in a stressful work environment, nondrinkers are more likely to be absent from work than moderate drinkers. Alcohol may also have a buffering effect between stress and sickness. In addition, nondrinkers are 27 percent more likely to be disabled compared to moderate drinkers. Incidentally, moderate drinkers may have higher incomes than teetotalers. However, excess alcohol consumption is associated with depression and negative feelings rather than pleasurable effects.[19]

> Moderate drinkers have better perceptions of good health and psychological well-being, as well as better coping skills to deal with work-related stress, than abstainers.

It has been well established in the medical literature that people who consume alcohol in moderation have a lower risk of developing anxiety and depression than heavy drinkers. Interestingly, in one study based on a survey of 38,930 subjects, the authors observed that people who do not drink (lifelong abstainers) are at a higher risk of anxiety and depression than people who consume alcohol in moderation. However, with an excessive drinking habit, the risks of anxiety and depression are increased significantly.[20] In another study, the authors reported that compared to abstainers, occasional drinkers (drinking once a month or less, consuming two or fewer drinks per occasion) showed a 21 percent lower prevalence of depression and generalized anxiety disorder. In addition, people who consumed alcohol regularly

> Occasional and moderate drinkers have a lower prevalence of depression and anxiety disorders compared to abstainers. However, heavy and excessive drinkers have a much higher prevalence of depression and anxiety disorders than abstainers.

but in moderation (up to fourteen drinks per week for males, up to seven drinks per week for females) showed a 51 percent lower prevalence of depression and generalized anxiety disorder compared to abstainers. In contrast, excessive drinkers (more than forty-two drinks per week for males, more than twenty-eight drinks per week for females) showed a 54 percent higher prevalence of anxiety or depression compared to abstainers.[21]

In a study involving subjects from fourteen countries, the authors concluded that light to moderate consumption of alcohol was associated with a lower incidence of depression and anxiety disorder compared to abstainers, while heavy consumption of alcohol was associated with a higher incidence of depression.[22] Heavy drinkers who quit drinking and become abstainers in order to avoid the negative effects of heavy drinking are often referred to as "sick quitters." Interestingly, in one study based on 4,527 women and a fourteen-year follow-up, the authors concluded that previous drinkers who became abstainers did not show a higher risk of symptoms of anxiety or depression than teetotalers. Therefore, the higher risk of depression and anxiety for heavy drinkers can be reversed if they quit drinking alcohol and become teetotalers. In addition, the authors confirmed that women who were light or moderate drinkers had a lower risk of developing anxiety and depression compared to abstainers, but heavy drinkers showed a higher risk of depression and anxiety than abstainers.[23]

Menopause is a difficult time in women's life because symptoms and stress during menopause have a negative impact on overall well-being. However, moderate consumption of alcohol may improve perceptions of well-being in these women. In one study based on 438 urban Australian women aged forty-five to fifty-five years during enrollment and an eight-year follow-up, the authors concluded that women who consumed alcohol in moderation had higher well-being scores than nondrinkers, provided they were also nonsmokers and exercised weekly or more.[24]

> Moderate alcohol consumption contributes positively to women's well-being through the menopausal transition.

Elderly people may also benefit from drinking in moderation. A Spanish study reported that moderate alcohol consumption, especially drinking wine, was associated with a more active lifestyle and better perceptions of health in elderly subjects.[25] In another study based on 6,005 individuals fifty years of age or older, the authors observed that for both men and women, better cognition and subjective well-being and fewer depressive symptoms were observed in subjects who consumed alcohol in moderation compared to teetotalers. The authors concluded that for middle-aged and older men and women, moderate levels of alcohol consumption are associated with better cognitive health than abstinence.[26]

Age-related dementia and Alzheimer's disease are neurodegenerative diseases associated with advanced age. Alzheimer's disease is a devastating neurological disorder affecting one in ten Americans over the age of sixty-five and almost half of all Americans over eighty-five years old. Moderate alcohol consumption can dramatically reduce the risk of age-related dementia and Alzheimer's disease. The triggering agent for Alzheimer's disease is β-amyloid peptide (Aβ-aggregates), which alters the synaptic activity and disrupts the neurotransmission mediated by N-methyl-D-aspartate receptors in the brain. Alcohol in low dosages can prevent formation of Aβ-aggregates, thus delaying or preventing the onset of Alzheimer's disease. Moreover, low to moderate consumption of alcohol is associated with reduced risk of other neurodegenerative diseases, as evidenced by data from several large clinical trials.[27] Dietary compounds (polyphenols) found in grapes have some protective effect against Alzheimer's disease because these compounds interfere with the generation and aggregation of β-amyloid peptide. Resveratrol, a compound found in abundance in red wine and also in grapes, provides protection against Alzheimer's disease.[28]

> Drinking in moderation improves cognitive function in elderly people and also reduces the risk of neurodegenerative diseases such as age-related dementia and Alzheimer's disease. Red wine may provide additional protection due to the presence of resveratrol, which is present in grape skin.

Parkinson's disease is also a neurodegenerative disease, but moderate alcohol consumption (wine or liquor) has no protective effect against this illness. In contrast, beer drinkers (one to three beer drinks per month to one to three beer drinks per week) have an approximately 30 percent lower incidence of Parkinson's disease than non–beer drinkers. Because this lower risk is not observed in wine or liquor drinkers, it is possible that some components of beer rather than alcohol are responsible for this effect. Serum uric acid levels increase after beer drinking, and uric acid is an excellent antioxidant. Increased uric acid concentration may be responsible for the reduced risk. Cigarette smoking and caffeine consumption are associated with a decreased incidence of Parkinson's disease.[29] Another study reported no association between the risk of Parkinson's disease and moderate alcohol or coffee consumption. However, drinking two or more cups of tea per day or two or more cola drinks per day was associated with a reduced risk of Parkinson's disease. The authors also observed protective effects of cigarette smoking against Parkinson's disease.[30] However, this author strongly discourages anyone from starting smoking to get a protective effect against Parkinson's disease because the benefits are less compared to the many health hazards associated with cigarette smoking.

> Drinking beer, but not any other type of alcoholic beverage, reduces the risk of Parkinson's disease.

ALCOHOL AND THE HUMAN BRAIN

The tension-reduction hypothesis has been historically and cross-culturally a predominant explanation for why people consume alcohol. In general, the word "tension" refers to several unpleasant feelings, such as anxiety, fear, frustration, and stress. The tension reduction hypothesis is based on two assumptions. First, alcohol can reduce tension and, second, people consume alcohol to reduce tension. People who are exposed to high stress levels or who are anxiety prone may consume excess alcohol to reduce stress or unpleasant feelings, but such a habit may also increase the risk of excess alcohol consumption.[31]

After consumption, alcohol crosses the blood-brain barrier and interacts with various neurotransmitter systems of the central nervous system (CNS), including the glutamatergic, GABA (gamma-aminobutyric acid), dopaminergic, opioid, serotonergic, and endocannabinoid systems. Alcohol inhibits the glutamate system, the major excitatory neurotransmitter system, by inhibiting N-methyl-D-aspartate (NMDA) receptors. This effect causes mild sedation and muscle relaxation but may also impair learning, even at a low blood alcohol concentration (0.03 percent). Inhibition of NMDA is more significant with higher alcohol consumption, which results in disorientation, blurred speech, and even blackout. Alcohol also stimulates the GABA neurotransmitter system, which is the main inhibitory neurotransmitter system in the brain. As a result, concentrations of the neurotransmitter GABA are increased because alcohol inhibits the degradation of this neurotransmitter by interacting with GABA receptors. GABA reduces stress, anxiety, and depression and promotes a good night's sleep. GABA deficiency is associated with anxiety, depression, and insomnia, while the anxiolytic effects of the benzodiazepine class of drugs (Valium, Xanax, Halcion, etc.) are due to their interaction with the GABA neurotransmitter system, which restores normal GABA levels in the brain. Relief of stress and anxiety after consumption of moderate amounts of alcohol is due to its effect on the GABA neurotransmitter system. Moreover, such interactions are responsible for relaxation and disinhibition after alcohol consumption.

> Stress and anxiety relief after moderate consumption of alcohol is due to stimulation of the GABA neurotransmitter system.

The pleasurable effect of alcohol when consumed in moderation is also due to its interaction with the dopaminergic and opioid neurotransmitter systems. Alcohol in moderate concentrations triggers the release of dopamine, a neurotransmitter in the limbic system of the brain that stimulates pleasurable and rewarding experience after moderate drinking. Interestingly, the effect of alcohol on the dopaminergic neurotransmitter system indirectly activates serotonergic pathways, which are also associated with mood elevation and subjective feelings of well-being.

Alcohol acts directly on opioid receptors present in the brain, especially mu-receptors (other opioid receptors are delta and kappa receptors), causing a pleasurable effect and euphoria.[32] Alcohol also increases endogenous opioid peptides such as beta-endorphins, which are associated with pleasurable experience after moderate consumption of alcohol.[33] Long-distance running is associated with increased levels of beta-endorphin, which is responsible for "runner's high." In addition, alcohol interacts with the endocannabinoid system (cannabinoid receptor 1: CB1 and endogenous endocannabinoids). Animal studies have shown that after short-term exposure to moderate blood alcohol levels, brain endocannabinoid concentrations (anandamide and 2-arachidonoylglyceraol) are reduced, but after chronic alcohol administration, brain endocannabinoid levels are increased. A study using human subjects also showed decreased blood levels of endocannabinoids after consumption of 250 mL of red wine.[34] Alcohol addiction and tolerance are related to the interaction of alcohol with the endocannabinoid system. Important interactions of alcohol with major neurotransmitter systems are summarized in table 9.3.

Table 9.3. Important interactions of alcohol with major neurotransmitter systems in the brain

Neurotransmitter System	Effect	Comments
Glutamate (glutamatergic)	Inhibition of N-methyl-D-aspartate (NMDA) receptors	At low blood alcohol concentration, this inhibition causes mild sedation and muscle relaxation, but at high blood alcohol levels the effects are disorientation, blurred speech, and even blackout.
GABA	Stimulation	Stress and anxiety reduction after moderate consumption.
Dopaminergic	Stimulation	Increased dopamine levels in the limbic system of the brain, associated with pleasure.
Serotonergic	Indirect stimulation related to stimulation of the dopaminergic system by alcohol. Alcohol mostly interacts with the serotonin receptor 5-HT$_3$.	Mood elevation and subjective feelings of well-being.
Opioid	Interacts with mu-opioid receptors.	Pleasure and relaxation. Alcohol also increases endogenous opioids known as endorphins that cause euphoria. Runner's high is also associated with endorphin release.
Endocannabinoid	Interacts with the CB1 (cannabinoid-1) receptor.	Alcohol tolerance and addictions may be related to the interaction of alcohol with the endocannabinoid system.

PHYSICAL HEALTH BENEFITS OF MODERATE DRINKING

In addition to reducing stress and anxiety, alcohol, if consumed in moderation, has many physical health benefits. These benefits include the following:

- Lower risk of cardiovascular diseases, including heart attack and heart failure
- Lower mortality in survivors of heart attack
- Lower risk of stroke
- Lower risk of type 2 diabetes
- Lower risk of certain types of cancer
- Lower risk of rheumatoid arthritis

- Increased longevity
- Red wine may protect from the common cold

Probably the number-one benefit of drinking in moderation is reduced risk of cardiovascular diseases, including heart failure and heart attack (myocardial infarction). The relationship between alcohol consumption and cardiovascular diseases was examined in the original Framingham Heart Study, which showed a U-shaped curve indicating that moderate alcohol consumption reduces the risk of cardiovascular diseases, but heavy alcohol consumption increases the risk. Smoking is a risk factor for developing cardiovascular diseases, but moderate alcohol consumption also reduces the risk of cardiovascular diseases in smokers.[35] Interestingly, women just need to drink one standard drink once a week for protection against heart diseases, while men may need to drink one standard drink more often for protection.[36]

In one review article, the authors commented that habitual light to moderate drinking lowers the rate of death due to coronary artery disease (heart attack is a coronary artery disease), congestive heart failure, diabetes mellitus, and stroke. In general, men older than age fifty get more favorable effects of consuming alcohol in moderation than younger men, but women of any age get the favorable effects of moderate alcohol consumption. Unfortunately, the cardioprotective effect of alcohol has not been documented in epidemiological studies using populations from India and China.[37] In one study based on 58,827 individuals and 11.6-year follow-up, the authors observed that light to moderate consumption of alcohol was associated with a lower risk of heart attack.[38] Light to moderate consumption of alcohol also increased the chance of survival after a first heart attack in study subjects.

> Women get cardioprotection by just consuming one drink per week, while men need to drink in moderation more often. Moderate alcohol consumption also lowers the risk of heart attack, as well as the risk of mortality after a first heart attack. However, epidemiological studies indicate that Indians and Chinese may not get cardioprotection from moderate consumption of alcohol.

There are several hypotheses on how moderate drinking can reduce the risk of developing cardiovascular diseases. In general, at moderate concentration, alcohol increases the concentration of good cholesterol known as HDL cholesterol (high-density lipoprotein cholesterol) in the blood. However, studies have also indicated that the level of increased HDL cholesterol in the blood may explain 50 percent of the protective effect of alcohol against cardiovascular diseases, and the other 50 percent may be partly related to antioxidant, anti-inflammatory, and antiplatelet effects due to the presence of many beneficial organic compounds (other than alcohol) present in beer and wine, known as polyphenolic and phenolic compounds. These chemicals are naturally present in barley, hops, and grapes. However, these beneficial organic compounds are lost during distillation, which is essential to increase the alcohol content of liquor, but during the aging of distilled liquors in wood barrels some polyphenolic compounds present in the wood may leak into the liquor.

Based on a study of 3,176 elderly men and women (mean age 69.1 years), the authors observed that moderate drinkers (two or fewer drinks per day of beer, wine, or liquor) had an approximately 50 percent lower risk of having an ischemic stroke (most strokes, approximately 85 percent, are ischemic strokes, where an artery that supplies oxygen-rich blood to the brain is blocked) compared to nondrinkers. The maximum protection was observed in individuals who consumed only 1.2 drinks per day. However, consuming more than two drinks a day was associated with a trend toward increased risk of hemorrhagic stroke (less common, but it occurs when an artery in the brain leaks blood or ruptures).[39]

Moderate consumption of alcohol reduces the risk of developing type 2 diabetes (non-insulin dependent diabetes), most probably by increasing insulin sensitivity. Based on fifteen studies conducted in the United States, Finland, the Netherlands, Germany, the United Kingdom, and Japan, with 369,862 men and women and an average follow-up of twelve years, the authors reported that light drinkers and moderate drinkers had an approximately 30 percent lower risk of type 2 diabetes compared to nondrinkers. It made little difference whether an individual consumed beer, wine, or spirits.[40]

Moderate consumption of alcohol may reduce the risk of certain types of cancer because wine and beer contain anticarcinogenic (anticancer) compounds and antioxidants. In the California Men's Health Study using 84,170 men aged between forty-five and sixty-nine, the consumption of one or more drink of red wine per day was associated with an approximately 60 percent reduced lung cancer risk, even in smokers.[41] Moderate consumption of alcohol may also reduce the risk of head and neck cancer as well as renal cell carcinoma (the most common type of kidney cancer). Although heavy alcohol consumption increases the risk of breast cancer and many other types of cancer, whether moderate alcohol consumption also increases the risk of breast cancer is controversial due to conflicting reports. However, in one study the authors concluded that the consumption of fewer than three alcoholic drinks per week is not associated with an increased risk of breast cancer, but consuming three to six drinks per week may be associated with a small increase in risk.[42]

Moderate alcohol consumption reduces the risk of rheumatoid arthritis. In one study based on 2,908 patients suffering from rheumatoid arthritis, the authors reported that occasional or daily consumption of alcohol reduced the progression of the disease as determined by radiological studies (x-ray). The best results were observed in male patients.[43] In a large study using 4,272 faculty and staff of five Spanish universities, the investigators observed that total alcohol intake from drinking beer and spirits had no protective effect against the common cold, whereas moderate wine consumption was associated with reduced risk of common cold.[44]

Because moderate consumption of alcohol can prevent many diseases, it is expected that moderate drinkers may live longer than lifetime abstainers from alcohol. In the Physicians' Health Study involving 22,071 male physicians in the United States between the ages of forty to eighty-four with no history of myocardial infarction, stroke, or cancer during enrollment and then ten years of follow-up, the authors observed that men who consumed two to six drinks per week had the most favorable results (20–28 percent lower mortality rate compared to people who consumed one drink per week). In contrast, people who consumed more than two drinks per day had an approximately 50 percent higher risk of mortality than people who consumed just one drink per week.[45]

WHAT TO DRINK: BEER, WINE, OR LIQUOR?

Beer and wine, in addition to alcohol, contain many beneficial organic compounds. The approximate calories from drinking one serving of beer, white wine, or red wine are 153, 121, and 125 calories, respectively. Only beer contains beneficial soluble dietary fiber. Both beer and wine are rich in antioxidants. The major antioxidants present in beer include xanthohumol, 8-prenylnaringenin, flavones, and proanthocyanidins, while the major antioxidants present in wine include resveratrol (red wine), tyrosol (white wine), anthocyanins, flavanols, and catechins. Beer but not wine is a good source of silicone, which promotes good bone health. Small amounts of vitamin B complex and minerals are present in both beer and wine, but folate content is much higher in beer. Beer, wine, and liquor do not contain any cholesterol.

The French paradox was first described by Professor Serge Renaud. In most countries, eating foods rich in fat increases mortality from cardiovascular diseases, but the situation in France is paradoxical because the mortality from cardiovascular diseases is relatively low in France compared to other industrialized countries. Professor Renaud attributed this paradox to the regular consumption of wine by French people.[46] Although according to the French paradox, drinking wine, especially red wine, is superior to beer or liquor, in one study, the authors commented that beer and wine may have similar cardioprotective effects because a 25 percent risk reduction was observed in wine drinkers and a 23 percent risk reduction was observed in beer drinkers.[47]

Overall, men prefer drinking beer, and women prefer wine. For men younger than fifty years of age, drinking beer in moderation is fine. However, for older men, especially men over sixty-five years of age, drinking wine, especially red wine, has more benefits, including a significant reduction in the risk of dementia and Alzheimer's disease. Moreover, wine consumption in the elderly population is associated with overall perceptions of good health, but drinking beer or spirits does not provide that benefit. Therefore, drinking more wine than beer or spirits may be beneficial for elderly people.

For women who prefer drinking wine, please continue your choice. Both white and red wine have health benefits. If you prefer to drink beer, please consider drinking wine (especially red wine) occasionally. For elder women, drinking wine has more benefits. Therefore, consider drinking wine more often than beer or cocktails. For everyone, although drinking liquor should provide many health benefits associated with alcohol, beer and wine may provide additional benefits due to the presence of antioxidants. The key is drinking in moderation. A comparison of beer, wine, and spirits for various health benefits associated with moderate consumption of alcoholic beverages is summarized in table 9.4. This author suggests drinking beer and wine more often than liquor. For elderly people, drinking wine, especially red wine, is recommended.

Table 9.4. Comparison of beer, wine, and spirits for various health benefits associated with moderate consumption of alcoholic beverages

Health Benefit	Beer	Wine	Liquor	Comments
Reduced overall risk of cardiovascular disease	++	++	+	Any alcoholic beverage increases HDL cholesterol (good cholesterol), but beer and wine, especially red wine, seem to be superior to liquor due to the presence of antioxidants.
Reduced mortality in survivors of heart attack	++	++	+	Although alcohol content is partly responsible for protection, antioxidant compounds present in beer and especially red wine provide additional protection.
Reduced risk of ischemic stroke	++	++	++	Consuming any alcoholic beverage is associated with decreased risk because alcohol is responsible for this effect.
Reduced risk of type 2 diabetes	++	++	++	Consuming any alcoholic beverage is associated with decreased risk.
Protection from certain types of cancer	+	++	—	Polyphenolic compounds present in beer and wine may reduce the risk of certain types of cancer, but wine may be more effective.
Reduced risk of rheumatoid arthritis	++	++	++	Consuming any alcoholic beverage is associated with decreased risk.
Reduced risk of forming gallstones	++	++	++	Consuming any alcoholic beverage is associated with decreased risk.
Protection from common cold	—	+	—	Only wine drinking is associated with protection from the common cold.
Better bone health	++	+	+	Silicon, which is present in beer but not in wine or liquor, has a beneficial effect on bone health.
Protection from age-related dementia and Alzheimer's disease	+	++	+	Resveratrol, found in abundance in grape skin and red wine, has protective effects, although the alcohol content of a drink provides some protection.
Increased longevity	++	+	+	Drinking in moderation increases longevity, but red wine may be slightly better.
Perception of good health	—	++	—	Only drinking wine is associated with subjective perception of good health.

++ Significant effect, + Positive effect

ADVERSE HEALTH EFFECTS OF HEAVY DRINKING

All physical and mental health benefits of drinking in moderation disappear with heavy drinking. Alcohol abuse affects multiple organ systems, including the brain, heart, bone, immune system, and endocrine system. Major adverse effects of chronic alcohol consumption include decreased life span, increased risk of cardiovascular diseases (including heart attacks), increased risk of violent behavior, alcoholic liver diseases including cirrhosis of the liver, mood disorder, and significantly increased risk of various cancers. As mentioned earlier, drinking during pregnancy is associated with a poor outcome in pregnancy, including fetal alcohol syndrome. The legal age of drinking is twenty-one years because consuming alcohol below the legal age of drinking causes significant brain damage, as the adolescent brain is still developing. Girls are more affected than boys by underage drinking. Significant impairment of learning abilities and memory may occur due to underage drinking, especially teenage drinking. Excess alcohol consumption also causes damage to the adult brain.

Adverse effects of alcohol are observed when a person consumes any amount of alcohol exceeding the guidelines of moderate drinking. In one study, the authors commented that above a threshold of seven to thirteen drinks per week for women and fourteen to twenty-seven drinks per week for men, there is a risk of developing alcohol-related liver problems. The greater sensitivity of women to alcohol toxicity may be related to a genetic predisposition of the process of metabolizing alcohol in women, where more oxidative by-products of alcohol are formed compared to men. Consumption of coffee may protect males against alcohol-induced liver damage, but no such data are currently available for females.[48] The major health hazards associated with heavy drinking are listed in table 9.5. A detailed discussion of the health hazards of excessive drinking is beyond the scope of this book. Interested readers on this topic may see my earlier book, *The Science of Drinking*.[49]

Table 9.5. Adverse effects of heavy consumption of alcohol

Adverse Outcome of Heavy Drinking	Comments
Hangover	A hangover consists of unpleasant physical and mental symptoms that occur after drinking too much alcohol. The most common symptoms are headache, muscle ache, excessive thirst, redness of eyes, and increased sensitivity to light and sound. Typically a hangover occurs several hours after drinking, when the blood alcohol level is reduced from the initial high blood alcohol level, for example in the early morning after heavy drinking the night before. Although hangover most commonly occurs in women after three to five drinks in one night and in men after five to seven drinks, studies have shown that people who consume more than nine drinks per week are at higher odds of experiencing hangover.
Alcohol withdrawal symptoms	Heavy consumption of alcohol for weeks to months may cause alcohol withdrawal symptoms if a person stops drinking. The symptoms may be similar to hangover or more severe and may be associated with convulsion, requiring immediate medical attention. Alcohol withdrawal is similar to drug withdrawal, requiring alcohol detoxification under medical supervision. Severe alcohol withdrawal symptoms may be fatal if medical care is not provided in a timely manner.
Fatty liver disease	Fatty liver is the first symptom of liver toxicity associated with drinking. One study indicates that above a threshold of seven to thirteen drinks per week for women and fourteen to twenty-seven drinks per week for men, there is a risk of developing some alcohol-related liver disease.
Cirrhosis of the liver	A lifetime ingestion of 100 kg of alcohol (average of 3.9 drinks a day for approximately five years) is needed to develop cirrhosis of the liver. This disease may be fatal or may require liver transplant. However, a patient must show complete abstinence before a liver transplant.
Brain damage in adolescents	Early onset of drinking around age thirteen has devastating effects on the developing brain that may persist for a lifetime. Teenagers and young adults below the age of twenty-one should not drink at all. Girls are more susceptible than boys.
Brain damage in adults	Alcohol can cause smaller brain volume in both men and women, with accompanying mental impairment and cognitive difficulties. However, women are affected more than men.
Korsakoff syndrome	This disease observed in alcoholics is mainly due to thiamine (vitamin B_1) deficiency. Severe dementia is the major observation, but abstinence from alcohol and proper treatment may be able to reverse some symptoms.
Wernicke-Korsakoff syndrome	In addition to dementia and confusion, visual problems and muscle weakness (difficulty walking, etc.) are observed. Thiamine deficiency is the major cause of this disease.
Mood disorders, anxiety, and depression	Although drinking in moderation is associated with pleasure and euphoria, depression and mood disorders may be observed with blood alcohol levels above 0.08 percent. Chronic heavy consumption of alcohol is associated with mood disorders and major depression in both young adults and the elderly.

Adverse Outcome of Heavy Drinking	Comments
Increased risk of suicide	Alcohol abuse may increase the risk of late-life suicide.
Increased risk of cardiovascular diseases, including heart attack and heart failure	Consuming more than three drinks each day on a regular basis may cause some damage to the heart. Heavy drinking is also associated with hypertension, heart failure, alcoholic cardiomyopathy, and increased risk of death after heart attack. Women are more susceptible to alcohol-induced heart damage than men.
Increased risk of stroke	Consuming twenty-one or more drinks weekly on a regular basis increases risk of stroke, especially hemorrhagic stroke (stroke due to rupture or leak of blood vessels in the brain).
Increased risk of cancer	Excessive alcohol consumption is associated with cancer of the mouth, pharynx, larynx, and esophagus. Alcoholics may develop cirrhosis of the liver, which may progress to liver cancer. Heavy drinking may also cause pancreatic cancer.
Damage to the immune system	Alcohol reduces immunity; as a result, individuals consuming excessive amounts of alcohol are more prone to both viral and bacterial infections.
Progression of AIDS	Even consuming two or more drinks per day on a regular basis may harm an HIV patient despite receiving treatment.
Damage to the endocrine system	High alcohol concentration in the blood may interfere with proper secretion of hormones from endocrine glands. Pseudo-Cushing's disease, which has all the symptoms of Cushing's disease, may be observed in alcoholics.
Impaired fertility	Alcohol abuse is associated with fertility problems in both men and women.
Bone damage	Heavy consumption of alcohol may reduce bone mass, thus increasing the risk of fracture after a fall.
Fetal alcohol spectrum of disorders and fetal alcohol syndrome	Pregnant women and women planning to be pregnant should not consume any alcohol.
Weight gain	Heavy alcohol consumption (over thirty grams a day, more than two drinks) is associated with significant weight gain.
Violent behavior	Alcohol abuse may cause aggressiveness and violent behavior. According to the U.S. Bureau of Justice, approximately 37 percent of state prison inmates and 21 percent of federal prison inmates serving time for violent crimes were under the influence of alcohol when they committed their crimes.
Reduced life span	Consuming alcohol exceeding the upper limit of moderate drinking, and especially binge drinking, may reduce life span. People drinking nine or more drinks on one occasion have a high risk of death following injury after a binge-drinking episode.

CONCLUSION

Drinking in moderation (up to two drinks per day for males and up to one drink per day for females) has many physical and mental health benefits. Drinking in a social context facilitates communication and enhances friendship. Drinking in moderation, along with regular exercise and a balanced diet, is the best approach to living healthily. Good physical health also increases overall feelings of psychological well-being. However, drinking in excess and even occasional binge drinking is injurious to your health. Therefore, if you know anyone with a drinking problem, please encourage that person to seek professional help immediately. Alcohol abuse is a psychiatric illness that can be cured with proper treatment.

Stress Relief and Other Health Benefits of Chocolate

Chocolate is a popular confection not only in the United States but also worldwide. According to one study, chocolate is the most commonly craved food among college students, especially among women.[1] Although chocolate is most often consumed for pleasure, it may also be considered a functional food because research from the past ten years has clearly indicated that moderate consumption of chocolate, especially dark chocolate, has protective effects against the development of cardiovascular disease (heart disease), which is the number-one killer in the United States and also in other developed countries.[2] Cardiovascular diseases include a range of conditions that ultimately affect the heart. These diseases include coronary artery disease (narrowing of the coronary arteries due to deposits of lipids and other materials, a process also known as atherosclerosis, which may eventually cause a heart attack if not treated), heart rhythm problems (arrhythmias), heart failure, and related disorders. Congenital heart diseases may also be categorized under cardiovascular diseases.

Chocolate is an excellent stress buster due to the presence of several psychoactive compounds. Moreover, chronic stress increases free radical production in the body, which increases oxidative stress. Dark chocolate, rich in antioxidants, is very effective in reducing oxidative stress. In fact, many health benefits of chocolate are due to its excellent antioxidant property. Chocolate

Table 10.1.   Health benefits of chocolate (dark chocolate)

Health Benefit	Comments
Protection against cardiovascular diseases, including heart attack and heart failure	Chocolate protects the heart by multiple mechanisms.
Stress relief and elevated mood	Chocolate contains psychoactive compounds that can provide stress relief and improve feelings of well-being.
Lower blood pressure	Eating chocolate may be beneficial for people with hypertension because chocolate reduces blood pressure by increasing serum nitric oxide levels.
Improved insulin sensitivity/ antidiabetic effect	Chocolate increases nitric oxide bioavailability in endothelial cells, thus improving insulin sensitivity.
Protection against stroke	Daily chocolate consumption reduces the likelihood of a stroke. The mechanisms include antioxidant effect, preventing blood clot formation, improving endothelial function, and lowering blood pressure.
Anticancer property	Some evidence indicates that chocolate has anticancer properties, but the mechanism is not clearly understood. However, the antioxidant properties of chocolate may provide protection against cancer because increased oxidative stress may increase the risk of certain types of cancer.
Favorable effect on pregnancy	Dark chocolate is effective in protecting pregnant woman against preeclampsia. Eating chocolate during pregnancy also leads to infants with good temperament.
Weight loss	Chocolate reduces appetite, reduces digestion and absorption of fats as well as carbohydrates, and increases satiety.
Protection from age-related dementia	Chocolate intake increases cerebral blood flow and may protect against age-related dementia.
Recovery after exercise	Eating chocolate before exercise results in rapid recovery from postexercise physiological and metabolic changes.
Reduced symptoms of chronic fatigue syndrome	High coca liquor/polyphenol-rich chocolate (dark chocolate) may reduce the burden of symptoms in subjects suffering from chronic fatigue syndrome.

can lower blood pressure and inhibit platelet activation, thus making blood thinner (which may indirectly protect against heart attack), and it has anti-diabetic and antitumor properties, as well as anti-inflammatory effects. The health benefits of chocolate are summarized in table 10.1.

Although chocolate is most commonly consumed as a confection, historically cocoa was consumed as a beverage for centuries and was not used as a confection until the nineteenth century. The first solid dark chocolate was produced in 1847 by adding cocoa butter to ground roasted cocoa beans and also adding sugar. Milk chocolate, prepared by mixing cocoa with sugar and condensed milk powder, was originally invented in Switzerland.

HISTORY OF CHOCOLATE

Chocolate is derived from cocoa beans, which are the fruit of the cacao tree. The cacao tree (*Theobroma cacao*) grows in the cocoa belt, which is a tropical belt straddling the equator—between 10 and 20 degrees north and south. The biological name of the cacao tree was given by Swedish naturalist Carl von Linné (1707–1778), which literally translates into "food of the gods." The fruit contains twenty to forty seeds, which are also known as cocoa beans. An ancient tribe (1200 BC–300 BC) of Mexico known as the Olmecs knew about this plant and used the beans. These ancient tribal people called the bitter beans

> Switzerland, the birthplace of milk chocolate, reports the highest per capita consumption of chocolate in the world. Milk chocolate is more popular in the United States and Europe, but dark chocolate has more health benefits.

"kakawa" or "cacao." The Maya archaeological site at Colha in northern Belize, Central America, has yielded several spouted ceramic vessels that contain residue from the preparation of food and beverages. Analysis of dry residue specimens obtained from fourteen of these vessels by a sophisticated analytical method (high-performance liquid chromatography coupled with atmospheric pressure chemical ionization mass spectrometry) confirmed consumption of cacao (chocolate) as early as 600 BC by chemically identifying theobromine in the residue. Although cacao contains more than five hundred different chemical compounds, theobromine is present in significant amounts in cacao, and *Theobroma cacao* is the only Mesoamerican plant that contains theobromine as the primary methylxanthine.[3]

Cacao trees were probably routinely cultivated during the Mayan civilization around 400 AD. At that time, cocoa beans were ground and dissolved in water to prepare a chocolate drink, but to hide the bitter taste, cinnamon and pepper were added. When Aztecs dominated the Mayan civilization around 1500 AD, Emperor Montezuma

> Ancient Mayans as early as 600 BC consumed cacao (chocolate).

probably consumed dozens of cups of chocolate drinks each day. At that time, cocoa beans were considered as valuable as gold and precious stones and were used as currency. The elites of the Aztec civilization from the twelfth to the

sixteenth centuries drank chocolate derived from cocoa beans and also offered chocolate to the Aztec gods.

In 1502 when Christopher Columbus landed in the island of Guanaja, Hon-
duras, he received a cup of chocolate as a gift from the native people.[4] Following the Spanish conquest of Mexico, cocoa beans
were brought back to Spain in 1528, and over the
next one hundred years, in order to improve the
bitter taste, sugar, vanilla, cinnamon, and other
ingredients were added to the chocolate. In 1657,
the first chocolate house was opened in London;
chocolate was introduced in North America around the mid-1800s.[5] In 1884,
Milton S. Hershey founded the Hershey Chocolate Company, which is now
the largest chocolate manufacturer in the United States.

> The word "chocolate" was probably derived from the word "xocolati," meaning "bitter water" in the Aztec language.

DIFFERENT TYPES OF CHOCOLATE

Today, the Ivory Coast and Ghana are the two countries that cultivate cacao
trees (*Theobroma cacao*) more than any other countries. In general, 80–90
percent of cocoa comes from small family-run farms, and there are approximately five to six million cocoa farmers worldwide.[6] Cacao trees produce
berry-like fruits, also known as cocoa pods, which when ripe have a yellow-
orange color. Then the pods are broken to obtain the seeds (cocoa beans), and
the pulps are removed. The cocoa beans are fermented, dried, and roasted at
100–150°C (212–302°F) in order to prepare the precursor of chocolate. Then
the shells of the roasted cocoa beans are removed to produce cacao nibs. The
nibs are then ground to cocoa mass, which is usually liquefied and is called
chocolate liquor but contains no alcohol. The chocolate liquor contains cocoa
solids (the nonfat component) and cocoa butter (the fatty content). Then
cocoa powder is prepared by mechanical pressing, which removes the cocoa
butter, but the cocoa powder retains some residual cocoa butter, usually
10–12 percent. The cocoa powder (mostly cocoa solids) contains most of the
polyphenolic antioxidants present in cocoa beans and also retains the characteristic chocolate flavor. In general, cocoa solids are primarily used in dark
chocolate making or as cocoa powder for cooking and drinks.

Cocoa is sometimes Dutched, a technique developed in the 1820s and still
used today. This process darkens the cocoa and changes the taste by reducing
its bitterness. This process involves treatment with alkali, but U.S. regulations

require that Dutched cocoa powder or cocoa liquor be labeled as "treated with alkali." In general, alkaline cocoa powder and alkalized chocolate liquors are not commonly used in making chocolate because this process destroys many of the antioxidants present in the cocoa beans. However, some brands of dark chocolate still use this ingredient because of its superior taste and texture. Much of the chocolate consumed today

> Dark chocolate has the most health benefits.

is in the form of dark sweet chocolate (combining cocoa solids, cocoa butter or other fat, and sugar), milk chocolate, and white chocolate. Milk chocolate is sweet chocolate that also contains milk powder or condensed milk. White chocolate contains cocoa butter, sugar, and milk but no cocoa solids. White chocolate has little health benefit.

BIOACTIVE COMPOUNDS PRESENT IN CHOCOLATE

Cocoa butter contains both saturated fatty acids (most commonly palmitic and stearic acids) and unsaturated fatty acids (mostly oleic acid, which is also found in abundance in olive oil). Although cocoa butter is high in saturated fats, chocolate contains mostly stearic acid, which does not increase cholesterol. Moreover, the human liver transforms stearic acid into oleic acid, a beneficial monounsaturated fatty acid. When volunteers consumed a high proportion of stearic acid expected to be present in milk chocolate, no significant change in cholesterol or low-density lipoprotein choles-

> Eating chocolate, which is high in saturated fats, does not increase cholesterol because chocolate mostly contains stearic acid.

terol (bad cholesterol) in their plasma (the aqueous part of the blood) was observed.[7] Most of the fiber present in cocoa beans is lost in the preparation of chocolate, but dark chocolate contains some fiber, mostly insoluble fiber. Chocolate, however, is not a source of dietary fiber in the American diet. Chocolate also contains various minerals, including potassium, phosphorus, copper, zinc, and magnesium.

Cocoa beans are rich in antioxidants, and dark chocolate contains more antioxidants than tea or wine. More than two hundred polyphenolic antioxidants are present in cocoa beans, but the main polyphenolic antioxidants present in cocoa beans are subclassified as flavanols, also known as flavan-3-ols. The main flavanols found in chocolate are epicatechin, catechin, and procyanidins (oligomers and polymers of epicatechin and catechin). In addition to polyphenols, chocolate contains methylxanthine compounds, mostly theobromine. A small amount of caffeine is also present in chocolate. Theobromine has antioxidant effects similar to caffeine. Other psychoactive compounds are present in very small amounts.[8]

In general, dark chocolate contains considerably higher amounts of flavanols than milk chocolate. Valeric acid, which acts as a stress-reducing agent, is also present in chocolate.[9] Various organic compounds found in chocolate are listed in table 10.2. Although significant amounts of polyphenolic antioxidants present in cocoa beans are lost during normal processing, if cocoa nibs, cocoa powder, or

> Flavanols are responsible for the bitter astringent flavor of chocolate because these compounds form complexes with proteins present in saliva.

chocolate liquor are treated with alkali (the Dutching process), further loss of beneficial antioxidants may occur.

Table 10.2. Various compounds found in chocolate

Class/Type of Compound	Specific Compound
Fatty acid	The fatty acid composition of dark chocolate consists of 33 percent oleic acid, 33 percent stearic acid, and 25 percent palmitic acid
Minerals	Potassium, phosphorus, copper, zinc, iron, and magnesium
Flavonoids (flavanols)	Epicatechin, catechin, and procyanidins
Methylxanthine	Theobromine, caffeine, which may be responsible for the acquired taste of dark chocolate
Stress-reducing agent and psychoactive compounds	Methylxanthines, biogenic amines, endogenous cannabinoid-like fatty acids, valeric acid

CHOCOLATE FOR STRESS REDUCTION

Psychological stress, commonly known as stress, induces cortisol secretion though the activation of the hypothalamic-pituitary-adrenal axis (HPA axis) (see chapter 1). Cortisol is the major stress hormone, along with epinephrine and norepinephrine (epinephrine and norepinephrine are also called catecholamines). Consumption of chocolate, especially dark chocolate, results in reduced secretion of cortisol under stress. One study using thirty human subjects observed that daily consumption of 40 grams (1.4 ounces) of dark chocolate for fourteen days was effective in reducing urinary secretion of the stress hormones cortisol and catecholamines in people who felt highly stressed. Moreover, consumption of dark chocolate for two weeks was effective in partially correcting other stress-related biochemical imbalances in such subjects.[10]

It is well accepted in the scientific community that medical students experience a high level of stress, especially before exams. In one study based on sixty second-year medical students (thirty males and thirty females), the authors observed that consumption of dark chocolate and milk chocolate (40 grams, or 1.4 ounces, of chocolate every day) for two weeks was effective in reducing the perception of stress in medical students. Interestingly, the stress reduction capacity of chocolate was more obvious in female students than male students. However, the consumption of white chocolate was not effective in reducing stress. The authors further demonstrated that the stress-reducing effects of both dark chocolate and milk chocolate were due not to the sweet taste but to the cocoa solids, which were present in both dark and milk chocolate but not in white chocolate.[11]

> Dark chocolate and milk chocolate can reduce stress, but white chocolate may not be effective.

It has been well established that dark chocolate consumption reduces the risk of cardiovascular diseases, including myocardial infarction (heart attack). Psychosocial stress, especially chronic stress, is associated with increased risk of cardiovascular diseases due to activation of the HPA axis, which is associated with increased secretion of cortisol and other stress hormones. One study hypothesized that dark chocolate exerts its protection against cardiovascular diseases by blunting the physiological response to stress. The authors divided sixty-five subjects into two groups: a dark chocolate group (thirty-one subjects) and a placebo group (thirty-four subjects). Subjects in the dark chocolate group consumed 50 grams (1.75 ounces) of dark chocolate containing 125 mg of epicatechin. All subjects underwent a Trier Social Stress Test (TSST), which combined a three-minute preparation phase after a short introduction, a five-minute mock job interview, and a five-minute mental arithmetic task in front of an audience. All subjects were exposed to the psychological stressor two hours after ingestion of the chocolate or placebo, which was optically identical to the dark chocolate. The authors observed that only subjects who consumed dark chocolate showed significantly blunted cortisol and epinephrine reactivity to psychosocial stress compared to the placebo group. Moreover, subjects with higher plasma epicatechin levels showed lower stress reactivity, as revealed by lower secretion of the stress hormones cortisol and epinephrine. However, no difference was observed in the level of adrenocorticotropic hormone (ACTH), which stimulates adrenal glands to secrete cortisol due to activation of the HPA axis under stress. Therefore, dark chocolate is capable of reducing stress by blunting the effect of ACTH on the adrenal glands; as a result, less cortisol is secreted in response to stress.[12]

Another research group studied the effect of chocolate in reducing stress in pregnant women. Mothers also rated infant temperament after six months. The authors studied 305 mother-infants dyads and reported that mothers who consumed chocolate daily during pregnancy reported their infant's behavior more positively than mothers who never consumed or seldom consumed chocolate during pregnancy. Another intriguing finding was that maternal chocolate consumption also provided favorable effects on infants even in the most stressed mothers. It has been known that maternal stress may have a negative effect on an infant's behavior. The authors speculated that the active components of chocolate, such as methylxanthine, biogenic amines, and cannabinoid-like fatty acids, may play a mediating role in the association between maternal chocolate consumption and positive temperament of infants.[13]

> Maternal consumption of chocolate may be associated with positive temperament in infants.

Based on a study of one hundred pregnant women with uncomplicated pregnancy, the authors observed that maternal ingestion of dark chocolate induced much more reactivity in female fetuses than male fetuses, indicating innate gender differences for the effects of chocolate during the fetal period.[14] Chocolate also has other beneficial effects on pregnancy, including reduced blood pressure and better glycemic control and liver function in pregnant women.[15]

Chocolate Improves Mood and Subjective Well-Being

There are several studies in which investigators reported a potential link between eating chocolate and positive mood and subjective well-being. In one study involving twenty-seven healthy normal-weight women who ate a chocolate bar, apple, or nothing and recorded their subjective mood five, thirty, sixty, and ninety minutes after eating, the authors observed that women who ate an apple or chocolate reported reduced hunger and elevated mood, but the mood-elevating capacity of chocolate was more significant than the apple. Moreover, positive mood after eating chocolate lasted longer compared to eating an apple.[16]

In another study, negative, positive, or neutral mood was induced in subjects (forty-eight subjects randomly assigned to different groups) by showing them emotive film clips. Negative mood was induced in some subjects by showing them a sad sequence from a popular film, *The Champ*, in which a boy cried at the death of his father (duration of the clip: 2:51 minutes). Positive mood was induced by showing a clip from the movie *When Harry Met Sally* in which a woman and a man discussed an orgasm (duration: 2:35 minutes). For inducing neutral mood, a documentary on processing and usage of copper was shown (duration: 2:02 minutes). After watching movie clips, all subjects rated their momentary mood using a twenty-five-point scale, where scores between 21 and 25 were considered very good, between 16 and 20 good, between 11 and 15 medium, between 6 and 10 bad, and between 1 and 5 very bad. The authors observed that subjects who ate chocolate reported improved self-rated mood after watching the sad film clip compared to subjects who drank a mouthful of water, indicating that negative mood was reduced in chocolate eaters. In addition, after watching the happy film clip, mood ratings tended to be higher in the subjects who ate chocolate than in subjects who drank water. In a separate experiment using 113 subjects, the authors further investigated the capability of palatable versus unpalatable chocolate on reducing negative mood and observed that negative mood was only ameliorated in subjects who consumed palatable chocolate.[17] One published report concluded that consumption of cocoa flavonoids resulted in improvement in mood and cognitive performance during sustained mental effort.[18]

Chocolate consumption is associated with happiness and subjective well-being in older men. In one study involving older men (average age: seventy-six years), where 860 men preferred eating chocolate and 399 men preferred other types of candy, the authors observed that men who preferred chocolate had better health and psychological well-being. In addition, men preferring chocolate showed lower body mass index and waist circumference, indicating that they were healthier at the time of the study compared to elderly men who preferred other types of candy. The authors concluded that in the socioeconomically homogenous male cohort, chocolate preference in old age was associated with better

> Eating chocolate improves mood and feelings of well-being and may lower the risk of cognitive decline in elderly people.

health, optimism, and better psychological well-being.[19] Chocolate may also act as an antidepressant.[20] Chocolate consumption is associated with lower risk of cognitive decline in elderly subjects aged sixty-five years and over.[21]

Psychoactive Compounds Present in Chocolate

Methylxanthines (theobromine and caffeine) are present in chocolate. Theobromine (3, 7-dimethylxanthine) is also a metabolite of caffeine (1, 3, 7-trimethylxanthine), but in chocolate a higher amount of theobromine is found compared to caffeine. In 50 grams (1.75 ounces) of dark chocolate, 237–519 mg of theobromine may be present. The psychoactive properties of caffeine have been well studied, but there are relatively few studies regarding the psychoactive effects of theobromine. Caffeine, even at a lower dosage, increases alertness and mental energy as well as a subjective feeling of well-being. In one study, the authors showed that both the theobromine and the caffeine present in chocolate have psychostimulant effects, as evidenced by similar positive mood construct and cognitive function after subjects consumed either cocoa powder or a similar amount of caffeine and theobromine in combination. Moreover, additional experiments showed that the amount of methylxanthines present in dark chocolate and milk chocolate was sufficient to improve cognitive function in the subjects who volunteered for the study. However, white chocolate consumption showed no effect.[22] In another study, the authors speculated that methylxanthines in amounts found in 50 grams of chocolate may be responsible for the acquired taste for dark chocolate.[23]

Chocolate and cocoa contain chemicals (N-acyl-ethanolamines) that are chemically and pharmacologically related to endogenous cannabinoid anandamide ("anandamide" means internal bliss). The euphoric effect of smoking marijuana is due to interaction of the active ingredients of marijuana (delta-9-tetrahydrocannabinoid; THC) with the cannabinoid receptors present in the human brain. Anandamide is the endogenous equivalent of THC, which is also capable of interacting with cannabinoid receptors, thus mimicking the psychoactive effects of smoking marijuana. The two N-acetyl-ethanolamines (N-oleoyl-ethanolamine and N-linoleoyl-ethanolamine) present in chocolate appear to interfere with the brain's ability to degrade anandamide by hydrolysis, thus prolonging the blissful effect of anandamide and producing a sense of well-being and positive mood after eating chocolate. However, some investigators argue that the low amounts of these active compounds present in chocolate may not be sufficient to induce this neurochemical effect.[24]

Some organic compounds such as phenylethylamine and tyramine are also present in chocolate, which may be involved in mood-elevating effects after eating chocolate. However, the role of these biogenic amines as psychoactive compounds in chocolate is controversial because these compounds are present in low concentrations. Valeric acid present in chocolate is also a stress reducer.[25] Chocolate stimulates the release of endorphins, which are the endogenous equivalent of opiates, with mood-elevating properties. Chocolate also reduces stress and elevates mood by prompting serotonin production. Serotonin is a neurotransmitter that has a calming effect.[26] Many antidepressants (e.g., SSRIs: selective serotonin reuptake inhibitors) act by increasing serotonin concentrations in the brain (at synapses) by inhibiting the uptake of serotonin by serotonin transporters. The bioactive compounds present in chocolate are summarized in table 10.2. The mechanisms of the stress-relieving and mood-enhancing properties of chocolate include the following:

- Chocolate reduces the secretion of the stress hormone cortisol.
- Epicatechin present in chocolate may blunt the effect of ACTH on the adrenal glands in response to stress; as a result, smaller amounts of cortisol are secreted.
- Theobromine and caffeine present in dark chocolate may have psychoactive properties and are also responsible for the acquired taste of dark chocolate.
- The two N-acetyl-ethanolamines (N-oleoyl-ethanolamine and N-linoleoyl-ethanolamine) present in chocolate appear to interfere with the brain's ability to degrade endogenous cannabinoid (anandamide), thus producing a sense of well-being and positive mood after eating chocolate.
- Valeric acid present in chocolate is a stress reducer.
- Eating chocolate stimulates the release of endorphins, which are the endogenous equivalent of opiates and have mood-elevating effects.
- Chocolate also promotes serotonin production. Serotonin is a neurotransmitter that can improve mood.
- Dark chocolate and milk chocolate, but not white chocolate, can reduce stress and enhance mood. However, dark chocolate is best for reducing stress.

ANTIOXIDANT EFFECT OF CHOCOLATE

It has been well documented in the medical literature that psychological stress (simply referred to as stress) results in activation of the hypothalamic-pituitary-adrenal axis (HPA axis), which produces cortisol and other stress hormones. Elevated cortisol levels are associated with increased oxidative

stress, and many ill health effects of chronic stress are related to increased oxidative stress as a result of the increased production of free radicals. Therefore,
foods rich in antioxidants have beneficial effects in reducing oxidative stress
in people who are experiencing chronic stress. Many fruits and vegetables
are rich in antioxidants, and consumption of these foods has many health
benefits. In addition, tea and coffee are rich in antioxidants (see chapter 8).
Chocolate is rich in antioxidants due to the presence of many natural antioxidant phytochemicals. Thus the stress-relieving effects of chocolate are partly
due to its antioxidant properties.

The epicatechin and catechin found in cocoa are monomeric compounds,
but these molecules are also the building blocks of procyanidins, which are
oligomers and polymers of catechin and epicatechin. All of these compounds
are strong antioxidants. However, epicatechin, catechin, and related polyphenolic compounds are also found in other plant-based foods. Tea contains
the highest amount of catechin (102–418 mg/L), but red wine is another rich
source of catechin (27–96 mg/L).[27] In one study, the authors reported that
the amount of catechin was 6.0 mg/gm in cocoa extract, 1.2 mg/gm in cocoa
powder, and 0.6 mg/gm in dark chocolate, while the epicatechin level was
59.0 mg/gm in cocoa extract, 2.5 mg/gm in cocoa powder, and 1.85 mg/gm
in dark chocolate.[28] Therefore, 40 grams of dark chocolate should contain approximately 24 mg of catechin and 74 mg of epicatechin.

Another study showed that when subjects ate chocolate, plasma epicatechin levels increased from 22 mmol/L (millimoles/liter) to 257 mmol/L,
and the antioxidant capacity of plasma was also increased by 31 percent two
hours after eating chocolate. Moreover, thiobarbituric acid reactive substance (malondialdehyde), a marker of oxidative stress in the blood, was reduced by 40 percent, indicating superior antioxidant properties of the blood
after eating chocolate. Plasma epicatechin levels and plasma antioxidant
capacity returned to the baseline value six hours after eating chocolate. The
authors concluded that consumption of chocolate can result in significant
increases in plasma epicatechin concentrations as well as increased antioxidant capacity of the blood.[29]

A very common assay known as oxygen radical absorption capacity
(ORAC) is used to determine the antioxidant content of a food. This assay
is based on the capacity of a food to neutralize oxygen radicals generated by
a chemical process during the assay procedure. In general, a higher ORAC

value indicates the higher antioxidant capacity of a food. However, there are controversies regarding the use of ORAC values to assess the antioxidant capacity of food because the ORAC assay estimates the in vitro antioxidant capacity of a food, which may be different when the food is consumed by humans. Nevertheless, ORAC values provide a rough guide of the antioxidant capacity of various foods.

The ORAC values for dark chocolate, milk chocolate, unsweetened chocolate, baking chips, and natural coca powders have been reported in one study. In addition, researchers measured the epicatechin, catechin, and procyanidin content of these chocolate products. The authors analyzed five different commercially available dark chocolates (dark chocolates 1–5), three different brands of white chocolate, and several brands of baking chips, natural powder, and unsweetened chocolate. The catechin level varied from 0.11 to 0.33 mg/gm (4.4–16 mg in a 40-gram bar) in dark chocolate and from 0.05 to 0.12 mg/gm (7.2–9.6 mg in a 40-gram bar) in milk chocolate. Similarly, epicatechin and total procyanidins were higher in dark chocolates compared to milk chocolates. As expected due to the higher content of antioxidant compounds, the ORAC values of all five different brands of dark chocolate were significantly higher than the milk chocolate.[30] White chocolate, though, is a poor source of antioxidants.[31]

> Dark chocolate has more antioxidant compounds than milk chocolate. White chocolate is a poor source of antioxidants.

CHOCOLATE PROTECTS THE HEART

Probably the most cited benefit of eating chocolate is protection against cardiovascular diseases (heart diseases). Chronic stress increases the risk of cardiovascular diseases, including heart attack, because chronic stress significantly increases oxidative stress. Excess production of free radicals increases oxidative stress, and these very reactive free radicals chemically modify the structure of lipids (lipid peroxidation), making stable lipid molecules unstable. In general, the oxidation of low-density lipoprotein cholesterol (LDL cholesterol: bad cholesterol) significantly increases the risk of cardiovascular diseases because these oxidized lipids tend to deposit in the coronary arteries, making such arteries narrower and thus restricting blood flow.

Antioxidants present in chocolate act as scavengers of free radicals and prevent lipid peroxidation. In one study, the authors conducted a clinical trial where forty-five nonsmoker health volunteers consumed 75 grams (2.6 ounces) of dark chocolate, dark chocolate enriched with cocoa polyphenols (high-polyphenol chocolate), or white chocolate for three weeks. The authors observed that the concentration of high-density lipoprotein cholesterol (HDL cholesterol: good cholesterol) was increased by 11.4 percent in subjects who ate dark chocolate and by 13.7 percent in subjects who ate high-polyphenol chocolate, but it was decreased by 2.9 percent in subjects who ate white chocolate. However, the concentration of serum low-density lipoprotein-diene, a marker of lipid peroxidation, was reduced by 11.9 percent in all three groups. White chocolate contains cocoa butter but no cocoa solids. Some cocoa butter is also added to dark chocolate. Therefore, the beneficial fatty acid present in cocoa butter may inhibit lipid peroxidation.[32]

Eating smaller amounts of chocolate also has health benefits. In one study, the authors measured blood pressure at the beginning of the study and after five years in 470 elderly men who were free from chronic diseases. In addition, the authors investigated causes of death during fifteen years of follow-up. One-third of the subjects did not eat any cocoa products, but other subjects consumed cocoa by eating a variety of cocoa-containing foods, including dark chocolate and milk chocolate. Daily cocoa intake was determined through the cocoa content of each food. The median cocoa intake was 4.18 grams per day (9.7 grams/.03 ounces of dark chocolate or 14 grams/.05 ounces of milk chocolate per day) in subjects who consumed the highest amount of cocoa, and this group showed significantly lower blood pressure than people who did not use any cocoa products. Moreover, in this group, mortality from cardiovascular diseases was reduced by approximately 50 percent compared to elderly men who did not consume any cocoa-containing products.[33] Chocolate consumption also reduces mortality following a first heart attack.

Chocolate protects against heart failure. In a study based on 31,823 women aged forty-eight to eighty-three years without any history of diabetes, heart failure, or heart attack, the authors reported that compared to women who did not eat any chocolate, the rate of heart failure was 26 percent lower among women who consumed one to three servings of chocolate per month and 32 percent lower among women who consumed one to two servings of chocolate per week.[34] The mechanisms by which chocolate protects the heart are summarized in table 10.3.

> Eating one to two servings of chocolate per week or even consuming one to three servings of chocolate per month protects against heart failure.

Table 10.3.   How chocolate protects the heart

Proposed Mechanism	Comments
Chocolate is rich in antioxidants, and eating chocolate reduces oxidative stress	Eating chocolate reduces oxidative stress and protects the heart. Interestingly, white chocolate, which contains cocoa butter, can also reduce lipid peroxidation, although it is generally accepted that dark chocolate is superior to milk chocolate for protecting the heart while white chocolate has few benefits.
Increasing HDL cholesterol	Dark chocolate can significantly increase the concentration of HDL cholesterol (good cholesterol), which protects the heart, but white chocolate has no such beneficial effect.
Stress-relieving effect of chocolate	Chronic stress increases the risk of cardiovascular diseases. Chocolate is very effective in reducing stress.
Lowering blood pressure	Chocolate reduces blood pressure through a variety of mechanisms, including increased serum nitric oxide levels, which improve endothelial function and restore normal blood flow. Lower blood pressure also protects the heart.
Inhibiting platelet activation/aggregation	Chocolate reduces platelet activation, thus preventing clot formation (aspirin-like effect in protecting the heart).
Anti-inflammatory effect	Chocolate polyphenols have an anti-inflammatory effect and reduce C-reactive protein concentrations. Higher levels of C-reactive protein in the blood increase the risk of heart attack.
Anti-diabetic effect	Diabetes increases the risk of heart attack. Chocolate improves insulin sensitivity and thus protects against metabolic syndrome and diabetes.

CHOCOLATE REDUCES BLOOD PRESSURE AND LOWERS THE RISK OF DIABETES

Decreased nitric oxide levels in the blood are associated with endothelial (the inner lining of blood vessels) dysfunction, which is the earliest triggering event in atherosclerosis. Such endothelial dysfunction may increase the risk of hypertension, high cholesterol, and diabetes. Insulin sensitivity also depends on nitric oxide bioavailability. Cocoa and chocolate increase serum nitric oxide levels, thus correcting endothelial dysfunction and restoring normal blood flow. Chocolate may lower blood pressure by acting as an angiotensin-converting enzyme inhibitor (several blood pressure–lowering drugs act through this mechanism) and may also reduce inflammation. In one study involving nineteen hypertensive male patients with impaired glucose tolerance (prediabetic), the authors showed that eating 100 grams of dark chocolate per day for fifteen days was associated with lowered blood pressure and improved insulin sensitivity. However, eating white chocolate did not improve insulin sensitivity. In addition, subjects who ate dark chocolate showed a reduction in serum cholesterol and LDL cholesterol (bad cholesterol).[35]

Other studies have shown an association between long-term chocolate consumption and lower risk of diabetes. In one study involving 7,802 subjects, the author showed that the best effect was observed in subjects who ate chocolate (one ounce; approximately 28 grams) two to six times per week, where the risk of diabetes was lowered by 34 percent.[36]

CHOCOLATE MAY REDUCE THE RISK OF STROKE

Several studies have indicated that regular consumption of chocolate may reduce the risk of stroke in both men and women. Larsson et al., based on a study of 37,103 men during 10.2 years of follow-up, reported that the risk of stroke was reduced by 17 percent in men who consumed an average of 62.9 grams (2.2 ounces) of chocolate peer week compared to men who did not eat any chocolate. The authors speculated that the beneficial polyphenolic compounds present in chocolate, such as epicatechin, catechin, and procyanidins, may reduce the risk of stroke by several mechanisms, including antioxidant, antiplatelet, and anti-inflammatory effects, as well as by lowering blood pressure and improving endothelial functions.[37]

CHOCOLATE FOR WEIGHT LOSS

Eating one standard chocolate bar (40–50 grams) is associated with intake of approximately 200–250 calories. Therefore, common sense tells us that eating chocolate on a regular basis may be associated with weight gain. However, research indicates that eating chocolate in moderation may actually help in losing weight. Chocolate may act as an appetite suppressant.[38] A study with twelve normal-weight healthy females showed that eating dark chocolate (30 grams; 1.1 ounces) decreased hunger and increased satiety (the sense of being full after eating). A study with male volunteers also showed that eating dark chocolate (100 grams; 3.5 ounces) before eating a meal ad libitum (at one's pleasure) decreased food intake and prompted a higher satiety score when compared with eating 100 grams (3.5 ounces) of white chocolate before a meal. Another study showed that people who ate chocolate had a lower body mass index (BMI). Several mechanisms, including decreasing the expression of genes involved in fatty acid synthesis, reducing the digestion and absorption of fats and carbohydrates, and increasing satiety, may explain the association between eating chocolate and the modulation of body weight.[39]

OTHER HEATH BENEFITS OF CHOCOLATE

Chocolate may have some anticancer effect. One study has shown that the flavanols and procyanidins of cocoa and chocolate inhibit the growth of human colonic cancer cells. Chocolate reduces the likelihood of preeclampsia (elevated blood pressure and excretion of protein in the urine during pregnancy; if not treated, it may have an adverse outcome). In one study based on 2,291 pregnant women, the authors showed that compared to women who consumed less than one serving of chocolate per week, women who ate five or more servings of chocolate per week had 30 percent less chance of developing preeclampsia during the last three months of pregnancy.[40]

Chocolate may reduce the risk of preeclampsia.

Chocolate reduces the risk of dementia and may protect against Alzheimer's disease. Chocolate flavanols are absorbed after eating chocolate and penetrate as well as accumulate in the regions of the brain (especially the hippocampus) involved in learning and memory and promote neurogenesis (the process by which nerve cells are generated). Chocolate also improves blood flow in the brain and promotes angiogenesis (the formation of new blood vessels from existing blood vessels) in the brain and sensory system. As a result, chocolate consumption improves cognitive performance and protects against developing age-related dementia.[41]

Prolonged exercise increases oxidative stress, but eating dark chocolate before exercise may counteract increased oxidative stress and normalize plasma glucose levels.[42] In one study, the authors showed that eating high cocoa liquor/polyphenol-rich chocolate (usually dark chocolate) may reduce the burden of symptoms of chronic fatigue syndrome.[43]

DARK OR WHITE CHOCOLATE AND HOW MUCH?

Eating dark chocolate provides more health benefits than consuming white chocolate, but the question is how much chocolate a day. There is some confusion because many studies published in the literature are short-term studies where subjects ate 40–100 grams of chocolate (one to three chocolate bars) per day for one or two weeks. However, long-term studies indicate that eating chocolate every day is not needed for obtaining health benefits. In fact, consuming a high amount of chocolate every day may not provide any health benefits but may be a health risk because chocolate is high in calories and high in potassium. Eating too much chocolate each day for a prolonged period of time may cause weight gain instead of weight loss, and high potassium may adversely affect people with kidney problems.

There is no clear-cut guideline in the medical literature for optimum consumption of chocolate. C-reactive protein is a marker of inflammation, and a higher blood level of C-reactive protein significantly increases the risk of cardiovascular diseases, including heart attack. In one study, the authors showed that eating moderate amounts of chocolate lowered blood levels of C-reactive protein, but with higher consumption, C-reactive protein levels were increased. The best effect was observed with consumption of up to 6.7 grams of chocolate every day or consuming 20 grams of chocolate every three days.[44] A standard chocolate bar usually contains 40–50 grams of chocolate, while a small square may contain 6 grams of chocolate. For getting health benefits, eating one small cube of chocolate (6 grams) daily or a 40-gram chocolate bar up to twice a week is sufficient. If you are feeling stressed, you can eat one bar of dark chocolate (40–50 grams; 1.4–1.75 ounces) to improve your mood, but do not make it a regular habit. For a person experiencing chronic stress or depression, chocolate is not going to cure that problem; in this situation, medical help is needed.

CHOCOLATE CRAVING/INDULGENCE

Chocolate is a comfort food and also a food craved by both men and women. In general, more women crave chocolate than men, and eating candies or sweets may not be good enough to satisfy that craving. In one study, the authors reported that approximately half of American women crave chocolate most commonly around the onset of menstruation. If it is hypothesized that the craving for chocolate is a direct hormonal effect in women, then it is expected that there should be a 38 percent decline in chocolate craving among women after menopause. However, the authors observed a 13.4 percent decline in craving in postmenopausal women, indicating that the craving could also be related to a response to acute stress and other factors.[45] Although chocolate craving is common, sometimes guilt is also associated with eating chocolate, especially because there is a common perception that eating chocolate is associated with increased body weight. However, studies clearly indicate that

> The craving for chocolate in women may increase around the onset of menstruation.

moderate consumption of chocolate is not associated with weight gain but in fact may help in losing weight.

People often crave chocolate when feeling depressed or sad. In one study when music was used to induce a happy or sad mood, chocolate intake (but not the intake of chocolate substitute) was increased in those who heard the sad music.[46] "Chocolate addiction" or "chocoholic" are common media terms, but chocolate craving is not related to craving for an illicit drug. Cravers for chocolate usually consume twelve bars of chocolate per week and crave chocolate about six times a week. Usually the cause of addiction is the taste, smell, and texture of chocolate. Craving chocolate may be considered an eating disorder, and eating such high amounts of chocolate is not good for one's health. Dieters and secret eaters may also feel guilty after eating chocolate.[47]

CONCLUSION

Chocolate, especially dark chocolate, has a stress-reducing effect as well as many other health benefits. The most well-documented health benefit of eating chocolate in moderation is protection against cardiovascular diseases, including heart attack and heart failure. Chocolate may protect pregnant woman against preeclampsia and may also have positive effects on infants. In general, eating just 20 grams of chocolate every three days or eating only 6 grams of chocolate per day is sufficient to get the beneficial effects of eating chocolate. Eating excessive amounts of chocolate (several chocolate bars every day for a prolonged time) is not beneficial for health because chocolate is high in calories. There are also controversies regarding the positive effect of chocolate on skin health. Although some studies have reported that chocolate provides protection from UV-induced skin damage (sunburn), other studies have failed to report such positive findings. In one study, the authors reported that dark chocolate, when consumed in normal amounts for four weeks, exacerbated acne in male subjects.[48]

Notes

CHAPTER 1. ADVERSE EFFECTS OF STRESS ON MIND AND BODY

1. P. M. Goodnite, "Stress: A concept analysis," *Nursing Forum* 49, no. 1 (January–March 2014): 71–74.

2. S. Cohen and D. Janicki-Deverts, "Who's stressed? Distributions of psychological stress in the United States, in probability samples from 1983, 2006 and 2009," *Journal of Applied Social Psychology* 42, no. 6 (June 2012): 1320–34.

3. "Stress in America: 2017 Snapshot," American Psychological Association, http://www.stressinamerica.org, and other reports related to stress published by the American Psychological Association, accessed March 31, 2017.

4. American Psychological Association, "The impact of stress: 2011," http://www.apa.org/news/press/releases/stress/2011/impact.aspx, accessed March 31, 2017.

5. "The burden of stress in America," NPR/Robert Wood Johnson Foundation/Harvard School of Public health report, media.npr.org/documents/2014/july/npr_rwfj_harvard_stress_poll.pdf, accessed March 31, 2017.

6. A. Nerukar, A. Bitton, R. B. Davis, R. S. Phillips, et al., "When physicians counsel about stress: Results of a national study," *JAMA Internal Medicine* 173, no. 1 (January 2013): 76–77.

7. F. S. Dhabhar, "A hassle a day may keep the doctor away: Stress and augmentation of immune function," *Integrative Comparative Biology* 42, no. 3 (July 2002): 556–64.

8. J. R. Edward and C. L. Cooper, "The impact of positive psychological states on physical health: A review and theoretical framework," *Social Science and Medicine* 27, no. 12 (December 1988): 1447–559.

9. R. S. Lazarus, "Toward better research on stress and coping," *American Psychologist* 55, no. 6 (June 2000): 665–73.

10. M. Kumar, S. Sharma, S. Gupta, S. Vaish, et al., "Effect of stress on academic performance in medical students: A cross sectional study," *Indian Journal of Physiology and Pharmacology* 58, no. 1 (January–March 2014): 81–86.

11. S. S. Adaramola, "Job stress and productivity increase," *Work* 41, no. S1 (2012): S2955–88.

12. B. L. Simmons and D. L. Nelson, "Eustress at work: The relationship between hope and health in hospital nurses," *Healthcare Management Review* 26, no. 4 (Fall 2001): 7–18.

13. G. Gustafsson, B. Persson, S. Eriksson, A. Norberg, et al., "Personality traits among burnt out and non-burnt out healthcare professionals at the same workplace: A pilot study," *International Journal of Mental Health Nursing* 18, no. 5 (October 2009): 336–48.

14. K. L. Zellars, W. A. Hochwarter, P. L. Perrewe, M. Hoffman, et al., "Experiencing job burnout: The roles of positive and negative traits and states," *Journal of Applied Social Psychology* 34, no. 5 (May 2004): 887–911.

15. B. Campos, S. W. Wang, T. Plaksina, R. L. Repetti, et al., "Positive and negative emotion in daily life of dual earner couples with children," *Journal of Family Psychology* 27, no. 1 (February 2013): 76–85.

16. A. Steptoe, K. O'Donnell, M. Marmot, and J. Wardle, "Positive affect, psychological well-being, and good sleep," *Journal of Psychosomatic Research* 64, no. 4 (April 2008): 409–15.

17. B. L. Fredrickson, "What good are positive emotions?" *Review of General Psychology* 2, no. 3 (September 1998): 300–319.

18. M. A. Cohen, B. L. Fredrickson, S. L. Brown, and J. A. Mikels, "Happiness unpacked: Positive emotions increase life satisfaction by building resilience," *Emotions* 9, no. 3 (June 2009): 361–68.

19. B. L. Fredrickson, M. M. Tugade, C. E. Waugh, and G. R. Larkin, "What good are positive emotions in crisis? A prospective study of resilience and emotions

following terrorist attacks on the United States on September 11th, 2001," *Journal of Personality and Social Psychology* 84, no. 2 (February 2003): 365–76.

20. C. T. Gloria and M. A. Steinhardt, "Relationships among positive emotions, coping, resilience and mental health," *Stress and Health* 32, no. 2 (April 2016): 145–56.

21. B. L. Fredrickson, M. A. Cohn, K. A. Coffey, J. Pek, et al., "Open hearts build lives: Positive emotions, induced through loving-kindness meditation, building consequential personal resources," *Journal of Personality and Social Psychology* 95, no. 5 (November 2008): 1045–62.

22. C. Mogilner, "The pursuit of happiness: Time, money and social connection," *Psychological Science* 21, no. 9 (September 2010): 1348–54.

23. J. Quoidbach, E. W. Dunn, K. V. Petrides, and M. Mikolajczak, "Money giveth, money taketh away: The dual effect of wealth on happiness," *Psychological Science* 21, no. 6 (June 2010): 759–63.

24. E. W. Dunn, L. B. Aknin, and M. L. Norton, "Spending money on others promotes happiness," *Science* 319, no. 5870 (March 2008): 1687–88.

25. D. Kahneman and A. Deaton, "High income improves evaluation of life but not emotional well-being," *Proceedings of the National Academy of Sciences, USA* 107, no. 38 (September 2010): 16489–93.

26. G. L. Matheny, "Money not key to happiness, survey finds," *Physician Executive* 34, no. 6 (November–December 2008): 14–15.

27. M. Kalia, "Assessing the economic impact of stress: The modern day hidden epidemic," *Metabolism* 52, no. 6, S1 (June 2002): S49–54.

28. M. D. Seidman and R. T. Standring, "Noise and quality of life," *International Journal of Environmental Research and Public Health* 7, no. 10 (October 2010): 3730–38.

29. B. D. Buller, V. Cokkinides, H. I. Hall, A. M. Hartman, et al., "Prevalence of sunburn, sun protection and indoor tanning behaviors among Americans: Review from national surveys and case studies of 3 states," *Journal of American Academy of Dermatology* 65, no. 5, S1 (November 2011): S114–23.

30. P. M. Mannucci, S. Harari, I. Martinelli, and M. Frachini, "Effects on health of air pollution: A narrative review," *Internal and Emergency Medicine* 10, no. 6 (September 2015): 657–62.

31. M. A. McGuigan, "Common culprits in childhood poisoning: Epidemiology, treatment and parental advice for prevention," *Pediatric Drugs* 1, no. 4 (October–December 1999): 313–24.

32. S. Patra, G. Sikka, A. K. Khaowas, and V. Kumar, "Successful intervention in a child with toxic methemoglobin due to nail polish remover poisoning," *Indian Journal of Occupational and Environmental Medicine* 15, no. 3 (September 2011): 137–38.

33. M. Kaess, P. Parzer, L. Mehl, L. Weil, et al., "Stress vulnerability in male youth with Internet gaming addiction," *Psychoneuroendocrinology* 77 (March 2017): 244–51.

34. T. DeAngelis, "Is Internet addiction real?" *Monitor on Psychology* 31, no. 4 (April 2000): 1–5.

35. J. B. Grubbs, N. Stauner, J. J. Exline, K. I. Pargament, et al., "Perceived addiction to Internet pornography and psychological distress: Examining relationships concurrently and over time," *Psychology of Addictive Behavior* 29, no. 4 (December 2015): 1056–67.

36. D. N. Greenfield and R. A. Davis, "Lost in cyberspace: The web@work," *Cyber Psychology and Behavior* 5, no. 4 (August 2002): 347–53.

37. E. Aboujaoude, L. M. Koran, N. Gamel, M. D. Large, et al., "Potential markers for problematic Internet use: A telephone survey of 2513 adults," *CNS Spectrums* 11, no. 10 (October 2006): 750–55.

38. M. A. Moreno, L. Jelenchick, E. Cox, H. Young, et al., "Problematic Internet use among US youth: A systematic review," *Archives of Pediatric and Adolescence Medicine* 165, no. 9 (September 2011): 797–805.

39. H. Odaci and M. Kalkan, "Problematic Internet use, loneliness and dating anxiety among young adult university students," *Computers and Education* 55, no. 3 (November 2010): 1091–97.

40. F. Lin, Y. Zhou, Y. Du, L. Qin, et al., "Abnormal white matter integrity in adolescents with Internet addiction disorder: A tract based spatial statistics study," *PLoS One* 7, no. 1 (January 2012): e30253.

41. J. A. Roberts, L. H. Yaya, and C. Manolis, "The invisible addiction: Cell-phone activities and addictions among male and female college students," *Journal of Behavioral Addiction* 3, no. 4 (December 2014): 254–65.

42. P. Smetaniuk, "A preliminary investigation into the prevalence and prediction of problematic cell phone use," *Journal of Behavioral Addiction* 3, no. 1 (March 2014): 41–53.

43. J. De-Sola Gutierrez, F. Rodriguez de Fonseca, and G. Rubio, "Cell-phone addiction: A review," *Frontiers in Psychiatry* 24, no. 7 (October 2016): 175.

44. M. L. Pettit and K. A. DeBarr, "Perceived stress, energy drink consumption, and academic performances among college students," *Journal of American College Health* 59, no. 5 (2011): 335–41.

45. G. S. Trapp, K. Allen, T. A. O'Sullivan, M. Robinson, et al., "Energy drink consumption is associated with anxiety in Australian young adults," *Depression and Anxiety* 31, no. 5 (May 2014): 420–28.

46. G. Richards and A. P. Smith, "A review of energy drinks and mental health, with a focus on stress, anxiety and depression," *Journal of Caffeine Research* 6, no. 2 (June 2016): 49–63.

47. P. Sood, S. Priyadarshini, and P. Aich, "Estimation of psychological stress in humans: A combination of theory and practice," *PLoS One* 8, no. 5 (May 2013): e63044.

48. C. Kirschbaum, K. M. Pirke, and D. H. Hellhammer, "The Trier Social Stress Test: A tool for investigating psychobiological stress response in a laboratory setting," *Neuropsychology* 28, nos. 1–2 (1993): 76–81.

49. J. Campbell and U. Ehlert, "Acute psychological stress: Does the emotional stress response correspond with physiological response," *Psychoneuroendocrinology* 37, no. 8 (August 2012): 1111–34.

50. M. Gunnar and K. Quevedo, "The neurobiology of stress and development," *Annual Review of Psychology* 58 (January 2007): 145–73.

51. A. Dasgupta and K. Klein, *Antioxidants in foods, vitamins and supplements: Prevention and treatment of disease* (Waltham, MA: Elsevier, 2014), 97–110.

52. M. F. Juruena, "Early life stress and HPA axis trigger recurrent adulthood depression," *Epilepsy and Behavior* 38 (September 2014): 148–59.

53. Z. Bhagwagar, S. Hafizi, and P. J. Cowen, "Increased salivary cortisol after waking in depression," *Psychopharmacology* (Berlin) 182, no. 1 (October 2005): 54–57.

54. M. Prussner, D. H. Hellhammer, J. C. Prussner, and S. J. Lupien, "Self-reported depressive symptoms and stress levels in healthy young men: Associations with the cortisol response to awakening," *Psychosomatic Medicine* 65, no. 1 (January–February 2003): 92–99.

55. Z. N. Mannie, C. J. Harmer, and P. J. Cowen, "Increased salivary cortisol levels in young people at familial risk of depression," *American Journal of Psychiatry* 164, no. 4 (April 2007): 617–21.

56. G. Grossi, A. Perski, M. Ekstedt, T. Johansson, et al., "The morning salivary cortisol response in burnout," *Journal of Psychosomatic Research* 59, no. 2 (August 2005): 103–11.

57. F. Hardeveld, J. Spijker, S. A. Vreeburg, R. D. Graaf, et al., "Increased cortisol awakening response was associated with time to recurrence of major depressive events," *Psychoneuroendocrinology* 50 (December 2014): 62–71.

58. D. B. O'Connor, H. Hendrickx, T. Dadd, T. D. Elliman, et al., "Cortisol awakening rise in middle aged women in relation to psychological stress," *Psychoneuroendocrinology* 34, no. 10 (November 2009): 1486–94.

59. J. M. Violanti, D. Fekedulgen, M. E. Andrew, T. A. Hartley, et al., "The impact of perceived stress intensity and frequency of police work occupational stressors on the cortisol awakening response (CAR); findings from BCOPS study," *Psychoneuroendocrinology* 75 (January 2017): 124–31.

60. S. M. Staufenbiel, B. W. Penninx, A. T. Spijker, B. M. Elzinga, et al., "Hair cortisol, stress and mental health in humans: A systematic review," *Psychoneuroendocrinology* 38, no. 8 (August 2013): 1220–35.

61. S. Iglesias, D. Jacobsen, D. Gonzalez, S. Azzara, et al., "Hair cortisol: A novel tool for evaluating stress in programs of stress management," *Life Sciences* 141 (November 2015): 188–92.

62. S. Schiavone, V. Jaquet, L. Trabace, and K. H. Krause, "Severe life stress and oxidative stress in the brain: From animal models to human pathology," *Antioxidant and Redox Signaling* 18, no. 12 (April 2013): 1475–90.

63. E. S. Epel, E. H. Blackburn, J. Lin, D. Dhabhar, et al., "Accelerated telomere shortening in response to life stress," *Proceedings of the National Academy of Sciences, USA* 101, no. 49 (December 2004): 17312–15.

64. K. Aschbacher, A. O'Donovan, O. M. Wolkowitz, F. S. Dhabhar, et al., "Good stress, bad stress, and oxidative stress: Insights from anticipatory cortisol activity," *Psychoneuroendocrinology* 38, no. 9 (September 2013): 1689–708.

65. M. D. De Bellis and A. Zisk, "The biological effects of childhood trauma," *Child and Adolescent Psychiatric Clinic of North America* 23, no. 2 (April 2014): 185–222.

66. C. Hammen, "Depression, and stressful environments: Identifying gaps in conceptualization and measurement," *Anxiety Stress and Coping* 29, no. 4 (July 2016): 335–51.

67. C. Hammen, "Stress and depression," *Annual Review of Clinical Psychology* 1 (April 2005): 293–319.

68. E. S. Sheets and W. E. Craighead, "Comparing chronic interpersonal and noninterpersonal stress domains as predictors of depression recurrence in emerging adults," *Behavior Research and Therapy* 63 (December 2014): 36–42.

69. S. Vrshek-Schallhorn, C. B. Stroud, S. Mineka, C. Hammen, et al., "Chronic and episodic interpersonal stress as statistically unique predictors of depression in two samples of emerging adults," *Journal of Abnormal Psychology* 124, no. 4 (November 2015): 918–32.

70. M. F. Marin, C. Lord, J. Andrews, R. P. Juster, et al., "Chronic stress, cognitive functioning and mental health," *Neurobiology of Learning and Memory* 96, no. 4 (November 2011): 583–95.

71. A. Ambelas and M. George, "Individualized stress vulnerability in manic depressive patients with repeated episodes," *Journal of the Royal Society of Medicine* 81 (August 1988): 448–49.

72. J. A. Hardway, N. A. Crowley, C. M. Bulik, and T. L. Kash, "Integrate circuits and molecular components for stress and feeding: Implications for eating disorders," *Genes, Brain and Behavior* 14, no. 1 (January 2015): 85–97.

73. P. K. Priya, M. Rajappa, S. Kattimani, P. S. Mohanraj, et al., "Association of neurotrophins, inflammation and stress with suicide risk in young adults," *Clinica Chimica Acta* 457 (June 2016): 41–45.

74. M. Pompili, L. Sher, G. Serafini, A. Forte, et al., "Posttraumatic stress disorder and suicide risk among veterans: A literature review," *Journal of Nervous and Mental Disease* 201, no. 9 (September 2013): 802–12.

75. J. P. Herman, N. K. Mueller, and H. Figueiredo, "Role of GABA and glutamate circuitry in hypothalamo-pituitary-adrenocortical stress integration," *Annals of the New York Academy of Science* 1018 (June 2004): 35–45.

76. A. S. Zannas, D. R. McQuoid, M. E. Payne, D. C. Steffens, et al., "Negative life stress and longitudinal hippocampal volume changes in older adults with and without depression," *Journal of Psychiatry Research* 47, no. 6 (June 2013): 829–34.

77. P. J. Gianaros, J. R. Jennings, L. K. Sheu, P. J. Greer, et al., "Prospective reports of chronic life stress decreased gray matter volume in the hippocampus," *NeuroImage* 35, no. 2 (April 2007): 795–803.

78. S. Chetty, A. R. Friedman, K. Taravosh-Lahn, E. D. Kirby, et al., "Stress and glucocorticoids promote oligodendrogenesis in the adult hippocampus," *Molecular Psychiatry* 19, no. 12 (December 2014): 1275–383.

79. E. B. Ansell, K. Rando, K. Tuit, J. Guarnaccia, et al., "Cumulative adversity and smaller gray matter volume in medial prefrontal, anterior cingulate and insula region," *Biological Psychiatry* 72, no. 1 (July 2012): 57–64.

80. B. L. Ganzel, P. Kim, G. H. Glover, and E. Temple, "Resilience after 9/11: Multimodal imaging evidence for stress-related change in healthy adult brain," *NeuroImage* 40, no. 2 (April 2008): 788–95.

81. H. J. Kang, B. Violeti, T. Hajszan, G. Raijkowska, et al., "Decreased expression of synapse related genes and loss of synapses in major depressive disorders," *Nature Medicine* 18, no. 9 (September 2012): 1413–17.

82. F. Calabrese, R. Molteni, G. Racagni, and M. A. Riva, "Neural plasticity: A link between stress and mood disorders," *Psychoneuroendocrinology* 34, no. S1 (December 2009): S208–17.

83. G. M. Lawson, J. S. Camins, L. Wisse, J. Wu, et al., "Childhood socioeconomic status and childhood maltreatment: Distinct associations with brain structure," *PLoS One* 12, no. 4 (April 2017): e0175690.

84. M. M. Riem, L. R. Alnik, D. Out, M. H. Van Ijzendoorn, et al., "Beating the brain about abuse: Empirical and meta-analytic studies of the association between maltreatment and hippocampal volume across childhood and adolescence," *Developmental Psychopathology* 27, no. 2 (May 2015): 507–20.

85. A. L. van Harmelen, M. J. van Tol, N. J. van deer Wee, D. J. Veltman, et al., "Reduced medial prefrontal cortex volume in adults reporting childhood emotional maltreatment," *Biological Psychiatry* 68, no. 9 (November 2010): 832–38.

86. H. Iso, C. Date, A. Yamamoto, H. Toyoshima, et al., "Perceived mental stress and mortality from cardiovascular disease among Japanese men and women: The Japan collaborative cohort study for evaluation of cancer risk sponsored by Monobusho (JACC Study)," *Circulation* 106, no. 10 (September 2002): 1229–336.

87. H. Nabi, M. Kivimaki, G. D. Batty, M. J. Shipley, et al., "Increased risk of coronary heart disease among individuals reporting adverse impact of stress on their

health: The Whitehall II prospective cohort study," *European Heart Journal* 34, no. 34 (September 2013): 2697–705.

88. J. Li, M. Zhang, A. Loerbroks, P. Angerer, et al., "Work stress and the risk of recurrent coronary heart disease events: A systematic review and meta-analysis," *International Journal of Occupational Medicine and Environmental Health* 28, no. 1 (January 2015): 8–19.

89. A. Rozanski, J. A. Blumenthal, and J. Kaplan, "Impact of psychological factors on the pathogenesis of cardiovascular disease and implications for therapy," *Circulation* 99, no. 16 (April 1999): 2192–217.

90. Ibid.

91. S. L. Risemberg, G. E. Miller, J. M. Brehm, and J. C. Celedon, "Stress and asthma: Novel insights in genetic, epigenetic and immunological mechanisms," *Journal of Allergy and Clinical Immunology* 132, no. 5 (November 2014): 1009–15.

92. N. Schneiderman, G. Ironson, and S. D. Siegel, "Stress and health: Psychological, behavioral and biological determinants," *Annual Review of Clinical Psychology* 1 (2005): 607–38.

93. J. Kruk and H. Y. Aboul-Enein, "Psychological stress and the risk of breast cancer: A case controlled study," *Cancer Detection and Prevention* 28, no. 6 (2004): 399–408.

94. F. Pouwer, N. Kupper, and N. C. Adriaanse, "Does emotional stress cause type 2 diabetes mellitus? A review from the European Depression in Diabetes (EDID) Research Consortium," *Discovery Medicine* 9, no. 45 (February 2010): 112–18.

95. E. A. Mayer, "The neurobiology of stress and gastrointestinal disease," *Gut* 47, no. 6 (2000): 861–69.

96. T. Janevic, L. G. Kahn, P. Landsbergis, P. M. Cirillo, et al., "Effects of work and life stress on semen quality," *Fertility and Sterility* 102, no. 2 (August 2014): 530–38.

97. L. D. Hamilton and C. M. Meston, "Chronic stress and sexual function in women," *Journal of Sexual Medicine* 10, no. 10 (October 2013): 2443–554.

98. K. M. Hasan, M. S. Rahman, K. M. Arif, and M. E. Sobhani, "Psychological stress and aging: Role of glucocorticoids (GCs)," *Age* 34, no. 6 (December 2012): 1421–33.

99. A. Keller, K. Litzelman, L. E. Wisk, T. Maddox, et al., "Does the perception that stress affects health matter? The association with health and mortality," *Health Psychology* 31, no. 5 (September 2012): 677–84.

100. J. L. Harding, K. Backholer, E. D. Williams, A. Peeters, et al., "Psychosocial stress is positively associated with body mass index gain over 5 years: Evidence from the longitudinal AusDiab study," *Obesity* (Silver Spring) 22, no. 1 (January 2014): 277–88.

101. B. Smith, K. Metzker, R. Waite, and P. Gerrity, "Short-form mindfulness-based stress reduction reduces anxiety and improves health-related quality of life in an inner city population," *Holistic Nursing Practice* 29, no. 2 (March–April 2015): 70–77.

102. M. Lozada, N. Carro, P. D'adamo, and C. Barclay, "Stress management in children: A pilot study in 7 to 9 years olds," *Journal of Developmental Behavior Pediatrics* 35, no. 2 (February–March 2014): 144–47.

103. Y. Kotozaki, H. Takeuchi, A. Sekiguchi, Y. Yamamoto, et al., "Biofeedback-based training for stress management in daily hassles: An intervention study," *Brain and Behavior* 4, no. 4 (July 2014): 566–79.

104. E. Levy-Gigi, C. Sazbo, O. Kelemen, and S. Keri, "Association among clinical response, hippocampal volume and FKBP5 gene expression in individuals with posttraumatic stress disorder receiving cognitive behavioral therapy," *Biological Psychiatry* 74, no. 11 (December 2013): 793–800.

105. K. S. Young, L. J. Burklund, J. B. Torre, D. Saxbe, et al., "Treatment for social anxiety disorder alters functional connectivity in emotion regulation neural circuitry," *Psychiatric Research* 261 (March 2017): 44–51.

106. J. L. Phillips, L. A. Batten, F. Aldosary, P. Tremblay, et al., "Brain volume increases with sustained remission in patients with treatment resistant unipolar depression," *Journal of Clinical Psychiatry* 73, no. 5 (May 2012): 624–31.

107. R. Smith, L. Chen, L. Baxter, C. Fort, et al., "Antidepressant effects of sertraline associated with volume increases in dorsolateral prefrontal cortex," *Journal of Affective Disorders* 146, no. 3 (April 2013): 414–19.

108. G. D. Shapiro, W. D. Fraser, M. G. Frasch, and J. R. Seguin, "Psychosocial stress in pregnancy and preterm birth: Associations and mechanisms," *Obstetrical and Gynecological Survey* 41, no. 6 (November 2013): 631–45.

109. S. Babbar and J. Shyken, "Yoga in pregnancy," *Clinical Obstetrics and Gynecology* 59, no. 3 (September 2016): 600–612.

110. S. Ertekin-Pinar, O. Duran-Aksoy, G. Daglar, Z. B. Yurtsal, et al., "Effect of stress management training on depression, stress and coping strategies in pregnant women: A randomized controlled trial," *Journal of Obstetrics and Gynecology* (May 2017): 1–8 [electronic publication ahead of print].

CHAPTER 2. DO WOMEN HAVE BETTER COPING SKILLS IN RESPONSE TO STRESS?

1. M. C. Davis, K. A. Matthews, and E. W. Twamley, "Is life more difficult on Mars or Venus? A meta-analytical review of sex differences in major and minor life events," *Annals of Behavioral Medicine* 21, no. 1 (January 1999): 83–97.

2. L. Wiegner, D. Hange, C. Bjorkelund, and G. Ahlborg Jr., "Prevalence of perceived stress and association to symptoms of exhaustion, depression, and anxiety in working age population seeking primary care: An observational study," *BMC Family Practice* 16 (March 2015): 38.

3. N. M. Tyan, "Stress coping strategies identified from school age children's perspective," *Research in Nursing Health* 12, no. 2 (April 1989): 111–22.

4. L. Dusselier, B. Dunn, Y. Wang, M. C. Shelley, et al., "Personal health, academic, and environmental predictors of stress for residence hall students," *Journal of American College Health* 54, no. 1 (July–August 2005): 15–24.

5. R. Misra and M. McKean, "College students' academic stress and its relationship to their anxiety, time management and leisure satisfaction," *American Journal of Health Studies* 16, no. 1 (January 2000): 41–51.

6. American Psychological Association, "Stress in America," http://www.apa.org/news/press/release/2010/gender-stress.aspx, accessed October 2, 2016.

7. American Psychological Association, "Stress and Gender," http://www.apa.org/news/press/releases/stress/2011/gender.aspx, accessed October 2, 2016.

8. D. Coperland and B. L. Harbaugh, "Differences in parenting stress between married and single first time mothers at six to eight weeks after birth," *Issues in Comprehensive Pediatric Nursing* 28, no. 3 (July–September 2005): 139–52.

9. U.S. Bureau of Labor Statistics, February 2013, http://www.bls.gov.

10. O. Evans and A. Steptoe, "The contribution of gender role, orientation, work factors and home stressors to psychological well-being and sickness absences in male- and female-dominated occupational groups," *Social Science and Medicine* 54, no. 5 (February 2002): 481–92.

11. A. B. Jena, D. Khullar, O. Ho, A. R. Olenski, et al., "Sex differences in academic rank in US medical schools in 2014," *Journal of American Medical Association* 314, no. 11 (September 2015): 1149–58.

12. S. L. Brewer and L. B. Mongero, "Women in perfusion: A survey of North American female perfusionist," *Journal of Extra Corporal Technology* 45, no. 3 (September 2013): 173–77.

13. Indiana University, "Women in mostly male workplaces exhibit psychological stress response," *Science Daily*, August 24, 2015, www.sciencedaily.com/releases/2015/08/150824130459.htm.

14. S. M. Townsend, B. Major, C. E. Gangi, and W. B. Mendez, "From 'in the air' to 'under the skin': Cortisol response to social identity threat," *Personality and Social Psychology Bulletin* 37, no. 2 (February 2011): 151–64.

15. D. Stevens-Watkins, B. Perry, E. Pullen, J. Jewell, et al., "Examining the associations of racism, sexism, and stressful life events on psychological distress among African-American women," *Cultural Diversity and Ethnic Minority Psychology* 20, no. 4 (October 2014): 561–69.

16. C. Kane-Urrabazo, "Sexual harassment in the workplace: It is your problem," *Journal of Nursing Management* 15, no. 6 (September 2007): 608–13.

17. J. A. Richman, K. M. Rospenda, S. J. Nawyn, J. A. Flaherty, et al., "Sexual harassment and generalized abuse among university employees: Prevalence and mental health correlates," *American Journal of Public Health* 89, no. 3 (March 1999): 358–63.

18. J. Khubchandani and J. H. Price, "Workplace harassment and morbidity among U.S. adults: Results from the National Health Interview Survey," *Journal of Community Health* 40, no. 3 (June 2015): 555–63.

19. G. M. Svare, L. Miller, and G. Ames, "Social climate and workplace drinking among women in a male dominated occupation," *Addictive Behaviors* 29, no. 8 (November 2004): 1691–98.

20. M. B. Nielsen and S. Einarsen, "Prospective relationship between workplace sexual harassment and psychological distress," *Occupational Medicine* (London) 62, no. 3 (April 2013): 226–28.

21. N. G. Choi and J. H. Ha, "Relationship between spouse/partner support and depressive symptoms in older adults: Gender difference," *Aging and Mental Health* 15, no. 3 (April 2011): 307–17.

22. P. K. Deka and S. Sharma, "Psychological aspects of infertility," *British Journal of Medical Practitioners* 3, no. 3 (September 2010): a336.

23. L. Genesoni and M. A. Tallandini, "Men's psychological transition to fatherhood: An analysis of the literature 1989–2008," *Birth* 36, no. 4 (December 2009): 305–18.

24. L. Vismara, L. Rolle, F. Agostini, C. Sechi, et al., "Perinatal parenting stress, anxiety, and depression outcome in first time mothers and fathers: A 3–6 month postpartum follow-up study," *Frontiers in Psychology* 7 (June 2016): 938.

25. M. S. Epifanio, V. Genna, C. De Luca, M. Roccella, et al., "Paternal and maternal transition to parenthood: The risk of postpartum depression and parenting stress," *Pediatric Report* 7, no. 2 (June 2015): 5872.

26. X. Cong, S. M. Ludington-Hoe, N. Hussain, R. M. Cusson, et al., "Parental oxytocin responses during skin to skin contact in pre-term infants," *Early Human Development* 97, no. 7 (July 2015): 401–6.

27. M. Bertrand, E. Kamenica, and J. Pan, "Gender identity and relative income within households," *Quarterly Journal of Economics* 130, no. 2 (2015): 571–614.

28. T. Kushnir and R. Kasan, "Major sources of stress among women managers, clerical workers and working single mothers: Demands vs. resources," *Public Heath Review* 20, nos. 3–4 (1992–1993): 215–29.

29. C. Emslie, K. Hunt, and S. Macintyre, "Gender, work-home conflict and morbidity amongst white collar bank employee in the United Kingdom," *International Journal of Behavioral Medicine* 11, no. 3 (March 2004): 127–34.

30. F. Eek and A. Axmon, "Gender inequality at home is associated with poorer health for women," *Scandinavian Journal of Public Health* 43, no. 2 (March 2015): 176–82.

31. L. Berntsson, U. Lundberg, and G. Krantz, "Gender differences in work-home interplay and symptom perception among Swedish white-collar workers," *Journal of Epidemiology and Community Health* 60, no. 12 (December 2006): 1070–75.

32. J. Roberts, R. Hodgson, and P. Dolan, "'It's driving her mad': Gender differences in the effects of commuting on psychological health," *Journal of Health Economics* 30, no. 5 (September 2011): 1064–76.

33. N. R. Lighthall, M. Mather, and M. A. Gorlick, "Acute stress increases sex differences in risk seeking in the balloon analogue risk task," *PLoS One* 4, no. 7 (July 2009): e6002.

34. S. E. Taylor, L. C. Klein, B. P. Lewis, T. L. Gruenewald, et al., "Biobehavioral responses to stress in females: Tend-and-befriend, not flight or fight," *Psychological Review* 107, no. 3 (July 2000): 411–29.

35. D. Maestripieri, "Gender differences in response to stress: It boils down to a single gene," *Psychology Today*, March 17, 2012, https://www.psychologytoday.com/blog/games-primates-play/201203/gender-differences-in-responses-stress-it-boils-down-single-gene, accessed October 3, 2016.

36. G. W. Bird and R. L. Harris, "A comparison of role strain and coping strategies by gender and family structure among early adolescents," *Journal of Early Adolescence* 10, no. 2 (May 1990): 141–58.

37. R. T. Rada, D. R. Laws, and R. Kellner, "Plasma testosterone levels in rapist," *Psychosomatic Medicine* 38, no. 4 (July–August 1976): 257–68.

38. D. Jezova, E. Jurankova, A. Mosnarova, M. Kriska, et al., "Neuroendocrine response during stress with relation to gender," *Acta Neurobiologiae Experimentalis* 56, no. 3 (1996): 779–85.

39. I. Schneiderman, O. Zagoory-Sharon, J. F. Leckman, and R. Feldman, "Oxytocin during the initial stages of romantic attachment: Relations to couples interactive reciprocity," *Psychoneuroendocrinology* 37, no. 8 (August 2012): 1277–85.

40. N. Magon and S. Kaira, "The orgasmic history of oxytocin: Love, lust and labor," *Indian Journal of Endocrinology and Metabolism* 15, no. S3 (September 1011): S156–61.

41. J. A. Rash and T. S. Campbell, "The effect of intranasal oxytocin administration on acute cold pressor pain: A placebo-controlled, double-blind, within participants crossover investigation," *Psychosomatic Medicine* 76, no. 6 (July–August 2014): 422–29.

42. M. Olff, J. L. Frijling, L. D. Kubzansky, B. Bradly, et al., "The role of oxytocin in social bonding, stress regulation and mental health: An update on the moderating effects of context and interindividual differences," *Psychoneuroendocrinology* 38, no. 9 (September 2013): 1883–94.

43. M. Heinrichs, T. Baumgartner, C. Kirschbaum, and U. Ehlert, "Social support and oxytocin interact to suppress cortisol and subjective response to psychosocial stress," *Biological Psychiatry* 54, no. 12 (December 2012): 1389–98.

44. B. Ditzen, M. Schaer, B. Gabriel, G. Bodernmann, et al., "Intranasal oxytocin increases positive communications and reduces cortisol levels during couple conflict," *Biological Psychiatry* 65, no. 9 (May 2009): 728–31.

45. J. Lee and V. R. Harley, "The male fight-flight response: A result of SRY regulation of catecholamines," *Bioessays* 34, no. 6 (June 2012): 454–57.

46. R. F. Baumeister and K. L. Sommer, "What do men want? Gender differences and two spheres of belongingness: Comment on Cross and Madison (1997)," *Psychological Bulletin* 122, no. 1 (July 1997): 38–44.

47. S. E. Taylor, L. C. Klein, B. P. Lewis, T. L. Gruenewald, et al., "Sex differences in biobehavioral response to threat: Reply to Geary and Flinn (2002)," *Psychological Review* 109, no. 4 (October 2002): 751–53.

48. C. Kieschbaum, B. M. Kudielka, J. J. Gabb, N. C. Schommer, et al., "Impact of gender, menstrual cycle phase, and oral contraceptives on the activity of the hypothalamic-pituitary-adrenal cortex," *Psychosomatic Medicine* 61, no. 2 (March–April 1999): 154–62.

49. M. A. Stephens, P. B. Mahon, M. E. McCaul, and G. S. Wand, "Hypothalamic-pituitary-adrenal axis response to acute psychosocial stress: Effects of biological sex and circulating sex hormones," *Psychoneuroendocrinology* 66 (April 2016): 47–55.

50. Y. Huang, R. Zhou, M. Wu, Q. Wang, et al., "Premenstrual syndrome is associated with blunted cortisol reactivity to TSST," *Stress* 18, no. 2 (April 2015): 160–68.

51. S. R. Lindheim, R. S. Legro, L. Bernstein, F. Z. Stanczyk, et al., "Behavioral stress responses in premenopausal women and postmenopausal women and the effects of estrogen," *American Journal of Obstetrics and Gynecology* 16, no. 6 (December 1992): 1831–36.

52. E. M. Glover, T. Jovanovic, K. B. Mercer, K. Kerley, et al., "Estrogen levels are associated with extinction deficits in women with posttraumatic stress disorder," *Biological Psychiatry* 72, no. 1 (July 2012): 19–24.

53. Z. Pan and C. Chang, "Gender and the regulation of longevity: Implications for autoimmunity," *Autoimmune Review* 11, no. 6–7 (May 2012): A393–A403.

54. D. Mozaffarian, E. J. Benjamin, A. S. Go, D. K. Arnett, et al., "Heart disease and stroke statistics—2015 update: A report from the American Heart Association," *Circulation* 131, no. 4 (January 2015): e29–e322.

55. Y. Sofer, E. Osher, R. Limor, G. Shefer, et al., "Gender determines serum free cortisol: Higher levels in men," *Endocrine Practice* 22, no. 12 (December 2016): 1415–21.

56. L. Manenschijn, L. Schaap, N. M. van Schoot, S. van der Pass, et al., "High long term cortisol levels, measured in scalp hair, are associated with a history of

cardiovascular disease," *Journal of Clinical Endocrinology and Metabolism* 98, no. 5 (May 2013): 2078–83.

57. NCSR (by age and sex), Health Care Policy, Harvard Medical School, https://www.hcp.med.harvard.edu/ncs/ftpdir/NCS-R_Lifetime, accessed May 12, 2017.

58. K. Petrowski, U. Herold, P. Joraschky, H. U. Wittchen, et al., "A striking pattern of cortisol non-responsiveness to psychosocial stress in patients with panic disorder with concurrent normal cortisol awakening response," *Psychoneuroendocrinology* 35, no. 3 (April 2019): 414–21.

59. D. A. Bangsser, "Sex differences in stress related receptors: 'Micro' difference with 'macro' implications for mood and anxiety disorder," *Biological Sex Difference* 4, no. 1 (January 2013): 2.

60. J. Wang, M. Koeczykpwski, H. Rao, Y. Fan, et al., "Gender difference in neural response to psychological stress," *Social Cognitive and Affective Neuroscience* 2, no. 3 (September 2007): 227–39.

61. S. Nolen-Hoeksema, "Gender differences in depression," *Current Directions in Psychological Science* 10, no. 5 (October 2001): 173–76.

62. S. Nolen-Hoeksema, J. Larson, and C. Grayson, "Explaining the gender difference in depressive symptoms," *Journal of Personality and Social Psychology* 77, no. 5 (November 1977): 1961–72.

63. R. Garfield, "Male emotional intimacy: How therapeutic men's group can enhance couples therapy," *Family Process* 49, no. 1 (March 2010): 109–22.

64. T. David-Barrett, A. Rotkirch, J. Carney, I. Behncke-Izquierdo, et al., "Women favor dyadic relationships, but men prefer clubs: Cross-cultural evidence from social networking," *PLoS One* 10, no. 3 (March 2015): e0118329.

CHAPTER 3. PETS ARE NATURAL STRESS BUSTERS

1. R. L. Matchock, "Pet ownership and physical health," *Current Opinion in Psychiatry* 28, no. 5 (September 2015): 386–92.

2. https://www.avma.org/KB/Resources/Statistics/Pages/Market-research-statistics-US-Pet-Ownership-Demographics-Sourcebook.aspx.

3. S. L. Triebenbacher, "Pets as transitional objects: Their role in children's emotional development," *Psychological Reports* 82, no. 1 (February 1998): 191–200.

4. C. Eisley-Curtiss, L. C. Holley, and S. Wolf, "The animal-human bond and ethnic diversity," *Social Work* 51, no. 3 (July 2006): 257–68.

5. R. Schoenfeld-Tacher, L. R. Kogan, and M. L. Wright, "Comparison of strength of the human-animal bond between Hispanic and non-Hispanic owners of pet dogs and cats," *Journal of the American Veterinary Medical Association* 236, no. 5 (March 2010): 529–34.

6. E. A. Clancy, A. S. Moore, and E. R. Bertone, "Evaluation of cat owner and owner characteristics and their relationship to outdoor access of owned cats," *Journal of the American Veterinary Association* 222, no. 1 (June 2003): 1541–45.

7. F. Nightingale, *Notes on Nursing* (New York: Dover, 1969) [originally published in 1860].

8. B. M. Levinson and G. P. Mallon, *Pet-oriented child psychotherapy* (Springfield, IL: Charles C. Thomas, 1997) [originally published in 1969].

9. M. O'Haire, "Companion animals and human health: Benefits, challenges and the road ahead," *Journal of Veterinary Behavior* 5, no. 5 (September–October 2010): 226–34.

10. A. A. Driscoll, D. W. Macdonald, and S. J. O'Brien, "From wild animals to domestic pets, an evolutionary view of domestication," *Proceedings of the National Academy of Sciences, USA* 106, no. S1 (June 2009): S9971–78.

11. E. O. Wilson, *Biophilia* (Cambridge, MA: Harvard University Press, 1984).

12. M. Borgi and F. Cirulli, "Pet face: Mechanisms underlying human-animal relationships," *Frontiers in Psychology* 7 (March 2016): 278.

13. K. Hirsh-Pasek and R. Treiman, "Doggerel: Motherese in a new concept," *Journal of Child Language* 9, no. 1 (February 1982): 229–37.

14. E. Prato-Previde, G. Fallani, and P. Valsechi, "Gender difference in owners interacting with a pet dog: An observational study," *Ethology* 112, no. 1 (January 2006): 64–73.

15. A. Beetz, K. Unvas-Moberg, H. Julius, and K. Kotrschal, "Psychological and psychophysiological effects of human-animal interactions: The possible role of oxytocin," *Frontiers of Psychology* 9, no. 3 (July 2012): 234.

16. J. S. Odendaal, "Animal-assisted therapy—magic or medicine?" *Journal of Psychometric Research* 49, no. 4 (October 2000): 275–80.

17. A. R. McConnell, C. M. Brown, T. M. Shoda, L. E. Stayton, et al., "Friends with benefits: On the positive consequences of pet ownership," *Journal of Personality and Social Psychology* 101, no. 6 (December 2011): 1239–52.

18. L. Woods, K. Martin, H. Christian, A. Nathan, et al., "The pet factor: Companion animals as a conduit for getting to know people, friendship formation and social support," *PLoS One* 10, no. 4 (April 2015): e0122085.

19. H. Rothgerber and F. Mican, "Childhood pet ownership, attachment, and subsequent meat avoidance: The mediating role of empathy towards animals," *Appetite* 79 (August 2014): 1–17.

20. J. McNicholas and G. M. Collis, "Dogs as catalysts for social interactions: Robustness of the effect," *British Journal of Psychology* 91, no. 1 (February 2000): 61–70.

21. D. L. Wells, "The facilitation of social interactions by domestic dogs," *Anthrozoos* 17, no. 4 (April 2004): 340–52.

22. N. Gueguen and S. Ciccotti, "Domestic dogs as facilitators in social interaction: An evaluation of helping and courtship behavior," *Anthrozoos* 21, no. 4 (December 2008): 339–49.

23. K. Hodgson, L. Barton, M. Darling, V. Antao, et al., "Pet's impact on your patient's health: Leveraging benefits and mitigating risk," *Journal of American Board of Family Medicine* 28, no. 4 (July–August 2015): 526–34.

24. A. H. Kidd and R. M. Kidd, "Benefits and liabilities of pets for the homeless," *Psychological Reports* 74, no. 3 (June 1994): 715–22.

25. L. Irvine, K. N. Kahl, and J. M. Smith, "Confrontation and donations: Encounters between homeless pet owners and the public," *Sociological Quarterly* 53, no. 1 (January 2012): 25–43.

26. H. Rhoades, H. Winetrobe, and E. Rice, "Pet ownership among homeless youth: Associations with mental health service utilization and housing status," *Child Psychiatry and Human Development* 46, no. 2 (April 2015): 237–44.

27. M. Mullersdorf, F. Granstrom, L. Sahlqvist, and P. Tillgren, "Aspects of health, physical/leisure activities, work and socio-demographics associated with pet ownership in Sweden," *Scandinavian Journal of Public Health* 38, no. 1 (February 2010): 53–63.

28. R. E. Zasloff and A. L. Kidd, "Loneliness and pet ownership among single women," *Psychological Reports* 75, no. 2 (October 1994): 747–52.

29. I. H. Stanley, Y. Conwell, C. Bowen, and K. A. Van Orden, "Pet ownership may attenuate loneliness among older adult primary care patients who live alone," *Aging and Mental Health* 18, no. 3 (2014): 394–99.

30. S. Shiloh, G. Sorek, and J. Terkel, "Reduction of state anxiety by petting animals in a controlled laboratory experiment," *Anxiety, Stress and Coping* 16, no. 4 (December 2003): 387–95.

31. N. Epley, S. Akalis, A. Waytz, and J. T. Cacioppo, "Creating social connection through influential reproduction: Loneliness and perceived agency in gadgets, gods and greyhounds," *Psychological Science* 19, no. 2 (February 2008): 114–20.

32. J. M. Siegel, F. J. Angulo, R. Detels, J. Wesch, et al., "AIDS diagnosis and depression in the multicenter AIDS cohort study: The ameliorating impact of pet ownership," *AIDS Care* 11, no. 2 (April 1999): 157–70.

33. H. E. Wright, S. Hall, J. Hardiman, R. Mills, et al., "Acquiring a pet dog significantly reduces stress of primary carers for children with autism spectrum disorder: A prospective case control study," *Journal of Autism and Developmental Disorders* 45, no. 8 (August 2015): 2531–40.

34. G. K. Carlisle, "The social skills and attachment to dogs of children with autism spectrum disorder," *Journal of Autism and Developmental Disorders* 45, no. 5 (May 2015): 1137–45.

35. S. B. Baker, J. S. Knisely, N. L. McCain, and A. M. Best, "Measuring stress and immune response in healthcare professionals following interaction with a therapy dog: A pilot study," *Psychological Reports* 96, no. 3 (June 2005): 713–39.

36. C. A. Krause-Parello, J. Tyschowski, A. Gonzalez, and Z. Boyd, "Human-canine interaction: Exploring stress indicators response patterns of salivary cortisol and immunoglobulin A," *Research and Theory for Nursing Practice: An International Journal* 26, no. 1 (January 2012): 24–40.

37. R. Viau, G. Arsenault-Lapierre, S. Fecteau, N. Champagne, et al., "Effect of service dogs on salivary cortisol secretion in autistic children," *Psychoneuroendocrinology* 35, no. 8 (September 2010): 1187–93.

38. K. M. Allen, J. Blascovich, J. Tomaka, and R. M. Kelsey, "Presence of human friends and pet dogs as moderators of autonomic responses to stress in women," *Journal of Personality and Social Psychology* 61, no. 4 (October 1991): 582–89.

39. K. Allen, J. Blascovich, and W. B. Mendes, "Cardiovascular reactivity and the presence of pets, friends and spouses: The truth about cats and dogs," *Psychosomatic Medicine* 64, no. 5 (September–October 2002): 727–39.

40. K. Allen, B. E. Shykoff, and J. L. Izzo, "Pet ownership but not ACE inhibitor therapy blunts home blood pressure responses to mental stress," *Hypertension* 38, no. 4 (October 2001): 815–20.

41. G. N. Levine, K. Allen, L. T. Braun, H. E. Christian, et al., "Pet ownership and cardiovascular risk: A scientific statement from the American Heart Association," *Circulation* 127, no. 33 (June 2013): 2353–63.

42. K. Arhant-Sudhir, R. Arhant-Sudhir, and K. Sudhir, "Pet ownership and cardiovascular risk reduction: Supportive evidence, conflicting data and underlying mechanism," *Clinical and Experimental Pharmacology and Physiology* 38, no. 11 (November 2011): 734–38.

43. E. Friedman and S. A. Thomas, "Pet ownership, social support, and one year survival after acute myocardial infarction in the cardiac arrhythmia support trial (CSAT)," *American Journal of Cardiology* 76, no. 17 (December 1995): 1213–17.

44. E. Friedman, A. H. Katcher, J. J. Lynch, and S. A. Thomas, "Animal companionship and one-year survival of patients after discharge from a coronary care unit," *Public Health Report* 95, no. 4 (July–August 1980): 307–12.

45. E. D. Williams, E. Stamatakis, T. Chandola, and M. Hamer, "Physical inactivity behavior and coronary heart disease mortality among South Asian people in the UK: An observational longitudinal study," *Heart* 97, no. 8 (April 2011): 655–59.

46. E. M. Murtagh, L. Nichols, M. A. Mohammed, R. Holder, et al., "The effect of walking on the risk factors for cardiovascular disease: An updated systematic review and meta-analysis of randomized trials," *Preventive Medicine* 72 (March 2015): 34–43.

47. H. Christian nee Cutt, B. Giles-Corti, and M. Knuiman, "'I'm just a walking the dog': Correlates of regular dog walking," *Farm and Community Health* 33, no. 1 (January–March 2010): 44–52.

48. C. Lentino, A. J. Visek, K. McDonnell, and L. Dipietro, "Dog walking is associated with a favorable risk profile independent of a moderate to high volume of physical activity," *Journal of Physical Activities and Health* 9, no. 3 (March 2012): 414–20.

49. C. Westgarth, J. Liu, J. Heron, A. R. Ness, et al., "Dog ownership during pregnancy, maternal activity and obesity: A cross-sectional study," *PLoS One* 7, no. 2 (February 2012): e31315.

50. J. R. Sirard, C. D. Patnode, M. O. Hearst, and M. N. Laska, "Dog ownership and adolescent physical activity," *American Journal of Preventive Medicine* 40, no. 3 (March 2011): 334–37.

51. B. H. Headey and M. M. Grabka, "Pets and human health in Germany and Australia: National Longitudinal Results," *Social Indicators Research* 80, no. 2 (January 2007): 297–311.

52. J. M Siegel, "Stressful life events and use of physician services among the elderly: The moderating role of pet ownership," *Journal of Personality and Social Psychology* 58, no. 6 (June 1990): 1081–86.

53. I. Ogechi, K. Snook, B. M. Davis, A. R. Hansen, et al., "Pet ownership and the risk of dying from cardiovascular diseases among adults without major chronic medical conditions," *High Blood Pressure and Cardiovascular Prevention* 23, no. 3 (2016): 245–53.

54. A. I. Quereshi, M. Z. Memon, G. Vazquez, and M. F. Suri, "Cat ownership and the risk of fatal cardiovascular disease: Results from the second national health and nutrition examination study mortality follow-up study," *Journal of Vascular and Interventional Neurology* 2, no. 1 (January 2009): 132–35.

55. E. A. Los, K. L. Ramsey, I. Guttmann-Bauman, and A. J. Ahmann, "Reliability of trained dogs to alert to hypoglycemia in patients with type 1 diabetes," *Journal of Diabetes Science and Technology* 11, no. 3 (2016): 506–12.

56. G. dee Meer, B. G. Toelle, K. Ng, E. Tovey, et al., "Presence and timing of cat ownership by age 18 and the effect on atopy and asthma at age 28," *Journal of Allergy and Clinical Immunology* 113, no. 3 (March 2004): 433–38.

57. B. Brunekreef, B. Groot, and G. Hoek, "Pets, allergy and respiratory symptoms in children," *International Journal of Epidemiology* 21, no. 2 (April 1992): 338–42.

58. M. J. Gilmer, M. N. Baudino, A. T. Goddard, D. C. Vickers, et al., "Animal-assisted therapy in pediatric palliative care," *Nursing Clinics of North America* 51 (2016): 381–95.

59. D. Snipelisky and M. C. Burton, "Canine-assisted therapy in the inpatient setting," *Southern Medical Journal* 107, no. 4 (April 2014): 265–73.

60. M. F. Stasi, D. Amati, C. Costa, D. Resta, et al., "Pet therapy: A trial for institutionalized frail elderly patients," *Archives of Gerontology and Geriatric* 38, no. S9 (September 2004): S407–12.

61. E. Lust, A. Ryan-Haddad, K. Coover, and J. Snell, "Measuring clinical outcomes of animal-assisted therapy: Impact on resident medication usage," *Consultant Pharmacists* 2, no. 7 (July 2007): 580–85.

62. F. Moretti, D. De Ronchi, V. Bernabei, L. Marchetti, et al., "Pet therapy in elderly patients with mental illness," *Psychogeriatrics* 11, no. 2 (June 2011): 125–29.

63. M. Churchill, J. Safaoui, B. W. McCabe, and M. M. Baun, "Using a therapy dog to alleviate the agitation and desocialization of people with Alzheimer's disease," *Journal of Psychosocial Nursing and Mental Health Services* 37, no. 4 (April 1999): 16–22.

64. S. L. Filan and R. H. Llewellyn-Jones, "Animal-assisted therapy for dementia: A review of literature," *International Psychogeriatrics* 18, no. 4 (December 2006): 597–611.

CHAPTER 4. CHILD DEVELOPMENT AND SOCIAL INFLUENCES ON STRESS: RELIEF THROUGH SOCIAL NETWORKING, VOLUNTEERING, LAUGHTER, AND TAKING A VACATION

1. C. A. Sandman, L. Glynn, C. D. Schetter, P. Wadhwa, et al., "Elevated maternal cortisol early in pregnancy predicts third trimester level of placental corticotropin releasing hormone (CRH) priming the placental clock," *Peptides* 27, no. 6 (June 2006): 1457–63.

2. E. P. Davis, L. M. Glynn, F. Waffarn, and C. A. Sandman, "Prenatal maternal stress programs infant stress regulation," *Journal of Child Psychology and Psychiatry* 52, no. 2 (February 2011): 119–29.

3. M. I. Bolten, N. S. Fiunk, and C. Stadler, "Maternal self-efficacy reduces the impact of prenatal stress on infant's crying behavior," *Journal of Pediatrics* 161, no. 1 (July 2012): 104–9.

4. H. Wurmser, M. Rieger, C. Domogalla, A. Kahnt, et al., "Association between life stress during pregnancy and infant crying in the first six months postpartum: A prospective longitudinal study," *Early Human Development* 82, no. 5 (May 2006): 341–49.

5. M. O. Huttunen and P. Niskanen, "Prenatal loss of father and psychiatric disorder," *Archives of General Psychiatry* 35, no. 4 (April 1978): 429–32.

6. L. Hohwu, L. Li, J. Olsen, T. I. Sorensen, et al., "Severe maternal stress exposure due to bereavement before, during and after pregnancy and risk of overweight and obesity in young adult men: A Danish National Cohort Study," *PLoS One* 9, no. 5 (May 2014): e97490.

7. J. K. Rilling, "The neural and hormonal bases of human parental care," *Neuropsychologia* 51, no. 4 (May 2013): 731–47.

8. R. Feldman, I. Gordon, I. Schneiderman, O. Weisman, et al., "Natural variations in maternal and paternal care are associated with systematic changes in oxytocin following parent-infant contact," *Psychoneuroendocrinology* 35, no. 8 (September 2010): 1133–41.

9. I. Gordon, O. Zagoory-Sharon, J. F. Leckman, and R. Feldman, "Oxytocin and the development of parenting in humans," *Biological Psychiatry* 68, no. 4 (August 2010): 377–82.

10. R. Feldman, A. Weller, O. Zagoory-Sharon, and A. Levine, "Evidence for a neuroendocrinological foundation of human affiliation: Plasma oxytocin levels across pregnancy and the postpartum period predict mother-infant bonding," *Psychological Science* 18, no. 11 (November 2007): 965–70.

11. B. L. Mah, "Oxytocin, postnatal depression and parenting: A systematic review," *Harvard Review of Psychiatry* 24, no. 1 (January–February 2016): 1–13.

12. A. A. Bryan, "Enhancing parent-child interaction with a prenatal couple intervention," *American Journal of Maternal and Child Nursing* 25, no. 3 (May–June 2003): 139–44.

13. S. Schiavone, M. Colaianna, and L. Curtis, "Impact of early life stress on the pathogenesis of mental disorder: Relation to brain oxidative stress," *Current Pharmaceutical Design* 21, no. 11 (November 2015): 1404–12.

14. M. D. Ainsworth, "Attachments across the life span," *Bulletin of the New York Academy of Medicine* 61, no. 9 (November 1985): 792–812.

15. D. Lenzi, C. Trentini, R. Tambell, and P. Pantano, "Neural basis of attachment-caregiving systems interactions: Insights from neuroimaging studies," *Frontiers in Psychology* 6 (August 2015): 1241.

16. Ibid.

17. Z. Kamalak, N. Kosus, D. Hizli, B. Akcal, et al., "Adolescent pregnancy and depression: Is there any association?" *Clinical and Experimental Obstetrics and Gynecology* 43, no. 3 (March 2016): 427–30.

18. M. D. Ainsworth, "Patterns of infant-mother attachments: Antecedents and effects on development," *Bulletin of the New York Academy of Medicine* 61, no. 9 (November 1985): 771–91.

19. M. Martin and J. Solomon, "Procedures for identifying infants as disorganized/ disoriented during the Ainsworth Strange Situation," in *Attachment in the preschool years: Theory, research and intervention*, ed. M. Greenberg, D. Cicchetti, and E. M. Cummings (Chicago: University of Chicago Press, 1990), 121–60.

20. M. Fuertes, A. Faria, M. Beeghly, and P. Lopes-Dos-Santos, "The effect of parental sensitivity and involvement in caregiving on mother-infant and father-infant attachment in a Portuguese sample," *Journal of Family Psychology* 30, no. 1 (February 2016): 147–56.

21. K. Bernard and M. Dozier, "Examining infant's cortisol response to laboratory tasks among children varying in attachment disorganization: Stress reactivity or return to baseline?" *Developmental Psychology* 46, no. 6 (November 2010): 1771–78.

22. K. Lyons-Ruth, L. Alpern, and B. Repacholi, "Disorganized infant's attachment classification and maternal psychosocial problems as predictors of hostile aggressive behavior in the preschool classroom," *Child Development* 64, no. 2 (April 1993): 572–85.

23. E. Lewis-Morrarty, K. A. Degnan, A Chronis-Tuscano, D. S. Pine, et al., "Infant attachment security and early childhood behavioral inhibition to predict social anxiety symptoms," *Child Development* 86, no. 2 (March 2015): 598–613.

24. S. E. Anderson and R. C. Whitaker, "Attachment security and obesity in US preschool aged children," *Archives of Pediatric and Adolescent Medicine* 165, no. 3 (March 2011): 235–42.

25. M. W. Clearfield, A. Carter-Rodtiguez, A. R. Merali, and R. Shober, "The effect of SES on infant and maternal diurnal salivary cortisol output," *Infant Behavior and Development* 37, no. 3 (August 2014): 298–304.

26. W. K. Silverman, A. M. La Greca, and S. Wasserstein, "What do children worry about? Worries and their relation to anxiety," *Child Development* 66, no. 3 (June 1995): 671–86.

27. G. Shamir-Essakow, J. A. Ungerer, and R. M. Rapee, "Attachment, behavioral inhibition and anxiety in preschool children," *Journal of Abnormal Child Psychology* 33, no. 2 (April 2005): 131–43.

28. S. Smeekens, J. Marianne-Riksen-Ealraven, and H. J. van Bakel, "Cortisol reactions in five-years-old to parent-child interaction: The moderating role of ego-resiliency," *Journal of Child Psychology and Psychiatry* 48, no. 7 (July 2007): 649–56.

29. G. Hornor, "Reactive attachment disorder," *Journal of Pediatric Health Care* 22, no. 4 (July–August 2008): 234–39.

30. C. A. Taylor, J. A. Manganello, S. J. Lee, and J. C. Rice, "Mothers' spanking of 3-year-old children and subsequent risk of children's aggressive behavior," *Pediatrics* 125, no. 5 (May 2010): e1057–65.

31. L. O. Linares, K. C. Stovall-McClough, M. Li, N. Morin, et al., "Salivary cortisol in foster children: A pilot study," *Child Abuse and Neglect* 32, no. 6 (June 2008): 665–70.

32. M. Dozier, M. Manni, M. K. Gordon, E. Peloso, et al., "Foster children's diurnal production of cortisols: An exploratory study," *Child Maltreatment* 11, no. 2 (May 2006): 189–97.

33. M. R. Gunnar, S. J. Morison, K. Chisholm, and M. Schuder, "Salivary cortisol in children adopted from Romanian orphanages," *Developmental Psychopathology* 13, no. 3 (Summer 2001): 611–28.

34. E. M. Hetherington, "Divorce and adjustment of children," *Pediatrics Review* 26, no. 5 (May 2005): 163–69.

35. L. J. Luecken, M. J. Hagan, A. A. Wolchik, I. N. Sandler, et al., "A longitudinal study of the effects of child-reported maternal warmth on cortisol stress response 15 years after parental divorce," *Psychosomatic Medicine* 78, no. 2 (February–March 2016): 163–70.

36. L. R. Martin, H. S. Friedman, K. M. Clark, and J. S. Tucker, "Longevity following the experience of parental divorce," *Social Science and Medicine* 61, no. 10 (November 2005): 2177–89.

37. L. J. Seltzer, T. E. Zigler, and S. D. Pollak, "Social and vocalization can release oxytocin in humans," *Proceedings of the Royal Society of Biological Sciences* 277, no. 1694 (September 2010): 2661–66.

38. S. L. Brown, J. A. Teufel, D. A. Burch, and V. Kancherla, "Gender, age and behavior differences in early adolescent worry," *Journal of School Health* 76, no. 8 (October 2006): 430–37.

39. J. R. Doom, C. M. Doyle, and M. R. Gunner, "Social stress buffering by friends in childhood and adolescence: Effects on HPA and oxytocin activity," *Social Neuroscience* 12 (2017): 8–21.

40. K. M. Keyes, M. L. Hatzenbuehler, B. F. Grant, and D. S. Hasin, "Stress and alcohol: Epidemiological evidence," *Alcohol Research* 34, no. 4 (2012): 391–400.

41. C. Liberwirth and Z. Wang, "The neurobiology of pair bonding formation, bond disruption and social buffering," *Current Opinion in Neurobiology* 40 (October 2016): 8–13.

42. S. Gordon and T. A. Wills, "Stress, social support and the buffering hypothesis," *Psychological Bulletin* 98, no. 2 (September 1985): 310–57.

43. C. S. Lee and S. Goldstein, "Loneliness, stress and social support in young adulthood: Does the source of support matter?" *Journal of Youth and Adolescence* 45, no. 3 (March 2016): 568–80.

44. A. A. Haydon and C. T. Halpern, "Older romantic partners and depressive symptoms during adolescence," *Journal of Youth and Adolescence* 39, no. 10 (October 2010): 1240–51.

45. B. Soller, "Caught in a bad romance: Adolescent romantic relationship and mental health," *Journal of Health and Social Behavior* 55, no. 1 (March 2014): 56–72.

46. J. Yang, J. T. Schaefer, N. Zhang, T. Covassin, et al., "Social support from the athletic trainer and symptoms of depression and anxiety at return to play," *Journal of Athletic Training* 49, no. 6 (December 2014): 773–79.

47. A. Inoue, N. Kawakami, H. Eguchi, and A. Tsutsumi, "Buffering effect of workplace social capital on the association of job insecurity with psychological distress in Japanese employees: A cross-sectional study," *Journal of Occupational Health* 58, no. 5 (September 2016): 460–69.

48. C. Aslund, P. Larm, B. Starrin, and K. W. Nilsson, "The buffering effect of tangible social support on financial stress: Influence of psychological well-being and psychosomatic symptoms in a large sample of adult general population," *International Journal of Equity and Health* 13, no. 1 (September 2014): 85.

49. J. C. Lee, A. M. Chong, O. T. Siu, P. Evans, et al., "Social network characteristics and salivary cortisol in healthy older people," *Scientific World Journal* 2012 (March 2012): 929067.

50. M. Sanchez-Martinez, E. Lopez-Garcia, P. Guallar-Castillon, J. J. Cruz, et al., "Social support and ambulatory blood pressure in older people," *Journal of Hypertension* 34, no. 10 (October 2016): 2045–52.

51. T. F. Robles and K. Kiecolt-Glaser, "The physiology of marriage: Pathways to health," *Physiology and Behavior* 79, no. 3 (August 2003): 409–16.

52. C. A. Schoenborn, "Marital status and health: United States, 1992–2002," *Advance Data from Vital and Health Statistics* 351 (December 2004): 1–32.

53. R. M. Kaplan and R. G. Kronick, "Marital status and longevity in the United States population," *Journal of Epidemiology and Community Health* 60, no. 9 (September 2006): 760–65.

54. G. M. Egeland, A. Tverdal, H. E. Meyer, and R. Selmer, "A man's heart and a wife's education: A 12-year coronary heart disease mortality follow-up in Norwegian men," *International Journal of Epidemiology* 31, no. 4 (August 2002): 799–805.

55. L. C. Gallo, W. M. Troxel, L. H. Kuller, K. Sutton-Tyrrell, et al., "Marital status, marital quality and atherosclerotic burden in postmenopausal women," *Psychosomatic Medicine* 65, no. 6 (December 2003): 952–62.

56. J. A. Rosenfeld, "Maternal work outside the home and its effect on women and their families," *Journal of the American Medical Women's Association* 47, no. 2 (March–April 1992): 47–53.

57. J. Holt-Lunstad, W. Birmingham, and B. Q. Jones, "Is there something unique about marriage? The relative impact of marital status, relationship, and network social support on ambulatory blood pressure and mental health," *Annals of Behavioral Medicine* 35, no. 2 (April 2008): 239–44.

58. R. De Vogli, T. Chandola, and M. G. Marmot, "Negative aspects of close relationships and heart disease," *Archives of Internal Medicine* 167, no. 18 (October 2008): 1951–57.

59. D. Oman, C. E. Thoresen, and K. McMahon, "Volunteerism and mortality among the community-dwelling elderly," *Journal of Health Psychology* 43, no. 3 (May 1999): 301–16.

60. P. A. Thoits and L. N. Hewitt, "Volunteer work and well-being," *Journal of Health and Social Behavior* 42, no. 2 (July 2001): 115–31.

61. J. Wilkins and A. J. Eisenbraun, "Humor theories and the physiological benefits of laughter," *Holistic Nursing Practice* 23, no. 6 (December 2009): 349–54.

62. P. Wooten, "Humor: An antidote for stress," *Holistic Nursing Practice* 10, no. 2 (January 1996): 49–56.

63. R. Mora-Ripoll, "The therapeutic value of laughter in medicine," *Alternative Therapy in Health and Medicine* 16, no. 6 (December 2010): 56–64.

64. L. S. Berk, S. A. Tan, W. F. Fry, B. J. Napier, et al., "Neuroendocrine and stress hormone changes during mirthful laughter," *American Journal of Medicine* 298, no. 6 (December 1989): 390–96.

65. K. Hayashi, I. Kawachi, T. Ohira, K. Kondo, et al., "Laughter is the best medicine? A cross-sectional study of cardiovascular disease among older Japanese adults," *Journal of Epidemiology* 26, no. 10 (October 2016): 546–52.

66. G. Strauss-Blasche, C. Ekmekcioglu, and, W. Marktl, "Does vacation enable recuperation? Changes in week being associated with time away from work," *Occupational Medicine* (London) 50, no. 3 (April 2000): 167–72.

67. B. B. Gump and K. A. Matthews, "Are vacations good for your health? The 9-year mortality experience after the multiple risk factors intervention trial," *Psychosomatic Medicine* 62, no. 2 (September–October 2000): 608–12.

68. G. Strauss-Blasche, B. Reithofer, W. Schobersberger, C. Ekmekcioglu, et al., "Effect of vacation on health: Moderating factors of vacation outcome," *Journal of Travel Medicine* 12, no. 2 (March–April 2005): 94–101.

69. M. Toda, H. Makino, H. Kobayashi, and K. Morimoto, "Health benefits for women staying with their husbands during a long-term trip to a hot spring spa," *Archives of Environmental and Occupational Health* 63, no. 1 (Spring 2008): 37–40.

CHAPTER 5. EXERCISE, YOGA, AND MEDITATION FOR STRESS MANAGEMENT

1. World Health Organization, "Global recommendation on physical activity for health: 2010 guidelines," http://whqlibdoc.who.int/publications/2010/9789241599979_eng.pdf.

2. C. M. Tipton, "The history of 'exercise is medicine' in ancient civilization," *Advances in Physiology Education* 38, no. 2 (June 2014): 109–17.

3. U.S. Department of Health and Human Services, *2008 Physical Activity Guidelines for Americans*, http://health.gov/paguidelines/pdf/paguide.pdf.

4. P. T. Williams, "Advantage of distance- versus time-based estimate of walking in predicting adiposity," *Medical Science of Sports and Exercise* 44, no. 9 (September 2009): 1728–37.

5. P. T. Williams and P. D. Thompson, "Walking versus running for hypertension, cholesterol and diabetes mellitus risk reduction," *Arteriosclerosis, Thrombosis and Vascular Biology* 33, no. 5 (May 2013): 1085–91.

6. R. R. Rosenkranz, M. J. Duncan, C. M. Caperchione, G. S. Kolt, et al., "Validity of the stage of changes in steps instrument (SoC Step) for achieving the physical activity goal of 10,000 steps per day," *BMC Public Health* 15 (November 2015): 1197.

7. J. D. Pillay, H. P. van der Ploeg, T. L. Kolbe-Alexander, K. I. Proper, et al., "The association between daily steps and health, and the mediating role of body composition: A pedometer-based, cross-sectional study in an employed South African population," *BMC Public Health* 15 (February 2015): 174.

8. B. Ewald, J. Attia, and P. McElduff, "How many steps are enough? Dose-response curves for pedometer steps and multiple health markers in a community-based sample of older Australians," *Journal of Physical Activity and Health* 11, no. 3 (March 2014): 509–18.

9. H. Arem, S. C. Moore, A. Patel, P. Hartge, et al., "Leisure time physical activity and mortality: A detailed pooled analysis of the dose response relationship," *JAMA Internal Medicine* 175, no. 6 (June 2015): 959–67.

10. D. Hupin, F. Roche, V. Gremeaux, J. C. Chatard, et al., "Even low dose of moderate to vigorous physical activity reduces mortality by 22% in adults aged ≥60 years: A systematic review and meta-analysis," *British Journal of Sports Medicine* 49, no. 19 (October 2015): 1262–67.

11. D. E. Warburton, C. W. Nicol, and S. S. Bredin, "Health benefits of physical activity: The evidence," *Canadian Medical Association Journal* 174, no. 6 (March 2006): 801–9.

12. M. Hamer, E. Stamatakis, and A. Steptoe, "Dose-response relationship between physical activity and mental health: The Scottish health survey," *British Journal of Sports Medicine* 43, no. 14 (December 2009): 1111–14.

13. M. R. Marselle, K. N. Irvine, and S. L. Warber, "Walking for well-being: Are group walks in certain types of natural environments better for well-being than

group walks in urban environments?" *International Journal of Environmental Research and Public Health* 10, no. 11 (October 2013): 5603–28.

14. M. Rogerson, D. K. Brown, G. Sandercock, J. J. Wooler, et al., "A comparison of four typical green exercise environments and prediction of psychological health outcomes," *Perspectives in Public Health* 136, no. 3 (March 2016): 171–80.

15. J. T. Coon, K. Boddy, K. Stein, R. Whear, et al., "Does participating in physical activity in outdoor natural environments have a greater effect on physical and mental wellbeing than physical activity indoors? A systematic review," *Environmental Science and Technology* 45, no. 5 (March 2011): 1761–72.

16. C. Thogersen-Ntoumani, E. A. Loughren, F. E. Kinnafick, I. M. Taylor, et al., "Changes in work affect in response to lunchtime walking in previously physically inactive employees: A randomized trial," *Scandinavian Journal of Medical Sciences and Sports* 25, no. 6 (December 2015): 778–87.

17. P. Bernard, G. Ninot, P. L. Bernard, M. C. Picot, et al., "Effects of a six-month walking intervention on depression in inactive post-menopausal women: A randomized controlled trial," *Aging and Mental Health* 19, no. 6 (2015): 485–92.

18. D. Julien, L. Gauvin, L. Richard, Y. Kestens, et al., "The role of social participation and walking in depression among older adults: Results from the VoisiNuAge study," *Canadian Journal of Aging* 32, no. 1 (March 2013): 1–12.

19. T. R. Prohaska, A. R. Eisenstein, W. A. Satariano, R. Hunter, et al., "Walking and the preservation of cognitive function in older populations," *Gerontologist* 49, no. S1 (June 2009): S86–93.

20. M. N. Silverman and P. A. Deuster, "Biological mechanisms underlying the role of physical fitness in health and resilience," *Interface Focus* 4, no. 5 (October 2014): 20140040.

21. A. H. Goldfarb and A. Z. Jamurtas, "Beta-endorphin response to exercise: An update," *Sports Medicine* 24, no. 1 (July 1997): 8–16.

22. W. D. Killgore, E. A. Olson, and M. Weber, "Physical exercise habits correlate with gray matter volume of the hippocampus in healthy adult humans," *Scientific Reports* 3 (December 2013): 3457.

23. K. I. Erickson, C. A. Raji, O. L. Lopez, J. T. Becker, et al., "Physical activity predicts gray matter volume in late adulthood: The cardiovascular health study," *Neurology* 75, no. 16 (October 2010): 1415–22.

24. S. J. Colcomber, K. I. Erickson, P. E. Scalf, J. S. Kim, et al., "Aerobic exercise training increases brain volume in aging humans," *Journal of Gerontology A: Biological Science and Medical Science* 61, no. 111 (November 2006): 1166–70.

25. K. I. Erickson, M. W. Voss, R. S. Prakash, C. Basak, et al., "Exercise training increases size of hippocampus and improves memory," *Proceedings of the National Academy of Sciences, USA* 108, no. 7 (February 2011): 3017–22.

26. H. Johansson, K. Norlander, H. Hedenstrom, C. Janson, et al., "Exercise-induced dyspnea is a problem among the general adolescent population," *Respiratory Medicine* 108, no. 6 (June 2014): 852–58.

27. F. Sanchis-Gomar, A. Santos-Lozano, N. Garatachea, H. Pareja-Galeano, et al., "My patient wants to perform strenuous endurance exercise: What's the right advice?" *International Journal of Cardiology* 197 (October 2015): 248–53.

28. K. D. Dunn, "A review of the literature examining the physiological processes underlying the therapeutic benefits of hatha yoga," *Advances in Mind Body Medicine* 23, no. 3 (Fall 2008): 10–18.

29. H. Cramer, R. Lauche, J. Langhorst, and G. Dobos, "Is one yoga style better than another? A systematic review of associations of yoga style and conclusions in randomized yoga trial," *Complementary Therapies in Medicine* 25 (April 2016): 178–87.

30. C. L. Park, K. E. Riley, E. Bedesin, and V. M. Stewart, "Why practice yoga? Practitioners' motivation for adopting and maintaining yoga practice," *Journal of Health and Psychology* 21, no. 6 (June 2016): 887–96.

31. J. Thirthalli, G. H. Naveen, M. G. Rao, S. Varambally, et al., "Cortisol and antidepressant effects of yoga," *Indian Journal of Psychiatry* 55, no. S3 (July 2013): S405–8.

32. A. Ross and S. Thomas, "The health benefits of yoga and exercise: A review of comparison studies," *Journal of Alternative and Complementary Medicine* 16, no. 1 (January 2010): 3–12.

33. C. C. Streeter, T. H. Whitfield, L. Owen, T. Rein, et al., "Effects of yoga versus walking on mood, anxiety, and brain GABA levels: A randomized controlled MRS study," *Journal of Complementary Medicine* 16, no. 111 (November 2010): 1145–52.

34. J. A Smith, T. Greer, T. Sheets, and S. Watson, "Is there more to yoga than exercise?" *Alternative Therapies in Health and Medicine* 17, no. 3 (May–June 2011): 22–29.

35. F. J. Huang, D. K. Chien, and U. L. Chung, "Effects of hatha yoga on stress in middle-aged women," *Journal of Nursing Research* 21, no. 1 (May 2013): 59–66.

36. R. Fang and X. Li, "A regular yoga intervention for staff nurse sleep quality and work stress: A randomized controlled study," *Journal of Clinical Nursing* 24 (December 2015): 3374–79.

37. S. L. Lin, C. Y. Huang, S. P. Shiu, and S. H. Yeh, "Effects of yoga on stress, stress adaption, and heart rate variability among mental health professionals: A randomized controlled trial," *Worldviews on Evidence-Based Nursing* 12, no. 4 (August 2015) 236–45.

38. A. Michalsen, P. Grossman, A. Acil, J. Langhorst, et al., "Rapid stress reduction and anxiolysis among distressed women as a consequence of a three-month intensive yoga program," *Medical Science Monitor* 11, no. 12 (December 2005): CR555–61.

39. D. L. Berger, E. J. Silver, and R. E. Stein, "Effects of yoga on inner-city children's well-being: A pilot study," *Alternative Therapy Health and Medicine* 15, no. 5 (September–October 2009): 36–42.

40. J. Medina, L. Hopkins, M. Powers, S. O. Baird, et al., "The effects of a hatha yoga intervention on facets of distress tolerance," *Cognitive Behavior and Therapy* 44, no. 4 (May 2015): 288–300.

41. R. K. Yadav, R. B. Ray, B. Vempati, and R. L. Bijlani, "Effect of a comprehensive yoga-based lifestyle modification program on lipid peroxidation," *Indian Journal of Physiology and Pharmacology* 49, no. 3 (July–September 2005): 358–62.

42. S. Sinha, S. N. Singh, Y. P. Monga, and U. S. Ray, "Improvement of glutathione and total antioxidant status with yoga," *Journal of Alternative and Complementary Medicine* 13, no. 10 (December 2007): 1085–90.

43. R. Pal, S. N. Singh, K. Halder, O. S. Tomer, et al., "Effects of yogic practice on metabolism and antioxidant redox status of physically active males," *Journal of Physical Activity and Health* 12, no. 4 (April 2015): 579–87.

44. S. Mayor, "Yoga reduces cardiovascular risk as much as walking or cycling, study shows," *British Medical Journal* 349 (December 2014): g7713.

45. S. M. Chimkode, S. D. Kumaran, V. V. Kanhere, and R. Shivanna, "Effect of yoga on blood glucose levels in patients with type 2 diabetes," *Journal of Clinical and Diagnostic Research* 9, no. 4 (April 2015): CC01–3.

46. T. Field, "Yoga research review," *Complementary Therapy in Clinical Practice* 24 (August 2016): 145–61.

47. V. R. Hariprasad, S. Varambally, V. Shivakumar, S. V. Kalmady, et al., "Yoga increases the volume of the hippocampus in elderly subjects," *Indian Journal of Psychiatry* 55, no. S4 (July 2013): S394–96.

48. M. Sharma and S. E. Rush, "Mindfulness-based stress reduction as a stress management intervention for healthy individuals," *Journal of Evidence-Based Complementary and Alternative Medicine* 19, no. 4 (October 2014): 271–86.

49. M. Goyal, S. Singh, E. M. Sibinga, N. F. Gould, et al., "Meditation programs for psychological stress and well-being: A systematic review and meta-analysis," *JAMA Internal Medicine* 174, no. 3 (March 2014): 357–68.

50. K. J. Kemper, D. Powell, C. C. Helms, and D. B. Kim-Shapiro, "Loving-kindness meditation's effect on nitric oxide and perceived well-being: A pilot study in experienced and inexperienced meditators," *Explore* (New York) 11, no. 1 (January–February 2015): 32–39.

51. S. G. Hoffman, P. Grossman, and D. E. Hinton, "Loving-kindness and compassion meditation: Potential for psychological interventions," *Clinical Psychology Review* 31, no. 7 (November 2011): 1126–32.

52. J. E. Bormann, T. L. Smith, S. Becker, M. Gershwin, et al., "Efficacy of frequent mantra repetition on stress, quality of life and spiritual well-being in veterans: A pilot study," *Journal of Holistic Nursing* 23, no. 4 (December 2005): 395–414.

53. J. E. Borman, D. Oman, J. K. Kemppainen, S. Becker, et al., "Mantram repetition for stress management in veterans and employees: A critical incident study," *Journal of Advanced Nursing* 53, no. 5 (March 2006): 502–12.

54. W. Turakitwanakan, C. Mekseepralard, and P. Busarakumtragul, "Effects of mindfulness meditation on serum cortisol of medical students," *Journal of the Medical Association of Thailand* 96, no. S1 (January 2013): S90–95.

55. S. Brand, E. Holsboer-Trachsler, R. Naranjo, and S. Schmidt, "Influence of mindfulness practice on cortisol and sleep in long-term and short-term meditators," *Neuropsychobiology* 65, no. 3 (April 2012): 109–18.

56. Y. Fan, Y. Y. Tang, and M. I. Posner, "Cortisol level modulated by integrative meditation in dose-dependent fashion," *Stress and Health* 30, no. 1 (February 2014): 65–70.

57. R. Jevning, A. F. Wilson, and J. M. Davidson, "Adrenocortical activity during meditation," *Hormones and Behavior* 10, no. 1 (February 1978): 54–60.

58. C. Mahagita, "Roles of meditation on alleviation of oxidative stress and improvement of antioxidant system," *Journal of Medical Association of Thailand* 93, no. S6 (November 2010): S242–54.

59. D. H. Kim, Y. S. Moon, H. S. Kim, J. S. Jung, et al., "Effect of Zen meditation on serum nitric oxide activity and lipid peroxidation," *Progress in Neuropsychopharmacology and Biological Psychiatry* 39, no. 2 (February 2005): 327–31.

60. E. Luders, A. W. Toga, N. Lepore, and C. Gasser, "The underlying anatomical correlates of long-term meditation: Larger hippocampal and frontal volume gray matter," *NeuroImage* 45, no. 3 (April 2009): 672–78.

61. C. M. Samart, S. J. B. P. Mulligan, J. Koudys, et al., "Mindfulness training for older adults with subjective cognitive decline: Results from a pilot randomized study," *Journal of Alzheimer's Disease* 52, no. 2 (April 2016): 757–74.

62. B. K. Holzel, J. Carmody, M. Vangel, C. Congleton, et al., "Mindfulness practice leads to increase in regional brain gray matter density," *Psychiatry Research* 191, no. 1 (January 2011): 36–43.

63. O. Singleton, B. K. Jolzel, M. Vangel, N. Brach, et al., "Change in brainstem gray matter concentration following a mindfulness-based intervention is correlated with improvement in psychological well-being," *Frontiers in Human Neuroscience* 18, no. 8 (February 2014): 33.

64. R. A. Gotink, R. Meijboom, M. W. Vernooij, M. Smits, et al., "8-week mindfulness based stress reduction induces brain changes similar to traditional meditation practice: A systematic review," *Brain and Cognition* 108 (October 2016): 32–41.

65. E. Luders, F. Kurth, E. A. Mayer, A. W. Toga, et al., "The unique brain anatomy of meditation practitioners: Alteration in cortical gyrification," *Frontiers in Human Neuroscience* 6 (February 2012): 34.

66. V. Jindal, S. Gupta, and R. Das, "Molecular mechanism of meditation," *Molecular Neurobiology* 48, no. 3 (December 2013): 808–11.

67. E. Luders, "Exploring age-related brain degeneration in meditation practitioners," *Annals of the New York Academy of Science* 1307 (January 2014): 82–88.

68. D. J. Kearney, C. A. Malte, C. McManus, M. E. Martinez, et al., "Loving-kindness meditation for posttraumatic stress disorder: A pilot study," *Journal of Traumatic Stress* 26, no. 4 (August 2013): 426–34.

69. S. Hemelstein, "Meditation research: The state of the art in correctional settings," *International Journal of Offender Therapy and Comparative Criminology* 55, no. 4 (June 2011): 646–61.

70. J. Lagopoulos, J. Xu, I. Rasmussen, A. Vik, et al., "Increased theta and alpha EEG activity during nondirective meditation," *Journal of Alternative and Complementary Medicine* 15, no. 11 (November 2009): 1187–92.

71. H. A. Pasquini, G. K. Tanaka, L. F. Basile, B. Velasques, et al., "Electrophysiological correlates of long-term *Soto Zen* meditation," *Biomedical Research International* 2015 (January 2015): 598496.

72. T. W. Kjaer, C. Bertelsen, P. Piccini, D. Brooks, et al., "Increased dopamine tone during meditation-induced change in consciousness," *Cognitive Brain Research* 13, no. 2 (April 2002): 255–59.

73. R. P. Brown and P. L. Gerbarg, "Yoga breathing, meditation and longevity," *Annals of the New York Academy of Science* 1172 (August 2009): 54–62.

74. C. N. Alexander, E. J. Langer, R. I. Newman, H. M. Chandler, et al., "Transcendental meditation, mindfulness and longevity: An experimental study with the elderly," *Journal of Personality and Social Psychology* 57, no. 6 (December 1989): 950–64.

75. D. Orme-Johnson, "Medical care utilization and the transcendental meditation program," *Psychosomatic Medicine* 49, no. 5 (September–October 1987): 493–507.

76. K. Walton, R. H. Schneider, and S. Nidich, "Review of controlled research on the transcendental meditation program and cardiovascular disease: Risk factors, morbidity and mortality," *Cardiology Review* 12, no. 5 (September–October 2004): 262–66.

77. M. K. Koika and R. Cardoso, "Meditation can produce beneficial effects to prevent cardiovascular disease," *Hormone Molecular Biology and Clinical Investigation* 18, no. 3 (June 2014): 137–43.

78. G. Dobos, T. Overhamm, A. Bussing, T. Ostermann, et al., "Integrating mindfulness in supportive cancer care: A cohort study on a mindfulness-based day

care clinic for cancer survivors," *Supportive Care in Cancer* 23, no. 10 (October 2015): 2945–55.

79. S. W. Robb, K. Benson, L. Middleton, C. Meyers, et al., "Mindfulness-based stress reduction teachers, practice characteristics, cancer incidence, and health: A nationwide ecological description," *BMC Complementary and Alternative Medicine* 14 (February 2015): 15–24.

CHAPTER 6. AROMATHERAPY, MASSAGE, REIKI, AND MUSIC FOR STRESS MANAGEMENT

1. University of Maryland Medical Center, "Aromatherapy."

2. M. A. Halm, "Essential oils for management of symptoms in critically ill patients," *American Journal of Critical Care* 17, no. 2 (March 2008): 160–63.

3. J. Vassilliou, "The history of massage," *Ezine Articles*, August 2009, http://EzineArticles.com/expert/Joe_Vassilliou/377331.

4. P. Miles and G. True, "Reiki-review of a biofield therapy history, theory, practice and research," *Alternative Therapies in Health and Medicine* 9, no. 2 (April 2003): 62–72.

5. N. J. Conard, M. Malina, and S. C. Muzel, "New flutes document the earliest musical tradition in Southwestern Germany," *Nature* 460, no. 7256 (August 2009): 737–40.

6. I. Morley, "A multi-disciplinary approach to the origins of music: Perspectives from anthropology, archaeology, cognition and behavior," *Journal of Anthropological Science* 92 (2014): 147–77.

7. A. Butje, E. Repede, and M. M. Shattell, "Healing scents: An overview of clinical aromatherapy for emotional distress," *Journal of Psychosocial Nursing* 46, no. 10 (October 2008): 46–52.

8. D. Bickers, P. Calow, H. Greim, J. M. Hanifin, et al., "A toxicological and dermatological assessment of linalool and related esters when used as fragrance ingredients," *Food Chemistry and Toxicology* 41, no. 7 (July 2003): 919–42.

9. Y. Zhang, Y. Wu, T. Chen, L. Yao, et al., "Assessing the metabolite effects of aromatherapy in human volunteers," *Evidence-Based Complementary and Alternative Medicine* 2013 (2013): 356381.

10. Y. Shiina, N. Funabashi, K. Lee, T. Toyoda, et al., "Relaxation effects of lavender aromatherapy improve coronary flow velocity reserve in healthy men evaluated by

transthoracic Doppler echocardiography," *International Journal of Cardiology* 129, no. 2 (September 2008): 193–97.

11. T. Atsumi and K. Tonosaki, "Smelling lavender and rosemary increases free radical scavenging activity and decreases cortisol level in saliva," *Psychiatry Research* 150, no. 1 (February 2007): 89–96.

12. M. Toda and K. Morimoto, "Effect of lavender aroma on salivary endocrinological stress markers," *Archives of Oral Biology* 53, no. 10 (October 2010): 954–68.

13. M. Toda and K. Morimoto, "Evaluation of effects of lavender and peppermint aromatherapy using sensitive salivary endocrinology stress markers," *Stress and Health* 27, no. 5 (December 2011): 430–35.

14. W. Sayorwan, V. Siripornpanich, T. Piriyapunyaporn, T. Hongratanaworakit, et al., "The effect of lavender oil inhalation on emotional states, autonomic nervous system, and brain electrical activity," *Journal of the Medical Association of Thailand* 95, no. 4 (April 2012): 598–606.

15. E. Watanabe, K. Kuchta, M. Kimura, H. W. Rauwald, et al., "Effects of bergamot (Citrus bergamia (Risso) Wright & Arn.) essential oil aromatherapy on mood states, parasympathetic nervous system activity and salivary cortisol levels in 41 healthy females," *Forschende Komplementarmedizin* 22, no. 1 (2015): 43–49.

16. M. C. Chen, S. H. Fang, and L. Fang, "The effects of aromatherapy in relieving symptoms related to job stress among nurses," *International Journal of Nursing Practice* 21, no. 1 (February 2015): 87–93.

17. S. H. Liu, T. H. Lin, and K. M. Chang, "The physical effects of aromatherapy in alleviating work-related stress on elementary school teachers in Taiwan," *Evidence-Based Complementary and Alternative Medicine* 2013 (October 2013): 853809.

18. S. K. Tang and M. Y. Tse, "Aromatherapy: Does it help to relieve pain, depression, anxiety, and stress in community-dwelling older persons?" *Biomed Research International* 2014 (2014): 430195.

19. T. C. Goes, F. R. Ursulino, T. H. Almeida-Souza, P. B. Alves, et al., "Effect of lemongrass aroma on experimental anxiety in humans," *Journal of Alternative and Complementary Medicine* 21, no. 12 (December 2015): 766–73.

20. T. C. Goes, F. D. Antunes, P. B. Alves, and F. Teixeira-Silva, "Effect of sweet orange aroma on experimental anxiety in humans," *Journal of Alternative and Complementary Medicine* 18, no. 8 (August 2012): 798–804.

21. J. Lehrner, G. Marwinski, S. Lehr, P. Johren, et al., "Ambient odors of orange and lavender reduce anxiety and improve mood in a dental office," *Physiology and Behavior* 86, no. 1–2 (September 2005): 92–95.

22. P. Conrad and C. Adams, "The effects of clinical aromatherapy for anxiety and depression in the high risk postpartum women: A pilot study," *Complementary Therapies in Clinical Practice* 18, no. 3 (August 2102): 164–68.

23. M. Kianpour, A. Mansouri, T. Mhrabi, and G. Asghari, "Effect of lavender scent inhalation on prevention of stress, anxiety and depression in postpartum period," *Iranian Journal of Nursing and Midwifery Research* 21, no. 2 (March–April 2016): 197–201.

24. F. Rashidi-Fakari, M. Tabatabaeichehr, and H. Mortazavi, "The effect of aromatherapy by essential oil of orange on anxiety during labor: A randomized clinical trial," *Iranian Journal of Nursing and Midwifery Research* 20, no. 6 (November–December 2015): 661–64.

25. T. Filed, T. Field, C. Cullen, S. Largie, et al., "Lavender bath oil reduces stress and crying and enhances sleep in very young infants," *Early Human Development* 84, no. 6 (June 2008): 399–401.

26. T. Hongratanaworakit, "Aroma therapeutic effects of massage blended essential oils on humans," *Natural Product Communication* 6, no. 8 (August 2011): 1199–204.

27. T. Hongratanaworakit, "Relaxing effect of rose oil on humans," *Natural Product Communication* 6, no. 8 (February 2009): 291–96.

28. T. Hongratanaworakit, "Relaxing effect of ylang ylang oil after transdermal absorption," *Phytotherapy Research* 20, no. 9 (September 2006): 758–63.

29. T. Hongratanaworakit, "Stimulating effect of aromatherapy massage with jasmine oil," *Natural Product Communication* 5, no. 1 (January 2010): 157–62.

30. M. Cooke, K. Jolzhauser, M. Jones, C. Davis, et al., "The effect of aromatherapy massage with music on the stress and anxiety levels of emergency nurses: Comparison between summer and winter," *Journal of Clinical Nursing* 16, no. 9 (September 2007): 1695–703.

31. M. Imura, H. Misao, and H. Ushijima, "The physiological effects of aromatherapy-massage in healthy postpartum mothers," *Journal of Midwifery and Women's Health* 51, no. 2 (April 2006): e21–27.

32. K. H. Rho, S. H. Han, K. S. Kim, and M. S. Lee, "Effects of aromatherapy massage on anxiety and self-esteem in Korean elderly women: A pilot study," *International Journal of Neuroscience* 116, no. 2 (December 2006): 1447–55.

33. E. Hwang and S. Shin, "The effects of aromatherapy on sleep improvement: A systematic literature review and meta-analysis," *Journal of Alternative and Complementary Medicine* 21, no. 2 (February 2015): 61–68.

34. L. W. Chien, S. L. Cheng, and C. F. Liu, "The effect of lavender aromatherapy on autonomic nervous system in midlife women with insomnia," *Evidence-Based Complementary and Alternative Medicine* 2012 (2012): 740813.

35. S. Kim, H. J. Kim, J. S. Yeo, S. J. Hing, et al., "The effect of lavender oil on stress, bispectral index value and needle insertion pain on volunteers," *Journal of Alternative and Complementary Medicine* 17, no. 9 (September 2011): 823–26.

36. T. M. Marzouk, A. M. El-Nemer, and H. N. Bakara, "The effect of aromatherapy abdominal massage on alleviating menstrual pain in nursing students: A prospective randomized cross-over study," *Evidence-Based Complementary and Alternative Medicine* 2013 (2013): 742421.

37. R. Kazemzadeh, R. Nikjou, M. Rostamnegad, and H. Norouzi, "Effect of lavender aromatherapy on menopause hot flashings: A crossover randomized clinical trial," *Journal of the Chinese Medical Association* 79, no. 9 (September 2016): 489–92.

38. J. R. Johnson, R. L. Rivard, K. H. Griffin, A. K. Kolste, et al., "The effectiveness of nurse-delivered aromatherapy in acute care settings," *Complementary Therapies in Medicine* 25 (April 2016): 164–69.

39. F. Barati, A. Nasiri, N. Akbari, and G. Sharifzadeh, "The effect of aromatherapy on anxiety in patients," *Nephro-Urology Monthly* 8, no. 5 (July 2016): e38347.

40. E. Karadag, S. Samancioglu, D. Ozden, and E. Bakir, "Effects of aromatherapy on sleep quality and anxiety of patient," *Nursing in Critical Care* 25, no. 2 (2015): 105–12.

41. W. N. Setzer, "Essential oils and anxiolytic aromatherapy," *Natural Product Communication* 4, no. 9 (September 2009): 1305–16.

42. A. Seyyed-Rasooli, F. Salehi, A. Mohammadpoorsasl, S. Goliaryan, et al., "Comparing the effects of aromatherapy massage and inhalation aromatherapy on

anxiety and pain in burn patients: A single-blind randomized clinical trial," *Burns* 42, no. 8 (2016): 1774–80.

43. J. Imanishi, H. Kuriyama, I. Shigemori, S. Watanabe, et al., "Anxiolytic effect of aromatherapy massage in patients with breast cancer," *Evidence-Based Complementary and Alternative Medicine* 6, no. 1 (March 2009): 123–28.

44. K. Boehm, A. Bussing, and T. Ostermann, "Aromatherapy as an adjuvant treatment in cancer care: A descriptive systematic review," *African Journal of Traditional Complementary and Alternative Medicine* 9, no. 4 (July 2012): 503–18.

45. J. Buckle, "Use of aromatherapy as a complementary treatment for chronic pain," *Alternative Therapies in Health and Medicine* 5, no. 5 (September 1999): 42–51.

46. A. Nasiri, M. A. Mahmodi, and Z. Nobakht, "Effect of aromatherapy massage with lavender essential oil on pain in patients with osteoarthritis of the knee: A randomized controlled clinical trial," *Complementary Therapy Clinical Practice* 25 (November 2016): 75–80.

47. B. Cetinkaya and Z. Basbakkal, "The effectiveness of aromatherapy massages using lavender oil as a treatment for infantile colic," *International Journal of Nursing Practice* 18, no. 2 (April 2012): 164–69.

48. Q. A. Nguyen and C. Paton, "The use of aromatherapy to treat behavioral problems in dementia," *International Journal of Geriatric Psychiatry* 23, no. 4 (April 2008): 337–46.

49. T. Field, "Massage therapy," *Medical Clinics of North America* 86, no. 1 (January 2002): 163–71.

50. H. Takeda, J. Tujita, M. Takemura, and Y. Oku, "Difference between the physiological and psychological effects of aromatherapy body treatment," *Journal of Alternative and Complementary Medicine* 14, no. 6 (July 2008): 655–61.

51. F. Labrique-Walusis, K. J. Keister, A. C. Russell, "Massage therapy for stress management: Implications for nursing practice," *Orthopedic Nursing* 29 (2010): 254–57.

52. M. Aourell, M. Skoog, and J. Carleson, "Effects of Swedish massage on blood pressure," *Complementary Therapies in Clinical Practice* 11, no. 4 (November 2005): 242–46.

53. I. H. Kim, T. Y. Kim, and Y. W. Ko, "The effect of a scalp massage on stress hormone, blood pressure, and heart rate of healthy females," *Journal of Physical Therapy Science* 28, no. 10 (October 2016): 2703–7.

54. T. Field, O. Quintino, T. Henteleff, L. Wells-Keife, et al., "Job stress reduction therapies," *Alternative Therapies in Health and Medicine* 3, no. 4 (July 1997): 54–56.

55. S. Leivadi, M. Hernandez-Reif, T. Field, M. O'Rourke, et al., "Massage therapy and relaxation effects on university dance students," *Journal of Dance Medicine and Science* 3, no. 3 (September 1999): 108–10.

56. T. Field, M. Diego, J. Deiter, M. Hernandez-Reif, et al., "Prenatal depression effects on the fetus and newborn," *Infant Behavior and Development* 27, no. 2 (May 2004): 216–29.

57. R. Adams, B. White, and C. Beckett, "The effects of massage therapy on pain management in the acute care setting," *International Journal of Therapeutic Massage and Bodywork* 3, no. 1 (March 2011): 4–11.

58. M. Adib-Hajbaghery, R. Rajabi-Beheshtabad, and A. Ardjmand, "Comparing the effect of whole body massage by a specialist nurse and patient's relatives on blood cortisol level in coronary patients," *ARYA Atherosclerosis* 11, no. 2 (March 2015): 126–32.

59. L. Corbin, "Safety and efficacy of massage therapy for patients with cancer," *Cancer Control* 12, no. 3 (July 2005): 158–64.

60. M. Juberg, K. K. Jerger, K. D. Allen, N. O. Dmitrieva, et al., "Pilot study of massage in veterans with knee osteoarthritis," *Journal of Alternative and Complementary Medicine* 21, no. 6 (June 2015): 333–38.

61. B. Garner, L. J. Phillips, H. M. Schmidt, C. Markulev, et al., "Pilot study evaluating the effect of massage therapy on stress, anxiety and aggression in a young adult psychiatric inpatient unit," *Australia, New Zealand Journal of Psychiatry* 42, no. 5 (May 2008): 414–22.

62. T. Field, S. Schanberg, and C. Kuhn, "Cortisol decreases and serotonin and dopamine increases following massage therapy," *International Journal of Neuroscience* 115, no. 10 (October 2005): 1397–413.

63. D. W. Wardell and J. Engebreston, "Biological correlates of Reiki Touch (sm) healing," *Journal of Advanced Nursing* 33, no. 4 (February 2001): 439–45.

64. R. M Rosade, B. Rubik, B. Mainguy, J. Plummer, et al., "Reiki reduces burnout among community mental health clinicians," *Journal of Alternative and Complementary Medicine* 21, no. 8 (August 2015): 489–95.

65. E. L. Bukowski and D. Berardi, "Reiki brief report: Using Reiki to reduce stress levels in a nine-year-old child," *Explore* (NY) 10, no. 4 (July–August 2014): 253–55.

66. K. Olson, J. Hanson, and A. Michaud, "A phase II trial of Reiki for the management of pain in advanced cancer patients," *Journal of Pain Symptoms and Management* 25, no. 5 (November 2003): 990–97.

67. E. Gillespie, B. Gillespie, and M. Stevens, "Painful diabetic neuropathy: Impact on an alternative approach," *Diabetes Care* 30, no. 4 (April 2007): 999–1001.

68. A. Vitale and P. O'Conner, "The effect of Reiki on pain and anxiety in women with abdominal hysterectomies: A quasi-experimental pilot study," *Holistic Nursing Practice* 20, no. 6 (November–December 2006): 263–74.

69. J. Joyce and G. P. Herbison, "Reiki for depression and anxiety," *Cochrane Database Systematic Review* 3, no. 4 (April 2015): CD006833.

70. M. S. Lee, M. H. Pittler, and E. Ernst, "Effects of Reiki in clinical practice: A systematic review of randomized clinical trials," *International Journal of Clinical Practice* 62, no. 6 (June 2008): 947–54.

71. A. Linnemann, J. Strahler, and U. M. Nater, "The stress-reducing effect of music listening varies depending on the social context," *Psychoneuroendocrinology* 72 (October 2016): 97–105.

72. M. V. Thoma, R. La Marca, R. Bronnimann, L. Finkel, et al., "The effect of music on the human stress response," *PLoS One* 8, no. 8 (August 2013): e70156.

73. W. E. Knight and N. S. Rickard, "Relaxing music prevents stress-induced increase in subjective anxiety, systolic blood pressure and heart rate in healthy males and females," *Journal of Music Therapy* 38, no. 4 (Winter 2001): 254–72.

74. H. Fukui and M. Yamashita, "The effects of music on visual stress on testosterone and cortisol in men and women," *Neurology and Endocrinology Letters* 24, nos. 3–4 (June–August 2003): 173–80.

75. E. K. Pauwels, D. Volterrani, G. Mariani, and M. Kostkiewics, "Mozart, music and medicine," *Medical Principles and Practice* 23, no. 5 (September 2014): 403–12.

76. J. Bradt, C. Dileo, and N. Potvin, "Music for stress and anxiety reduction in coronary heart disease patients," *Cochrane Database and Systematic Review* 28, no. 12 (December 2013): CD006577.

77. G. R. Watkins, "Music therapy: Proposed physiological mechanisms and clinical implications," *Clinical Nurse Specialist* 11, no. 2 (March 1997): 43–50.

CHAPTER 7. MAKING LOVE TO YOUR SPOUSE/ROMANTIC PARTNER— A GREAT STRESS BUSTER

1. G. A. Schuiling, "The benefit and the doubt: Why monogamy?" *Journal of Psychosomatic Obstetrics and Gynecology* 24, no. 1 (March 2003): 55–61.

2. L. J. Waite and M. Gallagher, *The case for marriage: Why married people are happier, healthier, and better off financially* (New York: Doubleday, 2000).

3. Wikipedia, s.v. "Legal status of polygamy."

4. S. Elbedour, A. J. Onwuegbuize, C. Caridine, and H. Abu-Saad, "The effect of polygamous marital structure on behavioral, emotional, and academic adjustment in children: A comprehensive review of the literature," *Clinical Child and Family Psychology Review* 5, no. 4 (December 2002): 2551–71.

5. K. L. Kramer and A. F. Russell, "Kin-selected cooperation without lifetime monogamy: Human insights and animal implications," *Trends in Ecology and Evolution* 29, no. 11 (November 2014): 600–606.

6. C. Opie, Q. D. Atkinson, R. I. Dunbar, and S. Shultz, "Male infanticide leads to social monogamy in primates," *Proceedings of the National Academy of Sciences, USA* 110, no. 33 (August 2013): 13328–32.

7. K. L. Kramer and A. F. Russell, "Was monogamy a key step on the hominin road? Reevaluating the monogamy hypothesis in the evolution of cooperative breeding," *Evolutionary Anthropology* 24, no. 2 (March–April 2015): 73–83.

8. H. Kaplan, K. Hill, A. Lancaster, and A. M. Hurtado, "A theory of human life history: Evolution, diet, intelligence and longevity," *Evolutionary Anthropology* 9, no. 4 (January 2000): 156–85.

9. M. Francesconi, C. Ghiglino, and M. Perry, "An evolutionary theory of monogamy," *Journal of Economic Theory* 166 (November 2016): 605–28.

10. L. Fortunato and M. Archetti, "Evolution of monogamous marriage by maximization of inclusive fitness," *Journal of Evolutionary Biology* 23, no. 1 (January 2010): 149–56.

11. C. T. Bauch and R. McElreath, "Disease dynamics and costly punishment can foster socially imposed monogamy," *Nature Communication* 7 (April 2016): 11219.

12. K. G. Seshadri, "The neuroendocrinology of love," *Indian Journal of Endocrinology and Metabolism* 20, no. 4 (July–August 2016): 558–63.

13. P. R. Shaver and C. Hazan, "A biased overview of the study of love," *Journal of Social and Personal Relationship* 5, no. 4 (November 1988): 473–501.

14. R. J. Sternberg, "A triangular theory of love," *Psychological Review* 93, no. 2 (April 1986): 119–35.

15. G. J. Fletcher, J. A. Simpson, L. Campbell, and N. C. Ovwerall, "Pair bonding, romantic love and evolution: The curious case of Homo Sapience," *Perspectives on Psychological* 10, no. 1 (January 2015): 20–36.

16. R. I. Dunbar, "The social brain hypothesis and its implications for social evolution," *Annals of Human Biology* 36, no. 5 (September–October 2009): 562–72.

17. D. C. Geary and M. V. Flinn, "Evolution of human parental behavior and the human family," *Parenting: Science and Practice* 1, nos. 1–2 (January–June 2001): 5–61.

18. A. Dixon and M. Anderson, "Sexual selection and the comparative anatomy of reproductions in monkeys, apes and human beings," *Annual Review of Sex Research* 12 (2001): 121–44.

19. B. Sillen-Tullberg and A. P. Moller, "The relationship between concealed ovulation and mating systems in anthropoid primates: A phylogenetic study," *American Naturalist* 141, no. 1 (January 1993): 1–25.

20. E. S. Walker, K. R. Hill, M. V. Flinn, and R. M. Ellsworth, "Evolutionary history of hunter-gatherer marriage practices," *PLoS One* 6, no. 4 (April 2011): e19066.

21. L. Fortunato, "Reconstructing the history of marriage strategies in Indo-European-speaking societies: Monogamy and polygamy," *Human Biology* 83, no. 1 (February 2011): 87–105.

22. A. de Boer, E. M. van Buel, and G. J. Ter-Horst, "Love is more than just a kiss: A neurobiological basis of love and affection," *Neuroscience* 201 (January 2012): 114–24.

23. L. J. Young, Z. Wang, and T. R. Insel, "Neuroendocrine basis of monogamy," *Trends in Neuroscience* 21, no. 2 (February 1998): 71–75.

24. S. Fink, L. Excoffier, and G. Heckel, "Mammalian monogamy is not controlled by a single gene," *Proceedings of the National Academy of Sciences, USA* 103, no. 29 (July 2008): 10956–60.

25. D. Scheele, A. Wille, K. M. Kendrick, B. Stoffel-Wagner, et al., "Oxytocin enhances brain reward system responses in men viewing the face of their female partners," *Proceedings of the National Academy of Sciences, USA* 110, no. 50 (December 2013): 20308–13.

26. D. Schelle, N. Striepens, O. Gunturkun, S. Deutschlander, et al., "Oxytocin modulates social distance between males and females," *Journal of Neuroscience* 32, no. 46 (November 2012): 16074–79.

27. W. Blaicher, D. Gruber, C. Bieglmayer, A. M. Blaicher, et al., "The role of oxytocin in relation to female sexual arousal," *Gynecologic and Obstetric Investigation* 47, no. 2 (1999): 125–26.

28. L. J. Young, Z. Wang, and T. R. Insel, "Neuroendocrine base of monogamy," *Trends in Neuroscience* 21, no. 2 (February 1998): 71–75.

29. H. K. Huynh, A. T. Willemsen, and G. Holstege, "Female orgasm but not male ejaculation activates the pituitary: A PET-neuro-imaging study," *NeuroImage* 76 (August 2013): 178–82.

30. F. Giuliano, "Neurophysiology of erection and ejaculation," *Journal of Sexual Medicine* 8, no. S4 (October 2011): 310–15.

31. S. Brody and T. H. Kruger, "The post-orgasmic prolactin increase following intercourse is greater than following masturbation and suggests greater satiety," *Biological Psychology* 71, no. 3 (March 2006): 312–15.

32. R. S. Edelstein, W. J. Chopik, and E. L. Kean, "Socio-sexuality moderates the association between testosterone and relationship status in men and women," *Hormones and Behavior* 60, no. 3 (August 2011): 248–55.

33. D. G. Blanchflower and A. J. Oswald, "Money, sex and happiness: An empirical study," *Scandinavian Journal of Economics* 106, no. 3 (September 2004): 393–415.

34. M. H. Burleson, W. R. Trevathan, and M. Todd, "In the mood for love or vice versa? Exploring the relations among sexual activity, physical affection, affect and stress in the daily lives of mid-aged women," *Archives of Sexual Behavior* 36, no. 3 (June 2007): 357–68.

35. B. Ditzen, I. D. Neumann, G. Bodenmann, B. von Dawans, et al., "Effects of different kinds of couple interactions on cortisol and heart rate response to stress in women," *Psychoneuroendocrinology* 32, no. 5 (June 2007): 565–74.

36. S. Brody, "Blood pressure reactivity to stress is better for people who recently had penile-vaginal intercourse than for people who had other or no sexual activity," *Biological Psychiatry* 71, no. 2 (February 2006): 214–22.

37. S. Brody and P. Weiss, "Simultaneous penile-vaginal intercourse orgasm is associated with satisfaction (sexual, life, partnership and mental health)," *Journal of Sexual Medicine* 8, no. 3 (March 2011): 734–41.

38. K. Klapilova, S. Brody, L. Krejcova, B. Husarova, et al., "Sexual satisfaction, sexual compatibility and relationship adjustment in couples: The role of sexual behavior, orgasms and men's discernment of women's intercourse orgasms," *Journal of Sexual Medicine* 12, no. 3 (March 2011): 667–75.

39. T. R. John, R. Menon, A. Bludau, T. Grund, et al., "Salivary oxytocin concentrations in response to running, sexual self-stimulation, breastfeeding and TSST: The Regensburg oxytocin challenge," *Psychoneuroendocrinology* 62 (December 2015): 381–88.

40. G. Alspach, "Hugs and healthy hearts," *Critical Care Nursing* 24, no. 3 (June 2004): 8–9.

41. K. M. Grewen, B. J. Anderson, S. S. Girdler, and K. C. Light, "Warm partner contact is related to lower cardiovascular reactivity," *Behavioral Medicine* 29, no. 3 (Fall 2003): 123–30.

42. K. M. Grewen, S. S. Girdler, J. Amico, and K. C. Light, "Effects of partner support on resting oxytocin, cortisol, norepinephrine, and blood pressure before and after warm partner contact," *Psychosomatic Medicine* 67, no. 4 (July–August 2005): 531–38.

43. K. C. Light, K. M. Grewen, and J. A. Amico, "More frequent partner hugs and higher oxytocin levels are linked to lower blood pressure and heart rate in premenopausal women," *Biological Psychology* 69, no. 1 (April 2005): 5–21.

44. S. A. Hall, R. Shacklton, R. C. Rosen, and A. B. Araujo, "Sexual activity, erectile dysfunction and incident of cardiovascular events," *American Journal of Cardiology* 105, no. 2 (January 2010): 192–97.

45. S. Ebrahim, M. May, Y. Ben Shlomo, P. McCarron, et al., "Sexual intercourse and risk of ischemic stroke and coronary heart disease: The Caerphilly study," *Journal of Epidemiology and Community Health* 56, no. 2 (February 2002): 99–102.

46. G. Davey Smith, S. Frankel, and J. Yarnell, "Sex and death: Are they related? Findings from the Caerphilly study," *British Medical Journal* 315, no. 7123 (December 1997): 1641–44.

47. E. B. Plamore, "Predictors of the longevity difference: A 25-year follow up," *Gerontologist* 22, no. 6 (December 1982): 513–18.

48. C. J. Charnetski and F. X. Brennan, "Sexual frequency and salivary immunoglobulin A (IgA)," *Psychological Reports* 94, no. 3 (June 2004): 839–44.

49. J. Frappier, I. Toupin, J. J. Levy, M. Aubertin-Leheudre, et al., "Energy expenditure during sexual activity in young healthy couples," *PLoS One* 8, no. 10 (October 2013): e79342.

50. S. Brody and T. H. Kruger, "Penile-vaginal intercourse decreases weight gain," *Medical Hypothesis* 71, no. 5 (November 2008): 812–13.

51. L. F. Marin, A. C. Felicio, and G. F. Prado, "Sexual intercourse and masturbation: Potential relief factors for restless leg syndrome," *Sleep Medicine* 12, no. 4 (April 2011): 422.

52. A. Hambach, S. Evers, O. Summ, I. W. Husstedt, et al., "The impact of sexual activity on idiopathic headaches: An observational study," *Cephalalgia* 33, no. 6 (April 2013): 384–89.

53. M. H. Burleson, W. L. Gregory, and W. R. Trevathan, "Heterosexual activity and cycle length variability: Effect of gynecological maturity," *Physiology and Behavior* 50, no. 4 (October 1991): 863–66.

54. M. F. Leitzman, E. A. Platz, M. J. Stammpfer, and W. C. Willett, "Ejaculation frequency and subsequent risk of prostate cancer," *Journal of the American Medical Association* 291, no. 13 (2004): 1578–86.

55. T. G. Murrell, "The potential for oxytocin (OT) to prevent breast cancer: A hypothesis," *Breast Cancer Research and Treatment* 35, no. 2 (August 1995): 225–29.

56. M. G. Le, A. Bachelot, and C. Hill, "Characteristics of reproductive life and risk of breast cancer in a case control study of young nulliparous women," *Journal of Clinical Epidemiology* 42, no. 12 (December 1989): 1227–33.

57. E. Laan and R. H. van Lusen, "Hormones and sexuality in postmenopausal women: A psychophysiological study," *Journal of Psychosomatic Obstetrics and Gynecology* 18, no. 2 (June 1997): 126–33.

58. C. M. Meston and D. M. Buss, "Why humans have sex," *Archives of Sexual Behavior* 36, no. 4 (August 2007): 477–507.

59. H. Wright and R. A. Jenks, "Sex on the brain: Association between sexual activity and cognitive function in older age," *Age and Aging* 45, no. 2 (March 2016): 313–17.

60. A. Nicolosi, E. D. Moreira, M. Villa, and D. B. Glasser, "A population study of the association between sexual function, sexual satisfaction and depressive symptoms in men," *Journal of Affective Disorders* 82, no. 2 (October 2004): 235–43.

CHAPTER 8. BALANCED DIET FOR PREVENTION OF CHRONIC DISEASES AND STRESS MANAGEMENT

1. B. W. Ward, J. S. Schiller, and R. A. Goodman, "Multiple chronic conditions among U.S. adults: A 2012 update," *Preventing Chronic Disease* 11 (April 2014): E62.

2. M. M. Wilson, J. Reddy, and S. M. Krebs-Smith, "American diet quality: Where it is, where it is heading and what it could be," *Journal of the Academy of Nutrition and Dietetics* 116, no. 2 (February 2016): 302–10.

3. R. W. Kimokoti and B. E. Millen, "Nutrition for prevention of chronic diseases," *Medical Clinical of North America* 100, no. 6 (November 2016): 1185–98.

4. J. Kimmons, C. Gillespie, J. Seymour, M. Serdula, et al., "Fruit and vegetable intake among adults in the United States: Percentage meeting individualized recommendations," *Medscape Journal of Medicine* 11, no. 1 (January 2009): 26.

5. T. Trivedi, J. Liu, J. Probst, A. Merchant, et al., "Obesity and obesity-related behaviors among rural and urban adults in the USA," *Rural and Remote Health* 15, no. 4 (October–December 2015): 3267.

6. D. Yu, J. Sonderman, M. S. Buchowski, J. K. McLaughlin, et al., "Healthy eating and risks of total and cause-specific death among low-income population of African-Americans and other adults in the Southeastern United States: A prospective cohort study," *PLoS Medicine* 12, no. 5 (May 2015): e1001830.

7. B. E. Harmon, C. J. Boushey, Y. B. Shvetsov, R. Etienne, et al., "Association of key diet quality index with mortality in the multiethnic cohort: The dietary patterns methods project," *American Journal of Clinical Nutrition* 101, no. 3 (March 2015): 587–97.

8. M. Leenders, I. Sluijs, M. M. Ros, H. C. Boshuizen, et al., "Fruit and vegetable consumption and mortality: European prospective investigation into cancer and nutrition," *American Journal of Epidemiology* 178, no. 4 (August 2013): 590–602.

9. O. Oyebode, V. Gordon-Dseagu, A. Walker, and J. S. Mindell, "Fruit and vegetable consumption and all cause, cancer and CVD mortality: Analysis of Health Survey for England data," *Journal of Epidemiology and Community Health* 68, no. 9 (September 2014): 856–62.

10. S. Liu, I. M. Lee, U. Ajani, S. R. Cole, et al., "Intake of vegetables rich in carotenoids and risk of coronary heart disease in men: The physician's health study," *International Journal of Epidemiology* 30, no. 1 (February 2001): 130–35.

11. K. J. Joshipura, F. B. Hu, J. E. Manson, M. J. Stampfer, et al., "The effect of fruit and vegetables intake on risk for coronary heart disease," *Annals of Internal Medicine* 134, no. 12 (June 2001): 1106–14.

12. F. J. He, C. A. Nowson, and G. A. MacGregor, "Fruit and vegetable consumption and stroke: Meta-analysis of cohort studies," *Lancet* 367, no. 9607 (January 2006): 320–26.

13. R. H. Liu, "Health-promoting components of fruits and vegetables," *Advances in Nutrition* 4, no. 3 (May 2013): S384S–92.

14. F. Turati, M. Rossi, C. Pelucchi, F. Levi, et al., "Fruit and vegetables and the cancer risk: A review of southern European studies," *British Journal of Nutrition* 113, no. S2 (April 2015): S102–10.

15. Y. Wu, D. Zhang, X. Jiang, and W. Jiang, "Fruit and vegetables consumption and risk of type 2 diabetes mellitus: A dose response meta-analysis of prospective cohort studies," *Nutrition Metabolism and Cardiovascular Diseases* 25, no. 2 (February 2015): 140–47.

16. J. Mann and D. Aune, "Can specific fruits and vegetables prevent diabetes?" *British Medical Journal* 341 (August 2010): c4395.

17. H. Boeing, A. Bechthold, A. Bub, S. Ellinger, et al., "Critical review: Vegetables and fruits in the prevention of chronic diseases," *European Journal of Nutrition* 41, no. 6 (September 2012): 637–63.

18. R. D. Whitehead, D. Re, D. Xiao, G. Ozakinci, et al., "You are what you eat: Within-subject increases in fruit and vegetable consumption confer beneficial skin-color changes," *PLoS One* 7, no. 3 (March 2012): e32988.

19. K. Pezdirc, M. J. Hutchesson, R. Whitehead, G. Ozakinci, et al., "Fruit, vegetables and dietary carotenoid intakes explain variation in skin color in young Caucasian women: A cross-sectional study," *Nutrients* 7, no. 7 (July 2015): 5800–5815.

20. B. A. White, C. C. Horwath, and T. S. Conner, "Many apples a day keep blues away: Daily experiences of negative and positive effect of food consumption in young adults," *British Journal of Health and Psychology* 18, no. 4 (November 2013): 782–98.

21. F. N. Jacka, J. A. Pasco, A. Mykletun, L. Williams, et al., "Association of Western and traditional diets with depression and anxiety in women," *American Journal of Psychiatry* 167, no. 3 (May 2010): 305–11.

22. C. Rahe, M. Unrath, and K. Berger, "Dietary patterns and the risk of depression in adults: A systematic review of observational studies," *European Journal of Nutrition* 53, no. 4 (June 2014): 997–1013.

23. J. S. Lai, S. Hiles, A. Bisquera, A. J. Hure, et al., "A systematic review and meta-analysis of dietary patterns and depression in community-dwelling adults," *American Journal of Clinical Nutrition* 99, no. 1 (January 2014): 181–97.

24. T. C. Chan, T. J. Yen, Y. C. Fu, and J. S. Hwang, "Click diary: Online tracking of health behaviors and mood," *Journal of Medical Internet Research* 17, no. 6 (June 2015): e147.

25. D. G. Blanchflower, A. J. Oswald, and S. Stewart-Brown, "Is psychological well-being linked to consumption of fruits and vegetables?" *Social Indicators Research* 114, no. 3 (December 2013): 785–801.

26. B. A. White, C. C. Horwath, and T. S. Conner, "Many apples a day keep the blues away: Daily experiences of negative and positive affect and food consumption in young adults," *British Journal of Health Psychology* 18, no. 4 (November 2013): 782–98.

27. T. S. Conner, K. L. Brookie, A. C. Richardson, and M. A. Polak, "On carrots and curiosity: Eating fruits and vegetables is associated with greater flourishing in daily life," *British Journal of Health Psychology* 20, no. 2 (May 2015): 413–27.

28. M. S. Morris, M. Fava, P. F. Jacques, J. Selhub, et al., "Depression and folate status in the US population," *Psychotherapy and Psychosomatics* 72, no. 2 (March–April): 80–87.

29. J. Seppala, H. Koponen, H. Kautiainen, J. C. Eriksson, et al., "Association between folate intake and melancholic depressive symptoms: A Finnish population-based study," *Journal of Affective Disorders* 138, no. 3 (May 2012): 473–78.

30. H. Watanabe, S. Ishida, Y. Konno, M. Matsumoto, et al., "Impact of dietary folate intake on depressive symptoms in young women of reproductive age," *Journal of Midwifery and Women's Health* 57, no. 1 (January–February 2012): 43–48.

31. L. Clement, M. Boylan, V. G. Miller, M. Rockwell, et al., "Serum levels of folate and cobalamine are lower in depressed than in nondepressed hemodialysis subjects," *Journal of Renal Nutrition* 17, no. 5 (September 2007): 343–49.

32. T. P. Ng, L. Feng, M. Niti, E. H. Kua, et al., "Folate, vitamin B12, homocysteine and depressive symptoms in a population sample of older Chinese adults," *Journal of American Geriatric Society* 57, no. 5 (May 2007): 871–76.

33. R. Evans-Olders, S. Eintracht, and L. J. Hoffer, "Metabolic origin of hypovitaminosis C in acutely hospitalized patients," *Nutrition* 26, nos. 11–12 (December 2010): 1070–74.

34. S. Gariballa, "Poor vitamin C status is associated with increased depression symptoms following acute illness in older people," *International Journal of Vitamin and Nutrition Research* 84, nos. 1–2 (2014): 12–17.

35. M. Zhang, L. Robitaille, S. Eintracht, and L. J. Hoffer, "Vitamin C provision improves mood in acutely hospitalized patients," *Nutrition* 27, no. 5 (May 2011): 530–33.

36. M. Gautam, M. Agrawal, M. Gautam, P. Sharma, et al., "Role of antioxidants in generalized anxiety disorder and depression," *Indian Journal of Psychiatry* 54, no. 3 (July 2012): 244–47.

37. M. Amr, A. El-Mogy, T. Shams, K. Vieira, et al., "Efficacy of vitamin C as an adjunct to fluoxetine therapy in pediatric major depressive disorder: A randomized double-blind placebo-controlled study," *Nutrition Journal* 12 (March 2013): 31.

38. E. R. Bertone-Johnson, S. I. Powers, L. Spangler, R. L. Brunner, et al., "Vitamin D intake from food and supplements and depressive symptoms in a diverse population of older women," *American Journal of Clinical Nutrition* 94, no. 4 (October 2011): 1104–12.

39. C. H. Wilkins, Y. I. Sheline, C. M. Roe, S. J. Birge, et al., "Vitamin D deficiency associated with low mood and worse cognitive performance in older adults," *American Journal of Geriatric Psychiatry* 14, no. 12 (December 2006): 1032–40.

40. Y. J. Bae and S. K. Kim, "Low dietary calcium is associated with self-rated depression in middle-aged Korean women," *Nutrition Research and Practice* 6, no. 6 (December 2012): 527–33.

41. E. R. Bertone-Johnson, S. E. Hankinson, A. Bendich, S. R. Johnson, et al., "Calcium and vitamin D intake and the risk of incident of premenstrual syndrome," *Archives of Internal Medicine* 165, no. 11 (June 2005): 1246–52.

42. T. Yari, S. M. Lehto, T. Tolmunen, T. P. Tuomainen, et al., "Dietary magnesium intake and the incidence of depression: A 20-year follow-up," *Journal of Affective Disorders* 193 (March 2016): 94–98.

43. E. K. Tarleton and B. Littenberg, "Magnesium intake and depression in adults," *Journal of American Board of Family Medicine* 28, no. 2 (March–April): 249–56.

44. D. Benton, "Selenium intake, mood and other aspects of psychological functioning," *Nutrition and Neuroscience* 5, no. 6 (December 2002): 363–74.

45. J. A. Pasco, F. N. Jacka, L. J. Williams, M. Evans-Cleverdon, et al., "Dietary selenium and major depression: A nested case-control study," *Complementary Therapies in Medicine* 20, no. 3 (June 2012): 119–23.

46. T. S. Conner, A. C. Richardson, and J. C. Miller, "Optimal serum selenium concentrations are associated with lower depressive symptoms and negative mood among young adults," *Journal of Nutrition* 145, no. 1 (January 2015): 59–65.

47. J. A. Tur, M. M. Bibilone, A. Sureda, and A. Pons, "Dietary sources of omega-3 fatty acids: Public health risks and benefits," *British Journal of Nutrition* 107, no. S2 (June 2012): S23–53.

48. K. D. Wenstrom, "The FDA's new advice on fish: It is complicated," *American Journal of Obstetrics and Gynecology* 211, no. 5 (November 2014): 475–78.

49. C. J. Passos, D. Mergler, M. Lemire, M. Fillion, et al., "Fish consumption and bio indicators of inorganic mercury," *Science of Total Environment* 373, no. 1 (February 2007): 68–76.

50. F. Li, X. Liu, and D. Zhang, "Fish consumption and risk of depression," *Journal of Epidemiology and Community Health* 70, no. 3 (March 2016): 299–304.

51. K. Hamazaki, T. Natori, S. Kurihara, N. Murata, et al., "Fish consumption and depressive symptoms in undergraduate students: A cross-sectional analysis," *European Psychiatry* 30, no. 8 (November 2015): 983–87.

52. M. Gispert-Llaurado, M. Perz-Garcia, J. Escribano, R. Closa-Monasterolo, et al., "Fish consumption in mid-childhood and its relationship to neuropsychological outcomes measured in 7–9 year old children using NUTRIMENTHE neuropsychological battery," *Clinical Nutrition* 35, no. 6 (December 2016): 1301–7.

53. R. K. McNamara, R. Jandacek, P. Tso, T. J. Blom, et al., "Adolescents with or at ultra-high risk of bipolar disorder exhibit erythrocyte docosahexaenoic acid

and eicosapentaenoic acid deficit: A candidate prodromal risk biomarker," *Early Intervention Psychiatry* 10, no. 3 (June 2016): 203–11.

54. M. C. Morris, D. A. Evans, C. C. Tangney, J. L. Bienias, et al., "Fish consumption and cognitive decline with age in a large community study," *Archives of Neurology* 62, no. 12 (December 2005): 1849–53.

55. C. Firk and C. R. Markus, "Mood and cortisol responses following tryptophan-rich hydrolyzed protein and acute stress in health subjects with high and low cognitive reactivity in depression," *Clinical Nutrition* 28, no. 3 (June 2009): 266–71.

56. G. Lindseth, B. Helland, and J. Caspers, "The effects of dietary tryptophan on affective disorders," *Archives of Psychiatric Nursing* 29, no. 2 (April 2015): 102–7.

57. R. Hakkarainen, T. Partonen, J. Haukka, J. Virtamo, et al., "Association of dietary amino acids with low mood," *Depression and Anxiety* 18, no. 2 (September 2003): 89–94.

58. R. J. Wurtman, J. J. Wurtman, M. M. Regan, J. M. McDermott, et al., "Effects of normal meals rich in carbohydrate or proteins on plasma tryptophan and tyrosine ratios," *American Journal of Clinical Nutrition* 77, no. 1 (January 2003): 128–32.

59. C. R. Markus, "Effects of carbohydrate on brain tryptophan availability and stress performance," *Biological Psychiatry* 76, nos. 1–2 (September 2007): 83–90.

60. F. Shabbir, A. Patel, C. Mattison, S. Bose, et al., "Effect of diet on serotonergic neurotransmission in depression," *Neurochemistry International* 62, no. 3 (February 2013): 324–29.

61. N. Kitano, K. Tsunoda, T. Tsuji, Y. Osuka, et al., "Association between difficulty initiating sleeping in older adults and the combination of leisure time physical activity and consuming milk or milk products: A cross-sectional study," *BMC Geriatrics* 14 (November 2014): 118.

62. M. aan het Rot, D. S. Moskowitz, G. Pinard, and S. N. Young, "Social behavior and mood in everyday life: The effects of tryptophan in quarrelsome individuals," *Journal of Psychiatry and Neuroscience* 31, no. 4 (July 2006): 253–62.

63. S. Steinberg, L. Annable, S. N. Young and N. Liyanage, "A placebo-controlled study of the effects of L-tryptophan in patients with premenstrual dysphoria," *Advances in Experimental Medical Biology* 467 (1999): 85–88.

64. A. Steptoe, E. L. Gibson, R. Vuononvitra, E. D. Williams, et al., "The effect of tea on psychopharmacological stress responsivity and post-stress recovery:

A randomized double blind trial," *Psychopharmacology* (Berlin) 190, no. 1 (January 2007): 81–89.

65. A. Steptoe and J. Wardle, "Mood and drinking: A naturalistic diary study of alcohol, coffee and tea," *Psychopharmacology* (Berlin) 141, no. 3 (January 1999): 315–21.

66. T. Garcia-Blanco, A. Davalos, and F. Visioli, "Tea, coffee and affective disorders: Vicious or virtuous cycle?" *Journal of Affective Disorders* (November 2016) [e-pub ahead of print].

67. A. Nehlig, "Effects of coffee/caffeine on brain health and disease: What should I tell my patients?" *Practical Neurology* 16, no. 2 (April 2016): 89–95.

68. J. Liu, X. Sui, C. J. Lavie, J. R. Hebert, et al., "Association of coffee consumption with all-cause and cardiovascular disease mortality," *Mayo Clinic Proceedings* 88, no. 10 (October 2013): 1066–974.

69. P. A. van den Brandt and L. J. Schouten, "Relationship of tree nut, peanut and peanut better intake with total and cause-specific mortality: A cohort study and meta-analysis," *International Journal of Epidemiology* 44, no. 3 (June 2015): 1038–49.

70. V. Vadivel, C. N. Kunyang, and H. K. Biesalski, "Health benefits of nut consumption with special reference to body weight control," *Nutrition* 28, nos. 11–12 (November–December 2012): 1089–97.

71. S. G. West, A. L. Krick, L. C. Klein, G. Zhao, et al., "Effects of diets high in walnuts and flax oil on hemodynamic responses to stress and vascular endothelial function," *Journal of American College of Nutrition* 29, no. 6 (December 2010): 595–603.

72. A. Sanchez-Villegas, P. Henriquez, M. Bes-Rastrollo, and J. Doreste, "Mediterranean diet and depression," *Public Health and Nutrition* 9, no. 8A (December 2006): 1104–9.

73. A. Dasgupta and K. Klein, *Antioxidants in foods, vitamins and supplements: Prevention and treatment of disease* (Waltham, MA: Elsevier, 2014), 209–53.

74. C. N. Black, M. Bot, P. G. Scheffer, P. Cuijpers, et al., "Is depression associated with increased oxidative stress? A systematic review and meta-analysis," *Psychoneuroendocrinology* 51, no. 1 (January 2015): 164–75.

CHAPTER 9. DRINKING IN MODERATION FOR STRESS RELIEF

1. B. L. Vallee, "Alcohol in the Western World," *Scientific American* 278, no. 6 (June 1998): 80–85.

2. R. Dudley, *The drunken monkey: Why we drink and abuse alcohol* (Berkeley: University of California Press, 2014).

3. A. Erol and V. M. Karpyak, "Sex and gender-related differences in alcohol use and its consequences: Contemporary knowledge and future research considerations," *Drug and Alcohol Dependence* 156 (November 2015): 1–13.

4. C. A. Marczinski, "Can energy drinks increase the desire for more alcohol?" *Advances in Nutrition* 6, no. 1 (January 2015): 96–101.

5. A. Lac and C. D. Donaldson, "Alcohol attitudes, motives, norms and personality traits longitudinally classify nondrinkers, moderate drinkers and binge drinkers using discriminant function analysis," *Addictive Behavior* 61 (October 2016): 91–98.

6. C. Baum-Baicker, "The psychological benefits of moderate alcohol consumption: A review of the literature," *Drug and Alcohol Dependence* 15, no. 4 (August 1985): 305–22.

7. R. Clarisse, F. Testu, and A. Reinberg, "Effect of alcohol on psycho-technical test and social communication in a festive situation: A chronopsychological approach," *Chronobiology International* 21, nos. 4–5 (August 2004): 721–38.

8. P. C. Dolder, F. Holze, E. Liakoni, S. Harder, et al., "Alcohol acutely enhances decoding of positive emotion and emotional concern for positive stimuli and facilitates the view of sexual images," *Psychopharmacology* (Berlin) 234, no. 1 (January 2017): 41–51.

9. B. T. Jones, B. C. Jones, A. P. Thomas, and J. Piper, "Alcohol consumption increases attractiveness ratings of opposite sex faces: A possible third route of risky sex," *Addiction* 98, no. 8 (August 2003): 1069–75.

10. M. J. Eckardt, S. E. File, G. L. Gessa, K. A. Grant, et al., "Effects of moderate alcohol consumption on the central nervous system," *Alcoholism: Clinical and Experimental Research* 22, no. 5 (August 1998): 998–1040.

11. S. Celik, M. Karapirli, E. Kandemir, F. Ucar, et al., "Fatal ethyl and methyl alcohol related poisoning in Ankara: A retrospective analysis of 10,720 cases between 2001 and 2011," *Journal of Forensic and Legal Medicine* 20, no. 3 (April 2013): 151–54.

12. A. W. Jones and K. A. Jonsson, "Food-induced lowering of blood ethanol profiles and increased rate of elimination immediately after a meal," *Journal of Forensic Sciences* 39, no. 4 (August 1994): 1084–93.

13. C. Caputo, F. Wood, and L. Jabbour, "Impact of fetal alcohol exposure on body system: A systematic review," *Birth Defect Research Part C: Embryo Today* 108, no. 2 (June 2016): 174–80.

14. A. M. Kiselica and A. Borders, "The reinforcing efficacy of alcohol mediates associations between impulsivity and negative drinking outcomes," *Journal of Study of Alcohol and Drugs* 74, no. 3 (May 2013): 490–99.

15. C. M. Young, A. M. DiBello, Z. K. Traylor, M. J. Zvolensky, et al., "A longitudinal examination of the association between shyness, drinking motives, alcohol use and alcohol related problems," *Alcohol Clinical and Experimental Research* 39, no. 9 (September 2015): 1749–55.

16. C. L. Lai, C. T. Yao, G. Y. Chau, L. F. Yang, et al., "Dominance of the inactive Asian variant over activity and protein contents of mitochondrial aldehyde dehydrogenase 2 in human liver," *Alcoholism Clinical and Experimental Research* 38, no. 1 (January 2014): 44–50.

17. T. L. Wall, S. H. Shea, S. E. Luczak, T. A. Cook, et al., "Genetic association of alcohol dehydrogenase with alcohol use disorders and endo phenotypes in white college students," *Journal of Abnormal Psychology* 114, no. 3 (August 2005): 456–65.

18. A. W. Jones, "Evidence-based survey of the elimination rates of ethanol from blood with applications in forensic casework," *Forensic Science International* 200, nos. 1–3 (July 2010): 1–20.

19. S. Peele and A. Brodsky, "Exploring psychological benefits associated with moderate alcohol use: A necessary corrective to assessments of drinking outcomes?" *Drug and Alcohol Dependence* 60, no. 3 (November 2000): 221–47.

20. J. C. Skogen, S. B. Harvey, M. Handerson, E. Stordal, et al., "Anxiety and depression among abstainers and low-level alcohol consumers: The Nord Trondelag study," *Addiction* 104, no. 9 (September 2009): 1519–29.

21. S. Bellos, P. Skapinakis, D. Rai, P. Zitko, et al., "Cross-cultural patterns of the association between varying levels of alcohol consumption and the common mental disorders of depression and anxiety: Secondary analysis of WHO collaborative study on psychological problems in general health care," *Drug and Alcohol Dependence* 133, no. 3 (December 2013): 825–31.

22. S. Bellos, P. Skapinakis, D. Rai, P. Zitko, et al., "Longitudinal association between different levels of alcohol consumption and a new onset of depression and generalized anxiety disorder: Results from an international study of primary care," *Psychiatry Research* 243 (September 2016): 30–34.

23. R. Alati, D. A. Lawlor, J. M. Najman, G. M. Williams, et al., "Is there really a 'J-shaped' curve in the association between alcohol consumption and symptoms of depression and anxiety? Findings from the Mater-University study of pregnancy and its outcomes," *Addiction* 100, no. 5 (May 2005): 643–51.

24. R. Alati, N. Dunn, D. M. Purdie, A. M. Roche, et al., "Moderate alcohol consumption contributes to women's well-being through the menopausal transition," *Climacteric* 10, no. 6 (December 2007): 491–99.

25. E. Gonzalez-Rubio, I. San Mauro, C. Lopez-Ruiz, L. E. Diaz-Prieto, et al., "Relationship of moderate alcohol intake and type of beverage with health behaviors and quality of life in elderly subjects," *Quality of Life Research* 25, no. 8 (August 2016): 1931–42.

26. I. Lang, R. B. Wallace, F. A. Huppert, and D. Melzer, "Moderate alcohol consumption in older adults is associated with better cognition and well-being than abstinence," *Age and Aging* 36, no. 3 (May 2007): 256–61.

27. J. Parodi, D. Ormeno, and L. D. Ochoa-de la Paz, "Amyloid pore channel hypothesis: Effect of ethanol on aggregation state using frog oocytes for an Alzheimer's disease study," *Biochemistry and Molecular Biology Report* 48, no. 1 (January 2015): 13–18.

28. G. M. Pasinetti, J. Wang, L. Jo, W. Zhao, et al., "Roles of resveratrol and other grape-derived polyphenols in Alzheimer's disease prevention and treatment," *Biochimica et Biophysica Acta* 1852, no. 6 (June 2015): 1202–8.

29. M. A. Hernan, H. Chen, M. A. Schwarzschild, and A. Ascherio, "Alcohol consumption and the incidence of Parkinson's disease," *Annals of Neurology* 54, no. 2 (August 2003): 170–75.

30. H. Checkoway, K. Powers, T. Smith-Weller, G. M. Franklin, et al., "Parkinson's disease risks associated with cigarette smoking, alcohol consumption and caffeine intake," *American Journal of Epidemiology* 155, no. 8 (April 2002): 732–38.

31. C. R. Kalodner, J. L. Delucia, and A. W. Ursprung, "An examination of the tension reduction hypothesis: The relationship between anxiety and alcohol in college students," *Addictive Behavior* 14, no. 6 (February 1989): 649–54.

32. J. V. Costardi, R. A. Nampo, G. L. Silva, M. A. Ribeiro, et al., "A review on alcohol: From central action mechanism to chemical dependency," *Revista Associacao Medica Brasileria* 61, no. 4 (July–August 2015): 381–87.

33. S. Jarjour, L. Bai, and C. Gianoulakis, "Effect of acute ethanol administration on the release of opioid peptides from the midbrain including the ventral tegmental area," *Alcoholism Clinical and Experimental Research* 33, no. 6 (June 2009): 1033–43.

34. M. Feuereker, D. Hauer, T. Gresset, S. Lassas, et al., "Effect of an acute consumption of moderate amount of ethanol on plasma endocannabinoid levels in humans," *Alcohol and Alcoholism* 47, no. 3 (May–June 2012): 226–32.

35. L. A. Friedman and A. W. Kimball, "Coronary heart disease mortality and alcohol consumption in Framingham," *American Journal of Epidemiology* 124, no. 3 (October 1986): 481–89.

36. J. Tolstrup, M. K. Jensen, A. Tjonneland, K. Overvad, et al., "Prospective study of alcohol drinking patterns and coronary heart disease in women and men," *British Medical Journal* 332, no. 7552 (May 2006): 1244–48.

37. J. H. O'Keefe, S. K. Bhatti, A. Bajwa, J. DiNicolantonio, et al., "Alcohol and cardiovascular health: The dose makes the poison or the remedy," *Mayo Clinic Proceedings* 89, no. 3 (May 2014): 382–93.

38. K. Gemes, I. Janszky, L. E. Laugsand, K. D. Laszlo, et al., "Alcohol consumption is associated with a lower incident of acute myocardial infarction: Results from a large prospective population-based study in Norway," *Journal of Internal Medicine* 279, no. 4 (September 2015): 365–75.

39. M. Elkind, R. Sciacca, B. Boden-Albala, T. Rundek, et al., "Moderate alcohol consumption reduces risk of ischemic stroke: The Northern Manhattan study," *Stroke* 37, no. 1 (January 2006): 13–19.

40. L. L. Koppes, J. M. Dekker, H. F. Hendriks, L. M. Bouter, et al., "Moderate alcohol consumption lowers the risk of type 2 diabetes: A meta-analysis of prospective observational studies," *Diabetes Care* 28, no. 3 (March 2005): 719–25.

41. C. Chao, J. M. Slezak, B. J. Caan, and V. P. Quinn, "Alcoholic beverage intake and risk of lung cancer: The California Men's Health Study," *Cancer Epidemiology Biomarkers and Prevention* 17, no. 10 (October 2008): 2692–99.

42. C. Pelucchi, I. Tramacere, P. Boffetta, E. Negri, et al., "Alcohol consumption and cancer risk," *Nutrition and Cancer* 63, no. 7 (July 2011): 983–90.

43. M. J. Nissen, C. Gabay, A. Scherer, and A. Finchk, "The effect of alcohol on radiographic progression in rheumatoid arthritis," *Arthritis and Rheumatology* 62, no. 5 (May 2010): 1265–72.

44. B. Takkouch, C. Regueira-Mendez, R. Garcia-Closas, A. Figueiras, et al., "Intake of wine, beer, and spirits and the risk of clinical common cold," *American Journal of Epidemiology* 155, no. 9 (May 2002): 853–58.

45. C. A. Camargo, C. H. Hennekens, J. M. Gaziano, R. J. Glynn, et al., "Prospective study of moderate alcohol consumption and mortality in US male physicians," *Archives of Internal Medicine* 157, no. 1 (February 1997): 79–85.

46. S. Renaud and M. De Lorgeril, "Wine, alcohol, platelet, and French paradox for coronary heart disease," *Lancet* 339, no. 8808 (June 1992): 1523–26.

47. E. B. Rimm and M. J. Stampfer, "Wine, beer and spirits: Are they really horses of a different color?" *Circulation* 105, no. 24 (June 2002): 2806–7.

48. K. Walsh and G. Alexander, "Alcoholic liver disease," *Postgraduate Medical Journal* 281, no. 8808 (June 2000): 280–86.

49. A. Dasgupta, *The science of drinking: How alcohol affects your body and mind* (Lanham, MD: Rowman & Littlefield, 2011), 77–100.

CHAPTER 10. STRESS RELIEF AND OTHER HEALTH BENEFITS OF CHOCOLATE

1. H. P. Weingarten and D. Elston, "Food craving in college students," *Appetite* 17, no. 3 (December 1991): 167–75.

2. G. Lippi, M. Franchini, M. Montagnana, E. J. Favaloro, et al., "Dark chocolate: Consumption for pleasure or therapy?" *Journal of Thrombosis and Thrombolysis* 28, no. 4 (November 2009): 482–88.

3. W. J. Hurst, S. M. Tarka, T. G. Powis, F. Valdez Jr., et al., "Cacao usage by the earliest Maya civilization," *Nature* 418, no. 6895 (July 2002): 289–90.

4. R. Verna, "The history and science of chocolate," *Malaysian Journal of Pathology* 35, no. 2 (December 2013): 111–21.

5. R. Lopez, *Chocolate: The nature of indulgences* (New York: Harry N. Abrams, 2002).

6. World Coca Foundation, "Coca market update," April 1, 2014, http://www.worldcocoafoundation.org.

7. P. M. Kris-Etherton and V. A. Mustad, "Chocolate feeding studies: A novel approach for evaluating the plasma lipid effects of stearic acid," *American Journal of Clinical Nutrition* 60, no. S6 (December 1994): 1029S–1036.

8. D. L. Katz, K. Doughty, and A. Ali, "Cocoa and chocolate in human health and disease," *Antioxidants and Redox Signaling* 15, no. 10 (November 2011): 2779–811.

9. R. Latif, "Chocolate/cocoa and human health: A review," *Netherland Journal of Medicine* 71, no. 2 (March 2013): 63–68.

10. F. P. Martin, S. Rezzi, E. Pere-Trepat, B. Kamlage, et al., "Metabolic effects of dark chocolate consumption on energy, gut bacteria, and stress-related metabolism in free-living subjects," *Journal of Proteomes Research* 8, no. 12 (December 2009): 5568–79.

11. A. Al Sunni and R. Latif, "Effects of chocolate intake on perceived stress: A controlled clinical study," *International Journal of Health Sciences* (Qassim University) 8, no. 4 (October–December 2014): 393–401.

12. P. H. Wirtz, E. von Kanel, R. E. Meister, A. Arpagaus, et al., "Dark chocolate intake buffers stress reactivity in humans," *Journal of American College of Cardiology* 63, no. 21 (June 2014): 2297–99.

13. K. Raikkonen, A. K. Personen, A. L. Jarvenpaa, T. E. Strandberg, "Sweet babies: Chocolate consumption during pregnancy and infant temperament at six months," *Early Human Development* 76, no. 2 (February 2004): 139–45.

14. A. L. Tranquilli, S. Lorenzi, G. Buscicchio, M. Di Tommaso, et al., "Female fetuses are more reactive when mother eats chocolate," *Journal of Maternal Fetal and Neonatal Medicine* 27, no. 1 (January 2014): 72–74.

15. G. C. Di Renzo, R. Brillo, M. Romanelli, G. Porcaro, et al., "Potential effects of chocolate on human pregnancy: A randomized controlled trial," *Journal of Maternal Fetal and Neonatal Medicine* 25, no. 10 (October 2012): 1860–67.

16. M. Macht and D. Dettmer, "Everyday mood and emotions after eating a chocolate bar or an apple," *Appetite* 46, no. 3 (May 2006): 332–36.

17. M. Macht and J. Mueller, "Immediate effects of chocolate on experimentally induced mood states," *Appetite* 49, no. 3 (November 2007): 667–74.

18. A. B. Scholey, S. J. French, P. J. Morris, D. O. Kennedy, et al., "Consumption of cocoa flavanols results in acute improvements in mood and cognitive performance during sustained mental efforts," *Journal of Psychopharmacology* 24, no. 10 (October 2010): 1505–14.

19. T. E. Strandberg, A. Y. Strandberg, K. Pitkala, V. V. Salomaa, et al., "Chocolate well-being and health among elderly men," *European Journal of Clinical Nutrition* 62, no. 2 (February 2008): 247–53.

20. G. Parker, I. Parker, and H. Brotchie, "Mood state effects of chocolate," *Journal of Affected Disorders* 92, nos. 2–3 (June 2006): 149–59.

21. A. Moreira, M. J. Diogenes, A. de Mendonca, N. Lunet, et al., "Chocolate consumption is associated with a lower risk of cognitive decline," *Journal of Alzheimer Disease* 53, no. 1 (May 2016): 85–93.

22. H. J. Smit, E. A. Gaffan, and P. J. Rogers, "Methylxanthines are the psycho-pharmacologically active constituents of chocolate," *Psychopharmacology* (Berlin) 176, nos. 3–4 (November 2004): 412–19.

23. H. J. Smit and R. J. Blackburn, "Reinforcing effects of caffeine and theobromine as found in chocolate," *Psychopharmacology* (Berlin) 181, no. 1 (August 2005): 101–6.

24. A. Scholey and L. Owen, "Effects of chocolate on cognitive function and mood: A systematic review," *Nutrition Review* 71, no. 10 (October 2013): 665–81.

25. J. Van Wensem, "Overview of scientific evidence for chocolate health benefits," *Integrative Environmental Assessment Management* 11, no. 1 (January 2015): 176–77.

26. D. Benton and R. T. Donohoe, "The effects of nutrients on mood," *Public Health and Nutrition* 2, no. 3A (September 1999): 403–9.

27. I. C. Arts, B. van De Outte, and P. C. Hollman, "Catechin contents of foods commonly consumed in the Netherlands. 2. Tea, wine, fruit juices and chocolate milk," *Journal of Agricultural and Food Chemistry* 48, no. 5 (May 2000): 1752–57.

28. P. R. Machonis, M. A. Jones, B. T. Schaneberg, and C. L. Kwik-Uribe, "Method for the determination of catechin and epicatechin enantiomers in cocoa-based ingredients and products by high-performance liquid chromatography: Single laboratory validation," *Journal of American Oil Chemist Society* 95, no. 2 (March–April 2012): 500–507.

29. D. Reid, S. Lotito, R. R. Holt, C. L. Keen, et al., "Epicatechin in human plasma: In vivo determination and effect of chocolate consumption on plasma oxidation status," *Journal of Nutrition* 130, no. S8 (August 2000): S2109–14.

30. L. Gu, S. E. House, X. Wu, B. Ou, et al., "Procyanidin and catechin content and antioxidant capacity of coca and chocolate products," *Journal of Agricultural and Food Chemistry* 54, no. 11 (May 2006): 4057–61.

31. C. C. Meng, A. M. Jalil, and A. Ismail, "Phenolic and theobromine contents of commercial dark, milk and white chocolate on the Malaysian market," *Molecules* 14, no. 1 (January 2009): 200–209.

32. J. Mursu, S. Vautilainen, T. Nurmi, T. H. Rissanen, et al., "Dark chocolate consumption increases HDL cholesterol concentration and chocolate fatty acids may inhibit lipid peroxidation in healthy humans," *Free Radical Biology and Medicine* 37, vol. 9 (November 2004): 1351–59.

33. B. Buijsse, E. J. Feskens, F. J. Kok, and D. Kromhout, "Cocoa intake, blood pressure, and cardiovascular mortality: The Zutphen elderly study," *Archives of Internal Medicine* 166, no. 4 (February 2006): 411–17.

34. E. Mostofsky, E. B. Levitan, A. Wolk, and M. A. Mittleman, "Chocolate intake and incidence of heart failure: A population-based prospective study of middle-aged and elderly women," *Circulation and Heart Failure* 3, no. 5 (September 2010): 612–16.

35. D. Grassi, G. Desideri, S. Necozione, C. Lippi, et al., "Blood pressure is reduced and insulin sensitivity increased in glucose-intolerant hypertensive subjects after 15 days of consuming high-polyphenol dark chocolate," *Journal of Nutrition* 138, no. 9 (September 2008): 1671–76.

36. J. A. Greenberg, "Chocolate intake and diabetes risk," *Clinical Nutrition* 34, no. 1 (February 2015): 129–33.

37. S. C. Larsson, J. Virtamo, and A. Wolk, "Chocolate consumption and risk of stroke: A prospective cohort of men and meta-analysis," *Neurology* 79, no. 12 (September 2012): 1223–29.

38. E. T. Massolt, P. M. van Haard, J. F. Rehfield, E. F. Posthuma, et al., "Appetite suppression through smelling of dark chocolate correlates with changes in ghrelin in young women," *Regulatory Peptides* 161, nos. 1–3 (April 2010): 81–86.

39. G. Farhat, S. Drummond, L. Fyfe, and E. A. Al-Dujaili, "Dark chocolate: An obesity paradox or a culprit for weight gain?" *Phytotherapy Research* 28, no. 6 (June 2014): 791–97.

40. E. W. Triche, L. M. Grosso, K. Belanger, A. S. Darefsky, et al., "Chocolate consumption in pregnancy and reduced likelihood of preeclampsia," *Epidemiology* 19, no. 3 (May 2008): 459–564.

41. A. N. Sokolov, M. A. Pavlova, S. Klosterhalfen, and P. Enck, "Chocolate and the brain: Neurobiological impact of cocoa flavanols on cognition and behavior," *Neuroscience and Biobehavioral Review* 37, no. 10 (December 2013): 2445–53.

42. G. Davison, R. Callister, G. Williamson, K. A. Cooper, et al., "The effect of acute pre-exercise dark chocolate consumption on plasma antioxidant status, oxidative stress and immunoendocrine response to prolonged exercise," *European Journal of Nutrition* 51, no. 1 (February 2012): 69–79.

43. T. Sathyapalan, S. Beckett, A. S. Rigby, D. D. Mellor, et al., "High cocoa polyphenol rich chocolate may reduce burden of the symptoms in chronic fatigue syndrome," *Nutritional Journal* 9, no. 55 (November 2010): 1186.

44. R. di Giusepper, A. Di Castelnuovo, F. Centritto, F. Zito, et al., "Regular consumption of dark chocolate is associated with low serum concentrations of C-reactive protein in a healthy Italian population," *Journal of Nutrition* 138, no. 10 (October 2008): 1929–45.

45. J. M. Hirmes and P. Rozin, "Perimenstrual chocolate craving: What happens after menopause?" *Appetite* 53, no. 2 (October 2009): 256–59.

46. P. Willner, D. Benton, E. Brown, S. Chheta, et al., "Depression increases craving for sweet rewards in animal and human model of depression and craving," *Psychopharmacology* (Berlin) 136, no. 3 (April 1998): 272–83.

47. M. M. Hetherington and J. I. MacDiarmid, "Chocolate addiction: A preliminary study of its description and its relationship to problem eating," *Appetite* 21, no. 3 (December 1993): 233–36.

48. S. Vongraviopap and P. Asawanonda, "Dark chocolate exacerbates acne," *Internal Journal of Dermatology* 55, no. 5 (May 2016): 587–91.

Index

acceptance-oriented approach to stress, 6

acetaldehyde, 219

actinic (solar) keratoses, 14

action-oriented approach to stress, 6

acute stress, 30–32; episodic, 30–32, 32*t*; symptoms of, 32*t*

adolescents: and cell phone addiction, 19; and Internet addiction, 17–18; and loneliness, 102; parental support and, 99–100

adrenocorticotropic hormone (ACTH), 26, 61

African Americans: and alcohol intolerance, 221; and pets, 70; racism and, 49, 101*t*; and stress in children, 97; and stress-related illnesses, 63; and touch, 179

age, and stress levels in women, 46–47

aggression, 56–57, 235*t*

AIDS, 39, 79, 235*t*

Ainsworth, Mary, 93–96

air pollution, 15

alcoholic beverages, 211–36; contraindications to, 218–19, 220*t*;

effects of, 216, 217*t*; guidelines for, 212–14; hazards of, 212, 215, 233, 234*t*–35*t*

alcohol intolerance, 219–21

alcohol poisoning, 215

alcohol withdrawal, 234*t*

allergies, pets and, 84–85

allostasis, 27

Alzheimer's disease, 33; chocolate and, 253; drinking and, 224

ambivalent attachment, 95, 95*t*

animals, 69–87; domestication of, 71–72

anthrozoology, 71

antidepressants, 42

antioxidants, 183, 192*t*, 206; in alcoholic beverages, 230–31; in chocolate, 237–38, 241, 247–50; in fruits, 208–10; and mood, 193

anxiety: aromatherapy and, 151, 154*t*; drinking and, 222–23; heavy drinking and, 234*t*; massage and, 158*t*; pets and, 78–79; and stress response, 7

arginine vasopressin (ARV), 26

About the Author

Amitava Dasgupta is a tenured full professor of pathology and laboratory medicine at the University of Texas McGovern Medical School in Houston. He has published 221 scientific papers; written many invited review articles and abstracts; and written, coauthored, edited, or coedited a total of twenty-one books. He is on the editorial board of five major medical journals, including the *American Journal of Clinical Pathology* and the *Archives of Pathology and Laboratory Medicine*. He is the recipient of the 2009 Irvine Sunshine Award from the International Association for Therapeutic Drug Monitoring and Clinical Toxicology. He also received the Outstanding Contribution to Education Award from the American Association for Clinical Chemistry in 2010. This is his second general-interest book published by Rowman & Littlefield. The first book, *The Science of Drinking: How Alcohol Affects Your Body and Mind*, was published in 2011.